An Invitation
to Philosophy

Nicholas Capaldi, Eugene Kelly,
and Luis E. Navia

Prometheus Books

700 East Amherst Street
Buffalo, N.Y. 14215

Nicholas Capaldi is Professor of Philosophy at Queens College of the City University of New York.

Luis E. Navia is an Associate Professor of Philosophy at the New York Institute of Technology.

Eugene Kelly is an Assistant Professor of Philosophy at the New York Institute of Technology.

Published 1981 by Prometheus Books
700 East Amherst Street, Buffalo, N.Y. 14215

Library of Congress Card Number 81-81131
ISBN 0-87975-162-2

Printed in the United States of America

We dedicate this book to our children,

Carolyn
Diana
Elizabeth
Jeffrey
Libusha
Meredith
Monica
Olga Lucia

Contents

Foreword

An Invitation to Philosophy has been written as an introductory text in philosophy for those college students who have little or no acquaintance with the subject and who are taking, either by choice or requirement, a basic course in philosophy. Ideally, this book should be used in conjunction with an anthology of primary sources in which the writings of the major philosophers are well represented. Our discussions and explanations of the chief ideas of these philosophers can become enriched and can be made more meaningful only by a careful reading of what they actually said and wrote, even if, at first sight, the study of their writings may seem a most difficult task. Philosophical sources are often characterized by an unusual degree of complexity and difficulty that may easily baffle and even discourage the beginning student. But he must bear in mind that this circumstance may well be the unavoidable result of the very nature and substance of the questions and problems with which philosophers must cope. Occasionally, however, the fact remains that certain philosophers are not as clear in expressing their thought as they could be. But, in either case, it is always a worthwhile enterprise to undertake the patient and thoughtful reading of the actual works of the major philosophers. We hope that the pages of *An Invitation to Philosophy* will make such an enterprise somewhat easier and more pleasant.

The title of this book is no accidental choice, as by entitling it *An Invitation to Philosophy* we mean, literally, "an invitation." We want to *invite* the student to partake in the grand enterprise of philosophical activity that has captivated and engaged the best and most powerful minds for the last twenty-five centuries. We want to invite the student to be a living part of the unending process of philosophical speculation and analysis that has been the human reaction *par excellence* in the presence of the mystery of the universe. We extend to the student our cordial invitation to think, speculate, examine, imagine, and create under the guidance of great thinkers. The pages of this book will surely assist him or her in the process of becoming a part of the philosophical enterprise.

Our book is divided into thirteen chapters, some of which deal with individual philosophers like Plato and Aristotle, others with aspects of philosophy (logic, ethics, political philosophy, epistemology, metaphysics, and the philosophy of religion), while others approach more general subjects (the rise of philosophy among the early Greeks, the philosophy of man, the contributions of Oriental philosophers, and the philosophical developments of the twentieth century). In most of the chapters, the student will find abundant references to specific sections of primary sources, and at the end of every chapter a series of questions will be found, by reference to which the student may measure his or her understanding of the material read. An extensive glossary at the end of the book will shed light on some of the most common meanings attached to philosophical concepts. The Bibliography will identify both a large number of primary sources and a select sample of secondary sources.

The authors of *An Invitation to Philosophy* have been teaching courses in philosophy for many years, and in writing this book we have made an effort to write in a way reminiscent of the way in which we ordinarily lecture in introductory courses; accordingly, clarity, precision, and comprehensiveness have been our primary goals. Although the three of us have worked closely together so that the book as a whole may be said to be the joint effort of all of us, each author has borne the main responsibility for specifically assigned chapters. Thus, Professor Capaldi is responsible for chapters 5, 8, 9, and 10; Professor Kelly for chapters 6, 11, 12, and 13; and Professor Navia for chapters 1, 2, 3, 4, and 7.

We wish to express our gratitude to Professors Richard E. Hart, Maxim Mikulak, Rama Puligandla, and Neil Rossman for having read and commented on several of the chapters. We also wish to thank Pamela Capaldi, Zuzana Kelly, and Alicia S. Navia for their invaluable and affectionate support.

1

The Meaning of Philosophy

The first and most obvious question that confronts us at the beginning of a course in philosophy is what are its meaning and scope. Without a clear understanding of these, our objectives are bound to be uncertain and vague, and our progress slow and insignificant. We must know what we are expected to learn, and what advantages, intellectual or practical, we are to derive from the study of philosophy. Surely, on countless occasions, we must have heard the word 'philosophy', and, undoubtedly, our general education has enabled us to identify certain great thinkers, like Plato and Aristotle, as 'philosophers'. But this cannot be enough. As we undertake the formal study of philosophy, we must command a far greater degree of precision in the meaning of the subject.

Unfortunately, we encounter at this point a number of initial difficulties peculiar to philosophy. For, unlike other fields of study, in philosophy to state a precise definition and a satisfactory stipulation of its scope is most difficult, if not impossible. Throughout the history of philosophy, several distinct definitions have been advanced, and from the point of view of different philosophers, the scope of philosophy is not always the same. In each instance, the preferred definition corresponds closely with the philosopher's intellectual orientation, with his training, and even with his cultural prejudices, and since all these come in all sorts of varieties, there is not at present, nor has there ever been, a general and compelling agreement about the meaning of philosophy. One may even be satisfied with saying that "philosophy is what philosophers think, write, and do," but such a definition can, in fact, shed little light on our own problem as students of philosophy.

In the sciences, especially the natural sciences, there is generally a consensus about what each science means and what its scope entails. Take, for instance, the case of astronomy. There is little difficulty in coming to an adequate definition of this science and to a practical specification of its scope. We know that astronomy investigates the nature, position, and behavior of objects like the moon, the sun, and the planets, stars, nebulae, and galaxies. We also know its basic methodology, which is observation together with a heavy dosage of theoretical and mathematical work. Furthermore, we recognize that in contemporary astronomy, as in other sciences, there is a body of generally accepted scientific knowledge that is the result of the labors of past and present astronomers. We should not hesitate to affirm that, in spite of the many areas that still remain unknown and mysterious, a competent astronomer of our time knows a great deal more about the heavens than an eminent astronomer of antiquity. Surely, progress has taken place in astronomy and the other natural sciences—progress in the sense that our present scientific explanations and theories, as well as our methodologies, are more adequate and comprehensive than those of the past.

But can we say the same about philosophy and philosophers? Is there in philosophy a body of generally accepted truths and knowledge? Are the insights and ideas of twentieth-century philosophers superior to those of the Greek philosophers? Is there a universal methodology in philosophical investigations? In a word, has there been real progress in this field?

The answers and solutions to these questions and problems depend heavily on one's own conception of what philosophy is. It is possible to argue, for example, that philosophical progress is a reality and that certain contemporary philosophical approaches are more adequate than those of Plato and Aristotle. But one can also argue that much contemporary philosophy represents a clear instance of cultural decadence in comparison to the accomplishments of Plato, Aristotle, and other ancient thinkers. In this case, one may be forced to conclude that, at least in a philosophical sense, today we know less about the universe and human existence than our predecessors. But again, such an assertion depends on one's understanding of philosophy. It is therefore useful at this point to review a number of possible definitions of our field.

Apparently, the origin of the word 'philosophy' is linked to the teachings of Pythagoras, the Greek mathematician of the sixth century B.C. The word itself comes from the Greek verb *philosophein*, which literally means 'to love wisdom'. Hence the noun 'philosophia' means 'the love of wisdom', and a philosopher is a person who loves or desires wisdom. According to ancient biographers, Pythagoras coined the word 'philosopher' in order to distinguish himself from those who were commonly known as 'sophists' or wise men. The word 'sophist' comes from the Greek word 'sophia', which means 'wisdom' or 'understanding', in the sense of being able to make sense of facts, experiences, or occurrences. Thus, for instance, when we *understand* the meaning of a poem or work of art, when we *grasp* the significance of a series of events, or when we *get the point* that a speaker seeks to convey, we have developed wisdom or *sophia* about our experiences. Knowing the poem by heart, remembering the name of the artist who painted the work of art, or even intelligently retaining the words of the speaker do not necessarily constitute wisdom or *sophia*. The early Greeks distinguished carefully between this wisdom and simple knowledge which they called *episteme*. A knowledgeable person may be well versed in facts, names, dates, processes, and situations, but the wise person *understands*. Accordingly, those men who among the Greeks were called 'sophists' had gained the reputation of being not only intelligent and knowledgeable but wise. Their ideas and teachings were the guiding light by which whole cultures lived, as from them there emanated a profound wisdom that was often deemed to be superhuman. Homer and Hesiod, for instance, were genuine sophists, since in their descriptions of gods and heroes, and in their accounts of the beginning and structure of the universe, the ordinary Greek found a rich source of knowledge and wisdom.

Pythagoras, however, must have felt uncomfortable with the designation of 'sophist', by which he was known to many. His knowledge and understanding of the world were surely remarkable, and his mathematical accomplishments impressive; yet, he knew that in the context of reality at large his wisdom was insignificant, for what he knew and understood was small compared with what surrounded him. He must have experienced that uncanny sense of wonder in the presence of the universe, a sense that, as Aristotle says, lies at the root of the philosophical impulse. Pythagoras then chose to call himself simply a lover of wisdom, that is, someone who devotes his life to the pursuit of understanding. In so doing, however, he gave birth to the word philosophy, since this word means, as we saw, 'the love of wisdom'.

The Greek philosophers in general understood philosophy in precisely this sense, as is obvious from the contributions of Plato and Aristotle. For them, the philosopher is literally 'a lover of wisdom', someone who has committed his or her life to the difficult task of clarifying and understanding the universe and human existence, and who, unwilling to abide by traditional dogmas and beliefs, undertakes the critical and rational evaluation of his or her experiences. Forgetful of religious creeds that sometimes blind and bind the mind, and willing to forsake emotional responses to the mystery of existence, the lover of wisdom, the philosopher, valiantly seeks to make sense of the universe. Undoubtedly, in spite of the many differences between one philosopher and another, between one philosophical system and another, this general conception of philosophy, which we owe to Pythagoras, has lived in every major philosophical mind. Every single philosopher discussed in the subsequent chapters has been, in one sense or another, a living personification of the Pythagorean ideal of philosophy.

Yet, for us who are about to begin the study of philosophy, this ideal as such remains very vague. After all, the idea of wisdom can be given a number of interpretations, and the objects about which we hope to become wise can be many. Moreover, the ways in which wisdom can be pursued are various. Thus, we are entitled to raise questions like these: What is the wisdom that the philosopher seeks? What sorts of objects does the philosopher endeavor to understand? What methods are to be employed in the pursuit of wisdom? But, to each one of these questions various and often mutually exclusive answers have been suggested in the history of philosophy, and it is for this reason that, as we said earlier, there are many conceptions of what philosophy is. Today, for instance, there are philosophers for whom the chief object of philosophical activity is the analysis of language. They argue that in and through the analysis of language we can find whatever wisdom may be attained in philosophy. Philosophy, for them, becomes reduced to the analytical examination of the utterances made by scientists and ordinary people, the end result of this examination being the elimination of ambiguities and obscurities that, they believe, are the root of most if not all philosophical problems. This conception of philosophy was sufficiently powerful to dominate an important segment of Anglo-American philosophy for several decades, although there are clear signs today that such domination is giving way.

Among the early Greek philosophers, especially those known as Milesian Rationalists, the analysis of language played a minor role. For them, the chief object of philosophy was the clarification of the universe at large, and for this reason they devoted themselves to cosmological speculation. The major philosophical issues that they endeavored to solve had to do with the origin and nature of the cosmos or universe, the constitution and structure of the primordial substance or substance of all things, and the harmony and balance of physical forces. Their philosophical systems, as far as we can reconstruct them, were systems of speculative cosmology. But in this they sought to find philosophical wisdom.

For Socrates, on the other hand, the chief object of philosophy was to make illuminating statements not about the universe at large or about the structure of matter, but about the meaning of human existence. The concepts that the philosopher examines are all related to human issues: virtue, happiness, value, goodness; the rest is mostly insignificant, if not outright impertinent. The answer to the question "How should I live my life?" was, for Socrates, the primordial question in the scheme of philosophy, and the proper method for answering this ethical question has little to do with observation of the physical world or the *bare* analysis of language. His method involved a great deal of self-examination and much discourse with his fellow human beings. Socratic philosophy is, more than anything else, a search for meaning: not only an intellectual search for the purpose of simply knowing or understanding what virtue, happiness, and goodness mean, but an existential search in order to become ourselves virtuous, happy, and good.

In the philosophy of Plato, we encounter elements reminiscent of both the Milesian Rationalists and of Socrates. The structure of the universe *and* the meaning of human existence appear prominently in Plato's *Dialogues*, but the real object of philosophical wisdom is, according to him, a realm of reality that transcends the physical world of sense experience. For him, as we are told in the *Phaedo*, the purpose of philosophy is to take us away from this material world into a sphere of being where there is no change or time. His method is, accordingly, neither observation nor the analysis of language, but thinking, meditation, and reflection, as his ideal is, as he hints in one of his letters, to enter into close communion with a perfectly spiritual world. In chapter 4 we will have an ample opportunity to examine the major elements of this Platonic philosophy, a philosophy that has undoubtedly exercised a profound and decisive influence in the development of Western civilization.

In medieval times, for instance, Plato's definition of philosophy as the search for wisdom about the transcendent world can be unmistakably detected in the writings of Saint Augustine, who found Plato and the Platonists the only ancient philosophers worthy of serious consideration. For Saint Augustine, as well as for many other medieval thinkers including Saint Anselm and Saint Thomas Aquinas, God, the soul, eternal salvation, and divine grace are the proper objects of the philosophical activity. The rest is either inconsequential or detrimental. Naturally, among medievals, philosophy becomes indistinguishable either from theology and religion or from the rational attempt to make sense of theological and religious contentions.

After medieval times, a number of old and new conceptions of philosophy arose in the minds of philosophers. Sometimes we find it defined as the attempt to make sense of the physical world; as the endeavor to gain clarity about the problem of God, the existence of the soul, and the reality of human freedom; as the analysis of the mind and the conditions of knowledge; as a science of all sciences in which scientific concepts are subjected to a critical evaluation; as a system of human and social values; as an examination of the human predicament, etc., etc. But diverse as these and other conceptions of philosophy may be, it is undeniable that they all express in their individual ways something that cannot but remind us of the Pythagorean idea of philosophy as the love of wisdom.

In the paragraphs that follow we propose to acquaint the student with a number of important themes and topics that will facilitate his or her understanding of our subsequent chapters and the primary sources that will be read throughout this course. We will begin by presenting a general outline of Aristotle's *concept* of philosophy (chapter 5 will be devoted to a concise exposition of Aristotelian philosophy). As we will presently see, Aristotle's concept of philosophy is sufficiently rich and wide to allow us to include in it practically all other concepts of what philosophical activity should entail. His concept of philosophy will be helpful in classifying, defining, and exemplifying those main branches or areas of philosophy that will be discussed in later chapters and will guide us in making a few pertinent remarks about the relationship between philosophy and science and between philosophy and religion. After this, we will proceed to give a brief outline of the major historical developments of Western philosophy in order to allow the student to place within a meaningful historical context the many philosophers who will be discussed in this book. Our emphasis throughout this text is Western philosophy, but this should not be taken to mean that philosophy is exclusively the contribution of Western minds. Non-Western philosophy is a rich field of speculations and accomplishments, and we hope that our chapter on oriental philosophy will tempt the student to undertake further investigations along these lines. As one studies the history of Western philosophy, one becomes immediately aware of the indirect influence that oriental philosophy has exercised on a number of philosophers and philosophical movements in the West.

1. ARISTOTLE'S CONCEPT OF PHILOSOPHY

At the beginning of the *Metaphysics,* Aristotle observes that "all men by nature desire to know." The human quest for knowledge and understanding is, according to him, our most fundamental characteristic and the trait that distinguishes us from all other living beings. It is something with which we are born, something which we possess "by nature." This desire to know can be nourished and strengthened by proper breeding and education or partly stifled and discouraged by unintelligent upbringing, but in the end it remains deeply ingrained in our human texture.

It is easy to verify the correctness of the Aristotelian remark as we observe the behavior of children. Their little minds seem to be filled with curiosity about the mysterious and unknown world that surrounds them. They want to know everything, and every object of their experience is something to be explored and investigated. As their language becomes more flexible and as they develop a greater sense of social independence, their curiosity forever finds new dimensions and fields for possible exploration. The sense experiences stored in their minds demand more and more complex explanations, and at one point, possibly before reaching adulthood, they feel the necessity to understand who they are and what the meaning of the world in which they live is. They then become young philosophers in the old Pythagorean sense of the word. Unfortunately, sometimes a lack of proper parental guidance, poorly structured educational systems, blinding social prejudices, or suffocating cultural restrictions may succeed in throwing formidable obstacles along the path of their development; they become intellectually stagnated and turn out to be the sort of people who know little and understand nothing. Their minds develop into storage rooms of disjointed and unrelated facts, usually gathered from television programs, newspaper columns, and neighborhood gossip. If one adds to this the socially promoted search for physical pleasure that is immeasurably enhanced by certain kinds of music, sports, sexual activities, and drugs, one succeeds in turning our once promising young philosophers into genuine caricatures of human beings from whom little can be expected in the way of true intellectual value.

These remarks should not be construed as implying that the search for knowledge and understanding ought to be the sole concern of human beings, for, after all, we are neither angelic creatures nor disembodied intelligences. Our mind is only a dimension of our being, and although its importance can never be exaggerated, its growth and development must be achieved in the context of other human dimensions such as our emotions, our bodies, and even our religious needs. It is, therefore, a matter of emphasis and balance, and Aristotle, perhaps more than any other major philosopher, would have gone along with this. Just as it is easy to stifle the mind by means of an exclusive pursuit of pleasure and physical satisfactions, the end result being a mindless and thick-headed person, it is easy to overlook the emotional and physical components of the human being for the exaggerated concern for purely intellectual matters. In the latter case, however, the outcome is just as lamentable: a person who has lost touch with an essential part of his or her being. An important element of philosophical development entails taking into account *all* that we are and all the aspects of the world in which we live, move, and have our being. Still, we must recognize the truth of the Aristotelian view that the search for wisdom constitutes the most typically human, and hence the most worthy, innate characteristic of the species to which we belong.

But now let us be more specific. When we say that all human beings by nature desire to know, we must ask two inevitable questions, namely, (1) What is it that human beings desire to know? and (2) What is the purpose of their desired knowledge?

From the point of view of its purpose, Aristotle distinguishes two kinds of knowledge, namely, practical and theoretical. Practical knowledge, as its name suggests, allows us to understand the world around us so that we may manipulate, control, change, and generally use the objects of our experience. This knowledge enables us to deal successfully with nature and empowers us to survive and compete successfully in our complex social world. In practical terms, it prepares us to obtain a creative and lucrative position in the world, as is the end of the so-called career-oriented education. The medical student, the young car mechanic, the architectural apprentice, the student of the various technologies—all of them undertake their studies with mainly one aim in mind: to do something practical with what they learn.

In practical knowledge the emphasis lies on *doing* something, ideally for the ultimate purpose of improving the condition of mankind and oneself. This kind of knowledge unquestionably constitutes a tremendous source of power, specifically the power to control and tame the unfriendly natural world with which we must cope both collectively and individually. The complexities of our present technological world and the enormous demands placed today upon each one of us by our bewildering socio-economic world have elevated all the branches of practical knowledge to an unprecedented level of importance, and this trend has been dramatically at work since the seventeenth century when Francis Bacon stated unequivocally that *knowledge is power.*

And yet, we must bear in mind that in antiquity things were otherwise. Among the Greeks, for instance, practical knowledge was invariably relegated to a second plane of importance. Occasionally, as in the case of Archimedes, it was referred to as something despicable and ignoble. Repudiating as sordid and degrading the whole trade of engineering, this great mathematician of the third century B.C. destroyed those works and designs of his that allowed him to construct formidable war engines for the defense of Syracuse against the invading Romans. The manipulation of things belonged exclusively to the slave classes, and few intelligent persons would stoop so low as to become involved in the practical applications of what they knew. Obviously, much can be said for and against this ancient contempt for applied knowledge, and it is not difficult to see how many sociological factors contributed to it. In an ecologically undisturbed world where vast numbers of uneducated human beings were forever available to do whatever simple physical labors had to be done, one cannot but expect to find a profound contempt for physical work and practical knowledge on the part of the few educated ones. As a faint vestige of this perhaps lamentable phenomenon, there remains today a certain discriminatory view of "blue collar" workers on the part of highly sophisticated people. Whether such a view is to be condemned or praised remains of course a matter of much controversy.

But, if for Archimedes practical knowledge was to be despised as sordid and base, what other kind of knowledge ought to be pursued by the philosophically minded? What could be the purpose of the philosopher's knowledge or wisdom? Here we come upon Aristotle's second kind of knowledge, a kind that he, not unlike other Greek philosophers, found to be infinitely superior to the practical kind. Theoretical knowledge is the goal of all philosophy, and this knowledge consists in knowing *for the sake of knowing alone.* It is, therefore, knowledge for its own sake. The English word 'theoretical' comes from a simple Greek word meaning 'view' or 'vision'. A *theoria* is, for example, the *view* we have as we climb a mountain peak: the panorama that unveils itself before our eyes is a *theoria.* Thus, in theoretical knowledge we seek to understand for the sake of understanding, to know for the sake of knowing, and any applications that our knowledge may have in the practical realm come in only incidentally and accidentally. The philosopher is, there-fore, a passive observer of reality, an intellectual eye that inspects every-thing, a mind that endeavors to understand the unfolding of reality: in a word, he is the consciousness of humanity.

In saying that all human beings by nature desire to know, what Aristotle means is that, aside from our natural inclination to become acquainted with things for strictly practical purposes, there is in each one of us an inborn yearning to know and understand the world simply for the purpose of becoming enlightened concerning its nature. This philosophical impulse, act-ing almost as a sixth sense, establishes an unbridgeable gap between us and other animals, and the contemplative mood to which it naturally leads us constitutes the worthiest style of life a human being may hope to follow. In itself, theoretical knowledge, which can now be called philosophical wis-dom, is thoroughly useless from the viewpoint of those for whom activity and practice are the substantive goals of knowledge. Like a genuine artist, for whom the purpose of art is art itself, the true philosopher rests satisfied on the notion that his or her activity will produce an adequate *view* or *theoria* of reality. It cannot be denied, however, that the philosopher's contemplative knowledge will inevitably fructify in the realm of practical concerns. Grand political systems, encompassing sociological ideas, compel-ling ethical imperatives, and incisive scientific explanations have grown out of pure philosophical speculation. Indeed, as we will see presently, according to Aristotle, a philosopher's life is bound to be profoundly affected by his or her contemplation of reality, so that philosophy must also be understood as a way of life, for a system of ideas that does not manifest itself in the domain of practical living has not really taken deep roots in the mind. Aristotle, like Socrates and Plato, believed in the integration of theory and practice, espe-cially in the sphere of ethics. The philosopher knows the good and must become thereby good himself. Thus here at least, the most theoretical inves-tigation finds a way to affect our daily activities, and almost paradoxically, it is precisely the most *useless* search for knowledge that turns out to be the most *useful.*

We can now summarize Aristotle's concept of philosophy in the following words: *Philosophy is the systematic attempt on the part of the human mind to know and understand reality in rational and human terms whenever this attempt has as its chief end the acquisition of knowledge and understanding for their own sake.*

2. THE BRANCHES OF PHILOSOPHY

Obviously, Aristotle's concept is as wide and rich as reality itself, including, as it does, all possible aspects of reality. Aiming at understanding all possible forms of existence, it must embrace a great multitude of investigations. His own voluminous works gave ample testimony of this. In more than two hundred works, he dealt extensively with areas as diverse as language, logical reasoning, scientific methodology, inference, deduction, induction, and probability; mathematics, physics, astronomy, cosmology, the generation and destruction of things, meteorology, optics, zoology, and botany, psychology, the meaning of dreams, memory, and physiognomy; ethics in general; education, economics, political science, music, poetry, drama, sports—and indeed many others. He devoted special attention to the clarification of the nature, sources, and process of knowledge (what today we call epistemology), and to the nature of reality or existence in itself (what has been called metaphysics). He wrote at length on issues and problems related to the existence and nature of God, the gods, and religious ideas (what became known as theological matters). In a word, practically nothing was left unanalyzed and untouched by his penetrating mind. Everywhere he sought to formulate the *principles,* unravel the *causes,* and identify the *elements* of each aspect of reality accessible to him, for, as he noted at the beginning of the *Physics,* "It is through acquaintance with these that knowledge, that is to say scientific or philosophical knowledge, is attained."

During Aristotle's time, and indeed for many centuries later, philosophy had this all-inclusive meaning. Any endeavor to obtain theoretical knowledge was simply called philosophical. An Alexandrian astronomer living in the second century B.C. who, like Hipparchus, spent his time observing, classifying, and giving an account of the stars, referred to his activities as philosophy. Likewise, a Stoic thinker of Roman times who investigated the nature of virtue and happiness was a philosopher. A Roman statesman who dealt with the problem of natural law looked upon himself as a philosopher, and the same can be said about medieval scholars like Saint Anselm and Saint Thomas Aquinas who lived more than one thousand years after Aristotle. We find that the great scientists of the seventeenth century, people like Galileo, Descartes, Huygens, and Newton, still called themselves simply philosophers.

With the immense growth of knowledge and the bewildering accumulation of information in the last three hundred years, the individual lines of investigation (the sciences) began to develop a certain sense of independence, not only from one another, but from the philosophical matrix from which they had been born in antiquity. Thus the sciences became partially disassociated from philosophy at large. Those specific investigations into limited aspects of reality, which Aristotle had classified as "speculative philosophies," developed into the distinct fields of scientific work that are known today as mathematics, physics, geology, astronomy, biology, chemistry, and the rest of the natural sciences. The disassociation of other sciences like psychology and the social sciences from philosophy took place a bit later, perhaps towards the middle of the nineteenth century. Still, as a vestige of a previous time, when under the Aristotelian view philosophy included all theoretical knowledge, doctoral degrees in the sciences and the humanities (Ph.D.'s) are said to be doctorates in philosophy.

We must now raise three important questions: (1) What are those aspects of theoretical knowledge that still belong to what academically goes by the name of philosophy? (2) What is at present the relationship between philosophy and the natural and social sciences? (3) Is the gap that separates philosophical speculation from scientific investigation a widening one, or are there indications that a return to the old Aristotelian concept is deemed desirable by present-day philosophers and scientists?

The chapters of this book will give the student an adequate idea of some of the major areas of contemporary philosophical work as they constitute in general the core of the academic and literary endeavors of twentieth-century philosophers. Each one of these areas can be treated in different ways, and the answers and solutions that have emerged from them are indeed quite varied, as chapter 13 will show. It will be more appropriate to leave the extensive discussion of each philosophical area to the individual chapters, and at this point we will limit ourselves to some very brief comments about some of them.

a. *Logic* is the aspect of philosophy that deals with the structure of arguments insofar as this is used as a vehicle for reasoning. The logician studies, for instance, the laws and forms of proper reasoning, as well as ordinary types of invalid or faulty reasoning that are known as logical fallacies. In logic, we discuss concepts such as inference, induction, validity, argument, and proof. Logic can be either deductive, as when we study the process by which we are able to draw particular or specific conclusions from general or universal statements, or inductive, as when we are concerned with the problem of making general inferences from the examination of particular cases. Even though logical issues are as old as human language and reasoning, it was Aristotle who succeeded in systematizing them into a scientific form. Aristotelian logic, also known as traditional logic, has exercised a profound development and remains today the matrix of scientific methodology. Since the middle of the last century, however, logic has been steadily moving along symbolic and mathematical lines, and fruitful approaches have been developed. Our chapter 6 will shed abundant light on the place of logic in philosophy and science.

b. *Ethics* is the area of philosophy in which we seek to investigate, understand, and clarify problems and issues specifically related to human values. Typically, the moral or ethical philosopher discusses questions such as the ideal life that human beings ought to pursue, the meaning of the good, the nature of virtue and righteousness, the basis of moral values, and the meaning of terms like 'good', 'evil', 'right', 'duty', 'responsibility', and others. It is now customary to distinguish three aspects of ethics: (1) descriptive ethics, in which the emphasis lies on the sociological and anthropological description of ethical systems and moral behavior; (2) metaethics, in which we devote ourselves to the analysis of the meaning and basis of ethical terms and utterances; and (3) normative ethics, in which the philosopher's main concern is to advance and justify specific moral values and precepts. A full discussion of ethics will be found in chapter 7.

c. *Political philosophy* deals with the human being insofar as he is a member of a social or political association. The political philosopher investigates problems such as the origins of the state, the nature and structure of political and social systems, the relationship between the individual and the state, the concept of civic responsibility, the notion of political liberty, the issue of human rights, and many others. As the chapter on ethics and political philosophy will show, the line of demarcation that separates ethics from political philosophy is often difficult to trace, since by nature everyone of us must forever function in the context of some social or political structure. The specific discussion of political philosophy will be found in chapter 8.

d. *Epistemology* represents one aspect of philosophy that has interested practically every major philosopher in the past and in the present. The word 'epistemology' comes from the Greek word for knowledge *(episteme)*. In epistemology, our chief concern is the clarification of basically four problems: (1) What is the nature of knowledge? (2) What kinds of knowledge are possible for the human mind? (3) What are the sources of knowledge? and (4) What are the limits of human knowledge? Obviously, these four intimately interrelated questions are fundamental in any philosophical *and* scientific endeavor, for the object of epistemological investigation is precisely the instrument that we, as human beings, must use to know and understand anything. This instrument, of course, is our very capacity to know. In epistemology, there are profoundly different philosophical schools, as the four questions stated above have been answered by different philosophers in radically different ways. This will become quite clear in chapter 9.

e. There are few concepts more difficult to define than *metaphysics*. In chapter 10 there will be an extensive presentation of what metaphysics, as an aspect of philosophy, entails. Let us note at this point that the word itself has an interesting origin. In editing the works of Aristotle, an Alexandrian scholar named Andronicus of Rhodes (first century B.C.) found an untitled book that apparently had been written or simply placed *after* the famous *Physics*. In this untitled work, Aristotle deals with a vast number of subjects that include the nature of being or existence, space and time, cause and motion, infinity, and many others. Andronicus chose to entitle this work *meta ta physica,* which literally means 'the after-the-physics', thus giving origin to the word 'metaphysics'. In philosophical usage, metaphysics itself has several meanings, chief among which are (1) the philosophical attempt to clarify the nature and structure of reality as a whole, in which case metaphysics is not altogether different from what Pythagoras would have meant by *philosophia;* (2) the study of being as such, or, in other words, existence itself, in which case metaphysics is what Aristotle called "first philosophy"; (3) as in the philosophy of Immanuel Kant (1724–1804), metaphysics could mean those lines of speculation in which we seek to answer questions concerning the existence of God, the human soul, and the problem of the freedom of the will.

f. Religion can perhaps be defined as a system of beliefs and practices accepted on faith and often strengthened by traditional and ritualistic institutions. In most instances, religious faith entails the *belief* in a non-physical realm of existence in which certain entities like God, gods, spirits, and souls occupy a prominent position. The religious person *binds* himself or herself to those beliefs and practices, something that explains the origin of the word 'religion'. This word comes from the Latin verb *religare,* which means 'to bind'. The *philosophy of religion,* on the other hand, is the aspect of philosophy in which religious statements and claims are subjected to a careful rational and critical appraisal. The philosopher of religion studies, for instance, the possibility of religious knowledge, the meaningfulness of religious language, the grounds (logical or otherwise) for believing in God, and the relationship between faith and reason. In the philosophy of religion, therefore, we do not argue either for or against religion in general or any religion in particular. Surely, since the religious experience has played so enormous a role in the development of mankind, it is natural to expect that most major philosophers have been keenly interested in the philosophy of religion. In chapter 11, the main issues confronted in the philosophy of religion will be explained.

g. *Aesthetics* does for art what the philosophy of religion does for religion. The philosophers who have devoted themselves to aesthetical studies have endeavored to come up with certain universal and rational criteria by which the activities of the artists may be philosophically assessed. In aesthetics, we analyze, for example, issues such as the meaning of art, beauty, and the relationship between art and human concerns.

So far we have made brief comments on several major philosophical areas, specifically on those to which entire chapters will be devoted. Of course, within the scope of contemporary philosophy there are many others to which reference will be made throughout this book. In all of them, we find a common denominator that, as an echo of the Pythagorean and Aristotelian ideas discussed earlier, is the chief characteristic of philosophy, perhaps the only element that allows us to define our subject. This common denominator is the commitment to understand and clarify the most significant aspects of human experience in a way that is rational and open. For the philosopher, ideally speaking, there are no sacred traditions, no infallible sources of authority, no unquestionable dogmas. In philosophy the often found "master-discipline" relationship does not, or rather should not, exist. Every philosopher, every thinker, and every student of philosophy cannot but feel forced to question not only the testimony of others, but his or her own experiences and thoughts. The love of wisdom must begin by making us free to seek knowledge and understanding in whatever direction our minds may choose to take us. The intellectual freedom, conceptual flexibility, and skeptical attitude so deeply ingrained in philosophy can thus explain the peculiar phenomenon that here, *perhaps* unlike in the sciences, the reality of progress (progress over many centuries, for instance) is not quite real; every major philosopher has had the strange feeling of being compelled to start the task of philosophy all over again. From this point of view, as we said at the beginning, it is pointless to ask questions such as, Does a contemporary philosopher know more than Plato or Aristotle? For in our search for wisdom, we have not come to accumulate a generally accepted body of truth. But, paradoxically, this is what constitutes the most challenging aspect of the discipline we are about to study.

3. PHILOSOPHY AND SCIENCE

In our brief discussion of Aristotle's concept of philosophy, we saw how according to this concept philosophy is conceived as an all-inclusive intellectual endeavor to understand and clarify all the domains of reality. Obviously then, the sciences, in which we study clearly delineated classes of things, belong to philosophy. But as we noted, the enormous growth of scientific information, the proliferation of scientific problems and theories, and the invention and development of scientific tools and instruments have made it necessary for philosophers, especially those interested in the investigation of the physical world, to become highly specialized in reasonably distinct fields of research. Already in the second part of the seventeenth century it was customary to distinguish "natural philosophy," signifying the natural sciences, from "speculative philosophy," reserved for theoretical investigations in the realm of ideas. Isaac Newton (1642–1727) entitled his major work *Mathematical Principles of Natural Philosophy,* a work in which we are introduced to hosts of physical, astronomical, and cosmological considerations. By the end of the nineteenth century, even the term "natural philosophy" was avoided, as the sciences sought to disassociate themselves from the old conceptual matrix from which they had emerged.

It is unquestionable that this disassociation had beneficial consequences, as there were practical factors that had made it inevitable. The strictly scientific world of the ancient Greeks, for instance, was more limited and restricted than that of the late nineteenth century. In a sense, there were fewer things to know then, so that *from the point of view of what today we mean by science,* a learned person could reach an encyclopedic level of knowledge: Aristotle was, besides being a metaphysician, a humanist, and a social scientist, a competent biologist, astronomer, cosmologist, physicist, mathematician, and physician. Encyclopedic competence in the sciences was even possible in the earlier decades of the seventeenth century, as the instances of Descartes, Galileo, and Locke clearly show. But as a consequence of the scientific revolution, the venerable ideal of antiquity became an impossible dream, since nobody could know and understand in depth the developing sciences as a whole; hence, specialization set in, and the natural philosophers began to move in divergent directions, each one exploring a given aspect or domain of the physical world, while the speculative philosophers were left with the task, among others, of discussing, analyzing, and assessing those underlying concepts that are at work in the various sciences. Thus, by the end of the nineteenth century, a new area of philosophy came into its own, namely, the *philosophy of science,* whose loosely defined goals included the formulation of adequate scientific methodologies, the examination of epistemological problems encountered in the individual sciences, and the clarification of scientific terms like 'fact', 'hypothesis', 'theory', 'proof', 'verification', 'confirmation', 'law', and others.

In some respects, we are living today in an age in which the disassociation of the sciences from philosophy is still a reality, a reality, however, that has grown in intensity as the sciences have become more complex and specialized, and as the perhaps fictitious demand for *practical* knowledge has infiltrated all areas of science. The once beneficial consequences of the disassociation of the sciences from philosophy are now transforming themselves into immensely detrimental results: the specialized scientist, whose intellectual grasp of science is no better than that of a limited technician, forms in his or her mind a fragmented and distorted image of reality, and as a half-educated barbarian, such a person forgets that all things are, after all, intimately interrelated. His doctoral degree in physics, biology, or astronomy, a degree that, as we saw, is nominally a doctorate in philosophy (Ph.D.), does not guarantee that his understanding of the world is more adequate than that of the most uneducated peasant. For when science forgets its philosophical roots and neglects the chief task that it is called upon to carry out, it gives birth to lamentable cases of myopic intellectualism. The presence of philosophy as an integral part of the required core of liberal arts studies in a university or college can go a long way in preventing, or at least diminishing, the detrimental consequences of a purely vocational education in which the emphasis is on career-oriented courses of study. In these, as we all know, the educational machinery is expected to produce technicians and manipulators of practical affairs and is urged to direct the unthinking masses of students along vocational avenues at the end of which the often chimerical promise of a job is set up as an allurement. All this is, of course, understandable for, after all, people need to make a living. On a deeper level of analysis, however, the eventual situation proves to be more complex. The vocationally trained student may find the desired job, and this will convince him that his education was truly worthwhile. But persons are more than the jobs they mechanically perform in the often unhappy routine of working conditions. We may work on a job thirty or forty hours per week, but we are forced to be ourselves every minute of our lives. Furthermore, jobs come and go, and often the vocational education that once occupied our college years is itself unable to find for us a reasonably decent place in the working force. In either case, whether vocationally successful or vocationally disappointed, it is indisputable that an education in which, together with practical training, we are exposed to the art of thinking critically about human and non-human issues, to the complexities of these conceptual, cultural, and historical issues that shape our own present world, to the major ideas of the philosophers who, long before us, attempted to cope with the same problems that are now besetting us—it is indisputable, we believe, that such an education is to be preferred to any other, as it gives us the necessary depth and flexibility to deal effectively with the issues and problems of our daily lives. Coming out of such an educational process, we will have grown up as persons, and then our vocational training will be of greater value to us and to the society to which we may belong.

It is for these and other reasons that the study of philosophy should occupy so important a place in all academic curricula and should constitute for every dedicated student a special area of concern and devotion. An introductory course in philosophy is often the one and only chance given a college student to come face to face with those perennial perplexities of human existence that engaged the imagination and genius of the most powerful minds of the past, and that still live in the foreground of consciousness of our most influential thinkers of today. If nothing else, it is a worthwhile occupation to find out what has agitated the minds of Socrates, Plato, Aristotle, Epicurus, Marcus Aurelius, Saint Augustine, Saint Thomas Aquinas, Francis Bacon, René Descartes, David Hume, Immanuel Kant, Karl Marx, Arthur Schopenhauer, Jeremy Bentham, John Stuart Mill, Friedrich Nietzsche, George Edward Moore, Ludwig Wittgenstein, Bertrand Russell, Martin Heidegger, Jean-Paul Sartre, and many others. Their preoccupations constitute what is known as philosophy, and the purpose of this book is to invite the students to partake in their activities.

4. THE HISTORY OF PHILOSOPHY

By its very nature, philosophy cannot be wholly separated from its history. Ideas have arisen in the context of long historical controversies and cannot be well understood and appreciated apart from them. Every major philosopher has taught us to see the world in a new way, and our own present human predicaments can become partially clarified by what can be found in the history of philosophy. Even though only some of the chapters of this book are historically oriented (chapters 2, 3, 4, 5, and 13), the student will find that throughout the entire book some emphasis has been made on the historical way in which philosophical systems and ideas have developed.

For the sake of convenience, the history of philosophy is divided into four major periods that can be generally characterized as follows:

a. *Ancient Philosophy* begins, as we will see in the following chapter, around the year 600 B.C. This period includes several developments: (1) *Pre-Socratic Philosophy* (600 B.C.–450 B.C.), in which the major philosophers are Thales, Anaximander, Anaxemines, Pythagoras, Parmenides, Heraclitus, Empedocles, Anaxagoras, and Democritus. The chief areas of concern among these early Greek thinkers were cosmological speculation and metaphysics (the understanding of reality at large). (2) *Socratic Philosophy* (450 B.C.–399 B.C.), which comprises the Sophists and Socrates. Here we find a decisive tendency to abandon cosmological investigation in favor of ethical, political, and social inquiries. (3) *Plato and Aristotle,* to whom we will devote separate chapters. (4) *Hellenistic Philosophy* (350 B.C. to the beginning of the Roman Empire), in which the major intellectual forces are Stoicism and Epicureanism (discussed in chapter 7) and Alexandrian science. (5) *Roman Philosophy* comprises whatever philosophical developments we find in late Roman times.

b. *Medieval Philosophy* (A.D. 400–1600), in which philosophy becomes largely subservient to theological and religious preoccupations, as the Church dominated the European world. The philosophers of this period are often members of the Catholic clergy (among the Christians) and devout religious scholars (among the Jews and Arabs). Saint Augustine (354–430), Saint Anselm of Canterbury (1033–1109), and Saint Thomas Aquinas (1225–1274) are among the major philosophers of the Middle Ages.

c. *Modern Philosophy* (1600–1900) was, among other things, a response to the increased prominence of science and technology in the aftermath of the Renaissance. Epistemological, metaphysical, ethical, and political questions were given a new orientation. The most prominent philosophers of modern times include Francis Bacon (1561–1626), René Descartes (1596–1650), John Locke (1632–1704), Thomas Hobbes (1588–1679), David Hume (1711–1776), Immanuel Kant (1724–1804), Georg F. Hegel (1770–1831), Karl Marx (1818–1883), Arthur Schopenhauer (1788–1860), Friedrich Nietzsche (1844–1900), and many others. Modern Philosophy covers the three hundred years between the Renaissance and our own present century and constitutes a fruitful period of philosophical activity in which a great number of important ideas and problems became the object of intense discussion. In many respects, the philosophical issues that contemporary philosophers approach today were raised in one way or another by their predecessors of the modern period.

d. *Contemporary Philosophy* comprises the philosophical developments of the twentieth century. As we will see in our last chapter, this period has seen the emergence of several major ways of interpreting and doing philosophy and of making sense of reality. Throughout this book, ample references will be made to many contemporary philosophers, and the last chapter will shed light on four major contemporary trends in philosophy: (1) Logical Analysis, (2) Linguistic Analysis, as this was developed by Ludwig Wittgenstein, (3) Dialectical Materialism, as this is embodied in Marxist philosophy, and (4) Phenomenology and Existentialism.

The ideas advanced in this introductory chapter should have given us a general notion concerning the meaning or meanings of philosophy. Still, we must bear in mind that it is through the patient and careful study of philosophical writings that a truly adequate understanding of philosophy can be obtained. Hence, as we said earlier, it is imperative to appeal to primary sources, that is, to the actual writings of the major philosophers. If this *Invitation to Philosophy* is wisely used in conjunction with a collection of primary sources, we can be reasonably sure of having led the students along the best possible way.

QUESTIONS FOR STUDY

1. What is the etymological origin of the word 'philosophy'? In what sense can we distinguish the ancient meaning attached to the word 'sophist' from what the early Greeks meant by 'philosopher'?

2. What was Aristotle's concept of philosophy? How do the sciences relate to philosophy in this sense?

3. What major factors do you think were at work in the process by which the sciences became disassociated from philosophy? Are these factors still present, and in your view, is such a disassociation something that we may regard as beneficial?

4. Define and explain some of the major branches of philosophy: logic, philosophy of science, ethics, political philosophy, epistemology, metaphysics, philosophy of religion, and aesthetics.

5. What are the main periods in the history of Western philosophy? Can you give a brief characterization of each one of them?

2

In the Beginning There Was Water

The rise of philosophy in the West is associated with the cosmological speculations of the early Greek philosophers. Its birthplace was the Ionian city of
Miletus, on the coast of Asia Minor; the time was the first decades of the sixth
century before Christ, and its father was Thales. This is where our long intellectual history began, where, for the first time, the human mind reached the
level of sophisticated thinking, and where the initial endeavors to understand the universe rationally and systematically were made. We must therefore turn our eyes to this crucial moment in the development of mankind, as
if from the specific events of that time and place, much of what has taken
place in the intervening twenty-five centuries was a logical and necessary
consequence. And it is most appropriate that we begin at the beginning, and
that we pay close attention to the process by which philosophy was born
among us, for, as Aristotle says, to understand the beginning is to understand the development. The themes, questions, and problems that actively
engaged the mind and imagination of the Milesian philosophers, no less than
the ideas, answers, and solutions advanced by them, have played a decisive
role in all subsequent attempts to explain the universe at large and the
human being in particular. In the study of philosophy, the acquaintance with
Thales and other pre-Socratics is equivalent to the learning of notes and
scales in the study of music. As such, then, it is something indispensable and
unavoidable.

We must observe at once, however, that when we speak of the birth of philosophy, we do not have in mind the idea of an *absolute* beginning, as if *nothing* of philosophical or scientific value had taken place before Thales. Surely, this cannot be the case, for if philosophy is defined simply as the love of wisdom, philosophy must be as old as our human species. As long as there have been thinking beings roaming this planet, and as long as a pair of intelligent eyes have been in the practice of inspecting the heavens, some kind of philosophical impulse must have been present. As an antidote to our unjustified, yet quite prevalent, sense of ethnocentric parochialism, we must always remember that the West is *not* the whole world, and that our cultural traditions are only a part of the human heritage. What we proudly call "the history of civilization" is not, after all, the real and complete history of human activity on this planet. The idea that civilization began only forty centuries before the birth of Christ may be a simplistic myth whose ideological roots can be easily traced to a certain narrow conception of history that comes to us from the writings of the German philosopher Hegel. But is it not possible that this conception may be mistaken? Is it not possible that in the more than two million years during which human beings have existed, many other, perhaps more advanced civilizations may have arisen, civilizations that the inexorable passage of time has erased completely? Is it not possible that the real history of mankind may be a repetitious and cyclical process in which cultural peaks are reached every so many thousand years? In such a case, great and insightful philosophical systems, as the necessary fruits of every well-developed civilization, must have grown in those faintly discerned cultures, and other "fathers of philosophy" like Thales must have commenced, each time anew, the process of thought. Perhaps the four periods of *our* philosophical history, of which we spoke in the previous chapter, may have repeated themselves countless times in an already forgotten past.

But even if we cast aside these and other speculative divagations and limit ourselves to the narrow Hegelian concept of history (as is the tendency among most academic historians), we must still remember that the Milesians belong to a not too distant past. Long before them, and even long before the Greeks learned to speak Greek, imposing philosophical insights, not only in ethics but in metaphysics and cosmology, had been developed in the West and elsewhere. The oldest texts of the Jews, Egyptians, and Hindus bear indubitable testimony in this regard. And the same thing can be said in reference to Greek writers who antedate the Milesians by many years. In quoting Homer, for instance, both Plato and Aristotle gave a sure indication of the philosophical import found in old sources; Homer, who in some sense was also a philosopher, expressed ethical views that found their way into Aristotle's *Nichomachean Ethics,* and his cosmological ideas can be discerned beneath the philosophy of Thales. Moreover, as we learn from ancient biographers, the Milesians and other Greek philosophers of antiquity were in the habit of journeying to Egypt and Babylonia, as if they expected to find in those lands certain bits of wisdom and knowledge that were lacking in their own native country. There are many important elements in the philosophical systems of the Greeks whose roots can only be found in Oriental sources, and the Greeks themselves were happy to acknowledge their debts to those whom they called "barbarians," a term which simply meant "foreigners." Thus, in speaking of the birth of philosophy, and in associating this birth with the Milesians in general and Thales in particular, we cannot reasonably have in mind the idea of an *absolute* beginning.

And yet, there is some justification in speaking of the birth of philosophy in a limited sense. There are basically two sets of considerations that sanction our practice of calling Thales "the father of philosophy." In the first place, it must be borne in mind that, aside from literary and religious texts, the fragment or fragments attributed to Thales are the oldest in Western civilization, specifically in what concerns the history of ideas. Our knowledge of what could have been said (from a scientific or philosophical viewpoint) about the world in ages that antedate Thales is practically nonexistent. Accordingly, Thales is our unavoidable starting point, as we have no earlier points of reference. He is our oldest *known* philosophical ancestor. Second, as we will see presently, as we seek to reconstruct his philosophy (a reconstruction that is the result of much speculation and guessing in the absence of definitive primary sources), we are inevitably struck by the fact that his way to confront the problem of the universe, that is, his philosophical stance, represents something altogether new, something different from anything that can be traced back to earlier times. With Thales, as we will soon explain, we learn to speak a new language and to see the world in a new way. The elements of Homeric, Egyptian, and Babylonian cultures that were inherited by him are raised in his philosophy to a radically different level. *In this sense,* Hegel was justified in saying that with Thales, we enter at once "into the realm of the mind," for, as we will see in chapter 6, Thales created a powerful new instrument for the expansion of human knowledge, and this instrument is *reason.* Such being the case, we feel compelled to abide by the practice of referring to him as the true father of philosophy, inasmuch as in philosophy, reason is the unavoidable basis of all our endeavors.

But in order to understand and appreciate adequately the place and importance of Thales, we must seek to clarify the temporal and geographical circumstances of his life, as well as the specific import of his philosophical contributions. Born around the year 625 B.C., Thales belongs to an age in Greek history in which few ideological changes had taken place since pre-Homeric days. An ordinary Greek of Thales' time would have found himself perfectly comfortable in the world of Homer and Hesiod. Between 1000 B.C. and 600 B.C., hardly anything had really changed: political institutions, religious cults, daily activities were all the same. Superstition and myth, anthropomorphism and fancy, distortion and exaggeration still dominated the foreground of human consciousness. The celestial bodies were still worshipped as divine beings, and the universe at large was still conceived as having come into being for the purpose of human needs and desires. In a world full of surprising events and miraculous occurrences that demanded immediate explanations, the human imagination was forced to produce hosts of invisible beings, such as gods and demons, who were made responsible for all that befell mankind. In Egypt, strange cults and rituals were used for the purpose of appeasing the inhabitants of the unseen world, while in Babylonia, reality was conceived as the battleground on which the supernatural forces of good and evil waged a never-ending war. The Jews, for their part, could not but see, amid their political tribulations, the invisible hand of a God who guided their destiny and who appeared to them as a sign of future deliverance. This was a time when myth and fantasy were the prevailing modes of giving an account of existence, and mankind lived, so to speak, as a child in whom imagination and ignorance combine to create a truly fantastic world.

In Greece, the land that was to become the cradle of intellectual enlightenment, things were not altogether different. The Homeric poems and the theogonies of Hesiod, memorized and recited by countless numbers of rhapsodists, remained the basis of what the Greeks knew about the world. In them, they found an infallible source of knowledge about the origin and structure of the universe, and their anthropomorphic accounts were faithfully repeated from generation to generation, as if they were sacrosanct verities. By the sixth century B.C., mystery religions had become popular, while political and religious affairs became intimately fused; the typical Greek city-state, the *polis,* functioned inevitably around the worship of the Olympian gods. Oracle consultation and divination were everywhere in use, and natural happenings (an earthquake, a storm, the singing of birds, etc.) were invariably seen as sure signs by reference to which human conduct could be guided, for the gods, it was believed, spoke through the processes of nature. Greece was, therefore, not unlike any other land, and the Greek mind reflected in its thought processes the same characteristics of the barbarian mind.

And yet, somewhere on the busy coasts of Asia Minor, something radically novel was beginning to take place, something like a fundamental departure from the immemorial traditions and beliefs that had controlled man's view of the world over thousands of years. A new approach to an old problem was discovered. At first, it was a localized and hardly noticeable movement that affected a very small number of people and left untouched the ordinary course of human events. Furthermore, this movement had to be conditioned by the prevailing cultural milieu out of which it was born, for no significant human contribution can ever come into being in a total cultural vacuum. Accordingly, it is not surprising to find that the language of the exponents of this movement is highly reminiscent of that of earlier times, when myth and legend constituted the chief modes of explanation. In due time, however, the new thinkers learned to speak their own language and were able to cast aside the mythical and legendary ideas of antiquity. As it became more sure of itself, it emerged eventually as a new way of looking at the world. Philosophy and science were its offspring, and our entire intellectual heritage proved to be its final outcome; for the history of Western philosophy and science can be conceived as the long and tortuous unfolding of what took place at that time.

The Ionian city-states of the coast of Asia Minor, and particularly Miletus, were the birthplace of this conceptual change. Between 600 and 450 B.C., several independent and bold thinkers made their entrance into the world of ideas, and most of them were connected, in one way or another, with those coastal cities. Thales, Anaximander, Anaxemines, Xenophanes, and Leucippus came from Miletus; Pythagoras from Samos; Heraclitus from Ephesus; Anaxagoras from Clazomenae; and Herodotus (of whom we will speak in chapter 6) from Halicarnassus. We will concentrate our attention on Thales and Anaximander, although a few passing remarks will be made about the others. From Thales we will learn a new way of approaching the problem of the universe, a way in which the emphasis will be on the *rational* search for a *principle* by reference to which all phenomena can be explained and understood. From Anaximander we will learn a number of important ideas both in science (astronomy) and philosophy. As we will see, Thales and Anaximander can be said to be the true founders of philosophy and science in the West, and their ideas constitute undoubtedly the beginning of our rational understanding of reality. This understanding, as we saw in the previous chapter, is not something stable and final. As the history of philosophy clearly shows, it is something dynamic and forever changing, something that develops in a multiplicity of forms that grow out of one another in a great variety of ways.

It is important to begin, however, with a brief examination of some of the historical, political, and cultural circumstances that contributed to the emergence of philosophy in Miletus at the beginning of the sixth century B.C. Founded around the tenth century B.C. by the Athenians, Miletus grew eventually into a major metropolis. Conveniently located as a haven for sailors and visitors from all parts of the Mediterranean, and easily accessible from Lydia, Persia, and Egypt, it enjoyed a constant flux of travelers and immigrants who brought to its markets and squares goods and ideas from the most remote lands. Its sophisticated circles were repeatedly exposed to new and foreign points of view, a circumstance that protected it from the provincialism that often characterized other Greek cities. Neither wholly Greek in character like Athens and Sparta, nor entirely foreign like Sardis, Miletus was able to take the best elements offered at that time by both Greeks and barbarians. We are told, for instance, that on its marketplace it was possible to hear a great variety of languages and dialects spoken at the same time. In its excellent harbor, Egyptian ships were always found, and through its gates, caravans of visitors from the Orient were always passing. Furthermore, certain political arrrangements with the neighboring Lydians, specifically with King Alyattes of Sardis, allowed the Milesians to live in an atmosphere of relative peace and security, which are so essential for any sort of intellectual growth. For the Milesians of the seventh century B.C., war was not the usual condition. This circumstance, in its turn, contributed to the rise of an intellectual class that was able to enjoy some degree of leisure, and that was in a position to devote itself to strictly speculative activities, especially as it enjoyed a great deal of affluence.

This exceptional and happy condition, however, did not last long. Already by the year 500 B.C., Miletus, like other Greek cities of Asia Minor, was deeply immersed in the nasty business of surviving amid dreadful dangers. Fear and insecurity replaced the serenity of former times, and many Greek Ionians were compelled to emigrate to the coast of southern Italy, as was the case with Pythagoras. In 494 B.C., Miletus was taken and destroyed by the invading Persians and their allies, and the destruction was so vast and brutal that the city was never able to recover completely. Eventually, several centuries later, Miletus died, and today it is only a collection of badly preserved archeological ruins. Not even the gulf of Latmos, on which it once proudly stood, is there; erosion and time have filled those parts that once bathed the Milesian port. Of course, the Milesian intellectual period coincides with its political golden age. The two philosophers who concern us here belong, therefore, to the sixth century, and reliable historical information allows us to place Thales' birth around the year 625 B.C., and that of Anaximander around 611 B.C. Both died in 547 B.C.

As one should expect, there are few historical facts about their lives, and it is not easy to separate their historical context from legendary accounts. Like many other ancient historical figures, Thales and Anaximander are extremely blurry images that are difficult to reconstruct. Obviously, our ideas concerning their philosophical and scientific systems can only be tentative and fragmentary, inasmuch as in either case we only have at our disposal collections of brief quotations from later sources. We know that both Thales and Anaximander were born in Miletus, and that the former was the latter's teacher. We also know that Thales traveled extensively, and that his travels took him to Egypt (where the Milesians kept a standing garrison at Naucratis) and to Babylonia. In Egypt he may have learned the rudiments of practical geometry, and from the Babylonians he could have obtained knowledge concerning the measurement of time (hours, days, years) and the art of predicting solar eclipses. In the neighboring kingdom of Lydia, he acted as the king's counselor at Sardis, and in Miletus, he took an active part in political affairs. His knowledge and influence earned for him a place among the so-called "Seven Wise Men" of antiquity.

Thales was the moving force of a fertile 'school' of philosophy with which many ancient philosophers became intimately associated. Anaximander

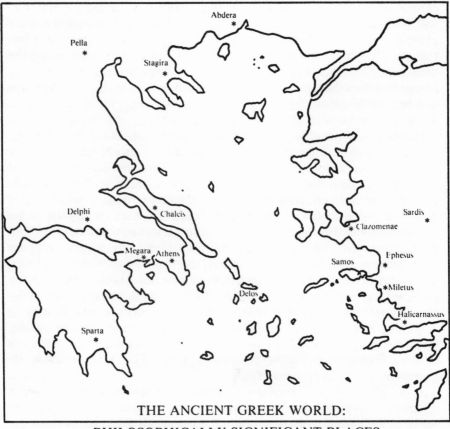

THE ANCIENT GREEK WORLD:

PHILOSOPHICALLY SIGNIFICANT PLACES

belonged to this school, and the testimony of some biographers make him out to be Thales' chief 'disciple'. We must bear in mind, however, that in philosophy we understand by 'disciple', not someone who repeats faithfully the ideas of another and who, out of reverence, refuses to question and challenge them, but someone who is willing to subject to criticism a set of philosophical tenets with which he finds himself in general agreement. It is in this sense, as we will see in chapter 4, that we can speak of Plato as being Socrates' disciple. Also, we must remember the etymology of the English word 'school', a word that comes from the Greek word for 'leisure'. Accordingly, when we speak of the Milesian school of philosophy, we should not conceive of a formalized and structured academic entity. As used in this context, 'school' simply means a loose association of persons who were in the habit of spending their *leisure* time exchanging, discussing, criticizing, and refining their ideas about the world.

Like Thales, Anaximander traveled to many distant lands, and there are sure indications that he spent time among the Babylonians. His interests were most varied, and his understanding of things quite remarkable. He explained the multiplicity of things that sense experience reveals in terms of a single *principle* that enigmatically he called "the infinite." He advanced a theory that can be seen as a rough anticipation of the evolutionary ideas of Charles Darwin and Lamarck. According to Anaximander, the human species is the evolutionary transformation of more primitive species that, in turn, are transformations of ancient aquatic creatures; the changes undergone by the surface of the earth have been responsible for these evolutionary developments. As an experienced traveler, Anaximander attempted the construction of the oldest map of the "inhabited" earth, giving birth, thereby, to scientific geography.

As we saw earlier, the general conception of the world that we find at the beginning of the sixth century B.C. is one that is thoroughly permeated by mythical descriptions of an anthropomorphic nature. But as long as the world is understood in terms of whimsical divinities for whom the universe is their playground, it is certainly futile to attempt to explain coherently and consistently the experiences revealed to us by our senses. The whole world is a constant miracle, and all its occurrences are miraculous. Things happen unexpectedly and by surprise at the command of a god or a demon. But since the will and design of the gods and demons are unpredictable from the human point of view, it is impossible to introduce some sense of order and predictability in the realm of natural phenomena. Reality remains on this level something utterly mysterious and enigmatic. This is, let us repeat, the pre-philosophical stage of the human consciousness, and it is precisely out of this stage that the Milesians were successful in taking us. When we stand in the presence of Thales and Anaximander, we realize at once that a new standpoint has been adopted. Homer and Hesiod, and along with them other mythical conceptions of reality, are partly cast aside in order to put forward a distinctly *rational* explanation of experience. Miracles, wonders, gods, and demons silently withdraw into the background, as the human mind decides that the universe can best be understood in terms of some universal *principle* that can be eventually elucidated by the power of *reason*. Now, as the anthropomorphic creations of former times lose significance, and the mind wakes up from its dreams, genuine philosophical concepts gain in value. The prophet, the visionary, and the sage are at last replaced by the philosopher.

But let us examine closely this conceptual transformation. According to Thales, beneath the ever-changing multiplicity of events and objects that we call the world, there is a universal and physical *element* or *principle* into which all things are ultimately resolvable. This element or principle (*arche*, to use Aristotle's language) manifests itself in different ways and forms, and its manifestations are subject to inflexible and rational processes. In fact, the universe at large is nothing but an ongoing process *(physis)* of regular and repetitious changes, of which gods, men, and things are an integral part. Our unrefined experiences reveal to us the existence of a great variety of many *different* things: fire, air, water, earth, clouds, mountains, lakes, plants, animals, human beings, celestial bodies, and terrestrial seas. We are empirically (that is, through sense perception) aware, moreover, that within the world things come into being and go out of existence: men are born, live for a short time, and then disappear into the earth, and plants and animals do likewise. Some things, like ants and bees, persist for a very short time, while others, like mountains and cities, enjoy longer periods of existence. But inexorably, all things perish in the end, some by death, others by transformation, others by dissipation; everything is the victim of a never-ending cycle of changes. But while this is an unquestionable truth from the point of view of ordinary sense experience, on a more sophisticated level of reflection the truth is quite otherwise. For as Heraclitus of Ephesus insisted, "The eyes and ears are bad witnesses," since what our senses reveal to us is *not* reality but a distorted and superficial representation of reality. Things *appear* to be many, *appear* to come into being and out of being, *appear* to be substantially different from one another. But *are* they really so? Appearance and reality may be, after all, two distinct dimensions of being. Is it then possible that amid change and multiplicity there may be *something* that remains forever the same, *something* out of which all things are made and into which they eventually return? Is there a substance that is permanent and that manifests itself in so varied a multiplicity of forms? Obviously, this substance cannot be subject to temporal changes and spatial determinations; it must be necessarily eternal and infinite, yet as material and physical as the objects that sense perception discloses to us. But what could this substance be?

These and similar considerations must have engaged Thales' imagination, until an answer dawned in his mind: this enigmatic something must be *water.* "All things are water," he flatly stated. The universal *arche* (substance) is everything, and everything is water. The things that surround us, as well as we ourselves, are nothing but water that, constantly undergoing specific and localized alterations, appears now as air, then as actual water, or fire, earth, rocks, and so on. Indeed, even the Olympian gods, if they exist, must also be water. There is, however, no way in which we can know how Thales explained the mechanism that is responsible for the transformations undergone by the primordial watery element that lies beneath all things; neither can we be certain about the reasons that led Thales to postulate water as opposed to something else. Possibly, as Aristotle suggests, he chose water on account of its importance in the processes of generation, or on account of the simple fact that water can be seen to assume different forms (ice, snow, water, vapor, etc.). In the absence of reliable primary sources, these questions cannot be really answered with finality. We know that in times long before Thales, water was vaguely conceived as some kind of original stuff out of which the universe emerged, as is the case, for instance, in certain Homeric passages.

But these secondary issues are not decisive for us. We will never know why

Thales chose water as the fundamental stuff of all things, or how he envisioned the physical processes at work in the transformations of water. But what we do know, however, is that at the beginning of the sixth century B.C., an attempt was made to find a universal element by reference to which all things can be rationally explained. As soon as this is done, reality becomes invested with rationality, and the universe ceases to be a mere collection of unrelated and disparate events. From a bewildering concatenation of surprising happenings in which no order can exist, the universe becomes for the first time a *cosmos,* that is, an ordered and predictable world. The Greek word *cosmos* means, among other things, something both beautiful and organized. The search for wisdom, which as we saw in chapter 1 is the basis of philosophy, becomes, as a result of Thales' bold statement, something possible, and science, originally in the form of speculative cosmology, is within the reach of reflective and intelligent human beings.

Thales' philosophy has been called "monistic," and this is most appropriate, for the idea of monism implies that all things are basically one *(monos),* and this is clearly maintained by Thales: All things are water. Now then, water, in the sense of a primordial and universal element, cannot be made or created out of something else, for what could this "something else" be? Water is therefore eternal, which implies that the universe is also eternal, not in the sense of "exceedingly old" as in Homer, but in the staggering sense of *timeless.* The universe has no time, has no beginning, has no end. We no longer need, as among the Jews and Hindus, the idea of a creator of the universe, for the universe was never created. A non-physical God who brought the physical universe out of nothing *(ex nihilo)* can have, therefore, no place in the cosmology of Thales, and this circumstance has led some historians to the conviction that his philosophy is basically an example of materialism. The materialist denies the existence of anything that is not in some sense physical, and in examining the claim of Thales, and the implications that can reasonably emerge from it, one cannot but be inclined to agree with such historians.

When we examine the contribution of Thales in the context of his own time, we cannot avoid a sense of admiration. In a world immersed in religious myths and fantastic legends in which the whims of the gods were seen as the ultimate explanation for all events, and in which the sayings of the prophets and sages were held to be sacrosanct, Thales had the courage to pursue another path of investigation: all things, let us repeat, are water. Now we can begin to impose on the multiplicity of our experiences some degree of order and arrangement according to a single and eternal element, namely, water. From this point on, we can begin to argue, as Thales' successors did, whether water is the true element, or whether something else can be chosen as the primordial *arche.* We can begin to ask the appropriate questions concerning the specific processes that are responsible for the multiplicity of things, and we can start to clarify issues concerning the relationship between what is and what appears to be. We can be sure, however, that whatever the universal processes may be, they must be universal and uniform, so that if we succeed in grasping what they are, the entire world will become intelligible and predictable.

And yet, the fact remains that the statement "All things are water" does sound paradoxical and strange. After all, we seem to know what water is, and can identify lakes, rivers, and seas as being made of water. But are rocks and stones, plants and animals, and the sun and the moon *also* water? Are we not forcing our ideas into avenues of thinking that openly contradict, not only traditional beliefs, but our most ordinary perceptions? Has Thales lost touch with reality, and like the character of Socrates in Aristophanes' *The Clouds,* is he not living on some imaginary cloud from which all things may appear to be *like* water to his deranged sense? Philosophers have the reputation of saying strange and bizarre things about the world, and the gap that separates them from ordinary people is often known to be wide. But the case of Thales clearly defies simple explanation!

With these understandable perplexities in mind, let us proceed to examine the value of Thales' famous statement in the light of philosophy in general and cosmology in particular. We can begin by noting that the course of scientific growth has fully confirmed the already quoted fragment of Heraclitus: "Eyes and ears are bad witnesses." What ordinary sense perception reveals about the world, and what the world actually is, are two vastly different things: the former is a subjectively distorted image of the latter. Our senses reveal to us a vague and unreliable representation of the real world, because what we know in empirical experience is necessarily conditioned by our senses, and these are limited by physiological, temporal, and spatial determinations. In the world of science, therefore, the testimony of the senses is used merely as a *basis,* never as a solid criterion of what the world is in itself. Philosophy and science are thus compelled to refine the data of sense experience, for otherwise the picture of the world that we would obtain would be a most unsophisticated one. We would have to say, for instance, that the sun actually moves from east to west; that the stars are smaller than the sun because their light is dimmer; that the earth does not move in space because we are not immediately aware of its motion; that light propagates itself instantaneously through space. The existence of things not immediately given to the senses would have to be denied, and the world would become a poor collection of surfaces.

But as the testimony of the senses is refined and artificially extended, the end result is often one that contradicts simple sense experience: the sun does not really move from east to west, some of the stars are thousands of times bigger than the sun, light travels at a finite velocity, etc. Ordinary things are made of atoms and molecules that the unaided eye cannot simply see. We can also say, albeit tentatively, that most of the observable universe is made of a single element, namely, hydrogen. But none of these statements is the *direct* result of ordinary perception. We will see in chapter 6 how in the logic of scientific discovery, simple observation must be transcended in order to arrive at meaningful insights into the nature of the physical world. Accordingly, the statement "All things are water," while appearing to defy what sense perception reveals, may be a useful instrument in the search for truth. Today we believe that more than 90 percent of the observable universe is made of hydrogen, even though this belief cannot be supported by *simple* observation. It is possible to say that all the known elements in nature are themselves transformations of hydrogen that under diverse physical conditions give rise to heavier atomic combinations. We also know, moreover, that the processes that bring about these changes are uniform, regular, and predictable, as they are the exemplifications of inflexible physical laws that, in principle, are capable of being known through rational and scientific investigation. Thus, *our* own view of the physical world is not entirely different from that of Thales. In both, it is possible to assume a monistic posture in order to speak in terms of *one* universal element; in both, we see the multiplicity of things, their diversity notwithstanding, as manifestations of the same primordial element; in both, we conceive of all physical transformations as being dictated by universal and uniform laws; and, lastly, in both, we assign to human reason the task of elucidating the processes and events of nature. It is, therefore, clear that in saying that all things are water, and in approaching the problem of reality from a rationalistic point of view, Thales struck the first note of a symphony that is still being played today. The themes of this symphony have been all related to each other, even though in vastly varied forms: Anaximander spoke of the "infinite" as the universal element, while Anaxemines chose air; Pythagoras spoke of number, while Leucippus and Democritus chose the atoms, and so on.

But more crucial than the choice of what constitutes the universal element is the ability of the human mind to raise itself to a level from which the mere idea of a universal element is somehow visible. Likewise, more crucial than the specific details of Thales' philosophy is his conviction that reason, rather than authority, superstition, or emotion, is the tool *par excellence* that human beings ought to employ in their search for wisdom. With Thales, then, the mind elevates itself to a high level of sophisticated speculation in which genuine philosophy is for the first time possible. The commitment to reason advocated by the Milesian philosophers in general and Thales in particular has remained a constant theme throughout the history of philosophy and science, and this is why, as we saw above, we are amply justified in calling Thales "the father of philosophy."

The years between the death of Thales and the appearance of Socrates saw the emergence of a great number of perceptive minds who endeavored to refine, correct, and extend the ideas to which Thales gave rise. In general, we can say that the two fundamental problems that engaged their thoughts were (1) whether the primordial substance *(arche)* is *one* or *many*, and (2) how the primordial substance or substances can become manifested in the immense multiplicity of things that we call the world. The attempts to cope with these two problems at first took the form of materialistic cosmologies, as was the case with Thales, Anaximander, and Anaxemines. Subsequently, metaphysical issues were inevitable, and grand metaphysical systems were created, as was the case with the speculations of philosophers like Parmenides of Elea. Obviously, what confronted the philosophical imagination at this point was the problem of the relationship between reality and appearance, a problem that, as we saw, had already been raised by Thales. Those who insisted on the notion that reality is basically *one* defended a *monistic* point of view (Thales, Anaximander, Anaxemines, and Parmenides). Those, for whom there were several substances *(archai)*, took a *pluralistic* stance: for Empedocles of Acragas, the substances were earth, water, air, and fire; for Anaxagoras, there was an infinite number of substances of infinite kinds; for Leucippus and Democritus, reality was made of an infinite number of atoms *(atoma* or exceedingly small and unbreakable bits of matter) of a finite number of types that floated aimlessly in empty space.

On several occasions, moreover, the monistic materialism of the early Milesians was challenged in the name of a distinctly *dualistic* metaphysical notion of reality, according to which there exist two fundamental kinds of existence, namely, physical existence and spiritual existence. Pythagoras of Samos was apparently inclined in this direction, as it was he who introduced in Western culture the idea of the human soul. In our subsequent chapter on Plato, we will have an opportunity to examine in detail this idea of the soul that, in Plato, is a clear manifestation of a Pythagorean influence on him. But the introduction of a spiritual element in existence on the part of Pythagoras and Empedocles should not make us forget that, as we said earlier, philosophy began its journey on an unquestionably *materialistic* basis, as for Thales only physical existence can be said to be truly real. The introduction of the idea of the soul, and the necessary introduction of a whole realm of non-physical existence in which a perfectly spiritual God becomes a real possibility, opened the door to a host of new and unsuspected problems and issues in philosophy that we are still attempting to clarify.

In general, we can say that the contributions of the early philosophers were marked by a spirit of *objectivism,* as their materialism would not have allowed anything else. For them (with some exceptions), the purpose of philosophy was the examination of the universe at large, a universe in which human beings did not occupy a privileged or special position. The world became the chief object of philosophical investigation, and the philosopher's task was to make meaningful statements about *this* world. Hence, the early philosophers have been called cosmologists or philosophical scientists. Their interest in astronomy, for instance, supports this way of speaking about them. All of them created complex and sophisticated systems of cosmology and cosmography in which they sought to clarify the nature of the earth and the heavens. In fact, for some of them, such a clarification was the true object of philosophy. It is recorded, for example, that, when asked what the purpose of life is, Anaxagoras of Clazomenae replied succinctly: "To investigate the sun, the moon, and the stars." Accordingly, ethical, political, and social investigations were not so crucial for him, and those specific aspects of existence in which human problems occupy the foreground were of secondary importance. The human being was conceived as just another object among objects, and the human species as just another kind of animal life. Anaximander's theory of evolution, which, as we saw, makes the human species emerge from certain aquatic forms as a result of ecological changes, is a clear example of the spirit of objectivity that, by and large, characterized early Greek philosophy.

This is important to bear in mind, especially as we are about to move into the chapter on Socrates. With the advent of the Sophists and Socrates, philosophy took a discernibly different direction, a direction away from *objectivity* towards *subjectivity*. For reasons that will become clear later on, the philosophers of the second half of the fifth century (450–399 B.C.) turned their attention towards questions of ethics and politics. If we had asked Socrates what the purpose of life is, he would have never answered: "To investigate the sun, the moon, and the stars" or "To know what the primordial substance is." He would have said: "The purpose of life is to learn the art of living ethically." Thus, with him and with his contemporaries, subjectivism replaced the objectivism of the Milesians, and ethics took the place of cosmology. In our chapter on Plato, we will see how an effort was made to integrate both objectivism and subjectivism, cosmology and ethics, into philosophy.

QUESTIONS FOR STUDY

1. Thales of Miletus has been called "the father of philosophy," and Miletus is often referred to as the cradle of philosophy and science. On what historical and cultural grounds are these statements justifiable?

2. There are certain distinct conditions which contributed to the rise of philosophical speculation among the Greeks of Asia Minor in general and the Milesians in particular. Can you explain what these conditions were?

3. What is the meaning of the statement "All things are made of water"? In what sense can we say that this idea reveals a great degree of conceptual sophistication?

4. Explain the sense in which materialism and monism can be predicated of the speculations of the Milesian philosophers.

5. The problem of the relationship between reality and appearance has occupied a prominent place in the history of philosophy. How does this problem first arise? How does Thales confront this issue?

6. In what sense are we justified in speaking of the early Greek philosophers as being *objectively* oriented?

3

A Certain Man Named Socrates

The last chapter has given us a general idea about the rise of philosophy in Miletus sometime towards the beginning of the sixth century B.C. We have made some comments about the cultural and historical circumstances that allowed the Greek colonies of Asia Minor to become a fertile soil for philosophical speculation, and these circumstances, let us recall, included affluence, prosperity, cosmopolitanism, and political security. But their happy conditions depended largely on the favorable political situation of the neighboring Lydians, with whom, as we saw, the Greeks had established friendly relations. Unfortunately, however, only one year after Thales' death, profound changes began to affect the Lydians. In 546 B.C., Sardis, the Lydian capital, was conquered by the Persians, who eventually came to dominate, at least in some respects, the Greek coastal cities. But the Ionian Greeks, accustomed to the enjoyment of political freedom, revolted against the Persian power in 499 B.C., and with the help of the Athenians, they once more succeeded in gaining their independence. By the year 494 B.C., however, the Greeks saw themselves attacked by a formidable enemy against whom they were virtually powerless. Thus it was that the Persian king Darius conquered and destroyed Miletus at this time. Great numbers of Greeks fled to the Greek mainland or the islands, or to the coasts of Italy. The following twenty years saw the conquest of Greece by the Persian army, as well as the eventual defeat of the Persians. By the year 479 B.C., Greece had regained its political independence, and the bulk of the invading forces of the Persians had been expelled. Still, the decades of the Persian War left a lasting mark on the history of Greece. In the first place, the colonies of Asia Minor lost their once privileged position, so that henceforth they became cities of minor importance; second, Athens emerged as the center of political and cultural life, as it was through the military power of the Athenians that the Persians were compelled to abandon their imperialistic ambitions.

By the middle of the fifth century, Athens had become the veritable center of Hellenic life. Its democratic institutions and its extraordinary affluence attracted a large number of people who came to seek, under the protecting shadow of the Acropolis, the security and opportunities that were difficult to find elsewhere. Art and architecture, poetry and drama, politics and rhetoric flourished in an unprecedented way, and under the tutelage of the great Pericles the Athenian world entered into an era of remarkable prosperity. Inevitably, however, deep within the Athenian worldly success the seeds of decadence and destruction lay engrained, and eventually these seeds brought about the confrontation of Athens with the Spartan power. By the time of Pericles' death (429 B.C.), the Greeks found themselves immersed once more in the deadly business of war. Twenty-five years later, the Spartan army marched into Athens, destroying thereby not only its democratic government, but all its chances for future grandeur. The Athens of Plato, Aristotle, and Epicurus was only a vestige of the great city in which Socrates was born. But in destroying Athens, the Spartans also destroyed the Hellenic world at large, and it is not unreasonable to say that the decadence of the Greek world, a decadence that lasted more than twenty-three centuries, was the result of the events of the Peloponnesian War (431–404 B.C.).

It is to be expected that a nation's era of power and affluence must manifest itself in the heightening of its culture, and that philosophy, as the highest expression of culture, should grow vigorously at that time. As we saw in chapter 2, such was the case of Miletus, and such was, also, the case of Athens. The second half of the fifth century, accordingly, was characterized by the arrival in Athens of several major philosophers who came to settle there. Anaxagoras of Clazomenae, for instance, whom we met earlier, made his home in Athens, where he developed a system of pluralistic philosophy. Widely influential among high political circles, Anaxagoras established a close relationship with Pericles. But political intrigues, mostly directed against Pericles, were successful in framing a legal case against the philosopher, who, as a result, was tried and convicted of atheism and impiety and eventually banished from the city. The same vicissitudes befell another eminent thinker who had come to take residence in Athens, namely, Protagoras of Abdera, an important exponent of a school of philosophy (the Sophists) to which we will devote considerable attention. Together with Anaxagoras and Protagoras, there were other notable foreign philosophers in Athens: Gorgias of Leontini, Hippias of Elis, Prodicus of Ceos, Thrasymachus of Chalcedon, and many others.

The philosophical activities of the early Milesians were centered, as we said, around cosmological and scientific questions such as the existence and nature of the primordial substance, and the structure of the universe. Their orientation was decidedly *objective*, inasmuch as the world in general was the main object of their preoccupation. The peculiar problems to which human existence gives rise, and the issues specifically related to the human being were, in their view, only one aspect of those questions to which the philosopher must direct his attention. But as the cultural climate of Greece in general and Athens in particular changed, it was inevitable that a new philosophical direction had to be taken. The Athenian of the fifth century faced typically human perplexities, and in his urgency to sort them out, he became somewhat oblivious of the old cosmological problems confronted by the Milesians. First, there was the ineludible necessity of coping with the responsibilities of direct democratic government: every citizen had to learn the art of participating meaningfully in the affairs of the city, and this entailed a thorough acquaintance with politics and rhetoric, as public discussions and debates took place everywhere. Then, there was the urgency of solving pressing political and social problems, which grew in intensity as a consequence of the Athenian imperialism; the problems of society took the place of old astronomical controversies. Furthermore, the confrontation with vast hordes of barbarians (who at one point had come to take over the city itself) opened the Athenian mind to hosts of new values and customs. As a result of these and other factors, then, Man, not the Universe; ethics, not cosmology; language, not astronomy, came to occupy the very foreground of philosophical interest. For, as Protagoras said, "Man is the measure of all things." We can apply to the Sophists in general what Cicero said about Socrates: "He called down philosophy from heaven, settled it in cities, introduced it into houses, and made it necessary for inquiries to be made on life and morals, good and evil."

Such was the birth of Sophism in the middle of the fifth century. It would be unwise at this point to seek the clarification of the ideas of the individual Sophists, since among them, there were many differences and often mutually exclusive viewpoints. But since, as we will presently see, a correct understanding of Sophism is essential for gaining an appreciation of Socrates, we will make a few general remarks about the Sophistical movement in order to bring to light some of its major characteristics.

1. As we said in the context of chapter 1, the word 'sophist' meant in ancient Greek 'wise man', as *sophia* meant 'wisdom'. By the time of Socrates, however, 'sophist' had come to mean something like 'traveling teacher' or 'someone who would go from place to place giving instruction to the youth for a certain fee'. Thus, the itinerant philosophers (Protagoras, Gorgias, etc.),

who visited Athens and who often made it their semipermanent home, were called 'Sophists'. *

2. But it was the specific kind of instruction imparted by the Sophists that really characterized them as such. According to Aristotle, they were concerned with teaching "the appearance, not the reality, of wisdom." Whether the Sophists were themselves *wise* or not is not the crucial issue; their concern was to teach others the art of *appearing* wise, for in a society like Athens, social appearance was more important than anything else. The Sophists were, therefore, able instructors of etiquette, manners, rhetoric, parliamentary procedure, and so on. When in the *Apology*, Socrates speaks of those whose only wish is to *appear* to be wise and good and who neglect the business of *being* actually wise and good, he is talking specifically about the Sophists, just as he does when he refers to those who charge exorbitant fees for instruction.

3. The goal of much of the activities of the Sophists was to ensure *the social and political success* of their pupils. They showed the Athenian youth how to succeed in the world, and this entailed the mastery of rhetoric, the aquaintance with legal and political processes, and the capacity of persuading public bodies of any idea one were to choose, no matter how bizarre it might be. When in the *Apology* Socrates begins by saying he is unacquainted with the way in which legal cases are tried in Athens, all he is saying is that he is *not* a Sophist or the pupil of a Sophist. *Persuasion,* regardless of the moral substance of that which is presented to the audience, was the goal of Sophistical teaching. In this regard there is an illuminating fragment attributed to Gorgias in which he praises "the power of speech":

> The power of speech over the constitution of the mind can be compared with the effect of drugs on the bodily state: just as drugs by driving out different humors from the body can put an end either to the disease or to life, so with speech: different words can induce grief, pleasure, or fear; or again, by means of a harmful kind of persuasion, words can drug and bewitch the mind.

It is not surprising, therefore, to find the Sophists actively engaged in political affairs and constantly caught in political turmoils, which explains why so many of them found themselves involved in dreadful political trials, of which Socrates' own trial was, *in a restricted way,* a lucid example.

4. Theoretically, Sophism gave rise to a great deal of *skepticism,* that is, the idea that there can be no absolute certainty about anything. This skepticism was effective in moving the Sophists away from strictly speculative endeavors in which neither certainty nor practical advantages can be found. In the political and ethical realms, there was no certainty either, but there was certainly a great deal of practical advantage. The skepticism of the Sophists appears quite clearly in the ideas of Protagoras who taught that "Every proposition can be shown to be equally true and equally false," which

is another way of saying that there is nothing true or false. Gorgias, for his part, took pride in proving three propositions: (1) nothing exists; (2) if anything existed, it could not be known; and (3) if it could be known, it could not be communicated to others. This implies a profound attachment to what can be characterized as philosophical nihilism, in the presence of which the only living option for an intelligent person is a complete commitment to the world of practical affairs.

5. More specifically, however, the skepticism of the Sophists took on four interrelated directions, that is, skepticism in metaphysics, in cosmology, in religion, and in ethics. In metaphysics, it led them to the conviction that the real world cannot be known, and that only appearance is accessible to us—something that explains their permeating interest in making things appear this way or that way depending on the audiences who came to hear them. In cosmology, their skepticism developed in them a certain disdain for scientific inquiries, a disdain that one can detect in Socrates' comments about Anaxagoras in Plato's *Phaedo*. Neither Socrates nor the Sophists were genuinely interested in scientific pursuits. In religion, Sophistical skepticism found expression in a certain indifference concerning theological questions, including the existence of God or gods. Protagoras, for instance, made the following most revealing comment:

> About the gods, I am not able to know whether they exist or do not exist, nor what they are like in form; for the factors preventing my knowledge are many: the obscurity of the subject, and the shortness of human life.

Lastly, in ethics, the skeptical attitude gave birth either to a relativistic view of values (all moral values depend on one's choices or feelings) or to a worship of those values or practices that ensure one's success in the turmoil of political and social relationships (might is right). We would like to quote a well-known passage from Plato's *Republic,* in which Thrasymachus of Chalcedon gives a most eloquent exposition of the typical ethical stance of many Sophists and their disciples. After accusing Socrates of naiveness and impracticality, the angry Thrasymachus goes on to say:

> Oh, no; and so entirely astray are you in your ideas about the just and unjust as not even to know that justice and the just are in reality another's good; that is to say, the interest of the ruler and stronger, and the loss of the subject and the servant; and injustice the opposite; for the unjust is lord over the truly simple and just: he is the stronger, and his subjects do what is for his interest, and minister to his happiness, which is very far from being their own. Consider further, most foolish Socrates, that the just is always a loser in comparison with the unjust. For first of all, in private contracts: whenever the unjust is the partner of the just you will find that, when the partnership is dissolved, the unjust man has always more and the just less. Secondly, in their dealings with the State: when there is an income-tax, the just man will pay more and the unjust less on the same amount

of income; and when there is anything to be received the one gains nothing and the other much. Observe also what happens when they take an office; there is the just man neglecting his affairs and perhaps suffering other losses, and getting nothing out of the public, because he is just; moreover he is hated by his friends and acquaintances for refusing to serve them in unlawful ways. But all this is reversed in the case of the unjust man. I am speaking, as before, of injustice on a large scale in which the advantage of the unjust is more apparent; and my meaning will be most clearly seen if we turn to that highest form of injustice in which the criminal is the happiest of all men, and the sufferers or those who refuse to do injustice are the most miserable—that is to say tyranny, which by fraud and force takes away the property of others, not little by little but wholesale; comprehending in one, things sacred as well as profane, private and public; for which acts of wrong, if he were detected perpetrating any one of them singly, he would be punished and incur great disgrace—they who do such wrong in particular cases are called robbers of temples, and man-stealers and burglars and swindlers and thieves. But when a man besides taking away the money of the citizens has made slaves of them, then, instead of these names of reproach, he is termed happy and blessed, not only by the citizens but by all who hear of his having achieved the consummation of injustice. For mankind censure injustice, fearing that they may be the victims of it and not because they shrink from committing it. And thus, as I have shown, Socrates, injustice, when on a sufficient scale, has more strength and freedom and mastery than justice; and, as I said at first, justice is the interest of the stronger, whereas injustice is a man's profit and interest.

Both in this chapter and in the chapter on Plato, we will see how Socrates endeavored to answer Thrasymachus' diatribe against those moral values for which Socrates stood, values that, needless to say, are far removed from the gross Machiavellian opportunism of some of the Sophists. For, as we will presently see, Socrates' philosophical association with Sophism was a superficial one, as he shared neither their practical goals nor their skeptical attitudes. It was indeed as a reaction to the decadent morality preached by the Sophists, and to their intellectual nihilism, that Socratic philosophy was born, even though, on the surface, this philosophy gave the appearance of being sophistical. But let us now turn our attention to Socrates himself.

There are abundant sources of information about him, as there are fewer historical characters who have attracted more philosophical and historical interest than Socrates. We learn about him in the writings of Plato, Xenophon, and Aristophanes. Practically every major philosopher and historian of antiquity has made extensive commentaries on him, and in modern times his life and philosophical outlook have been studied, reviewed, and criticized in a thorough way. The charm and intensity of his life have been held to be veritable paradigms of human excellence in general and philosophical worthiness in particular, and his ideas have been seen as a fertile soil out of which humanity has been able to derive the most advantageous and enlightening fruits. It is not an exaggeration to say that Socrates is philosophy itself, as in his own existence he was able to integrate, perhaps more than anyone else, the true spirit of philosophical curiosity that Aristotle made the distinguishing mark of a true philosopher. Socrates' influence runs powerfully throughout the entire history of ideas in Western culture, not only in the philosophies of Plato and the other ancient Socratic schools, but also in the Epicureans and Stoics, as well as other philosophical movements including those of the present time. The Delphian oracle called him the wisest of all men, and as "the enchanter of Greece," he was highly praised even by those who felt ill disposed towards him. Aristophanes, who in his *Clouds* sought to ridicule him, still had words of the highest encomium for him:

> O man that justly desirest great wisdom, how blessed will be thy life amongst Athenians and Greeks, retentive of memory and thinker that thou art, with endurance of toil for thy character; never art thou weary whether standing or walking, never numb with cold, never hungry for breakfast; from wine and from gross feeding and all other frivolities thou dost turn away.

There are many details of Socrates' life that can be historically ascertained. We know, for instance, that he was born in Athens in 469 B.C. His father was a sculptor named Sophroniscus, and his mother was a midwife. Early in his life, he was a student of a physicist by the name of Archelaus, and there are indications that he was interested in the philosophy of Anaxagoras. As a young man, he was engaged in the building and construction trade, but through the agency of the philosopher Crito (who was a wealthy man), Socrates was able to devote himself exclusively to philosophical pursuits. He was married to a woman named Xantippe and had either two or three sons. They are mentioned in the *Apology* when Socrates begs the Assembly to do him one special favor, namely, to punish his children if they grow up to be the sort of people who only seek to *appear* good and honest while neglecting the importance of *being* so; for honesty, sincerity, and authenticity were virtues that Socrates held to be essential for real progress in spiritual and philosophical matters.

Like other free Athenian citizens, Socrates took part in the defense of his country, and on at least two occasions he saw actual combat situations. In the battle of Delium, he managed to save Xenophon from death, and in the battle of Potidaea he displayed extraordinary courage and perseverance. Xenophon, who was later to become an Athenian general, never forgot his debt to him and wrote several works on his life and trial. Socrates' close friends included, not only military men like Xenophon and Alcibiades, but also many politicians, mathematicians, philosophers, and poets. It is said, for example, that he worked closely with Euripides, and that some of the plays written by the latter were the product of the cooperation of both men. But the list of his personal and professional enemies was not negligible. For reasons that will become apparent in the course of this chapter, there were many persons who felt uneasy in the presence of Socrates, and who eventually developed great hatred towards him. These people were successful in bringing charges against the philosopher, and these charges resulted in an indictment before the Assembly in 399 B.C. Like Anaxagoras, Socrates was accused of atheism, impiety, and the corruption of the young, and these grave accusations, brought by Anytus, Lycon, and Meletus, forced him into a trial in which he was found guilty and condemned to death. The Assembly, which acted as the jury and the judge, determined his guilt by a vote of 281 to 220, and the actual death sentence was passed by a wider margin (361 to 140). The vivid details of the trial were recorded first by Plato in the *Apology* and then by Xenophon in a work of the same title. There are indications that after Socrates' death, perhaps through the agency of Xenophon who, during the trial, had been waging war against the Persians, some of the accusers were banished, while Meletus was executed.

In the conduct of his life, Socrates exhibited certain virtues that are always associated with the highest human excellence. He was generally careless about those things that the vulgar and unsophisticated masses of human beings cherish so dearly: money, possessions, sensual pleasure, prestige, public honors, political power, and social influence. As an example of what Aristotle called "the high-minded man," Socrates was humble with the humble and proud and ruthless with the proud and ruthless. On repeated occasions, he displayed great contempt towards those who enjoyed political power *and* who abused such power. He publicly disobeyed and challenged the government when Critias and the generals ordered him to arrest a man named Leon of Salamis, and he was not afraid to take the side of unpopular and dangerous causes at the Assembly. Not even the natural fear of death could alter his convictions: during his trial, he refused to compromise with the wishes of his accusers, and, while in jail, he did not take advantage of Crito's offer to escape. As we will see in our subsequent exposition of Socrates' philosophy, moral integrity was the unshakable ground on which the philosopher stood as an unmovable rock, and not even the greatest danger could compel him to alter his uncompromising stance. But, of course, this rare attitude was bound to create an atmosphere of tension and distrust around him. Among the masses of ordinary human beings, who, as Schopenhauer says, are generally made up of rascals, opportunists, ragamuffins, ruffians, criminals, and morons, Socrates could not but appear as a kind of anomaly or deformity, and like a mistake of nature, he had to be eliminated, especially since he was in the dreadful habit of engaging other people in conversation and discussion. In the course of these, his most unusual character came at once to the surface.

Socrates' inveterate passion for conversing with others was indeed so deep and overwhelming that he observed that if he had money, he would gladly pay people to spend time with him talking about those values that constitute moral worth, and about the meaning of those virtues that make life worth living. Thus, in Plato's *Euthyphro,* we find him questioning Euthyphro about the meaning of piety and goodness; in the *Republic*, he challenges the old Cephalus to tell him what happiness is, and Thrasymachus what justice means; in the *Protagoras*, he wants to know from Protagoras himself what it is that the Sophists teach and know; and even in jail while awaiting execution, he insists on knowing from Crito why the offer of escape has been made to him; and in the *Phaedo*, that marvelous dialogue in which Plato recounts Socrates' death, he wishes to approach death while deeply engaged in discussions about pleasure, suicide, virtue, and death. As an annoying and incorrigible talker, Socrates spent countless hours at the marketplace, prating endlessly about, as Homer says, "whatsoever is good and evil in a house." Surely, from the viewpoint of the unthinking victims of his inquisitiveness, he must have appeared as a social menace, as a busybody, as a useless man, and, worse still, as a deranged person, as Aristophanes makes him out to be in the *Clouds*.

The systematic reconstruction of Socrates' philosophy is not an easy undertaking; perhaps it is an *unwise* undertaking. To begin with, there are no writings attributed to him, as writing, in which one confines ideas to a set and fixed form, was not part of his philosophical style. Claiming as he did to know nothing, what could he have written? Assuming the greatest ignorance about all things, what instructive writings could he have produced? Accordingly, what we know about Socrates' thought comes from the testimony of others, that is, from those who were close to him and were able to learn something from him. The problem is, however, that what these witnesses heard from the old prater is not always consistent, either because what he said was not always clear and consistent, or, more likely, because what *they* saw in him was not always the same. Different minds hear and receive even the most simple message in vastly different ways, just as different ears perceive musical sounds quite differently. What can a person raised amid the noise of rock music hear when Bach's music is played? Or what could have Mozart heard if he had been given a chance to hear the screamings and howlings that loudly pour from a rock band? Likewise, in the case of Socrates' speech, diverse audiences heard a variety of things. The uneducated crowds heard hair-splitting reasonings, idle talk, sneering remarks about this or that politician, or amusing and disrespectful comments about the poets; from the point of view of the masses, Socrates was then a silly and annoying man, one who deserved to be disliked, despised, and laughed at. Aristophanes and the adherents of the conservative party heard dangerous language and unsettling remarks about the democratic traditions of Athens, remarks that, *in their view*, were a threat to the security of the city-state; they also heard farfetched statements that were in little agreement with those expected from solid and law-abiding citizens like the Athenian equivalent of Archie Bunker; thus, unquestionably, Socrates deserved to be ridiculed on the stage, and if he persisted in his sophistical tricks, banished or even executed. The conservatives joined the uninstructed rabble in seeing in Socrates just another Sophist.

On the positive side, however, there was Xenophon, that most brave of Athenians, who eventually led ten thousand Greeks in the titanic effort to retreat safely from Persia. In his eyes, Socrates was a trusted friend, an honest citizen, a noble heart, and a meritorious man who displayed, both in words and actions, the noblest virtues to which a human being can aspire, and who was the victim of political intrigues that were never really directed against him. Philosophers like Aristippus of Cyrene, who had come to Athens attracted by the fame of Socrates, heard from Socrates words of praise with respect to pleasure and happiness and found in him the clear apprehension of the worthiness of human whims. Aristippus developed accordingly a 'Socratic' school of philosophy, in which pleasure was generally identified with the good. This school came to full fruition through the work and character of Epicurus (342–270 B.C.), about whom we will have much to say in our chapter on Ethics.

Antisthenes and the Cynics saw in Socrates a political and social rebel who, in the name of the most devastating individuality, had come into the world for the purpose of upsetting the social fabric, a fabric that they believed was made of artificial and pointless conventionalities with which the real philosophers should have little to do. The Cynics, whose name comes from the Greek word for 'dog', learned from Socrates a life devoted to reason, the recognition of Natural Law, the contempt for social and political institutions, and an existence devoid of as many physical and emotional needs as possible. Happily they would repeat the well-known anecdote about Socrates, namely, that "often when he looked at the multitude of wares for sale [at the marketplace], he would say to himself, 'How many things I can do without!'" Thus, the Cynics, whose ideas were later on taken over by the Stoics, appreciated immensely the spirit of negativity and individualism they detected in Socrates and made of this spirit the basis of their world view.

But surely Plato's view of Socrates must be explored in detail, not only because Plato was the most influential of all Socratic philosophers, but also because much of what we know about Socrates comes directly from the *Dialogues.* And yet, since the relationship between Socrates and Plato is a problematic and complicated one, we propose at this point to make no further comments about it and leave a fuller discussion of it for the first half of the chapter on Plato.

It would be useful now to give a varied *characterization* of Socrates' philosophy, a characterization that will avoid either a systematic approach or the exaggerated emphasis on any one single aspect of Socratic thought. Our characterization will address itself to a number of themes generally found in the several sources of testimony, principally in the early dialogues of Plato in which the spirit and character of Socrates appears to have been adequately captured. The biographical details of these dialogues, as well as the dialectical style, the unsettling inquisitiveness, and the open-minded uncertainty of their varied scenes, point undoubtedly to the fact that the Socrates portrayed in them must have been reasonably close to Socrates himself.

1. SUBJECTIVITY

As distinguished from the objective inclination of earlier philosophical activity in which, as we said, the emphasis lies on the objective world of things and events that we call the universe, there is in Socrates an unmistakable tendency towards *subjectivity,* if we understand this term in the restricted sense of enquiries directed to the elucidation of those issues and problems that primarily affect the *subject* of enquiry, namely the human being. This Socratic tendency is similar to that of Sophism in general. Accordingly, for Socrates, the chief object of philosophy is to investigate those problems that have an ethical, social, or political import, while other problems (for instance, those related to science and cosmology) become secondary and even inconsequential. Thus, Socrates' inquiries have to do with human beings, with their moral values, with the worth of their existence, with their progress towards virtue, with their political aspirations. The conduct of one's life and the rules for righteous living are the objects of Socratic interest, and from this point of view, it is not a mistake to affirm that for Socrates, the moral perplexity entailed in Euthyphro having indicted his own father on the charge of murder is far more transcendental than the search for the primordial substance that attracted Thales' interest. We find, therefore, that the initial issues with which Socrates confronts his contemporaries are ethical issues: What is the meaning of piety? What is the nature of happiness? Under what circumstances ought we to obey the laws? Are pleasure and goodness the same? How can *I* advance along the path that leads to wisdom and virtue? Is human life worth continuing at any cost? Is the life of the just man better or happier than that of the criminal? Is it possible to base our moral values on what religion teaches us about God and the gods? Does *my* life have a purpose, and if so, what can this purpose be?

There is a revealing passage in the *Phaedrus* (strictly speaking, not a Socratic dialogue), in which Socrates and his friends find themselves *outside* of the Athenian walls, that is, in the world of naked nature, where brooks and trees, birds and insects, the sun and the clouds have their empire, an empire in which the human presence is at most marginal. Phaedrus endeavors to call Socrates' attention to this and that detail of nature ("Do you see the tallest plane-tree in the distance?" "There are shade and gentle breezes, and grass on which we may either sit or lie down," etc.), but Socrates appears obviously to be ill at ease as he is not in familiar surroundings. But, let us ask, what are his familiar surroundings? These are the agora or marketplace, the city streets, the shops of the artisans, and the buildings where *human beings* live. Neither the sun nor the clouds, the trees nor the birds, can engage his imagination: nature remains for him unimportant. For this reason, he observes, he has hardly ever stepped outside the city walls, for as he says to Phaedrus,

> I am a lover of knowledge, and the men who dwell in the city are my teachers, and not the trees or the country.

And this Socratic attitude agrees fully with the command that, according to Socrates, Apollo, the Delphian god, gave him: "Know thyself," which does not enjoin Socrates to devote himself to the study of nature or the universe, but of himself, and in himself his fellow human beings. "Know thyself" entails directing our curiosity and inquisitiveness inwards, that is, towards our consciousness and conscience. But in this, the end result cannot be but the apprehension of philosophy as a human enterprise whose primary object is precisely the *subject* that conducts the enterprise. We are clearly justified in saying, therefore, that with Socrates philosophy became thoroughly *humanized* and internalized. We will see in chapter 4 how Plato sought to correct this perhaps one-sidedness of Socratic philosophy; Plato combined in a grand systematic whole the objective *and* subjective elements of his predecessors, as for him, *both* Man and the Universe were the proper subjects of philosophical investigation and discussion.

2. INTELLECTUAL OPTIMISM

The Sophistical movement had as its natural offspring a radical and thoroughgoing skepticism, according to which absolute knowledge, whether in cosmology, metaphysics, theology, or ethics, cannot be attained by the human being. This skepticism resulted in the consistent adoption of agnosticism (the denial of the possibility of knowledge), as well as in a pervasive attitude of intellectual pessimism. For some of the Sophists, the philosophical search for truth and knowledge, if taken seriously, had to be a futile and self-defeating enterprise, as the inexorable outcome of this search was (1) that nothing exists; (2) if anything existed, it could not be known; and (3) if it could be known, it could not be communicated to others in any way whatsoever. Hence, the Sophists devoted themselves to strictly practical concerns in which expediency, utility, and advantage were the only possible fruits. For them, it was enough to have and convey the *semblance* of certainty and the *appearance* of wisdom.

It is possible to find in Socratic utterances certain vestiges of this Sophistical pessimism manifested in agnostical pronouncements. In the *Apology*, for instance, Socrates repeatedly states the fact that he knows nothing except that he knows nothing, and that his reputation as a wise man (a 'sophist' in the old sense) is ill founded:

> Men of Athens, this reputation of mine has come to a certain wisdom which I possess. If you ask me what kind of wisdom, I reply, wisdom such as may be perhaps attained by man, for to that extent I am inclined to believe that I am wise . . . . And I am called wise, for my hearers always imagine that I myself possess the wisdom which I find wanting in others: but the truth is, O Men of Athens, that God only is wise . . . [for, in fact, human wisdom] is worth little or nothing.

And yet, it would be misguided to read in these lines the skepticism, agnosticism, and pessimism that permeated the thought of Sophism, because in Socrates, as we will presently show, the confession of ignorance and uncertainty, whether as an initial step or as a conclusion of his philosophical search, functioned in a way that was quite different from what we find in the Sophists. Socrates began and concluded all his activities on the clear assumption that knowledge is possible and attainable in principle, that reality is knowable, that moral values are universal and real, and that, in sum, the purpose of human existence can be somehow fathomed by the person who uses reason as a guide for thought. In these unshakable convictions, his ironic confession of ignorance notwithstanding, the presence of his intellectual optimism can be detected, and his exuberant and dynamic personality were sure manifestations of it. It was precisely this optimism that, acting as a living force, sustained him throughout the vicissitudes and aggravations entailed by his calling, and gave him the necessary courage to face death in a dignified and relaxed way. In his optimism, he was a genuine *skeptic,* if we use this term in its etymological sense, that is, in the sense of someone who is looking for something that he expects to find some day ('skeptic' comes from the Greek word for 'searching'). For, if it were otherwise, why would he have committed his entire life to the search for truth? Why would he have been willing to die, as he said in the *Apology,* one hundred times for his convictions? Why would he have neglected his private affairs and even his family in order to devote himself to the fulfillment of the god's command?

> And so I go about the world, obedient to the god, and search and make enquiry into the wisdom of any one, whether citizen or stranger, who appears to be wise; and if he is not wise, then in vindication of the oracle, I show him that he is not wise; and my occupation quite absorbs me, and I have no time to give either to any public matter of interest or to any concern of my own, but I am in utter poverty by reason of my devotion to the god.

3. THE SOCRATIC METHOD

Socrates' search for wisdom began as a result of a strange experience that, according to him, happened perhaps forty years before his trial. The Greeks were in the habit of consulting the will of Apollo by piously visiting the oracle at Delphi, where a priestess (perhaps under psychedelic conditions) spoke on behalf of the god. Such a practice was as old as Greek civilization itself, and the belief in the authenticity of the pronouncements made at Delphi was seldom doubted. Statesmen and politicians, Spartan kings and foreign despots, poets and rhetoricians, simple folks and sophisticated philosophers, all journeyed at one time or another to the slopes of Mount Parnassus in order to hear the divine utterances of the Delphian god. And Socrates, indeed, was no exception. On at least one occasion, he urged others to consult the oracle, as was the case when he advised Xenophon shortly before the expedition of the Ten Thousand. Obviously, his faith in Apollo was sincere and genuine, regardless of what certain contemporary historians may have said about it. These historians would like us to believe that Socrates' references to the oracle should be taken in a metaphorical sense only; but in this, they merely reveal their incapacity to take religious beliefs seriously, especially when they come from a philosopher of Socrates' great stature. But the facts are otherwise: Socrates believed in the authenticity of the oracle.

Both Plato and Xenophon report that a certain man named Chaerophon once visited the oracle and asked the priestess the following question: "Who is the wisest man in the world?" He was surprised to hear that the wisest of men was his friend Socrates of Athens, a simple artisan of no special pretensions. But more surprised still was Socrates himself when he was given the strange news. How, he must have said, can *I* be the wisest, if in fact I know little or nothing? Aren't the statesmen, the politicians, the poets, and the philosophers wiser than I? But if the god does not speak except the truth, how, then, can I be the wisest man? Such thoughts must have created in him a great deal of perplexity, especially since he chose to hold firmly to his faith in Apollo. Accordingly, he decided to interpret in a *critical* way the Delphian pronouncement and proceeded to verify the adequacy of his interpretation. Thus, he concluded that what the god meant was not that Socrates was the wisest of men in the sense that he possessed more knowledge than anyone else, for in such sense he was not the wisest. What Apollo meant was something else:

> By his answer, he [Apollo] intends to show that the wisdom of men is worth little or nothing; he is not speaking of Socrates; he is only using my name by way of illustration, as if he said, He, O men, is the wisest, who, like Socrates, knows that his wisdom is in truth worth nothing.

Here lies the root of the Socratic confession of ignorance, a confession that means, not that Socrates knows nothing (for this is obviously nonsense—he knew at least his name!), but that his knowledge, like the knowledge of other people, is inconsequential, insecure, uncertain, petty, and pointless in the context of so immense and complex a universe such as the one in which we live, move, and have our being. This is what Socrates meant when he baffled and annoyed those with whom he conversed by the declaration that he only knew that he knew nothing.

His ingenious way of verifying the adequacy of his interpretation of the oracle consisted in engaging other people in conversation in order to find out if, perchance, they knew more than he, but more specifically in order to force them to realize the emptiness of their pretended knowledge. Hence, after declaring himself ignorant, and postulating himself as their prospective disciple, he proceeded to entangle his victims in the net of their own contradictions. In the *Euthyphro,* after hearing that Euthyphro is about to bring charges of impiety against his own father, Socrates ironically says:

> And I, my dear friend, knowing this, am desirous of becoming your disciple . . . .
> And therefore, I adjure you to tell me the nature of piety and impiety, which you
> said that you knew so well, and of murder, and of other offences against the gods.

The dialogue began to reveal at once Euthyphro's own lack of *conceptual* clarity, for what Socrates wanted was not examples of piety, but the definition of the concept of piety. And every definition given by the confused Euthyphro proved to be either inadequate or in contradiction with earlier ones. At the end, much to Euthyphro's consternation, nothing is quite clear, except, of course, the profound state of intellectual confusion of those who, proud of their pretended knowledge, act impulsively on the basis of emotion, tradition, or social habituation. This explains Euthyphro's urge to bring the frustrating conversation to a speedy end: "Another time, Socrates; for I am in a hurry, and must go now." It also explains the animosity with which many looked upon the philosopher who, like a gadfly, compelled his hearers to wake up from the comfortable slumber of intellectual laziness. Those who like Crito loved Socrates came to the conclusion that it was better to argue no longer with him. Crito ended his pleas to move Socrates to accept his offer to escape from jail with these words: "I have nothing to say, Socrates." But others went away full of resentment and anger, like Euthyphro, Thrasymachus, and Gorgias, occasionally wishing upon the philosopher all kinds of calamities, even death itself.

Beginning thus with an ironic confession of ignorance, Socrates proceeded to interrogate all kinds of people, and his interrogation developed inexorably into a *dialectical* process in which the definition of ethical terms was demanded over and over again, each definition being found deficient because of a lack of clarity or because of its restricted applicability or because of the contradictions entailed by it. Piety, for instance, cannot be defined by merely pointing to one example of piety; it cannot be defined in terms of the will of the gods, and so on. Like other moral virtues, it must be defined in terms of certain universal and rational principles, which unfortunately Socrates was not willing to specify himself, as his task was not to instruct others in the style of the old poets or the Sophists but to compel others to seek the appropriate answers for themselves. His mother, let us remember, had been a midwife, that is, a woman who, while not giving birth herself, only aided other women to bring children into the world; likewise Socrates, while not willing to produce ideas and thoughts by himself, was solely interested in helping others in the often painful process of giving birth to ideas and thoughts. This aspect of Socratic philosophy may account for his unwillingness to confine his thought to the written expression, as he must have felt a marked predilection for the open-ended and free style of casual conversations and discussions.

4. UNCERTAINTY

The confession of ignorance has often stood as the basis of philosophical systems. We noted in chapter 1 how Pythagoras abandoned the flamboyant appellation of 'sophist' that was given to earlier philosophers, and how he chose to call himself simply a 'philosopher', that is, a lover of wisdom; surely, in refusing to be called 'wise' (sophist), he expressed the recognition of his own ignorance about those things that others claimed to know. In more recent times, moreover, other philosophers have emulated the Pythagorean practice and have commenced their philosophical journey by seeking to cleanse themselves of whatever bits of wisdom or knowledge they may have inherited from their predecessors. On account of this circumstance, the history of philosophy contains a manifold of examples in which a "new" beginning has been attempted, something that, as we also noted in chapter 1, does not characterize the history of science. The great philosophers of the Renaissance, Francis Bacon and René Descartes, made of uncertainty, as the natural offspring of ignorance, the foundation of their revolutionary systems. In Descartes, this gave rise to his methodic doubt, a methodological device by which the philosopher sought to test every idea and belief in his search for certainty, the natural offspring of knowledge. In his *Meditations,* he spoke of uncertainty when, at the beginning, he wrote:

> Several years have now elapsed since I first became aware that I had accepted, even from my youth, many false opinions for true, and that consequently what I afterward based on such principles was highly doubtful.

At one point, he was almost willing to conclude that "there is absolutely nothing certain," but eventually, the direction in which his methodic doubt took him saved him from the sort of nihilistic skepticism found among the Sophists of Socrates' time. The methodic doubt of Cartesianism was precisely the instrument that allowed Descartes to reach his desired goal: complete clarity and absolute certainty about questions pertaining to the existence of God, the immortality of the human soul, and even the general structure of physical reality.

In the instance of Socrates, on the other hand, the confession of ignorance did not function exclusively as a methodological device to cleanse the mind of preconceived and unjustified notions and ideas. In him, the confession of ignorance was the expression of intellectual honesty and humility that had been brought to the surface through the agency of the Delphian oracle. And contrary to what some of his contemporaries thought (those who saw in him a dishonest and clever fellow who would assume a posture of ignorance and uncertainty only for the purpose of confusing his dialectical adversaries), Socrates was a truly perplexed man: he was uncertain about most matters of philosophical importance. At the end of his life, as we are told in the *Apology*, he still failed to know what death is and entails:

> Either death is a state of nothingness and utter unconsciousness, or, as men say, there is a change and migration of the soul from this world to another.

Which of these two characterizations best describes death, Socrates did not know. He entertained the pious *hope* that the latter was the case, for, if so,

> I shall then be able to continue my search into true and false knowledge; as in this world, so also in the next; and shall find out who is wise, and who pretends to be wise and is not .... What infinite delight would there be in conversing with them [the souls of the dead] and asking them questions. In another world they do not put a man to death for asking questions: assuredly not. For besides being happier than we are, they will be immortal, if what is said is true.

Yes, but only "if what is said is true"! The problem is that he knew that neither he nor any other person truly ever knew "if what is said is true." This, nobody knows even now. But in spite of all this, we must not forget what we said earlier about the intellectual optimism that permeated the Socratic philosophy, otherwise we may fall into the lamentable temptation of viewing Socrates as just another skeptical Sophist; for *this*, he was not. His method of interrogating others and his inquisitiveness may have given the appearance of being Sophistical, and his individualism may have reminded his listeners of people like Protagoras and Gorgias. But the gap that separated him from them was nevertheless immense. There is a profound difference in maintaining, like Gorgias, that all knowledge is ultimately unattainable, or, like Protagoras, that all statements are equally true and false, or, like Thrasymachus, that moral values are expedient devices used by the powerful to control the weak, *and* confessing, in honesty and humility, that human knowledge is something that amounts to little or nothing.

5. MORAL CONFIDENCE

Socrates' confession of ignorance and attitude of uncertainty must, there-fore, be seen in the light of his overwhelming optimism, of which we spoke earlier. As we saw, it was this optimism that furnished him with enough spir-itual and intellectual energy to carry out his mission without much regard for practical concerns of a materialistic nature. But at the very root of his optimism, there was a conviction that moral values are universal and know-able, and that human life derives its only possible significance from the search for and realization of these values. Here, on the strictly ethical level, as Kierkegaard remarked, neither ignorance nor uncertainty has much rele-vance in Socratic philosophy. Here, he knew and was convinced of some-thing. Here, his confidence had no limits. More specifically, Socrates' moral convictions included (1) the belief that the welfare of one's soul is an affair that surpasses any other by far; in the *Apology*, he begs the jury to punish his sons, should they put aside the welfare of their spiritual life:

> When my sons are grown up, I would ask you, O my friends, to punish them; and I would ask you to trouble them, as I have troubled you, if they seem to care about riches, or anything, more than about virtue.

(2) The welfare of the soul is brought about by the practice of *virtue,* a con-cept that in Socratic philosophy stands for a life guided by reason, authen-ticity, and honesty. (3) More specifically, however, virtue takes on a more clear meaning as we consider our relations to others. For Socrates, as Plato reports in the *Gorgias,* to be virtuous means simply this: to be willing to suffer evil rather than to do evil to others. (4) Lastly, Socrates' moral convictions included his unshakable belief that evil is inevitably the result of igno-rance, and that to do evil is in every instance a manifestation of intellectual obscurity; hence, on the other side, *to know the good is to do the good.* In our chapter on Ethics, we will return to this most important Socratic theme, not only on account of the philosophical issues entailed in it, but also for its unmistakable influence on the development of Plato's moral philosophy. For the time being, let us remark that from the point of view of Socrates' belief that *to know the good is to do the good,* all his activities turn out to be mor-ally motivated. Why did he question Euthyphro about the indictment against his father? Why did he subject Crito to a barrage of questions about his motives for engineering Socrates' own escape from jail? Why did he question old Cephalus about the meaning of happiness, and Thrasymachus about the meaning of justice? In sum, why did he make of himself a veritable pest by interrogating countless people? We can only answer that the primary or per-haps the only purpose of his dialectical excursions was to compel others, as he had compelled himself, to see the inadequacy of traditional and conventional

ideas concerning the meaning of ethically relevant issues, in order to force them *thereby* to raise themselves, as he had raised himself, to an ethical level of existence. Their moral turpitude and ethical superficiality, he believed, were the outcome of their confused and misguided thoughts, and therefore their moral regeneration could only come from a consistent effort towards philosophical enlightenment.

6. INDIVIDUALISM

In speaking about Socrates' subjectivism, intellectual optimism, dialectical method, and moral confidence, the individualism of his general stance may have been sufficiently clarified; yet, a few additional remarks may be in order at this point. On the testimony of Plato and Xenophon, we know that since his early years, Socrates was visited by a peculiar experience, an experience that immediately set him aside from ordinary human beings. Often he spoke of a "voice" or "sign" that came to him with the specific purpose of warning him about situations that ought to be avoided. Always acting as a negative or dissuading guide, this "voice," also referred to as his "demon," told him what *not* to do, what *not* to say on a variety of occasions, but always as a perfectly private phenomenon. It was neither heard nor noticed by anybody else. Surely, such an experience must have added to the stock of social and public difficulties that surrounded Socrates from every side, since ordinary folks become uneasy in the presence of someone able to experience things that remain forbidden to others. In their eyes, such a person is a sort of visionary, a sort of weird character whom nobody can fully trust. After all, if public opinion or the authority of a judge should command him to do something, what guarantee is there that the mysterious "voice" may not intervene in some contrary direction? He becomes unmanageable, and his behavior turns out to be basically unpredictable: he is a social menace as he separates himself from the crowd in the name of some kind of private and secret source of authority. As Henri Charriere, the author of *Papillon,* remarked, there is nothing society hates more than a person who acts and thinks by reference to the dictates he hears within his inner self. In the case of Socrates, the Athenian society, unable to tolerate this unsettling circumstance, forced him to drink poison; thus it silenced him and his accursed "voice."

Much has been said and written about the actual meaning of the Socratic "voice." It has been identified with the voice of God—either Apollo or a higher deity. It has been referred to as Socrates' link to another dimension of being to which ordinary people generally have no access. There are those who see the philosopher as being able to go into altered states of consciousness, and one line from the *Symposium,* among others, is quoted as supportive of this view. Several persons have congregated in Agathon's house for the purpose of spending an evening drinking and conversing about a number of things. As Socrates appears to be late, Agathon sends someone to look for him. A moment later, he is told that Socrates is in the portico of a neighboring house. "There," the host is told, "he is fixed, and when I call to him he will not stir." Someone observes then that Socrates "has a way of stopping anywhere and losing himself without reason." Moments later, he joins the company of friends: "the fit, as usual, was not of long duration."

It was perhaps in these brief moments of inwardness that the phenomenon of the "voice" occurred, although it could have happened at other times. But as to what its real meaning was, and from what source it proceeded, it is not possible for us to advance a fully adequate answer. What we do know, however, is that it furnished the philosopher with a momentary access to an inner and private tribunal beyond which there was no appeal. Whether it was the voice of God or Apollo, or merely the promptings of *his* individual conscience, this tribunal removed him at once from the tribal or social restraints that control most people. In Socrates, therefore, we encounter a magnificent example of an individual who chooses to become an individual, and who chooses the course of his actions by reference to something that he carries deep within his inner self. The traditions and the beliefs of the community, the example of others, the injunctions of political tribunals, and the threats of almighty juries have no value if the secret "voice," heard only in the recesses of the spirit, points in the contrary direction. It deafens the spirit to the noises of the outside world and drowns out the chatter of human opinion, until it becomes a moving force of terrifying dimensions:

> This, dear Crito, is the voice which I seem to hear murmuring in my ears, like the sound of the flute in the ears of the mystic; that voice, I say, is humming in my ears, and prevents me from hearing any other.

Such was the source of the Socratic individualism, an individualism that the philosopher sought to instill in his listeners, and which the Cynics, for instance, learned to cherish and nourish. It is the same rugged individualism that meets us in the existentialist philosophy of Soren Kierkegaard (1813–1855) who believed that philosophical maturity can only be attained by a conscious choice to become an individual. It is the same individualism of other philosophers who, like Friedrich Nietzsche (1844–1900), have insisted on the notion that the philosopher is he who is willing and able to subject every idea, every belief, every practice to the most critical personal evaluation. From this point of view, then, the philosopher becomes, in a literal sense, his only source of valuations and his one and only judge. At bottom, the Socratic individualism derives its unsurpassed strength from its undeviating commitment to reason, a commitment that since Thales has been the animating force of all genuine philosophical minds. As one reviews the history of philosophy in general and the Socratic moment in particular, one cannot but remember the words with which Alfred North Whitehead (1861–1947) concluded his *Science and the Modern World:*

> The moral of the tale is the power of reason, its decisive influence on the life of humanity. The great conquerors, from Alexander to Caesar, influenced profoundly the lives of subsequent generations. But the total effect of this influence shrinks to insignificance, if compared to the entire transformation of human habits and human mentality produced by the long line of men of thought from Thales to the present day, men individually powerless, but ultimately the rulers of the world.

Let us now turn our attention to Plato, Socrates' most famous disciple. In him we will see how the Socratic philosophy underwent a wonderful transformation.

QUESTIONS FOR STUDY

1. What historical, political, and cultural circumstances may have been at work in the process by which philosophy moved from objectivity to subjectivity in the second half of the fifth century B.C.? Explain in clear terms what is meant by objectivity and subjectivity in this context.

2. Describe the major characteristics of Sophism, and contrast this movement with earlier philosophical movements such as Milesian Rationalism.

3. What common elements can we find in the Sophists *and* in Socrates? In what sense was the average Athenian partly justified in seeing in Socrates just another Sophist?

4. How did Socrates attempt to answer the challenge of Sophism, specifically with respect to the realm of ethical concerns?

5. How do you account for the fact that Socratic philosophy is open to so great a variety of interpretations that gave rise to a large number of Socratic schools?

6. After carefully reading one of the Socratic dialogues (the *Euthyphro,* for instance), explain how the elements of Socratic philosophy discussed in this chapter are manifested in it.

7. If you had been privileged enough to be a member of the Athenian Assembly at the time of Socrates' trial (399 B.C.), how would you have voted? Explain the reasons for your vote.

4

Plato: The Man Who Saw Beyond

"European philosophy," said Whitehead in his *Adventures of Ideas*, "is founded upon Plato's dialogues," in such a way that we are justified in looking upon the entire development of Western thought as if this were an extended footnote to Plato's philosophical system. For again, as Whitehead observed, "every problem which Plato discusses is still alive today," and this is true in every sphere of human interest, whether it be metaphysics, epistemology, cosmology, ethics, political science, aesthetics, or any other. In his philosophy Western culture reached perhaps its highest climax of intelligence and sophistication, and accordingly, the twenty-three centuries that have elapsed since his death are nothing but the slow unfolding of the questions, problems, and issues that his powerful mind attempted to resolve. It is therefore not surprising to find his influence in every realm of human activity, and to discover that every major philosopher, from Aristotle to Bertrand Russell, has naturally gravitated towards Platonic philosophy as if it constituted their natural center of gravity. In general, his influence has been regarded as beneficial and enlightening, although occasionally it has been viewed as detrimental and obscurantist. Karl Popper in his *The Open Society and Its Enemies* sees in Plato's political ideas the ancient seeds of totalitarian and oppressive political systems, and Lancelot Hogben in his *Mathematics for the Million* blames Plato's understanding of mathematics for the distaste with which many view the study of numbers, as "his influence on education has spread a veil of mystery over mathematics." But whether one's assessment of Plato's influence on Western culture be positive or negative, one thing is incontrovertible: for good or for ill, it was Plato who taught us how to think, and that it was he who determined, more than anyone else, the course taken by philosophy and science in the West.

As a person, Plato has been often regarded as someone who, on account of his natural gifts and his accomplishments, stands far above the ordinary human mold, for clearly he was not like the rest of men. Ancient biographers took pains in tracing his genealogy back directly to the Olympian gods, for in this way his almost superhuman character could be accounted for. We are even told that his birth was the result of the divine intervention of Apollo, through whose agency Plato's mother became pregnant. Thus, like Jesus of Nazareth, Plato could then be regarded as "the son of God." But even if respectfully we set aside these pious and edifying traditions, the fact remains that the philosopher's personality has been associated with the most exalted paradigms of human excellence and achievement. Nietzsche's remark in this respect is not altogether irrelevant: "The gap that separates Plato from the ordinary human being is far wider than the gap that separates the ordinary human being from the chimpanzee."

But *even* Plato had a human history. We know, for instance, that he was born in Athens in 427 B.C., only two years after Pericles' death, in the very midst of the Peloponnesian War of which we spoke in the previous chapter. His father's name was Ariston (if we abandon the idea of his having been conceived by Apollo), and his family belonged to the Athenian aristocracy (unlike the case of Socrates, whose family, while politically free, was of a humbler status). One of Plato's granduncles on his mother's side was a member of the council of thirty generals who ruled Athens shortly after the Spartan victory. Plato's real name was Aristocles, but on account of his strong physical frame (the result of his early interest in activities such as wrestling) he was given the nickname of 'platon', which best described his robust figure. In his early youth, he studied rhetoric and politics, as was expected of every aristocratic young man, until around his twentieth year when he came to be under the influence of Socrates. After this time, Plato devoted himself to the study of philosophy and gave up the political ambitions of his early years. The encounter with Socrates, then, constitutes the major turning point in Plato's life.

During the eight or nine years that Plato spent in close association with Socrates, he planted in his spirit the seeds of wisdom that were to flourish later in his own philosophical system. He began to appreciate the importance of critical analysis and reflective meditation, the value of intellectual honesty and moral authenticity, the transitory character of those possessions that the vulgar masses cherish (money, prestige, power, and pleasure), and the fact that only in virtue can a person find the fulfillment of human life. From Socrates he learned the rare art of developing in oneself a mature spirit of individuality and independence and the dangers inherent in democratic societies like the Athenian, in which public opinion and political success were held to be the sole criteria of human worth. He also learned the dialectical method of inquiry and the necessity of looking for truth in the intense intercourse of dialogue and conversation. He became eventually one of Socrates' most loyal friends, and as a respectful but critical disciple of the old gadfly, he inherited from him the understanding of life in general and philosophy in particular that characterizes the Socratic world view. During Socrates' trial, at which he was present, he must have felt the anguish and anger of those who helplessly witness a scene in which injustice and stupidity triumph over justice and intelligence. After Socrates' death, he left the city like others who had been associated with Socrates; their departure was occasioned by the atmosphere of hostility that Socrates' bad reputation had brought upon all his friends and associates. For Plato, this marked the beginning of a long series of journeys that took him to Megara (where he studied mathematics under Euclid), Cyrene (where he also studied mathematics), Italy (where he came in contact with the Pythagoreans), and finally Egypt (where he received instruction from the priests). As in the case of Thales (chapter 2), it is not easy to know exactly what Plato learned from the Egyptians, although, as we will see, there are certain elements in the *Dialogues* that betray an unmistakable Egyptian influence.

After perhaps ten years of traveling, Plato returned to Athens where he found a different political climate; even the persecutors of Socrates had been either banished or executed! He proceeded to establish a school of philosophy (the term 'school' being used in its etymological sense, as we explained in chapter 2), in a place near the Athenian walls that had been dedicated in former times to a hero named Hecademus. Thus, the name of the school, the Academy, can be traced back to this simple circumstance. There Plato spent the rest of his life, except for two or three brief periods of absence during which he attempted with no success to put into practice several political ideas advanced in the *Republic*. While at the Academy, he devoted himself to the writing of some twenty-four philosophical pieces that have come to be known as the *Dialogues*. But besides writing, there was also much teaching and instruction, together with long hours of casual conversations and discussions in the company of people who, attracted by his personality and reputation, had come to live in the Academy. The members of the school included a substantial number of prominent philosophers and scientists: mathematicians like Speusippus, astronomers like Eudoxus and Callippus, young philosophers like Aristotle, and so on. The range of studies in which, under Plato's guidance, they were immersed was quite varied, although the emphasis was always on the side of logic, mathematics, cosmology, and metaphysics. Religious practices, especially those honoring Apollo, were nicely mingled with relaxing social affairs, which even included wedding banquets for members of the school. It is interesting to observe that Plato, who chose to remain unmarried throughout his life, is said to have died while attending one of those banquets in 347 B.C. He was buried in the grounds of the Academy, although the exact place of his grave remains an archeological enigma.

After Plato's death, Aristotle left the Academy, while Speusippus was chosen to be the head of the school, a circumstance that accentuated the mathematical inclinations of the institution. The Academy continued to function as the center of intellectual life of the European world for more than nine hundred years, until the Byzantine emperor Justinian (483–565 A.D.) ordered its closing. But in no way did the unintelligent action of this emperor affect the influence that both Plato and the philosophers of the Academy were to have during subsequent times.

In seeking to give a systematic exposition of Plato's philosophy, one encounters a number of difficulties and obstacles that make this task specially hard. The recognized sources of this philosophy are basically the *Dialogues* and several letters written by Plato himself to friends of his in Syracuse, where he had tried his unsuccessful political experiments. In the seventh of these letters, there is a statement that deserves to be quoted in full, as it gives us a warning against the attempt to subject Plato's philosophy to a systematic presentation. Writing about his friend Dionysius (the king of Syracuse), Plato expresses himself thus:

> I hear too that he has since written on the subjects in which I instructed him at that time, as if he were composing a handbook of his own which differed entirely from the instruction he received. Of this I know nothing. I do know, however, that some others have written on these same subjects, but who they are they know not themselves. One statement at any rate I can make in regard to all who have written or who may write with a claim to knowledge of the subjects to which I devote myself—no matter how they pretend to have acquired it, whether from my instruction or from others or by their own discovery. Such writers can in my opinion have no real acquaintance with the subject. I shall certainly compose no work in regard to it, nor shall I ever do so in the future, for there is no way of putting it in words like other studies. Acquaintance with it must come rather after a long period of attendance on instruction in the subject itself and of close companionship, when, suddenly, like a blaze kindled by a leaping spark, it is generated in the soul and at once becomes self-sustaining.

What is said here is sufficiently clear: the subject to which Plato devoted his life, that is, philosophy, cannot be put into words like other studies; as a proof of this, Plato says, he himself has not written anything about it. Acquaintance with philosophy is a personal and spiritual matter that, after "a long period of attendance or instruction in the subject itself," is suddenly born in the soul where it becomes "self-sustaining." In the light of this, philosophy emerges then as some sort of mystical vision, as a flight into a transcendent realm of being, with respect to which, human language is totally useless: *it*, let us repeat, cannot be put into words like other subjects. But didn't Plato write the *Dialogues,* those profound and instructive collections of philosophical reflections in which we may confidently learn the elements of his philosophy? If now he says that he has not written, nor does he expect to write, anything about philosophy, what purpose and meaning can there be in his writings?

The answer to this and similar questions is neither easy nor simple, nor can we expect a unanimous approach to the problem on the part of those who have commented on Plato's philosophy. One reasonably comfortable (although probably unjustified) way of handling this perplexity is to say that the above quoted statement from the seventh letter should not be taken at face value: Plato did not mean what he said. But it is difficult to argue in this direction, first, because the philosopher was not the sort of person who is used to employ language lightly, and second, because the obviously autobiographical tenor of this most authentic of his letters points clearly in the opposite direction: Plato believed that his philosophy transcended language and cannot be communicated like other subjects. There is more justification, we think, in taking the statement at its face value, while at the same time making an effort to understand the *Dialogues* in the only possible avenue left, namely, as *preparatory exercises,* which, not unlike the Socratic conversations, may be of some use for those who are in the business of searching for wisdom and truth. *In this sense,* Plato appears once more to be under the influence of his philosophical preceptor; that is, he endeavored to do in writing what Socrates did in talking, and this is nothing else than the attempt to compel his readers to find for themselves the answers that he obscurely suggests in his dialectical exercises. The actual moment of philosophical illumination, the discovery of the truth, is something that is left entirely in our hands. If we fail, it is only our failure, not his; if we succeed, it is only our success, not his. It is we alone who must undertake the arduous journey.

But be it as it may, it is customary among academic philosophers to look upon some of the dialogues as being somewhat revelatory of Plato's philosophy, and this may be after all justifiable, in the sense that in those dialogues we may encounter here and there certain elements that may have constituted an important element of the Platonic vision of reality. The problem is, however, that the *Dialogues* were written over a period of forty years, during which Plato himself went through several stages of development. Thus, the Plato who speaks in the early dialogues is discernibly different from the Plato of the later ones. Furthermore, in a dialogue there are several participants, and it is not always easy or advisable to identify the author with this or that character. In all probability, the author of a dialogue, like the author of a play or novel, is all his characters at once; but since the diverse characters express divergent and often contradictory views, the author himself emerges as the conceptual matrix out of which a diversity of views have emanated. Had Plato written didactic works such as those of Aristotle or Kant, our problems would be substantially minimized, but since he did not, we must humbly accept our inevitable perplexities.

From the point of view of literary sequence, the *Dialogues* can be divided into three groups: (1) early, (2) middle, and (3) late. The early pieces, also known as Socratic dialogues, include, among others, the *Euthyphro*, the *Apology*, the *Crito*, and the first two books of the *Republic*. In these, the presence of the historical Socrates is immediately felt, and their character is evidently biographical. It is in them, as we saw in chapter 3, that we find abundant information about Socrates, as they reveal the major elements that are generally associated with him. Surely, they are not intended to be *verbatim* conversations in which Socrates took part, for, after all, they were all written years after his death, and even Plato's memory could have been subjected to distortions and changes. These Socratic dialogues, with the exception of the *Apology* in which a reasonably accurate account of the trial is given, are designed to give us an idea of the Socratic method, as well as an understanding of Socrates' personality. It is therefore safe to assert that the ideas expressed in them through the mouth of Socrates are not necessarily those of Plato, or at most, that they reflect a stage of Plato's life when his own philosophical views were not fully formed.

The dialogues of the middle period, on the other hand, do seem to represent philosophical views that can be associated directly with Plato, although, as we saw earlier, they should not be identified with his philosophy. These dialogues can themselves be divided into two subgroups: (1) those that deal with certain problems specifically posed by the Sophists (the *Protagoras*, the *Gorgias*, the *Meno*, the *Theaetetus*, the *Cratylus*, etc.), and (2) those that advance distinctly Platonic ideas (the *Republic*, the *Phaedrus*, the *Symposium*, the *Parmenides*, the *Sophist*, and surely the *Phaedo*). This last dialogue may well give the impression of being, like the *Apology* and the *Crito*, a Socratic dialogue since it contains biographical elements about Socrates' execution. In the *Phaedo*, we are made witnesses of Socrates' last hours in jail when, in the company of his most intimate friends, he discourses on the meaning of death. The dialogue ends with a graphic description of his death:

> Crito made a sign to the servant, who was standing by; and he went out, and having been absent for some time, returned with the jailer carrying the cup of poison. Socrates said: You, my good friend, who are experienced in these matters, shall give me directions how I am to proceed. The man answered: You have only to walk about until your legs are heavy, and then to lie down, and the poison will act. At the same time he handed the cup to Socrates, who in the easiest and gentlest manner, without the least fear or change of colour or feature, looking at the man with all his eyes, Echecrates, as his manner was, took the cup and said: What do you say about making a libation out of this cup to any god? May I, or not? The man answered: We only prepare, Socrates, just so much as we deem enough. I understand, he said: but I may and must ask the gods to prosper my journey from this to the other world—even so—and so be it according to my prayer. Then raising the cup to his lips, quite readily and cheerfully he drank off the poison. And hitherto most of us had been able to control our sorrow; but now

when we saw him drinking, and saw too that he had finished the draught, we could no longer forbear, and in spite of myself my own tears were flowing fast; so that I covered my face and wept, not for him, but at the thought of my own calamity in having to part from such a friend. Nor was I the first; for Crito, when he found himself unable to restrain his tears, had got up, and I followed; at that moment, Apollodorus, who had been weeping all the time, broke out in a loud and passionate cry which made cowards of us all. Socrates alone retained his calmness: What is this strange outcry? he said. I sent away the women mainly in order that they might not misbehave in this way, for I have been told that a man should die in peace. Be quiet then, and have patience. When we heard his words we were ashamed, and refrained our tears; and he walked about until, as he said, his legs began to fail, and then he lay on his back, according to the directions, and the man who gave him the poison now and then looked at his feet and legs; and after a while he pressed his foot hard, and asked him if he could feel; and he said, No; and then his leg, and so upwards and upwards, and showed us that he was cold and stiff. And he felt them himself, and said: When the poison reaches the heart, that will be the end. He was beginning to grow cold about the groin, when he uncovered his face, for he had covered himself up, and said—they were his last words—he said: Crito, I owe a cock to Asclepius; will you remember to pay the debt? The debt shall be paid, said Crito; is there anything else? There was no answer to this question; but in a minute or two a movement was heard, and the attendents uncovered him; his eyes were set, and Crito closed his eyes and mouth.

Such was the end, Echecrates, of our friend; concerning whom I may truly say, that of all men of his time whom I have known, he was the wisest and justest and best.

And yet, it would be a mistake to be guided by the mere appearance, for even though the *Phaedo* does contain biographical material such as the quoted scene, there are elements in it that transcend by far the limits of Socratic philosophy. For example, we may recall that, as we observed in chapter 3, Socrates was uncertain as to what the experience of death entails: is it the complete extinction of the self, or, as people say, is it the migration of the soul from this world into another? Socrates simply did not know. But the Socrates who speaks to us in the *Phaedo* is someone who *knows* that

if we would have pure knowledge of anything we must be quit of the body—the soul in herself must behold things in themselves; and then we shall attain the wisdom which we desire, and of which we say that we are the lovers; but not while we live, but after death.

In fact, the *Phaedo*'s fundamental aim is none other than to convince us that the real philosopher is he who constantly practices the art of dying, since this physical life, in which his true self must be confined to the prison of the body, is only a transitory condition of true being. The true self of a person is, unlike the body, immortal. We will presently see the role played by the idea of immortality in Plato's thought.

Lastly, there are those dialogues that belong to the late period. In these, we find Plato deeply immersed in cosmological speculations and in the attempt to make sense of ancient myths like that of the lost continent of Atlantis. His mind has taken by this late time a turn towards mysticism, and hosts of strange notions make their appearance. In these dialogues, even the presence of Socrates is hardly noticed, and no longer is he the protagonist of the early pieces: on occasion he is merely a quiet bystander. It would be a mistake to follow the directions suggested by some scholars to the effect that these mysterious late dialogues (the *Timaeus,* the *Critias*) do not reveal genuine philosophical views that should be associated with Plato, or that they do not represent what is best in Plato. This suggestion entails, we think, an unjustified value judgment. It is best to rest on the notion that everything written by Plato reflects aspects of his philosophical development, even though the very kernel of his philosophy may still transcend his actual writings. Accordingly, in our subsequent effort to outline his ideas, we will be taking into account elements from a variety of dialogues, regardless of the periods to which they may belong. His ideas were many, and they touched practically every sphere of human concern. Unlike his Milesian predecessors, he attached great importance to ethical concerns; but unlike Socrates and the Sophists, he was not willing to set aside the philosophical endeavor to investigate the nature of the universe at large. Consequently, there is in Plato's philosophy a systematic integration of fields like metaphysics, cosmology, epistemology, physics, psychology, ethics, politics, and aesthetics.

1. THE IMMORTALITY OF THE SOUL

We will begin our examination of Plato's ideas with the examination of his views on the human soul, not really because this subject stands in a position of logical priority with respect to the rest, but because its import is sufficiently clear and straightforward. As such, then, it may furnish us with a convenient point of departure. According to Plato, the human being is made up of two distinct and separable substances or elements, namely, the body and the soul, which coexist for a short time in the individual person, forming thereby an entity we call 'man'. The body, made up of matter, is subject to the laws that govern the material world: it comes into being at some definite point in time, grows and develops by the assimilation of new matter ("by the digestion of food, flesh is added to flesh and bone to bone"), and eventually dies when its parts are no longer held together. Its matter, like the matter of other physical things, was never created out of nothing: it always existed and will always exist, as the physical universe at large is eternal. The specific elements which enter into the formation of the human body are, as for Empedocles (see chapter 2), earth, water, air, and fire, and it is the mixture of these that accounts for the multiplicity of things that constitute the physical world. To the body there belong the appetites or natural tendencies: the need to eat, avoid pain, seek pleasure, and propagate. In this respect, the human body is similar to that of animals, no more and no less. Surely, if we define the human being as a body, and only as a body, death can only mean the total extinction of the person, although, obviously, not the extinction of the elements that constitute the body. If we are only bodies, our individual lives come to a total end upon death: we become, as Socrates says in the *Apology*, "nothingness and utter unconsciousness." At the moment of death, we would plunge ourselves into a condition of personal non-being, which is comparable to a dreamless sleep from which there is no awakening. We would be what we were before we were born or conceived: nothing; and the entire universe, with its Milky Way and galaxies, would also become nothing as far as we could be concerned. Human existence, seen from this materialistic viewpoint, could be likened to a momentary flash of consciousness amid an infinity of emptiness and nothingness.

We must observe at this point that many philosophers have been quite content with this materialistic view of man. Among the ancients, Democritus and Epicurus were inclined in this direction, Epicurean philosophy being designed as a way to remove from us the natural fear of not being. Among the Stoics, moreover, there were some who agreed with this idea. Marcus Aurelius, the Roman emperor of the second century A.D., asked in his *Meditations,*

> How can it be that the gods after having arranged all things well and benevolently for mankind, have overlooked this alone, that some men and very good men, and men who, as we may say, have had most communion with the divinity, and through pious acts and religious observances have been most intimate with the divinity, when they have once died should never exist again, but should be completely extinguished?

And his question can be brought home to each one of us. How is it possible that I, after several decades of effort to gain knowledge, to become virtuous and kind, to obtain a decent position in life, to create a family, to grow intellectually and spiritually, should one day become a heap of half-disintegrated bones? What purpose is there in such a life that is inexorably destined to nothingness? But materialistic philosophers, not only among the ancient but also among the moderns, have had apparently no great difficulty in escaping from the existential anguish that the prospect, nay, the certainty, of total extinction entails. Karl Marx was a materialist for whom death meant total destruction, and yet he worked for the creation of a new social order under socialism and communism. Some contemporary philosophers appear to see in the finitude of human existence a redeeming feature: life has meaning precisely because it must end at some point. The "now" emerges then as something precious, something that we cannot waste in any way.

But for Plato, the finitude of human existence applies only to the body. The soul, as a spiritual entity, does not belong to the physical world; hence it is not subject to its laws. It knows nothing about 'coming into being', and cannot experience destruction. Being a completely 'simple' substance, it has no parts, and having no parts, it cannot be broken apart like the body. One would be tempted to say that these ideas came from the writings of someone who, like Saint Thomas Aquinas, is endeavoring to explicate philosophically his religious convictions; after all, one of the fundamental tenets of traditional Christianity is precisely the separability of body and soul, and the immortality of the latter. Also, one would be tempted to see in Plato's ideas an anticipation of those of Descartes who sought to demonstrate the twofold nature of man (body=extended substance and soul=thinking substance). And in this, we would not be *entirely* astray. Medieval philosophers, like Saint Augustine, recognized their affinity with Plato, particularly with respect to the belief in the immortality of the soul, and it is for this reason that we read in Saint Augustine's *The City of God* "that it is especially with the Platonists that we [Christian philosophers] must carry on our disputations on matters of theology, [since] their opinions are preferable to those of other philosophers." The elements that they (the philosophers of medieval times and Descartes) have in common with Plato are many: the soul and the body are quite distinct, the soul is the seat of rationality and consciousness, the soul is unaffected by death, and so on. And yet, there is one chief point of difference: unlike them, Plato held that the soul is not only immortal but eternal; that is, the soul is not the special creation of God, but is a substance that, being beyond time, has neither a beginning nor an end. This view allowed Plato to sympathize with certain myths of reincarnation that he inherited from the Pythagoreans and the Egyptians.

In describing the soul and its relationship with the body, Plato made a constant appeal to the use of myths and allegories, a use that he did not restrict only to this aspect of his philosophy. Hence, his dialogues are filled with mythical accounts and allegorical tales, some of which come almost directly from religious traditions (the *hieros logos*) in which most ordinary Greeks had been raised. This is particularly true of the Orphic traditions and other mystery religions. The connection of Plato with these theosophic sources has been explored by many commentators, although the end result has invariably been disappointing, as there are areas that will probably remain forever outside of our knowledge. All that we wish to add in this respect is that the myth functions in Plato in a way similar to that in which poetical descriptions function in the case of the mystics: the myth takes over when conceptual understanding has reached its furthest limit, so that as a pointing sign, the myth allows us to look beyond what is empirically and intellectually in front of our eyes. Thus, his myths about the soul speak of death as the moment in which the soul is able to leave its prison (the body that has been nothing but a source of "endless trouble for us," and that as a nefarious infection has made the vision of true being blurred and distorted). Only after death, can the soul "behold things in themselves." While in *this* world, he wrote,

> I reckon that we make the nearest approach to knowledge when we have the least intercourse or communion with the body, and are not surfeited with the bodily nature, but keep ourselves pure until the hour when God himself is pleased to release us.

The key words to remember from this moving quotation from the *Phaedo* are "pure" and "release," for on them much of Plato's ethical views hinge. As we will presently see, he conceived human existence as a period of trial and imprisonment from which we may be *released* if and only if our conduct becomes *pure* in the practice of ascetic contemplation. The latter entails the avoidance of sensual pleasure in as much as our frail constitution allows us.

The reflective reader may ask at this point whether these elements of Platonism are not precisely the same that permeate the highest manifestation of the Christian faith, and the answer would have to be, perhaps to the unhappiness of some contemporary commentators, an affirmative one. Without much difficulty Plato could have understood the constant cry that is heard everywhere in the sacred music of Johann Sebastian Bach: "Come, sweet Death, come, release me, and set me free!" For Bach, like Plato, also looked upon the body as the unfortunate burden of the soul, and he, like Plato, devoted his life to the practice of dying, dying to this miserable world of shadows and appearances in which true being is reflected darkly, as if on a distorted and distorting mirror.

We must ask now, on what did Plato base his twofold vision of man and on what foundation did his belief in the soul rest? The arguments given by Socrates in the *Phaedo* in support of the immortality, or rather the eternal nature, of the soul may be taken at first to disclose for us such a foundation. But in so thinking, our judgment would be hasty and premature. The 'arguments' of the *Phaedo*, whatever their dialectical strength may be, are used there mostly as "comforting tales" with which the philosopher supports either an article of faith already accepted on some other basis or a more comprehensive view of reality, of which his ideas on the soul are only a part. And although both circumstances may be present in Plato, the latter is for us more worthy of attention, as it allows us to comment briefly on his view of reality at large.

2. THE THEORY OF TWO WORLDS

At the beginning of Book VII of the *Republic* there is a memorable passage in which Plato, by means of an allegory, sought to "show in a figure how far our nature is enlightened or unenlightened," that is, to present us with a graphic description of our human situation. This is the function of the famous "Allegory of the Cave." No student of philosophy should fail to read many times this most important and revealing section, as it contains, albeit in metaphorical language, the kernel of Plato's thought. Here, we are told of human beings who live since their birth in an underground den where, under physical restraints, they are only allowed to see the shadows that a fire projects onto the wall of the cave. Unable to recognize the shadows for what they are and ignorant of the existence of an outside world, the unfortunate prisoners call what they see "the real world." For them, only the shadows and echoes of the cave exist, although for *them,* these are neither shadows nor echoes: they are the real objects. At some point, a prisoner is *compelled* to free himself from the chains that have held him fixed to the ground of the cave. He is then *forced* to behold the fire and the objects that are the causes of shadows, and eventually he is "reluctantly *dragged* up a steep and rugged ascent, and *held* fast until he is *forced* into the presence of the sun himself." Dazzled and frightened by his experience (an experience that curiously enough was not the result of his choice, as the use of the Greek passive voice suggests in this passage—"is dragged," "is compelled," "is forced," etc.), the man is at first unable to see and distinguish the new objects. There, outside of the cave, he looks for the source of light that makes the outside world visible, just as the fire in the cave had made the shadows visible; he soon discovers the sun: "He would first see the sun and then reason about it," not the other way around. The remembrance of his old companions, those unfortunate wretches who remained in the cave, moves him to begin his "down-going," as Nietzsche would have said. At last, he finds himself once more in the cave; he has returned to announce to them the glad tidings: the world of the cave is an inside world beyond which there is another world of greater beauty and permanence—reality does not belong to passing and obscure shadows, nor to the fire of the cave; reality is waiting for them but only outside of the cave. He soon becomes a source of annoyance for the prisoners who find their comfort and distraction in the world of the shadows, and at last, becoming an intolerable gadfly, he, like Socrates, is killed by those to whom he had brought the light of the spirit.

The epistemological, metaphysical, and ethical implications of this allegory are obviously tremendous, and one could spend one's whole life exploring them. Fortunately for us, Plato himself undertook the translation of the mythical symbols of his allegory. The underground den and the prisoners represent ordinary human existence; the shadows and echoes projected onto the wall stand for the objects that sense perception discloses to us; the chains that fasten the prisoners to the ground of the cave and enable them to see only that which is presented to them on the wall are the limitations of time and space imposed by human sensibility; the fire that projects the shadows is the symbol for the sun that makes the visible world possible; the escape from the cave along that "rugged and steep ascent" is Plato's description of the journey undertaken by the philosophical mind in its search for truth; the reflections of objects that the released prisoner discovers on lakes and rivers are the objects of mathematics, objects that, according to Plato, stand closer to true being than the inconsistent perceptions of the senses; the actual objects of the world outside the cave are the allegorical symbols for the Ideas or eternal Forms, whose reality and permanence transcend by far those of the physical world; lastly, the sun itself, that glorious object that the prisoner must first *see* before he can *reason* about it, represents what Plato called "the Idea of the Good" *(to agathon),* "the universal author of things beautiful and right, parent of light and the lord of light in this visible world, and the immediate source of reason and truth in the intellectual." Several philosophers and commentators have opted for the notion that this "Idea of the Good" is none other than the very idea of God as it has been entertained by enlightened Christian thinkers, and they have argued that what Plato calls "the ascent of the soul into the intellectual world" is nothing but the flight of the philosophical mind towards the realm of spiritual reality, a realm, let us remember, in which often a mystical *vision* must precede the conceptual attempt to *reason* out its meaning; for, as the allegory puts it, the fortunate prisoner "would first see the sun and then reason about it." Surely, it would be unwise to speak dogmatically about the correctness of this spiritual interpretation of the Platonic tale, but if one keeps in mind the passage from the seventh letter quoted above, it is nevertheless a tempting and plausible way of translating Plato's meaning.

There are, of course, other elements in the allegory of the cave that create inescapable perplexities. It is unquestionable, for instance, that its cultural roots lie deep within certain Pythagorean and Orphic traditions with which Plato was in great affinity. The Orphics in their mystery cults also spoke of human existence as being akin to having fallen into a profound cave. Empedocles of Acragas stated that as we are born, "we have come into this roofed cavern." And the release of the prisoner is comparable to hosts of myths and legends of "rebirth" or "being born again" that have found their way even into the Christian gospels; thus, Jesus said to Nicodemus: "Verily, I say unto thee, except a man be born again, he cannot see the kingdom of God" (John 3:3–4). Also, there is the problem of the prisoner's *manner* of release: a careful reading of the Greek text reveals at once, as we intimated earlier, that he does not choose by himself to break the chains and leave the cave, as at every point he is reluctantly "compelled," "forced," "dragged" into a higher reality in which he is not at home. But who or what can be the compelling force be? Is he, like Socrates in the context of the Delphian oracle, acting under an ineludible *command?* And why was he chosen? Could he have chosen to be chosen? Lastly, why was he in the cave in the first place? Plato's myths, especially the one with which he concludes the *Republic,* may give us some hints to how these and similar perplexities could be resolved, and there again, the problem of interpretation is a formidable obstacle on our path. Ultimately, and indeed quite reluctantly, we may be forced to accept on its face value the quoted statement of the seventh letter: Plato's philosophy cannot be learned or communicated through language and discourse, but must be experienced in oneself—only then can our understanding of it become "self-sustaining."

And yet, it is still possible to make a number of pertinent statements about what Plato sought to inculcate upon us in passages such as the allegory of the cave. We can say, for instance, that according to him 'reality' is not a univocal term, inasmuch as the objects that we call 'real' can be classified along a vertical scale that contains *two* distinct levels. To its lower half, there belong those objects of sense perception (generally known as 'things') that constitute the physical world. To the upper half of the scale, there belong, on the other hand, those objects that, being devoid of matter, can only be grasped by the intellect. The former are perishable and transitory and are subject to the always changing conditions of empirical sensibility; their reality is trivial, and about them one is justified in saying with Protagoras that nothing is true and nothing is false. The objects of the intellect or soul are something quite different: they are changeless and eternal, and as immaculate prototypes of all existence they are the paradigms of reality. Physical objects stand related to the eternal Ideas in a relationship of participation *(methexis)*, an idea that Plato endeavored *with little success* to clarify by means of sundry analogies: things are to the Ideas as copies to originals, as shadows to objects, as a physical table to the idea of a table in the carpenter's mind, etc. We said just now "with little success" simply because no matter how we explore this highest Platonic idea, we are caught in inescapable difficulties. Indeed, Aristotle himself was ultimately unable to make much sense of it.

We are justified in calling Plato's philosophy a classic example of metaphysical *dualism*, for in it, reality is basically twofold: physical and intellectual or spiritual. Obviously, as we will presently see, his philosophical preference was always on the side of the upper half of the scale of being, although he was not altogether oblivious of the lower; his interest in astronomy, for instance, would not have allowed him to forget completely the physical world. Thus, he advanced interesting ideas concerning the sphericity of the earth, the structure of matter, and other physical problems in which the Milesian Rationalists would have felt more at home. But still, let us repeat, it was the realm of Ideas that captivated his imagination, for, after all, the soul, which for him was the essential part of man, was more akin to this realm than to the humble world of physical events. Plato's capital aim was to reach out for the upper world that was his true home and in which his soul had once participated. In the *Phaedrus,* he described the beatific visions beheld by the soul before it was unfortunate enough to be confined to a troublesome body. He spoke of the "heavenly highways on which the gods pass to and fro," and his spirit was filled with desire to come face-to-face with what he once knew. Physical beauty served him as a *reminder* of that heavenly beauty once present in the mind's eye, as we are told in the *Symposium*.

3. THE THEORY OF KNOWLEDGE

Our last comment can now give us a clue to the meaning of Plato's contention in the *Phaedo* that all *true* knowledge is a kind of recollection, a doctrine that obviously lends support to the idea that the soul has existed in some other world long before its association with the body:

> Cebes added: Your favourite doctrine, Socrates [Plato, in effect], that knowledge is simply recollection, if true, also necessarily implies a previous time in which we have learned that which we now recollect. But this would be impossible unless our soul had been in some place before existing in the form of man; here then is another proof of the soul's immortality [really, eternality].

But when Plato spoke of "true" knowledge, he must have done so in order to distinguish it from some other kind of knowledge, which he would have been compelled to call "untrue." And in fact, he did. Shortly before the allegory of the cave in the *Republic*, he introduced us to a less graphic, yet quite revealing allegory concerning human knowledge. In it, we are told that knowledge is like an unequally divided line, on the smaller and lower part of which we are to place the sensations of sense experience (dreams, hallucinations, as well as what we see, hear, smell, and touch), whereas the upper and bigger part belongs to the intelligible realm (that is, the Ideas or Forms). The former constitutes the world of human opinion that is characterized by a "want of clearness" and a perennial inconsistency, whereas the latter is the domain of true philosophical knowledge that is endowed with certainty and universality. In the former, there is nothing but fanciful opinion, since its objects are forever changing; here, we can hardly speak of knowledge, for the chief instrument that allows us to 'know' these objects is the body that, as we saw earlier, is the source of all our troubles:

> What again shall we say of the actual acquirement of knowledge?—is the body, if invited to share in the enquiry, a hinderer or a helper? I mean to say, have sight and hearing any truth in them? Are they not, as the poets are always telling us, inaccurate witnesses? and yet, if even they are inaccurate and indistinct, what is to be said of the other senses?—for you will allow that they are the best of them?

Thus, the knowledge that we obtain by the agency of our senses, those "inaccurate and indistinct" bodily witnesses, can only amount to humble opinion that under no circumstances can serve as the basis of philosophy or science. For Plato, empirical or *a posteriori* modes of knowledge, applying as they do to the world of change and multiplicity, must be distrusted, and in anticipation of lines of thinking that were later to be adopted by Descartes, he rejected categorically the claim of those empiricists who, like Aristotle, John Locke, and David Hume, based their epistemologies on the assumption that sense perception constitutes the true basis of human knowledge.

If any true knowledge is to be obtained by the human mind, this knowledge must be the result of mental operations in which sensibility has no decisive role to play. For the objects of true knowledge are by their very nature beyond the horizon of the senses. The Ideas or Forms, and even more the very Idea of the Good *(to agathon)*, are entities which disclose themselves only to the 'eye' of the soul ('soul', 'mind', and 'spirit' are English words that can be comfortably used to translate the Platonic notion of *psyche*). As such then, these objects can be grasped through *a priori* knowledge, to which the dialectical analysis of concepts, together with a moral and spiritual disposition of the soul, will lead us. This *a priori* knowledge obviously cannot be derived from our experiences of the physical world as *a priori* objects are far removed from physical reality. Our sense experiences, however, can act as reminders of the reality that the soul once was fortunate enough to behold before its descent into the body. For far from being a *tabula rasa* or blank slate, as Locke conceived the human mind at birth, the soul brings into this world an already completed stock of philosophical knowledge that has become partly or mostly forgotten through the contamination brought about by the body. Hence, as we saw, Plato was able to speak of true knowledge as a kind of recollection, that is, a process in which the soul brings to full consciousness its innate thoughts.

The crucial question is, of course, what the objects of true knowledge are. But, as we pointed out in our discussion of Plato's dualism, there is no easy and universally accepted answer. If we begin by assuming that all knowledge is somehow tied up with sense perception, as empirical philosophers have invariably done, Plato's Ideas or Forms transform themselves into hypostasized class concepts of no substantive reality, and like unreal and chimerical essences, they are inevitably relegated to the realm of philosophical imagination. Can there be such a thing as "the Idea of table" that exists independently of this or that physical table? Can we speak of the Idea of mud-itself, or of man-itself, or of justice-itself, if all that we can really know (assuming the correctness of the empirical standpoint) are concrete physical objects such as a table, a bit of mud, this-man-here, or a specific instance of justice? For Aristotle, for whom, as we will see in our next chapter, reality is always *this-thing-here-now*, Plato's Ideas or Forms had in themselves no reality: they were philosophical constructions that Plato's confusion had raised to the level of realities. But, of course, if we assume a position different from empiricism, the scene rearranges itself along lines far more favorable to Plato. For Saint Anselm of Canterbury, whom we will meet in chapter 11,

the *idea* of God as a being-anything-greater-than-which-cannot-be-conceived is
an idea that can be grasped by the mind in complete independence from sense
perception and, in fact, with far greater assurance than anything given to sensibility. His Platonism allowed him to 'behold' or 'see' the reality of God, and
like the man who escaped from the cave, he was able to first 'see' God in order
to reason about Him afterwards, and in no way was the non-observational
character of his idea of God a hindrance on his philosophical path.

It would not be a mistake to affirm that throughout the history of ideas in
Western civilization philosophers have belonged to either one of two distinct
ideological camps: Platonism or Aristotelianism. To the former, there belong
those who like Plato begin at the *top* of the conceptual process and, starting
with universal notions, descend reluctantly to the realm of particulars; for
them, *a priori* knowledge is the true knowledge, and they have little difficulty in accepting the reality of innate ideas, the existence of God and the
soul, and the primacy of the intellectual world. They often feel at home amid
mathematical divagations of the most abstract nature and are willing to lend
an attentive ear to religious, mystical, and metaphysical discourse. On this
Platonic camp, we can find a place for Plato himself, as well as for Plotinus
(205–270), who was allegedly able to leave his body on several occasions;
for Saint Augustine, whose entire being yearned for a union with God: *"Quia
fecisti nos ad te et inquietum est cor nostrum, donec requiescat in te"* ("for
thou madest us for thee, [Oh Lord,] and our heart is restless until it rests in
thee"); for Saint Anselm (1033–1109), whose "faith seeking understanding"
is a way to transcend the physical world; for Saint Thomas Aquinas (1225–
1274), whose mystical vision shortly before his death can remind us of
Plato's liberated prisoner; for Descartes, according to whom God is the ultimate reality, and who insisted on the innateness of notions like soul and on
the primacy of mathematical knowledge over physical knowledge; for Leib-
nitz (1646–1716), mathematician and metaphysician, who spoke of reality in
terms of spiritual monads; and indeed, for many others.

To the other camp, on the other hand, there belong those who, in the language of Plato's *Dialogues,*

> try to drag everything down to Earth out of heaven and the unseen, literally
> grasping rocks and trees in their hands, for they hold upon every stick and stone,
> and strenuously affirm that real existence belongs to that which can be handled
> and offers resistance to touch. They define reality as the same thing as body, and
> as soon as one of the opposite party [the Platonists] asserts that anything without
> body is real, they are utterly contemptuous and will not listen to another word.

Among them, we can find a place for Epicurus, who was in no way preoccu-
pied with problems belonging to non-physical existence; for John Locke
(1632–1704), who endeavored to do away with innate ideas by his insistence
on the primacy of empirical knowledge and by his definition of the mind at

birth as a *tabula rasa;* for David Hume (1711–1776), whose devastating attacks on the substantiality of the soul have created a lasting influence on philosophy and psychology; for the radical empiricists and logical positivists of our own time, whose efforts, as in the case of Moritz Schlick (1882–1936), have been directed towards the demolition of metaphysics; and, especially, for language philosophers who, in the tradition of the Sophists of Socrates' time, have converted the old Pythagorean vocation (philosophy as the search for wisdom) into a scholastic analysis of language. It remains for us to see whether Aristotle himself can find a place among the Aristotelians, but in our next chapter we will devote time to this curious question.

4. THE IDEAL STATE AND THE PERFECT SOUL

The three major elements of Plato's thought that we have discussed so far appear most clearly in his political and ethical ideas. These ideas can be found dispersed throughout the *Dialogues,* but it is in the *Republic,* we think, that they attained their highest expression. An adequate exposition of them would certainly take us far beyond the limits of this chapter, and since our present comments are meant to be only helping aids to those who are in the process of gaining access to primary philosophical sources, we feel at this point justified in merely summarizing Plato's political and ethical views, leaving for the student the task of extracting from Plato himself their fuller meaning.

a. *"To know the good is to do the good."* This fundamental Socratic idea found its way into Plato's philosophy. According to Plato, evil and impurity are the necessary consequences of ignorance and confusion. Hence, in the true philosopher, that is, in him whose *vision* of the Idea of the Good has become a self-sustaining reality, intellect, will, and appetite are in a lasting condition of harmony, a condition that Plato called *justice.* Injustice is, therefore, disharmony or disorientation, which is a condition typical of those in whom either the will or the appetite or both exercise a controlling power over the intellect; in them, obviously, the philosophical vision becomes blurred and distorted, and like blind men, they cannot but stumble into all sorts of depravities.

b. Consequently, the fundamental task of the philosopher is to *educate himself and those who share his social world.* Philosophy, as this is conceived in the *Republic,* is an educational process (using the word 'educational' in its old etymological sense of 'growing out') in which the philosopher, he who has attained wisdom, must rule, and rule absolutely, over all other human beings: he has been outside of the cave and is the only one who can lead the prisoners to their freedom. Any political system that fails to recognize the natural supremacy of the philosopher is bound to be a failure, and this is especially the case with democratic systems in which the rabble *(demos)* is given the right to govern. When the rabble governs, we can expect every sort of brutal appetite, every sort of animal instinct, and every sort of stupidity to come to the surface at once. As he sought to construct his ideal state, Plato reminded his listeners that

> until philosophers are kings, or the kings and princes of this world have the spirit and power of philosophy, and political greatness and wisdom meet in one, and those commoner natures who pursue either to the exclusion of the other are compelled to stand aside, cities will never have rest from their evils—no, nor the human race, as I believe.

Prophetic words, indeed! One only has to inspect our own political world, where all kinds of clowns and halfwits reach political prominence, in order to appreciate the import of Plato's frightening pronouncement!

c. *The gap that separates the realm of the ethical from the realm of the political is an illusory one,* for the State is nothing but a magnified individual, and the individual cannot exist apart from the political and social relationships that actually constitute the State. Justice and injustice are the same, whether in the person or in the State, and we can learn what they really are by studying them either in the individual or in the State. If, however, we study the meaning of justice and injustice as they pertain to the State, they will surely appear more discernible and distinct, as their features will be greatly enlarged. Thus, in the *Republic* Plato made an easy transition from the strictly ethical questions of the beginning of the work to the political considerations of its lengthier parts. The good person is by necessity a good citizen, and a good citizen is one who lives in a good State. Likewise, a good State can only exist if its citizens are good.

d. A good State is one in which the citizens operate justly, and this implies at the outset an adequate distribution of labor. This distribution assures that the needs of all are conveniently satisfied: *to each according to his need.* Moreover, given the absolute fact that no person is self-sufficient, as "being human" implies a life of social interrelations, each person must be prepared to do that job for which nature has made him fit: hence, *from each according to his capacity.* Human equality, that dreadful myth perpetrated by democratic ideologies, must be altogether abandoned as a political assumption. In the real world, different people are born and develop quite differently: some are born and remain stupid, while others are born and develop with great intellectual talents; some are born fit for combat, others for commerce, others for philosophy. Accordingly, like the organs of the body, the citizens must perform different functions in the State, and these functions can be classified along a vertical scale of importance and excellence. What would be the outcome if the toes decide to do the thinking, or the ears the seeing, or the brain the walking? Surely, in the context of the human organism, this would entail the individual's destruction. Likewise, when in political associations everybody decides to rule (as in democracies), anarchy will inevitably ensue, and enormous instances of injustice (like Socrates' execution) become a common occurrence. Under these circumstances the State falls into a condition of disharmony or injustice, and intellectual ragamuffins like Thrasymachus (chapter 3) have a free hand at political decisions.

e. We should not be afraid, therefore, to speak of the necessity of instituting *social classes* into which the citizens can be grouped, not necessarily by the specific station of their birth or their family's worth, but by the character with which they are endowed by nature. Their distinct character will emerge in the process of education, the chief purpose of which is to select the higher from the lower types of citizens. Eventually, three social classes will emerge from this selective process: *a class of producers, a class of soldiers, and a class of rulers,* each class being characterized by a virtue: temperance, courage, and wisdom respectively.

f. While the producers produce, the soldiers defend and guard the State, and while the latter do their job, *the philosopher-kings rule the affairs of the State with absolute power,* as the captain of a ship rules over the ship. The philosophers have attained the wisdom that comes from the contemplation of the Idea of the Good. They really know what is best for themselves and for everyone else, and their philosophical disposition has made them immune from the ordinary passions found among lower human types, such as the love for money, the abuse of power, the need for sensual pleasure. Their task is not only overseeing the affairs of the State, but also leading all the citizens onto a higher plane of existence, for politics is, according to Plato, essentially a spiritual concern.

g. Only under the aforementioned conditions can the State become just, as *justice is defined as a sort of social harmony,* comparable to the state of health that prevails in a body when all the organs are functioning well.

h. All the previous points can now be transferred to the realm of the ethical. In each person we can also distinguish three elements: the appetites, the will, and the soul or rational principle. Accordingly, we can promote in us the specific virtues that appertain to these elements: temperance, courage, and wisdom. *We become just or good when our appetites are healthy and are under the guidance of the will, and when our will is thoroughly subjected to our soul.* The just man is he who is in perfect harmony with himself and who has set all his affairs aright. He is happy because there is no turmoil within him; he is happy because he understands the meaning of his life; he is happy because he is spiritually healthy. Now we can answer fully Thrasymachus' diatribe against justice that we quoted in the previous chapter!

The Platonic spirit of idealism and rationalism in such a system of politics and ethics is undeniable. Far from being concerned with the way human affairs are in the actual physical world, far from committing himself to an empirical accommodation to the pragmatic needs of imperfect social structures, Plato created his perfect State, his Utopia, in strict compliance with absolute standards. He hoped, as is clear from many passages of the *Republic,* that mankind could perhaps approach, if ever so slightly, his ideal delineation. The thought that his ideas had no corresponding empirical actualization did not bother him in the least. His Utopia, he knew, was truly *utopic (ou*=no, *topos*=place, hence, 'no place' or utopic). True to his allegedly divine origin, he did not deal with the petty realities in which most people are so deeply engaged: he constructed a veritable heavenly city; and as an idealistic painter, he did not hesitate to sketch for us the outlines of a perhaps unattainable masterpiece that has served for over two thousand years as the standard of judgment according to which political and ethical accomplishments are assessed. As a person, he never attained political power and was the ruler of no nation. But as Whitehead told us in chapter 3, like Socrates and Aristotle and like other great philosophical minds, he is ultimately one of the true rulers of the world.

Let us now turn our attention to his most outstanding student, Aristotle of Stagira.

QUESTIONS FOR STUDY

1. The philosophy of Plato is said to be fundamentally based on the teachings of Socrates, and yet it is possible to discern clear differences between them. Explain the biographical relationship between them, and discuss, by making specific references to the *Dialogues,* the major contrasting features of their philosophical outlooks.

2. In his *Seventh Letter* Plato gives us some hints to how his *writings* are to be interpreted. Explain. How do the dialogue form and the appeal to myths help us in making sense of Plato's own assessment of his writings?

3. Explain Plato's views on the soul, and make specific reference to his doctrine of the eternality of the soul as this is advanced in the *Phaedo.*

4. Thales' philosophy is said to be monistic, whereas when we speak of Plato's we refer to it as dualistic. Explain.

5. Explain the meaning and significance of the "Allegory of the Cave." In particular, explain the epistemological and metaphysical import entailed in this allegory.

6. Describe and discuss the major features of Plato's political and ethical system as this is presented to us in the *Republic.* Do you agree with Karl Popper's statement to the effect that Plato's ideas contain the seeds of political totalitarianism?

5

Aristotle

LIFE

Aristotle was born in 384 B.C. at Stagira, a town in nothern Greece. His father was Nicomachus, the personal physician of the Macedonian king Amyntas III. His father died when Aristotle was still a child, and thereafter he was raised by a friend of the family. When he was eighteen, Aristotle was sent to Athens to study at Plato's Academy. But this was not Aristotle's last contact with Macedonia. Amyntas' son was the legendary Philip of Macedonia who, in turn, was the father of Alexander the Great. Aristotle would return one day to become the tutor of the future world conqueror.

Aristotle remained at the Academy for twenty years until Plato's death in 347 B.C. In 345 B.C. he moved to the island of Lesbos where he began his biological investigations. The two great influences on Aristotle's life had now commenced. He was deeply influenced by the philosophy of Plato, but Aristotle was no mere disciple. He would go on to create a new philosophy that clearly owed much to Plato, yet introduced major innovations of its own. Those innovations, as we shall see, stem from using biology instead of geometry as a model.

In 342 B.C. Philip of Macedonia invited Aristotle to become Alexander's tutor, and the invitation was accepted. Thus began one of the most intriguing

relationships in the whole of the classical world, subject to as much speculation as the relationship between Socrates and Plato. Aristotle returned to
Athens in 335 B.C. and set up a rival school of philosophy known as the
Lyceum. Later, it was referred to as the Peripatetic and its members as peri-
patetics. A great deal of research and scholarship was carried out at the
institution.

When Alexander the Great died unexpectedly in 323 B.C., there was a general uprising in Athens against anyone associated with the Macedonian
ruler. Not wishing to see "Athenians sin twice against philosophy" (an obvious reference to the trial and execution of Socrates), Aristotle fled to the
town of Chalcis in Euboea and died there just a year later in 322 B.C. In his
will, Aristotle requested that he be buried next to his long-dead wife.

PROBLEM OF INTERPRETATION

There are special problems involved in the interpretation of Aristotle's
philosophy. To put the problem succinctly, there is no general agreement
amongst scholars on what he did or did not write. To begin with, there were
so-called literary treatises written in dialogue form during the early part of
his career for a public audience. Unfortunately, these have all been lost.
What remains are bits and pieces, that is, references to them in the surviving
works of other ancient writers. For example, there are a few references to
Aristotle's lost works in the surviving works of Cicero. These early works, if
they had been available, might have been helpful in explaining the relation
between Aristotle and Plato.

When we turn to the works that are available, the so-called scholarly treatises, we have a different set of problems. These appear to be either lecture
notes or textbooks prepared for use within the Lyceum. They were written
over a long period of time during which the views expressed underwent
revision and a corresponding shift in emphasis. There is disagreement
among scholars as to whether all of these treatises were actually written by
Aristotle himself or by his associates or even his students. There is even disagreement about which pieces of manuscript go together with other pieces.
Aristotle's list of publications and the areas covered are so impressive and
vast that it is sometimes easier to think of him or his works, not as the product of an individual, but as the product of a research organization.

The subsequent history of Aristotle's works is also pertinent not only
because it reinforces the point that general agreement on their interpretation is hard to come by, but also because the influence of Aristotle has been
so great and varied over so long a period of time that the availability or
unavailability of some texts explains why Aristotle was differently interpreted.
The collection of Aristotle's works was given to his successor, Theophrastus,

on Aristotle's death. Theophrastus bequeathed them, in turn, to Neleus, who sold them to Appelicon. By this time, some of the manuscripts were badly damaged and deteriorating. Appelicon died in 86 B.C. Sulla then took the works from Athens to Rome, where they were published between 43 and 20 B.C. It is conceivable that there was no direct acquaintance with the manuscripts from 250 to 70 B.C. When all of the philosophical schools were ordered closed during Rome's imminent collapse in the sixth century A.D., only the logical treatises continued to be known. In the meantime, the main body of Aristotle's works were known and studied by Arab scholars, such as the famous Averröes, and it was only in the twelfth century that these works were once again known in the West. As in the case of Plato, there is an Aristotle legend that has perhaps been more influential on the development of Western civilization than the original intention of the author.

RELATION TO PLATO

There is a well-known statement, to which we have alluded already in the chapter on Plato, made by the great twentieth-century philosopher Whitehead, to the effect that all philosophy is a footnote to Plato. And, it is sometimes added, Aristotle has the largest piece of the footnote. There is also the famous quip that everybody is either a Platonist or an Aristotelian, and further, you can begin as an Aristotelian and later become a Platonist, but once a Platonist always a Platonist. All of this indicates that Aristotle must be seen against the background of Plato's thought.

We approach this issue by distinguishing between content and approach. From the point of view of content, there are innumerable items of Plato's work that Aristotle accepted as well as rejected. From the point of view of approach, there is a major difference between Plato and Aristotle. We take the position that Aristotle's originality consists in using biology as his philosophical model, and that he incorporates or rejects Platonic elements in terms of whether they fit that model. In addition, readers should be warned that great philosophers are not necessarily great or even fair scholars when it comes to interpreting the works of others. This means, for instance, that Aristotle reacts against what he takes Plato to be saying, and this is not how Plato may have understood what he was saying or how we would understand him. Moreover, Aristotle sometimes criticizes the followers of Plato, as when he talks about the "friends of the forms." Finally, many of the problems Aristotle raises about Plato's theories are problems that Plato himself had recognized and was among the first to articulate or to admit. Our purpose in this chapter is to try to understand Aristotle rather than to clarify or to defend Plato.

The major difficulty with Plato, according to Aristotle, lies in the theory of the forms. When Plato separated the forms from the ordinary objects of our world, he created two major problems. First, he could not explain, except by delightful but unhelpful metaphors, exactly how the forms were related to the actual objects of our experience. Second, he could not explain the precise manner in which forms could serve as ideals or standards for our actions in both the private and public world. Clearly, it is the separate existence of the forms from objects that creates the problem. One obvious solution is to reject this view and to argue that *forms cannot have a separate existence.* This is just exactly what Aristotle does.

The forms had played a key role in Plato's philosophy. Forms are the objects of knowledge, and they are the cause of the objects we experience being what they are and changing in the way they do. Therefore, any revision in the doctrine of forms will lead to revisions in the theory of knowledge and revisions in that cluster of related concepts of cause, change, and motion. With regard to knowledge, it is assumed by all of the parties involved that knowledge must be certain and unchangeable. Moreover, it is assumed that the properties of certainty and unchangeability must also belong to the objects of our knowledge. In order to preserve these properties, Plato had found it necessary to make the forms supersensible as well as universal. Aristotle will agree that forms must be universal but not supersensible. By arguing that forms are not outside the objects of daily experience, Aristotle made sense of the everyday reality of forms. But as a consequence, he will have to make a special effort to account for the permanence and the universality of the forms once he locates them in everyday objects that are not permanent. This, in turn, requires Aristotle to reinterpret permanence, and this he will do by arguing that *it is not "things" that are permanent but processes.* To make processes the home of the permanent will require a reinterpretation of those key concepts of change, motion, and cause.

THE MODEL OF BIOLOGY

It was in the study of biology that Aristotle found the solutions to what he took to be the problems generated by Plato's theory of forms. Biology is the study of life. In every instance life seems to be characterized by growth, development, and decay—in short, by a process of change. This process of change, whether in the passage of the seasons or the growth of a child into an adult, seems to be designed to achieve certain purposes. Nutrition, growth, and reproduction appear to be fundamental to all organic activity. These functions are present in all living things, plants as well as animals. At a higher level, animals exhibit the additional functions of sensation, desire, and locomotion (change of place). At a still higher level, some animals have the capacity for deliberate behavior, as when beavers build dams. When we come to the level of human beings, mankind has, in addition to all of the capacities already mentioned, the capacity for theoretical reasoning. What we have thus described is a *hierarchy* wherein each level contains all that we find on the lower levels, plus something additional and unique to that level. When Aristotle fully extends this hierarchy it eventually will look something like this:

DIVINE
↑
MAN
↑
ORGANIC (plants and animals)
↑
INORGANIC SUBSTANCES
↑
BASIC ELEMENTS (earth, air, fire, and water)
↑
PRIME MATTER (potential unformed matter)

Nature is, therefore, a graded series or hierarchy of existing things.

Another remarkable principle discovered from the observation of animals and plants is the *persistence of the form,* that is, the species, *through a changing succession of individuals.* For example, oak trees produce acorns, which in turn grow into oak trees, and these oak trees produce another generation of acorns, etc., etc. The original oak trees (or any later oak tree in the series) will eventually perish, but the form of being or developing into an oak tree is preserved for endless generations. Acorns do not, by the way, ever become maple trees or butterflies, etc. In human reproduction the same pattern is present. Aristotle did not, of course, know about genes, but he could observe that human beings produce only other human beings: that is why it is called *re*production, and why offspring clearly resemble their parents, and why the same traits are preserved through endless succeeding generations of a family. The traits are the forms, so to speak, but instead of existing outside the object they are somehow "transmitted" from generation to generation. So biology gives a clear case of embodied forms, somehow in the objects remaining permanent through a process that includes a succession of individuals.

Further, if we think of parents as the cause of children coming into existence, and if we remember that the form of being human persists through a succession of changing individuals and is transmitted, we arrive at the following conception of causation:

$$c\,\textcircled{P_1} \longrightarrow {}_E\textcircled{P_1}$$

C stands for the cause
E stands for the effect
P_1 stands for a particular property or trait

The children are the effects or products of their parents. The parents are the cause. Every trait of the child, that is, such properties, let us say, of being pug-nosed or having blue eyes, etc., is the result of that trait having been already present in the parents (or grandparents). There is no such thing as a totally new trait. Generalizing this point, we can say that in a causal sequence *the effect can have no property that is not already present in the cause.* Stated another way, if the effect has a particular property (or trait), we are justified in asserting that the cause must have had that property. This analysis of causation is not only crucial for Aristotle but totally dominates Western thought for two thousand years, right down to the eighteenth century.

One of the consequences of taking this view of causation is that it eliminates the possibility of evolution. Aristotle does not believe that new species or new forms can come into existence. Another point worth stressing is that Aristotle does not have a mechanical understanding of causation, and this too is a consequence of his biological model. Beavers, for example, do not just build dams; such dams are means toward the obtaining of food (nutrition). Nutrition is the end, goal, or purpose of the activity. Moreover, viewing the process as a whole, not just an isolated segment, nutrition is not just for survival but for growth, and when a beaver reaches maturity, it reproduces itself. Growth and reproduction may thus be interpreted as ends. The notion of viewing organic processes as goal-directed is fundamental to many biological investigations, and it can be extended in both directions. We can go backwards and investigate the anatomy of the beaver, e.g., its teeth, and when we explain the structure of the beaver's teeth, we say that the teeth have that structure in order to permit the beaver to build dams (by chewing and cracking twigs). We have explained the structure in terms of the goal. This is known as teleological biology, and a *teleological* explanation is an explanation of a process in terms of a goal or end.

Nobody pretends that individual teeth are conscious of the purpose. Some theorists would even argue that the beaver is not self-conscious of his activity. Nevertheless, it is plausible to explain structure and function in terms of goals. Another example would be the statement that the *function* of the heart is to pump blood to the vital organs. If the goal of a process need not necessarily be conscious, it is not unreasonable to extend this kind of teleological explanation back to inorganic matter. This is exactly what Aristotle will do in his physics. We can, even more plausibly, extend this analysis forward. So far we have talked about beavers. But what about man who is self-conscious? Aristotle will argue that human life has built-in goals, and the peculiar or unique capacity of mankind is that we can become conscious of them.

If we put this teleological conception of causation, namely, that we explain a process in terms of its goal, together with the hierarchy of nature, we have the following conception of nature. Every individual can be understood in two ways—every individual is both the fulfillment (end) of the purpose inherent in some other individual (as, e.g., the child is the end product of the parent) and at the same time the starting point for a development beyond itself (the child will become a parent of another child). Nature is thus a vast interlocking hierarchy of processes, in which things on one level are understood as means to things on another higher level.

To sum up, using teleological biology Aristotle is able to explain how forms are embodied, how they can be permanent through a succession of individuals, how it is the process of succession or change that is real (individual structure, function, and action only make sense as part of the process), and what it means for one thing to be the cause of another within a process.

KNOWLEDGE

We are now in a position to give a more detailed explanation of how Aristotle uses teleological biology as a model for explaining knowledge. Since it is human beings who possess knowledge, we would expect Aristotle to give us a biological account of the knowing process and its relation to the objects of knowledge. Aristotle's epistemology, that is, his theory of knowledge, is closely related to his psychology, his theory of human life.

The Greek word *psyche* (from which we get psychology) literally means soul, and soul is the form of a living object. For Aristotle, the soul is not separable from the body; rather, body and soul are two aspects of a single substance. More precisely, soul is related to body as form is to matter. Since forms are always embedded, the form (soul) cannot exist apart from body. But it should also be clear from our previous discussion that soul (as a form) cannot be reduced to or explained solely in terms of matter. Aristotle would reject a totally materialist explanation of life. Rather he will stress the goal of living processes and the hierarchical scheme of which it is a part.

As we have already discovered, human beings share a number of capacities with other living things, and at the same time we possess a unique capacity, one found for the first time on our level of the hierarchy. That capacity is our ability to reason. In Greek the word for the collection of intellectual powers unique to man is *nous*. We may now ask what is the relation of nous (reason) to psyche (the soul or form of the body)? The answer is that nous is the end or goal of one process, namely, the process that begins on the lower level with perception and is the beginning of a process reaching beyond itself.

Aristotle draws an analogy between thinking and perceiving. He also explains sensation in a manner analogous to the lower-level function of nutrition. In nutrition, the matter of an external object is literally taken into the body and transformed, as when we eat meat to obtain the protein for building our own tissues. In sensation, only the form, not the matter, is taken into the body. Aristotle gives us the example of a wax seal. We are familiar with the old process of sealing a document by dripping wax on it and then impressing on the wax a metal seal, usually with a design of some kind. In perception the sense organs separate out and take in the form in the same way as wax receives the imprint of the seal. But we do not absorb the object anymore than the metal seal is absorbed. Only the imprint is absorbed. When the sensory organs have absorbed the same form as exists in the object, our perception is in contact with reality. The mind can naturally assimilate the structure of the external world.

Thinking is like perceiving. A further faculty in the psyche unites the ideas derived from the separate senses and reconstructs them into something like a single object. This is called the "common sense." At this point there is a kind of awareness in the soul of these perceptual activities. *Nous* is in one part the ability to monitor our perceptual activity. Now we can distinguish between passive reason and the active intellect. On one level reason is passive: it receives the forms like a blank tablet. At another level it begins to do things and becomes an active intellect. As an active intellect it engages in the process of abstraction wherein it intuits self-evident truths or universal first principles. This activity is possible only once the forms themselves have been abstracted from the original matter.

Aristotle, like Plato, believed that there were universally true first principles, but he specifically denied that they were present at birth. These first principles are not directly apprehended in our experience, but they are arrived at by progressive acts of abstraction that begin with experience. How, then, does Aristotle explain the ability of reason to perform this feat? He seems to believe that there is a higher reason (divine reason) that is needed to actualize the power in us. This higher, divine reason accounts for both the intelligibility of the world and man's ability to grasp that intelligibility.

Two interpretations have prevailed on the exact status of this higher reason. One view is that the higher reason is within each person (immanent). This was the view of Aquinas. The other view is that the active intellect is transcendent (outside of man), and that when we are conscious of thinking we are conscious of God's thought, not our own. This was the view of Averröes and, in another form, the view of Hegel.

Given the foregoing account of how we acquire knowledge, namely, by abstraction originating in sense experience, we can summarize that process by saying that we pass from particular objects in sense experience to universal and necessary principles. Once we possess these universal, certain, and necessary truths we can have *science,* which is demonstrated (i.e., deductive) knowledge of the causes of things. The format of scientific exposition is a deductive argument in the form of a syllogism that begins with premises that are certain.

Premise: All men are mortal.
Premise: Socrates is a man.
Conclusion: Socrates is mortal.

How do we know the truth of the first premise, that "All men are mortal"? We know it because we have apprehended it by intuitive reason or *nous*. The name of the process of arriving at first principles is *induction*. Modern philosophers and readers are frequently disappointed that Aristotle did not spend more time explaining the process of induction. But if we accept Aristotle's theory of perception, we can see why this would be no problem for him. Because the moderns have a different theory of perception, the issue of induction becomes a problem for them. Aristotle's logic is a direct consequence of his view of the world as embodied form and his account of perception.

SCIENCE

Aristotle says that there are three kinds of knowledge, depending on the purpose for which they are pursued. Theoretical knowledge is pursued for its own sake; practical knowledge is pursued for the sake of action; productive knowledge is pursued in order to make something, as in the arts. Theoretical knowledge is subdivided into three parts: mathematics, physics, and metaphysics (or first philosophy). In mathematics we study what is unchangeable but cannot exist separately (e.g., a line with length but no width); physics studies what is changeable and separable; metaphysics studies what is unchangeable and can exist separately. Note that for Aristotle, physics is not practical. He did not have a technological view of science. The purpose of studying nature is to obtain knowledge, not control over it. There must be some permanent features of the world that remain unchangeable, and therefore uncontrollable, otherwise there would be no objective structure.

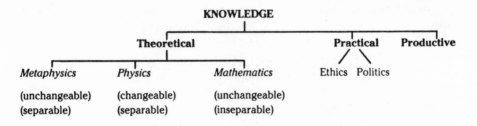

PHYSICS

The first thing to note about Aristotle's conception of physics is that it is not a branch of mathematics. This is in opposition to Plato. Mathematics, for Aristotle, is an abstraction from physics; it is not a separate realm from which physics can be deduced. The second thing to note about Aristotle's physics is that he is going to interpret physical change in terms of his biological model. This disorients many readers who are used to the modern notion that biology is to be explained in terms of chemistry and chemistry explained in terms of physics.

We identified Thales as the first philosopher, since he was the first of a long line of Greek thinkers to be concerned with defining the nature of reality. Despite giving divergent answers to the question, all of these thinkers agreed that some definitive statement could be given about the permanent nature of the real. One of the consequences of this assumption is that *change* becomes something of a problem. In our talk about things that change, we seem to be assuming that something remains permanent during the process of change. Moreover, if there is change, then there must be some permanent principles according to which change takes place. In short, Greek philosophers identified what was real with what was permanent, and they either denied the reality of what appears to change, or they interpreted change as a manifestation of what was unchanging.

Among Aristotle's predecessors, Parmenides had argued that change is impossible or an illusion since a thing had to be what it is. Aristotle claimed that change was real. The atomists and the Pythagoreans had postulated unchangeable elements combining and uncombining according to principles. Against them, Aristotle argued that change was not merely quantitative but qualitative as well. Moreover, Aristotle rejected the determinism of the atomists as well as their notion of a void (vacuum or empty space) in which atoms moved around. Finally, Aristotle rejected Plato's theory that things in the world imitated the separate forms.

Change is real. The most fundamental change is locomotion, change of place or location. What is the source of this change? It is, according to Aristotle, found within nature itself. There are four kinds of causes to which we must appeal when we explain change. But, we must remember that what is being explained is the process of change, not the objects.

1. *Material cause* (that of which a thing is made).
2. *Efficient cause* (that by which it comes into existence).
3. *Formal cause* (essence or structure).
4. *Final cause* (the end for which it exists).

In the case of natural objects, like an acorn, as opposed to the products of human art, such as a house, the last three causes coincide. That is, the efficient, formal, and final causes are the same.

To explain an acorn we might begin by describing the organic material of which it is made. But we would also note that an acorn comes from an oak tree. What happens to an acorn? It grows into an oak tree. Why does this all happen? It happens because the essence or form of an acorn is to become an oak tree. If we grasp the nature of the acorn, we can see that it must have come from an oak and that it is destined to become an oak tree. Such biological facts are generalized by Aristotle into a full-blown theory about how the universe works. In his language, the end or final cause of an object in nature is to realize its essence or formal cause. It also means that this formal cause or essence is embodied in another entity, which possesses an identical form or essence and serves as the efficient cause of its production. It is *this coincidence of formal and efficient causes that permits us to infer unerringly what a cause must necessarily be, from mere acquaintance with the effect.* The formal cause becomes, in practice, the basic explanatory principle, since what a thing is essentially is built into it.

Reality for Aristotle is the world of individual objects or substances. But we must be careful not to confuse substance with matter. Substance is *in*formed matter. The form is distinguishable in thought but not in fact. To think of the form as separate is to confuse an act of thought with reality itself. Matter and form must be thought of as *potentiality* and *actuality* in order to understand that a substance changes through time. *Entelechy* is the unconscious drive to achieve its end or purpose, and it is a property of form. What endures is the matter, what changes is the form. Development is change following a pattern in order to achieve an end.

How does this apply to the physical world? Every object on the earth has a natural place towards which it will move by rectilinear motion (straight line) if not hindered. Since the earth is finite in extent, every object must come to rest. Objects on the earth are thus perishable. Celestial objects, like planets, however, are eternal and therefore made of a different substance, the aether. Aristotle's physics thus sharply distinguishes the heavens from the earth.

The following summary of the physics can be given:

1. The world is intelligible as a whole (it is a *uni*verse).

2. The world is infinite in time, that is, eternal. It has neither a beginning nor an end. Why? A beginning or an end would be unintelligible, for we could always ask what was happening before or after, or what caused it to start. The world cannot, therefore, have been created (either in the sense of the book of Genesis or by Plato's Demiurge).

3. If the universe is eternal, and if time is the measure of change, then change is eternal.

4. Eternal motion must be circular motion *(cycle).* It cannot be motion in a straight line, because that would lead to the infinity of space. Aristotle rejects this idea as unintelligible. The universe is finite in space but eternal in time. The earth is the stationary center of the cosmos, and both it and the cosmos are spherical.

5. If change is eternal, then what causes change must be eternal.

6. The cause or causes of change of motion cannot form an infinite series. That is unintelligible. Hence, there must be a first or unmoved mover.

7. The *unmoved mover* must be eternal.

8. If the unmoved mover is eternal, it must be itself unchangeable, that is, have no potential for change. Since potentiality is a property of matter, the unmoved mover must be immaterial, that is, a pure unembodied form.

9. The unmoved mover is unextended (does not occupy space), because as an infinite (eternal) force it cannot have finite extension, and if the universe itself is finite, the unmoved mover cannot be infinite in size.

METAPHYSICS

Mention of the unmoved mover brings us to metaphysics or first philosophy. The main problem of understanding Aristotle here is that he appears to have two conceptions of metaphysics. On the one hand, he says that metaphysics is not one of the special sciences but the study of reality as a whole, in its totality. This is the study of "being as being." This part of metaphysics involves technical considerations of concepts like substance, essence, the relation of matter to form, etc., understood from a teleological point of view. On the other hand, metaphysics seems to be the study of separate and unchanging being, or what is called *theology:* the theory (logos) of God (theos), that is, the unmoved mover. The two views can be made consistent if one argues that a consideration of metaphysics in the first sense leads to a consideration of metaphysics in the second sense.

The unmoved mover or God is arrived at in two ways. First, it is the culmination of the analysis of the physical world. The unmoved mover is the supreme object of all knowledge. As such it has to be a substance, immune to change, good in the highest degree (as a goal). But Aristotle made clear that it is not a creator, not the efficient cause of the world, but its final cause. Neither is it a providence concerned for the well-being of the human race. It is not, in short, the Judaic or Christian God. Second, the unmoved mover as the divine is, from the biological point of view, the ultimate object of all desire. It moves things not as a physical object would move them but by being the perfect goal towards which they aspire. If you like, it is love of the divine that makes the world go round. As the next stage in the hierarchy beyond human reason, it would also have to be considered living and conscious. Since it does not have a body and sense organs, its thought is about thought itself. It is total self-consciousness.

ETHICS AND POLITICS

As a discipline, ethics has a practical aim: it is knowledge for the sake of action. The object of knowledge is the good for man. The good or end must be the full development of human nature. There is a distinction between what we seek and what we might think that we want. What we seek, if properly grasped, is rooted in our nature; it is a fact about us. It is given in our nature, there to be discovered, not arbitrarily chosen.

What is distinctive about us is our rational faculty, not our appetites. Our reason operates in two ways, first in the habitual subordination of appetite or passion to rational control, and second in the contemplation of truth. The first way comprises the moral virtues and involves the doctrine of the mean. Most moral virtues are means between extremes, as courage is the mean between being a coward and acting rashly. But virtuous action is not virtuous because it follows a mean, rather it is virtuous because it is consistent with reason (which routinely involves a mean).

The main ethical problem is, why do some people not choose to act consistently with their known good? Aristotle rejects the Platonic view that it is a kind of ignorance. Instead, he argues that virtuous conduct must be a result of habit, not just a natural event. We cannot, for example, just choose to change our behavior; we must first alter our habits. Aristotle has no conception of a radically free will. On the other hand, we are responsible for our behavior since it is not the product of bare necessity. Self-indulgence is as much a habit as anything else—it is not natural.

Since so much depends upon habit, and since habit is acquired within a social framework, the ethics cannot be intelligibly separated from the politics. The state exists for the good life; it is a necessary prerequisite for the full development of human nature. Aristotle's discussion of politics, like all of his philosophy, presupposes that we already are acquainted with a good state or what it is, and that it, along with other institutions in the community, has provided the background for proper habituation.

INFLUENCE

Along with Plato, Aristotle has been one of the two most influential philosophers in history. While his views on specific subjects have been more popular in some periods than in others, he has been influential even when he is the object of greatest criticism. The three notions that have been the most persistently influential are (a) the concept of teleology, (b) the analysis of causation, and (c) the analysis of knowledge in relation to perception.

QUESTIONS FOR STUDY

1. Aristotle has said that "ALL MEN *BY NATURE* DESIRE TO KNOW!" In what sense would this be true? Compare the statement to the following: "All men have two eyes."

2. What is the role of the unmoved mover in Aristotle's philosophy?

3. What is a teleological explanation? What is the difference between teleology and evolution?

4. Compare and contrast the theories of knowledge of Plato and Aristotle.

5. What is the relation between the formal and efficient causes? Give your own example.

6

Logic: The Study of Arguments

In the last four chapters, we have studied the development of philosophy during one of the greatest epochs of human civilization, the approximately two hundred fifty years from the time of Thales until the death of Aristotle. During this time, mankind in the West became more intensely aware of its natural and social environment than ever before. Before Thales, as we have seen, people had many beliefs about the world, their place in it, and their obligations to God and to each other. But they were dependent for those beliefs upon tradition and the authority of the ancient poets. With Thales, a powerful new instrument for the expansion of human knowledge was created. It is called *reason,* and by this name the ancients conceived of the power of the human mind to puzzle out the answers to the questions that troubled them, without reliance upon the received opinions of the time. Among the pre-Socratics, reason played the role of drawing out the consequences of clever and daring speculation about the nature of physical reality—what the Greeks called the cosmos. In Plato, reason took the form of *dialectic,* and with this method, Plato believed, a unique and almost mysterious realm of ideas could be explored. And in Aristotle, reason began with sense observation and attempted to draw conclusions about the nature of the substances we find about us in the world.

Of course, the expansion of knowledge and the intensification of man's conscious awareness of the world he inhabits was not confined to science and philosophy, even if we consider only the Greeks in that period. Profound advances were being made in sculpture and architecture, with the consequent deepening of man's esthetic awareness and of his knowledge of building materials, engineering techniques, and mathematics. The Greeks were also engaging in exchanges with foreign peoples—with Persians, Egyptians, Babylonians, and, perhaps even as early as Thales, with the Hebrews. They, perhaps more than any people before them, took the trouble to study carefully the beliefs and ways of other nations and to modify and adopt the best of their practices—even though, like most people, they looked upon all foreigners as inferior to themselves!

Such an expansion and intensification of knowledge was bound to lead to the most characteristically human form of consciousness, that of *self-consciousness*, or awareness of oneself as possessing beliefs, as seeking new knowledge, and as creating things of beauty. And the Greeks not only created reason and rational knowledge, they also created two characteristic forms that self-consciousness has taken since then. The first of these is *history*. Ages prior to the Greeks had their chroniclers, their lists of kings and patriarchs, but they did not attempt either to give a rational explanation of the course of events or to criticize the accounts of the participants in history. The first person to make both of these attempts was Herodotus, who described the Persian wars, the events leading up to them, and the customs and attitudes of the people who fought in them. And he was careful to distinguish between what seemed to him to be probable accounts and those that seemed improbable. A second historian was Thucydides, whose *History of the Peloponnesian War* depicts the course of, and the reasons for, the disaster that was to overtake Athens while Socrates was in the prime of life. The importance of the discovery of rational and critical history for mankind's understanding of itself cannot be overestimated. By writing of its history, a people recognizes itself as subject to change and development, and as being part of a larger community that influences it. Out of this use of reason to investigate mankind itself, not as it ought to be, but as it is, was later to come such sciences as economics, sociology, and political science.

The second great invention that was to expand mankind's self-consciousness was *logic*. Logic, at first, was conceived as *the attempt of reason to investigate the principles according to which it operates.* Since the time of Thales, thinking persons had advanced arguments, drawn conclusions, and developed reasons for their beliefs. The works of Plato, for example, are full of reasoned arguments; clearly some of them are more persuasive than others. But why should this be? Why should some arguments have a greater power to persuade than others? What is the nature of this new instrument, reason, that it sometimes gives clear and certain truth, and yet fails us at other times? This study, this attempt on the part of reason to lift itself up by its own bootstraps and investigate its own principles of operation, was *first* undertaken by Aristotle. His *Organon* is literally the creation of a new science out of nothing. Aristotle *invented* logic and left it in a form that was to endure, with only changes in detail, until the middle of the last century.

The present chapter is not a formal presentation of the concepts and structures of logic for their own sakes. Moreover, logic is too important a study to be of interest only to historians and specialists. The disciplined thinking it represents ought to be the property of everyone, not just of philosophers. And many people in all walks of life have noted how much they profited from a course in logic while at college. Although in a short chapter we cannot offer much *practice* in logical thinking, we will try to outline some of the principles of logic and observe them "in action," as it were. They lie at the root of rigorous thinking, even if we are usually not conscious of them, and make it possible for us to distinguish *good* reasoning from *bad* reasoning.

1. THE ELEMENTS OF LOGIC

A. Arguments.

The ideal of reason, first pursued by the ancient Greeks, can be stated as follows: always *give reasons* for your beliefs, and never accept any belief until you have explored the reasons for it! The process of giving reasons for a belief is called *argumentation.* An argument is defined as a *set of statements about which it is claimed that one of them is true because the others are.* The "others" are the reasons that are given in support of a belief. They are called the *premises* of an argument, while the statement that is based upon the premises is called the *conclusion.* There is an argument contained in the following simple assertions:

> "Charlie must not be in today, because he
> always leaves his coat on the rack above his
> desk, and I don't see any coat hanging there."

The *premises* of this argument are (1) "Charlie always leaves his coat on the rack above his desk"; and (2) "I don't see any coat hanging there." The *conclusion,* then, is (3) "Charlie must not be in today." The assumed truth of statements (1) and (2) are the reasons given for asserting truth of (3); (1) and (2) are claimed to *warrant* (3). *To decide whether or not, or the extent to which, a set of premises warrant a conclusion is the goal of logical analysis.* Before we begin a study of the typical forms arguments may take, and the logical analysis appropriate to each, we must first come to grips with the notion of a *statement.*

B. Statements.

Again, Aristotle's *Organon* contains the first known analysis of the structure of statements. There he considers only those statements that are of one simple type: those in which we assert some quality or characteristic of an entity. This process is called, in grammar, *predication:* I predicate something of a subject. Interestingly enough, Aristotle discovered that there are ten and only ten kinds of qualities or characteristics that we can predicate of a subject. He called these *categories.* Thus we can say of a thing that it is an independent entity or a *substance* ("Socrates"), and then predicate of it some *quantity* ("5'8" tall"), *relation* ("taller than Plato"), *quality* ("just," "healthy"), *activity* ("is speaking"), *passivity* ("is being spoken to"), *position* ("sitting"), *temporality* ("at noon"), *place* ("in the agora"), and *state* ("armed").

Not all *sentences* are *statements,* of course. If I say, for example, "please shut the door," I am uttering a sentence but am not making a statement in Aristotle's sense, for I am not predicating either openness or shutness (state) of the door; rather I am requesting that someone put it in the state of being shut. There are many kinds of sentences that are not statements. They may be distinguished according to their *uses.* "Please shut the door" is a *request* or *command.* Another kind of sentence is a question: "What time is it?" Other sentences are used to elicit information, perform a ceremony, pronounce judgment, evaluate works of art or the behavior of persons, or to make a promise or take an oath. But what distinguishes a statement from other kinds of sentences is that *statements are used to assert facts.* They therefore have the property of being either true or false, whereas questions and commands, for instance, are neither true nor false.

C. Truth.

The reader may, at this point, shrug his shoulders like Pilate and say, "What is truth?" And philosophers have wrestled with this question since the time of Plato. One of the theories of truth accepted by many philosophers today is the *correspondence theory of truth,* which says that a statement is true if it corresponds to some state of affairs. Thus the statement "Socrates is no longer alive" would be true only if Socrates once lived and is now dead, and false if Socrates either never lived or was still alive somewhere. Another way of expressing the idea behind this theory is that statements *describe* some aspect of the world, and a statement is true if it correctly describes what is the case. Statements are intended to "tell it like it is!" The question as to how we *know* whether a statement is in fact true is the question of *evidence,* about which there has again been a great deal of controversy. What is to count as a legitimate source of evidence? Intuition? Insight? The authority of ancient sages? The prophets who are said to have spoken with God? Let's get down to earth! What about statement (2) in the argument considered above: "I don't see any coat hanging there." The evidence in favor of the truth of that statement is simple *sense perception.* Most of us would say that no further evidence is needed in this case, although some philosophers—for example, Descartes—have argued that even in such cases I may be mistaken. After all, I could always be subject to some form of illusion and fail to see what is really there!

D. *A priori* Statements.

There seems to be another source of good evidence in addition to the evidence obtained by sense perception. Some statements do not refer to or describe the world at all but rather assert conceptual relationships. They may nonetheless be true or false. For example, "Today is Sunday or it is not Sunday" is a true statement, but not because it correctly describes some aspect of the world; this statement would be true regardless of what the calendar says. The truth of such statements depends upon the meanings of its component terms: today, Sunday, and the relationship "either A is true or A is false." Such statements are called *tautologies,* and we are said to know that they are true or false not by investigating the external world, but by reflecting upon the meanings involved in the terms they contain. Moreover *a priori* truths are *necessary* truths; their denial involves a contradiction. The concepts that are used to describe this difference are *a priori* (knowledge by reflection upon meanings), and *a posteriori* (knowledge by experience of the external world). Let us consider an example of how this distinction functions in logical thinking.

As we grow up, we learn a lot of things that we casually lump together as "facts." Most often, we take facts as they are given to us and rarely ask whether the fact in question is "in fact" true. Let us imagine that a first-grade teacher has just told her class that Columbus discovered America in 1492. One of her pupils, a bit cleverer and more aggressive than most, asks, "Why should I believe you, Miss Brubaker, when you tell us that?" If the teacher is not too surprised by the question, she will tell the child about log books and contemporary documents in archives in Spain and elsewhere. If the child asks why he should accept those documents as authentic, the teacher will have to refer him to the special science of historiography, which attempts to develop techniques for making accurate judgments about such matters. In any case, the *warrant* for the claim will be based upon an argument concerning some *experienceable* event, thing, or relation; if the child finally accepts the claim as true, it will be on the basis of *a posteriori* evidence.

What happens when our teacher tells the children that $2+2=4$? Again, our more clever child challenges her and demands evidence. "All right," says the teacher, "let's perform an experiment. You take these two apples. Place them next to two more apples. Count them all up. What do you get? Four apples. So 2+2=4." "But wait a minute," says our first grader. "Let's try another experiment. Here I have two eyedroppers. I squeeze out two drops of water from one, then two drops from the other. I let them roll together down the sides of this funnel. What do I get? *One* drop of water! Aha! I've just disproven that 2+2=4!" At this point most people would probably say that the experiment was *not relevant* to the truth or falsity of 2+2=4. The equation *can't* be disproven in that way. But if the child's experiment is not relevant, then the teacher's is not relevant either—or how do we decide on the basis of the formula which experiments are relevant and which not? To say that only those are relevant that result in a count of four would be to argue in a circle!

Fortunately, the teacher need not go into such subtleties. She might say to the child, "We are both wrong. *No* experiment is relevant to the truth or falsity of 2+2=4. I don't have to *give* you evidence to support the claim that 2+2=4. You have the evidence *in you* already! Just reflect on the meanings of '2' and '4' and '+' and '=,' and you will see with the eye of your mind that 2+2=4 is true, *must* be true if we retain the normal meanings of these terms." For the knowledge we have of such *tautalogous* expressions as 2+2=4 or "today is Sunday or it is not Sunday" is *a priori.*

This distinction that is made by logicians between knowledge that is *a posteriori* and knowledge that is *a priori* has played a great role in the history of philosophy and is of central concern today among those people who study the foundations of mathematics and the nature of human knowledge. We will encounter it again in later chapters. Here it is of importance to us for the *first* of the two branches of logic we will consider, the deductive or Aristotelian. For these arguments are said to warrant their conclusions "with necessity"—we can know *a priori* that *if* the premises of such arguments are true, the conclusion *must* be true.

2. DEDUCTIVE LOGIC

A typical *categorical* statement might be "Swans are white." Now Aristotle noted that statements like this one can vary in *quality* and *quantity*. By "quality" he means that the statement can be affirmed or denied; by "quantity," he means that we can speak of all swans or only some (at least one) of them. Thus a total of *four* statements can be generated from this one categorical statement: "All swans are white," "No swans are white (=All swans are not white)," "Some swans are white," "Some swans are not white." What has impressed so many philosophers is that some of these statements *imply* some of the others, and the implication is *a priori*. For example, if "Some swans are white" is true, then "No swans are white" *must* be false. Or, if

"Some swans are not white" is false, then "All swans are white" *must* be true. These relationships are called *immediate*. Thus it seemed to many people that our knowledge could be expanded by *thinking alone*, and that it contained an element of *certainty*. (Note figure on page 100.)

But this was only the beginning of deductive logic. For we do not as yet have an *argument*. Immediate inferences do not have premises and conclusions. But Aristotle noted that categorical statements can have relationships with other categorical statements that are purely *a priori*. For example,

> All white animals are birds
> All swans are white animals   (Premises)
>
> Therefore, all swans are birds   (Conclusion)

An argument of this kind is called a *categorical syllogism*. A *syllogism* is a *deductive* argument having two and only two premises. *A deductive argument asserts that if its premises are true, then its conclusion must be true.* The above argument is *categorical* because it refers to three and only three substances: swans, white animals, and birds. *Aristotelian logic is the critical analysis of categorical syllogisms.* It attempts to bring out the *a priori* nature of such reasoning and to develop a set of rules for deciding whether a given categorical syllogism is *valid*, that is, whether the assertion is true that if the premises are true, then the conclusion must be true. We should note two things about this undertaking.

A. Validity.

In order to be valid, a deductive argument must have premises that necessitate the conclusion. That is, it must not be possible for the premises to be true and the conclusion false. This restriction holds in our example. It could not be the case that swans are white and white animals are birds, and yet that some swans are not birds. This necessity is not due to any fact about birds or white animals or swans; it is *a priori* and founded in the very *structure* of the argument. Given that structure, the conclusion follows necessarily. No experiment, nothing *new* that we might learn about the three substances will limit that necessity.

But now observe an interesting fact: one of the premises is false! It is not true that all white animals are birds; look at rabbits, for example. But the conclusion is true, and our argument is valid! How is that possible? The answer is that our concept of validity refers only to the structure of the argument, not to the specific facts mentioned in the premises and the conclusion. Unless they are tautologies, the premises must be known to be true or false *a posteriori*. In the case of a valid argument, we can say *a priori* only that *if* the premises are true, then the conclusion must be true. However, if we have

FIGURE

Some of the immediate implications of categorical statements are expressed in a diagram known as the *Square of Opposition*. It looks like this:

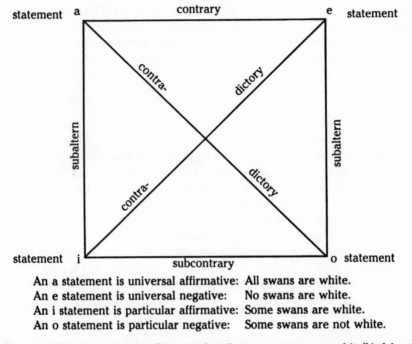

An a statement is universal affirmative: All swans are white.
An e statement is universal negative: No swans are white.
An i statement is particular affirmative: Some swans are white.
An o statement is particular negative: Some swans are not white.

Clearly, if "all swans are white" is true, then "some swans are not white" is false: the truth of a statement implies the falsity of its contradictory. As an exercise, try to work out the rules for each of the four types of immediate implication indicated on the Square. [Note: the truth of a statement may imply the falsity of one of its oppositional statements, but its *falsity* might still not imply the truth of that same oppositional statement.]

These oppositions are not the only examples of immediate implications. Another group of them includes the *converse* of a statement. The converse of "no swans are white" is "no white things are swans." Note that the truth or falsity of one of these statements implies the truth or falsity of the other. Is that true for the converse of "all swans are white"?

good *a posteriori* reason to believe that the premises of a valid argument are true, then we may have just as much confidence in the truth of the conclusion.

Valid deductive arguments, all of whose premises are true, are said to be *sound*. If the premises of a valid argument are tautologies, that is, are also true *a priori*, then we can speak of *proof*. *Geometry* is an example of a set of deductively valid arguments about abstract entities, in which each premise is true *a priori*. It is well known that the great philosopher Spinoza attempted to present his philosophical system in the form of a deductive proof from what he considered to be self-evident principles. He believed that only where such proof is possible can we have absolute confidence in the truth of philosophical doctrines. In modern times, the development of artificial symbolic languages, all of whose statements are deductive consequences of a single set of rules and definitions, has permitted the exact analysis of conceptual relations within a system of arithmetic or a physical theory.

Let us consider another example of the categorical syllogism.

Some women are French
All nuns are women

Therefore, some nuns are French

Here the premises are true, but the argument is invalid, for although the premises are true, the conclusion *might be* false. We can demonstrate this by developing another argument that is structurally parallel with it, and whose premises are also true, but whose conclusion is obviously false:

Some Europeans are German
All Greeks are European

Therefore, some Greeks are German (!)

An invalid argument thus fails to do what arguments are intended to do—namely, give a warrant for the conclusion—even though the conclusion may be true anyway!

B. Deductive Structures.

Although in our above example we refer to swans and birds and white animals, it is easier to see the *a priori* relationship between the premises and the conclusion if we abstract from specific classes of things and use capital letters in their place:

All P are M
All M are S

Therefore, all S are P

S and P are the subject and predicate, respectively, of the conclusion. M, which does not appear in the conclusion, is called the middle term; it provides the link between the subject and the predicate. Since each statement can have one of four forms, and since there are three statements in the argument, and since the three terms can be ordered in four different ways (these are called the four *figures* of the syllogism),

P – M	P – M	M – P	M – P
M – S	S – M	M – S	S – M
S – P	S – P	S – P	S – P

a total of 256 syllogisms are possible, of which 15 are valid. It is interesting to note that six and only six rules are necessary to distinguish valid from invalid syllogisms. In other words, if a syllogism breaks any one of these rules it will be invalid; if it conforms to all of them, it will be valid.

One of these rules is that *at least one* of the premises must be affirmative. For example,

> No Eskimos are icebox repairmen
> No icebox repairmen are under five years of age
>
> Therefore, no people under five years of age are Eskimos

This is obviously invalid! Try to construct a valid syllogism with two negative premises. You will not be able to do it. But can you explain *why* you cannot? Let us carry this question a bit further.

The idea of abstraction is an important one for critically evaluating deductive arguments; for if we can show that a deductive argument has an invalid *structure*, then it follows that the argument is also invalid. In the case of our earlier example,

> Some women are French
> All nuns are women
>
> Therefore, some nuns are French

we have the structure

> Some M are P
> All S are M
> Therefore, some S are P

Two of the rules of valid syllogisms are broken by this structure. Let us consider just one of them, that called *undistributed middle.* This means that neither premise refers to all members of the class of things M. Thus it is possible that we are referring to another part of that class in each premise. If that is the case, then the M class, our middle term, may not provide a link between the classes S and P. In our example, M in premise one refers to only those women that are nuns, and premise two refers only to those women who are French. And thus there *may* be no connection between being a nun and being French—although, of course some nuns are, in fact, French. But if we substitute "Jewish" for "French," we see how implausible is our conclusion on the basis of the information given! And similarly in the case of our syllogism with two negative premises: Since the first premise states that all or some P are excluded from all or some M, and the second premise states that all or some S are excluded from all or some M, no link can be established between S and P themselves. And it is this conceptual linkage that is at the root of deductive reasoning.

3. INDUCTIVE LOGIC

Valid deductive arguments have the virtue of warranting their conclusions with necessity, or *a priori,* as we have seen. However, the truth of the conclusion is no more certain than the truth of the premises. Where the premises are themselves *a priori,* as we have seen, we may speak of formal proof. But what if they are not *a priori?* And what if the premise is not supported by simple sense perception? Is there any way of evaluating arguments in support of *a posteriori* knowledge claims? Yes there is, and the study of the typical forms such arguments may take is called *inductive logic.*

Inductive logic includes many different tasks, all of which are related to this central concern of justifying *a posteriori* claims. We will consider two of these tasks: the study of *inductive generalization,* and the study of the logic of scientific discovery.

A. The Inductive Generalization

We have already observed that simple sense perception is normally accepted by most people as giving acceptable evidence for the truth of such statements as "This swan is white." I need only look in a certain direction to verify that statement. If I suspect that I may be subject to an illusion, I will perform some further tests, of course, but, again, they will normally involve a looking and seeing of some kind. However, *universal* or *general* statements ("All swans are white") have the peculiar property of "going beyond" what I can perceive to be the case. For the universal statement refers to *all* swans, past, present, and future, and I cannot directly examine all of them—especially not the future swans. However, I *can* submit a plausible argument in favor of my universal statement. That argument would take the form of an enumeration:

> Swan A is white
> Swan B is white
> Swan C is white
>
> $\vdots$
>
> Swan N is white
> _____
> Therefore, all swans are white

A better argument would enumerate areas of the world inhabited by swans and explored by zoologists—"All the swans in South America are white, all the swans in Europe are white . . . therefore, all the swans in the world are white." Most people would consider this to be a plausible argument and agree that it had established on reasonably firm ground that nature produces swans in one color only and not, like certain other species (such as the mamba snake or *Homo sapiens*), in several.

Unlike our deductive argument, the inductive argument gives us no *a priori* warrant of the truth of the conclusion. Therefore, an inductive argument can be contrasted with the deductive kind by noting that its conclusion may be false *even if* its premises are true. And, in fact, there are swans in Australia that are not white; they lived there unknown to zoologists, who had long accepted the generalization, "All swans are white." Again, since a valid argument is one whose conclusion must be true if the premises are, *we cannot speak of validity in the case of inductive arguments*. The warrant of an inductive argument is either strong or weak, and its strength will vary with the number of items mentioned in the premises—the more items mentioned, the stronger the warrant of the generalization.

So-called "laws of nature," which are supposedly "discovered" by scientists in their laboratories, are frequently general statements. Galileo's law of falling bodies is a general statement. It asserts that an object in a vacuum falling from rest near the surface of the earth will cover a distance s proportional to its acceleration and the time passed. The precise formulation, $s = \frac{1}{2}at^2$, refers to all bodies under those circumstances, past, present, and future. But Galileo would not have discovered that law if he had just made casual observations of things occurring in the world about him and then enumerated a set of relevant facts. The argument in favor of this law and the steps that led to its discovery are a bit more complex than inductive generalization. Let us examine Galileo's procedure, and then attempt to abstract some elements that are typical of reasoning in science in support of universal *a posteriori* statements.

B. The Logic of Scientific Discovery.

According to his own report, Galileo became interested in what we nowadays call dynamics or kinematics by observing the efforts of the military men of his day to solve the practical problem of placing a cannon in order to achieve a specific trajectory, given a specific powder charge and cannonball size. The proper placement for maximum trajectory, which was determined by trial and error, turned out to be a 45° angle, precisely halfway between the horizontal and the vertical. Now the question of the nature of motion—specifically, the motion of a projectile—had been considered since the time of Aristotle, who believed that motion was of two fundamental kinds: natural, or the motion of a freely falling object, which was seeking its "natural place"; and violent, or that produced by *another* movement—as the powder charge causes the cannonball to fly through space. Since all violent movement requires the continuous exertion of energy by another moving body, Aristotle speculated that projectiles were kept in motion by the force of the air behind them, which whips about from the front to the rear of the object as it moves through space. This clever analysis did not account for the fact that projectiles *slow down* (why should they, if the wind is constantly exerting a force upon them?)—as with the cannonball, which reaches a highest point and then falls to earth. To clarify this issue, medieval thinkers conceived of an energy substance they called *impetus,* which the explosive imparts to the cannonball, and which the cannonball then gives up as it moves through the air. Since both Aristotle and the impetus theorists denied that motion could be mixed—that is, motion in a curve produced by natural and violent forces acting simultaneously on a projectile—they conceived of the motion of the cannonball as traveling along two straight lines.

Such was the state of dynamics when Galileo began to study gunnery. If there is a "natural" and a "violent" component of the cannonball's trajectory, and if the path of the cannonball is the product of two forces acting upon it, one horizontal and the other vertical, then it might be possible to distinguish one of them from the other and assign a numerical value to the former. The search for an adequate solution to this problem took some thirty-eight years of Galileo's life, from the early *Mechanics* to the *Discourse on Two New Sciences,* and required major conceptual changes, that is, changes in *thinking* about the nature of motion, and how motion is best to be *described.* Specifically, the concept of impetus was abandoned, and the theory of inertia and momentum was developed. Galileo hypothesized that if a body acquires a velocity after falling some unit measure of time—let us say one second—then after t seconds its velocity will be the product of the number of seconds fallen and the velocity a it acquired in the first second. That velocity acquired during the first second we will call the object's *acceleration* and designate it by a. Thus, after t seconds, its velocity will be ta. Its average velocity at that time will be $\frac{1}{2}ta$. What distance will it have covered? If a distance s is covered in t seconds at an average velocity v, then $s = tv$. Substituting $(\frac{1}{2}ta)$ (the average velocity) for (v) in $(s = tv)$, we get $s = t(\frac{1}{2}ta) = \frac{1}{2}at^2$! A fine *hypothesis,* deducted *a priori* from the concepts of s, t, and a. But three questions remain: How can we test our hypothesis? What is the value of a near the surface of the earth? How can this formula *answer the question* with which we began, namely, what is the true nature of the trajectory of cannonballs?

The obvious test of the hypothesis would be to measure the "natural" acceleration imparted to the cannonball when it falls from rest, as from the top of a building. Alas, no clock possessed by Galileo was capable of measuring such speeds with any accuracy. but then Galileo came upon the idea of *diluting* natural impetus (what we today call gravity) by allowing a spherical object to roll down an inclined plane. The natural downward force imparted to the object would be the same as in free fall, of course, but it would require more time for the ball to travel from its starting point on the plane to a point on the horizontal at the foot of the plane. Galileo's apparatus had the following pattern:

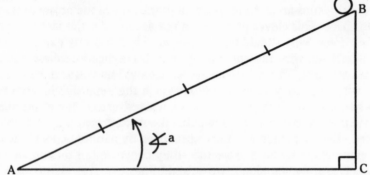

Galileo hypothesized that in traveling from B to A, the speed of the ball would continuously increase, if the force acting upon it is uniform and constant. The points marked on BA indicate a typical pattern of increase of the distances covered during some standard unit of time, such as a second, after the ball is released. Moreover, Galileo hypothesized that the rate of increase of velocity (acceleration) would itself increase as the angle a is increased and would approach the rate of increase imparted by natural impetus in free fall as ∡a approached 90°.

The experiment required the utmost care in preparation. An inclined plane had to be created that was exceedingly smooth, so as to minimize the effects of friction in slowing down the velocity of the ball. The ball itself had to be as round as possible. And, of course, the velocity had to be measured with great care. In order to do that, Galileo invented a rudimentary stopwatch. It consisted of an apparatus that was capable of allowing a constant flow of water from one receptacle to another. When the ball began to roll, the flow of water was begun; when the ball reached some measured point, the flow was stopped. The amount of water left in the receptacle could then be measured, weighed, and compared with some standard amount, or with the results of earlier measurements (would you have thought of such a device if you had been there?). After measuring the correlation between the angle of elevation (∡a) and the rate of acceleration for angles where the water clock was capable of measuring the times with great accuracy, Galileo was able to extrapolate a value of the acceleration a where ∡a=90°, that is, for free fall. On the basis of this procedure, he determined that a=32f/s². He was then able to explain the dynamics of falling bodies and clarify the problems raised by the experiments with ballistics. Specifically, he could deduce from his results that the trajectory of a cannonball would be a parabola, not two straight lines, and the mathematical analysis of that curve demonstrates that the maximum range of a cannon is obtained when it is set at 45°. Thus Galileo *explained* the phenomenon that had first started him thinking about dynamics.

A certain logical pattern underlies Galileo's experiments with inclined planes that is typical of most scientific work. The study of that pattern is, as we noted, one of the tasks of inductive logic.

1. The definition of the problem. Galileo was the kind of man who could see problems where few other people could. His observations of the flight of cannonballs were not casual; Galileo would ask himself questions about what he was observing. These questions were not just empty "why" questions—"Why does the cannonball fly that way, why not another way?" Such questions give the mind nothing to operate upon. Rather the scientist will ask himself whether what he is observing checks out with other facts he thinks he knows about the same or related phenomena. If it does not, why not? How are the two phenomena different? How similar? What other factors might be at play here to cause the discrepancy? You will note that such questioning always takes place upon the background of what was known at the time. Thus the impetus theory (and Aristotle's speculations, too, which Galileo generally rejected) formed the context in which Galileo first thought his problem through and made his advances in understanding motion—even though he was later to reject the impetus theory and introduce a new model of mechanical forces.

2. Hypothesis formation. It is well known that Galileo's first *correct* formulation of the law of motion followed from an *incorrect* conception of the nature of motion that Galileo had adopted while still a young man. By the time he came to test his hypothesis, some thirty years later, he was clear about his axioms and had correctly understood the nature of motion and acceleration, which had eluded even Descartes. How did he do this? How did he start from an incorrect appraisal of the forces involved in the trajectory problem and finally achieve clarity? How did he arrive at the incorrect conception and then go from there to the correct formulation of the law? Alas, he does not tell us. Quite probably, he could not himself have told us. For the making of hypotheses is a somewhat mysterious process. Many modern psychologists have studied and pondered the phenomenon of "creativity" or "genius" that lets one person see a possible solution to a problem where others see none. But one thing is clear: no purely mechanical solution to Galileo's problem is possible. He could not have put all the elements of the puzzle into some logical order and then derived or deduced the solution by applying some abstract pattern, for we cannot figure out what a "logical order" or relevant abstract pattern *is* until we have an inkling of a solution to the problem. Galileo had to see that the quantity a can be measured, and that it is a function of velocity and time. Once he had *seen* that, the formula "$s = \frac{1}{2}at^2$" follows *a priori*, that is, it can be deduced from the new conception of the interrelation of velocity, acceleration, distance, and time.

Of course, not all hypotheses depend upon a reformulation of concepts. Some require us to look at some set of facts in a new way. For example, Torricelli, a pupil of Galileo, was perplexed by the fact that water cannot be pumped from a well that is deeper than thirty-three feet below the surface of the earth. Galileo had hypothesized that a column of water longer than thirty-three feet would break up under its own weight, but this could not be shown. Torricelli then hypothesized that we are living under a "sea of air" that weighs down upon us from above with as much weight as would a column of water thirty-three feet long. At that depth, then, the two bodies, air and water, would be equal in weight, and the absence of air caused by the vacuum pump could no longer drive the water up the pipe! Here nothing is *deduced;* rather, Torricelli has seen a similarity between a body of water and a body of air and hypothesized that, like water, air too must exert a downward pressure.

Consider the following problem:

```
        •         •         •



        •         •         •



        •         •         •
```

Given this diagram, connect the dots by using four and only four connected straight lines. A *mechanical* attempt at solving this problem would draw the first line in one of the three possible directions beginning with the point on the upper left, then continue in one of the two possible remaining directions, and so on until the fourth line was complete. Since the attempt would meet with failure, we begin again with the same point in a different direction ... and so on, until we have exhausted all possibilities—which would take quite awhile. At that point, since we would still not have solved the problem, we would probably assume that no solution is possible! Our first try might look like this:

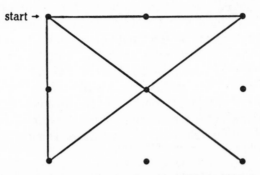

What is needed here is an *inductive leap,* a sailing of the imagination beyond the boundaries that the shape of the puzzle appears to impose upon us— but *not* so far as to break the rules stipulated by the problem! That inductive leap was taken by Galileo in his reformulation of the concept of acceleration and the resulting hypothesis. And it is taken by the person who sees that the lines need not be limited by the area enclosed by the dots, and who solves the problem this way:

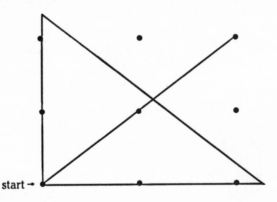

3. Deriving a test implication and conducting a test. A clever hypothesis must be put to an observable or *a posteriori* test. This is the principle that distinguishes the speculations of metaphysicians—which tend to be purely *a priori* and deductive—from that underlying the critical intelligence of scientists. In Galileo's case, he tested his hypothesis by using the inclined planes we mentioned before, and which he describes in great detail in his *Discourses.* The logic here is deductive in form. The first premise asserts that *if* a given hypothesis is true, then *if* I perform a given test, then a certain outcome will be obtained. Thus if the hypothesis $s = \frac{1}{2}at^2$ is true, then if I roll a ball down the apparatus, it will cover a certain distance s that will be a function of the angle of inclination and the time elapsed. It is easy to see that a large number of experiments could be performed upon Galileo's apparatus, each of which would be relevant to establishing the hypothesis. He could vary the angle of inclination, vary the size, weight, or density of the balls, or vary the position of the plane, or the length of its track. These are called the *independent variables,* for they are manipulated by the experimenter to see what the outcome, or the change in the *dependent variables,* will be. In this case, the dependent variable may be the rate of acceleration or the time it takes to pass between two points marked on the inclined plane.

The second premise states the outcome of the experiment. And the conclusion asserts the truth or falsity of the hypothesis. The logical pattern is as follows:

> If the hypothesis is true, then the test will have
> outcome A
> Outcome A is obtained
> _____
> Therefore, the hypothesis is true.

This argument form is an example of a *hypothetical syllogism*—a variant of the categorical syllogism we studied earlier. By using our method of analogy, it is easy to see that it is *invalid,* for the following argument has the same form:

> If a person is a nun, that person is a woman
> This person is a woman
> _____
> Therefore, this person is a nun

What a strange state of affairs! The test works out, but the argument is invalid! But remember that the fact that an argument is invalid does not mean that the conclusion is false, but only that it is not adequately supported by the premises. For this reason, again we say that *a posteriori* knowledge, such as the claim $s = \frac{1}{2}at^2$, is never known *with certainty,* but only inductively— that is, it is possible for a test that is implied by a hypothesis to come out as predicted, and yet for the hypothesis to be false. And this idea checks with our earlier observation that universal *a posteriori* claims always imply more than can be observed. After all, Galileo's theorem *need not* hold in places where it has not been tested—other worlds, other dimensions beyond our present horizons, even our own future—or do you think otherwise, do you think this law *must* hold always and everywhere, as $2+2=4$ holds always and everywhere? The logic of scientific discovery does not guarantee it, even if your own intuition does!

Still, the outcome of a prediction made on the basis of a relevant hypothesis is powerful evidence in favor of the hypothesis. And, of course, the experimenter does not have to confine himself to one test, or even to one kind of test. Many hypotheses have more than one test implication. For example, we spoke earlier of Torricelli's hypothesis of a sea of air. This hypothesis has the obvious test implication that air will support a column of water thirty-three feet high. Thus, Torricelli might have constructed a water pipe thirty-five feet long, sealed it at one end, placed it open end down in a pan of water, and then observed whether the level of water in the pipe fell to thirty-three feet. But the hypothesis also suggests that if such an apparatus only three feet long were filled with mercury, which is fourteen times heavier than water, the level of mercury would fall to twenty-eight inches. This idea led to the development of the mercury barometer. Moreover, the hypothesis implies that if such an apparatus was taken up the side of a mountain, the level of water or mercury would *decrease*, for the column of air that is counterbalancing it will be growing shorter. Similarly, the hypothesis implies that a balloon will expand as its altitude increases, that breathing is more difficult at the top of the mountain, and the like.

It is clear that the more new test implications derived from a given hypothesis check out as predicted, the stronger are our reasons for believing that the hypothesis is true. The reasoning here is still inductive, however, for it is always possible for any number of tests to work and for the hypothesis to be false. On the other hand, if the implications of the hypothesis do *not* work out as predicted, we may conclude *a priori* that our hypothesis is *false* as stated. Our argument in this case will be deductively valid:

> If the hypothesis is true, then the test will have outcome A
> The test does not have outcome A
> _____
> Therefore, the hypothesis is false.

This famous argument pattern is called *modus tollens*. A familiar example of it would be the following:

> If a person is Swiss, then he is European
> This person is not European
> _____
> Therefore, he cannot be Swiss.

Thus, we always have better evidence that a hypothesis is false than that it is true!

4. Applications. The immediate application of Galileo's hypothesis was to the phenomena of ballistics, which first inspired his researches. His theorem, now tested by repeated experiments and found to be probably true, could be used to explain the trajectory of cannonballs. Explanations, like the inductive reasoning whereby hypotheses are put to the test, have a simple pattern that logicians are able to analyze. In our example, the pattern would be as follows:

a. fact to be explained: The maximum trajectory of a cannonball occurs when the cannon is placed at 45°.

b. explanation

premise one: (law) If a body is subject to free fall and to a horizontal acceleration, then its trajectory will be a parabola whose greatest extent will be when the arc cuts the line parallel to the horizon at 45°. (To obtain this law, we apply the theorem $s = \frac{1}{2}at^2$ to the mathematical analysis of the resulting curve. The length of the trajectory will vary with the initial horizontal acceleration imparted by the powder charge.)

premise two: (fact) A cannonball is subject to free fall and to a horizontal acceleration.

Therefore, its trajectory will be a parabola whose greatest extent will be when the arc cuts the line parallel to the horizon at 45°.

This argument has the following logical structure:

If A is true, then B is true (statement of law)
A is in fact true   (statement of fact)

Therefore, B is true   (the fact to be explained)

This valid deductive pattern is called *modus ponens.* Here is a simple example whose validity is apparent:

If blue litmus paper is put in an acid, then
    it will turn red
This piece of blue litmus paper was put in acid

Therefore, this piece of blue litmus paper turned red.

The premises furnish an explanation demanded by the question, "How come this piece of paper turned red?" The argument is deductively valid, but remember that it may not be sound—that depends upon whether we've got our facts straight, and whether our law is in fact true—and the latter rests, of course, upon an inductive argument!

4. CONCLUSIONS

Since the time of Aristotle, logic has been considered a branch of philosophy. And professional philosophers today are making contributions to both the theory and the practice of logic. As we noted earlier, logicians have developed highly complex logical languages that can be used to understand the conceptual relationships in mathematical systems and in physical theories. And inductive logicians are concerned with the theory of probability, and with the logic of scientific discovery, as we have sketched it here. The latter study forms a part of the philosophy of science, which, however, is also concerned with questions about the nature and limits of scientific knowledge, with the interaction between science and society, and with the role of science in the realization of human values.

In philosophy itself, logic plays a somewhat different role. A philosophical theory is not a rigid mathematical structure nor a testable conceptual scheme, such as a theory in physics. In philosophy today, as in Aristotle's time, the logician reminds us that truth is only assured when we sift through arguments, our own and those of others; when we measure our evidence carefully and disclose the logical patterns we may be relying on; when we distinguish between kinds of statements, and separate statements of fact from statements of value; and when we ask always, What is the warrant for this belief? In the separate sections of this book we will subject to logical analysis many of the typical theories and speculations that have been developed by philosophers down through the ages. As you read further in philosophy, you will encounter persons who speculate about everything above the earth, upon it, or below it. Behind them stands the logician—or, if he is not there, we must place him there—acting as a sort of pedantic, overly fussy censor. He will never let us forget that beliefs must be founded in reasons, and that the connections between reasons and beliefs, premises and conclusions are complex, hard to identify, and often subject to error. But if we listen to him, he will help us develop that open-minded, optimistic, and cheerful skepticism that is a part of the Western tradition in philosophy at its best.

QUESTIONS FOR STUDY

1. Identify the Aristotelian categories demonstrated in the following statements:

    > The books are on the table.
    > He arrived at 2:15 P.M.
    > They ascended the staircase.
    > Two men were drinking whiskey.
    > The Bible was translated by Saint Jerome.
    > The naval battle will take place tomorrow.

2. Identify the following statements as *a priori* or *a posteriori*. If you find questionable cases, try to locate the ambiguity.

All violins have four strings.
All children have parents.
Gold is valuable.
The coffee is in the coffee can.
All books have pages.

3. Analyze the following syllogisms by identifying the patterns they represent, and then invent an analogous argument that is clearly valid or invalid.

All nurses are medical professionals
Some nurses are men
_____

Therefore, some men are medical professionals.

Some cheeses are made in France
No things made in France are inexpensive
_____

Therefore, some inexpensive things are not cheeses.

4. Imagine that you have been given a grant to investigate the influence of the full moon on violent behavior. Describe:

a. how you would define the problem (Hints: you must define violence in a way that is testable; you must state whether the moon must be both full and visible [no cloud cover?]);
b. what hypotheses would you develop;
c. what research would you conduct;
d. what results would have to be obtained before you assert that the full moon has an influence on violent behavior;
e. if the outcome is favorable, what applications might your knowledge of the moon's influence on violent behavior have?

5. Assume that you are asked to explain to a child why we see a rainbow at certain times. Distinguish general statements from specific facts in your explanation, and show how your explanation has the form of a deductive argument in *modus ponens*.

6. Do immediate implications involve tautologies? For example, is the statement "if all swans are white, then it is false that some swans are not white" a tautology? Show how its truth depends or does not depend upon the meanings of the component terms.

7

Ethics: The Search for the Good Life

Our last chapter has given us a good idea of philosophy's attempt to determine and clarify those rules and procedures that constitute sound and valid reasoning. Logic, with which that chapter dealt, represents the basis of all philosophical thinking, as it is in logic that we learn the art of judging which reasons are acceptable in order to give a firm foundation for our beliefs and ideas. Our concern in the present chapter will be an important area of human experience in which we are also compelled to adduce reasons for our contentions and assertions, and this area is ethics. Philosophers have been concerned with the general structure of the world at large and with the meaning of reality as this manifests itself to the human consciousness. But their preoccupations have extended themselves to those aspects of existence that specifically affect the human being, particularly those aspects that render human life meaningful, attractive, and worth living. Thus, besides seeking to describe existence in general and make sense of things as they are in fact, philosophers have sought to make relevant statements concerning the way things *ought* to be, especially when they are immediately related to human existence. Hence, there are statements that we call *de facto*, in which the characteristics of reality are described, and statements we call *de jure*, in which we enunciate the way things ought to be. The former statements belong either to speculative philosophy or to science, while the latter constitute the province of ethical discourse. In our chapter on the Milesian

115

Rationalists (chapter 2), we found abundant examples of *de facto* statements about the universe, such as Thales' statement that all things *are* made of water, and in our chapter on Socrates (chapter 3), we came across clearly *de jure* pronouncements, like the Socratic idea that one *ought* to choose suffering evil rather than doing evil. The emphasis in Socratic philosophy was assuredly on ethical matters, whereas that of his predecessors was on speculative or scientific domains.

Ever since the time of Socrates, ethics has occupied a prominent place in practically every major school or system of Western philosophy. The endeavor to advance and justify ethical values can be found, not only among Greek and Roman philosophers like Plato, Aristotle, Epicurus, Epictetus, and Marcus Aurelius, but also among medieval thinkers like Saint Augustine and Saint Thomas Aquinas, as well as among modern philosophers like Spinoza, Hume, Kant, Schopenhauer, Hegel, and Nietzsche. Utilitarianism, pragmatism, and existentialism, moreover, can be regarded as attempts on the part of recent philosophy to deal effectively with strictly ethical issues. And there is nothing surprising in all this, for, after all, what advantage could there be in understanding the world around us and in gaining valuable insights into the meaning of reality, if our own personal and public lives are in a lamentable state of moral disarray? What profit could there be in establishing grand cosmological theories, if we ourselves are unable to live a meaningful life? It is undoubtedly meritorious to know about the world and decipher the secrets of nature; but such accomplishments, which speculative philosophy and science promise to give us, are ultimately pointless if we lack the necessary presence of mind to know what constitutes genuine ethical values and to actualize those values in our own personal existence. And it is precisely in and through the study of ethics that we can hope to develop such essential knowledge in order to become good ourselves. For, let us emphatically point out, the study of ethics can have but one real goal, and that is the actualization of ethical values in our own lives. This idea was clearly stated in Aristotle's *Nicomachean Ethics* when he observed that the study of ethics

> is not, like other studies, purely speculative in its intention; for the object of our enquiry is not to know the nature of virtue but to become ourselves virtuous, as that is the sole benefit which it conveys.

The English word 'ethics' comes from an ancient Greek term *(ethos)*, which originally meant 'accustomed place' or 'abode', as when we speak of an animal's lair. In later times, certainly by the time of Homer, *ethos* came to be applied more specifically to the human context in the sense of 'custom' or 'habit'. For instance, the barbarians' custom of growing a beard was their distinctive *ethos*, as was the Spartan custom of killing deformed children. The Latin word *mos* seems to be an adequate translation of the Greek *ethos*, since the former may have also meant at some time 'accustomed place', as is clear from the Spanish derivative *morada,* which means 'dwelling'. The old meaning of *mos* underwent the same transformation as *ethos,* and eventually it came to mean 'custom' or 'habit'. Accordingly, the English words 'ethical' and 'moral' are etymologically equivalent, and from this point of view, the study of ethics and the study of morality are one and the same.

By the time of Plato, however, *ethos* had undergone yet another transformation, and from the designation of *any* human custom it passed on to designate certain distinct types of human conduct that in some sense could be regarded as more preferable than others. The *ethos* of the *good* man became the *ethos par excellence* that every rational being ought to emulate. Consequently, ethics developed into the philosophical discipline that studies the good, as this is clearly exemplified in Aristotle's use of the word 'ethical'. Among the Romans, moreover, an identical transformation took place, although at a much later time. Cicero (106–43 B.C.) is credited with coining the word *moralis* (moral) in order to create an equivalent Latin term for the Greek word for 'ethical'. Thus, among the later Romans, moral philosophy stood for the study of ethical values, and today, since our own Western languages are largely the offspring of the languages of Plato and Cicero, moral philosophy or ethics is defined as the branch of philosophy in which we undertake the study and analysis of issues specifically related to human values. In it, we raise questions such as, what is the meaning of human existence? what do we mean by concepts like 'good', 'evil', 'bad', 'right', 'wrong', 'happiness', 'duty', 'responsibility', and other ethically relevant concepts? is there an ideal human life, and if so, how can that life be actualized? on what are moral judgments based? are there absolute ethical values, or are all values relative to certain cultural circumstances? and so on.

The urgency and complexity of these and similar questions are surely undeniable. Each one of us has confronted ethical perplexities, sometimes dilemmas of perfectly innocuous consequences, and sometimes choices that entail tremendous ethical implications. All of us have been beset at least once by what is called in religious language "temptations" towards untruthfulness, infidelity, disregard for others, lack of integrity, and simply bad actions, and all of us have been compelled to make decisions of a clearly ethical texture. For the very essence of human existence implies the constant taking of moral (or immoral) stands, not only with respect to ourselves, but with respect to others. It is for this reason that we are constantly in the habit of praising, blaming, and criticizing. The complexity of moral issues is likewise easy to understand. Ordinary human beings, regardless of their cultural milieu, are much more inclined to stand in agreement about the way things are in the world, which explains why *de facto* matters can be generally brought to a satisfactory resolution, than about the way things ought to be, which accounts for the virtual impossibility of establishing a firm and abiding basis of agreement with respect to *de jure* or ethical questions. In what concerns science and speculative philosophy, the ordinary person is happy to admit the expertise of people like scientists or philosophers; but in the case of ethical disputes, it seems that everyone, even the half-wit, is an incontrovertible expert, for nobody is generally inclined to let others decide on what ought or ought not to be done. This latter circumstance has become more severe in those societies in which egalitarianism has succeeded in permeating all social relations. But aside from this, the very history of ethical thought exhibits the enormous complexity of moral issues, as among philosophers there has never been a common basis of agreement concerning human values. There is no ethical stance, no matter how bizarre or absurd, that has not been defended at least once by some prominent thinker, and the ethical systems or schools that have grown out of Western philosophy are not only most diverse in their content, but are often mutually exclusive.

All this may become understandable if we keep in mind the fact that the very subject of ethics, man himself, is the most complex of all possible subjects. The factors that determine and contribute to human existence are mysterious and complex, especially if the human being, as some believe, is truly able to make absolutely free choices. For in this case, the exactitude and precision that characterize some of the natural sciences must be precluded from ethical investigations, as Aristotle himself observed in his *Nicomachean Ethics*. But all these circumstances, instead of discouraging us from the systematic study of ethics, should act as a powerful incentive to seek some kind of clarity in a philosophical field in which urgency and complexity merge into a challenging undertaking.

As we pointed out in chapter 1, it is possible to distinguish three reasonably distinct aspects in ethics, namely, *descriptive ethics, normative ethics,* and *metaethics.* In descriptive ethics, the emphasis lies on the actual description, classification, and explanation of ethical values. Here, our concern is to find out what ideas human communities, past and present, have come to regard as ethically commendable. We are therefore interested in their customs and habits inasmuch as these are related to moral valuations. Often, we find that these customs and habits are those that affect the survival of the society and/or the individual, including those that prescribe rules of behavior concerning punishment, killing, sexual practices, contracts, and the like. Extraordinary examples of descriptive ethics can be found among the ancients, although they generally lack the systematic approach that today characterizes anthropological and sociological work. Herodotus, for instance, gave us a vivid account of the moral practices of the peoples who inhabited the coasts of northern Africa, from Egypt to Gibraltar, and from his lucid account one can readily come to the conclusion that human beings have taken, in different places and at different times, practically every conceivable kind of ethical stand. This fact is even more manifest today, as to our historical knowledge we can add the invaluable work done by contemporary anthropologists like Edward A. Westermarck (1862–1939) who in his studies of primitive marriage and in works like *The Origins and Development of the Moral Ideas* (1906–08) has given us a veritable wealth of information about the diversity of ethical and moral ideas and practices to which human beings are and have been attached.

The first thing that descriptive ethics teaches us is that other people and other cultures have defined the good in ways that are vastly different from ours. Our parochial ethnocentricity may easily convince us that our ways of determining moral values are universal, and that what we call good and bad are universal designations. But a glance at descriptive ethics will soon correct our myopic limitations. Both in Sparta and Rome, deformed children were killed by the father, who would have been surprised to hear that his action was immoral. Among certain Eskimo tribes, if the first child happened to be a girl, she had to be killed by the father, who again looked upon his action as quite commendable. In India, especially before the English arrived, it was the morally recognizable duty of the widow to burn herself alive next to the body of the husband. Among the Jews, the adulteress had to be stoned to death, while the adulterer had little to fear: the former was morally disgraced, while the latter, being a man, was merely doing his thing. The Nazis did not find anything ethically wrong as they proceeded to exterminate allegedly inferior peoples like Jews, gypsies, and the like, and the southern slave owner had no moral scruples about molesting and raping his slave women. In certain Asian cultures, girls must be circumcised in order to insure that they will never experience sexual pleasure, because sexual pleasure is a morally unacceptable experience for women. In ancient Sparta, every year the state would declare war against all slaves in order to allow any citizen to do away with any unruly slave. Virginity and chastity have been held to be worthy moral states in some cultures, whereas in others they are looked upon as disgraceful conditions. Today we are conscious of the moral implications of capital punishment, but we cannot overlook the fact that until quite recently, perhaps the middle of the nineteenth century, such moral implications were not recognized: even Plato himself believed that the State had the right to do away with troublesome citizens.

We could go on in this way, giving interesting examples of ethical diversity, but this is not really necessary. Most people today are quite aware of it, either because they have travelled to distant lands or because they have read something about other cultures past or present. What is important, however, is to raise at this point a fundamental question: In view of so bewildering a variety of ethical norms and standards, are we justified in saying that moral values are *merely* the conceptual manifestations of cultural customs and habits, and that, accordingly, all values are relative to the society from which they naturally spring? If our answer to this question is affirmative, we will be adopting a view known in ethics as *relativism*, which maintains that moral affirmations are meaningful only within the cultural and/or historical milieu that has brought them into being. Is it ethically good to kill a deformed child? Yes, but only if we are living in a society like that of ancient

Sparta. Should an adulteress be stoned to death? Yes, but only in a context similar to that of the biblical Jews. Is homosexuality morally wrong? Yes, if your upbringing and culture are Victorian or Catholic. Were the Germans justified in seeking the extermination of the Jews? Yes, as far as the Germans were concerned. Are there not, therefore, universal human values that apply to all rational beings, whether in ancient Sparta, in old Jerusalem, in New York, or in Munich? No, if, as relativism asserts, all moral values are relative to cultural and historical conditions. But what about allegedly universal precepts such as "Thou shalt not kill"? Even these precepts are relative to varying circumstances. The God who gave the Jews such a commandment as "Thou shalt not kill" did not neglect to institute countless exceptions: "Thou shalt kill the blasphemer, the adulteress, the Philistine, the atheist, and the murderer." "Thou shalt not kill" is therefore an empty moral precept unless one places it within some cultural setting. In such a setting, then, the precept emerges as the living manifestation of certain societal preferences that are themselves the expression of some vital need for survival and growth.

If we carry relativism one step further, moreover, we suddenly find ourselves in the presence of *ethical emotivism,* an allegedly metaethical view that maintains that all moral or ethical statements, such as "Killing deformed children is evil," are nothing but the expression of emotional responses to situations. As we will see later on, the emotivists, among whom we can find a place for Westermarck, insist that moral statements should be translated into psychological statements of the kind "I do not like the killing of deformed children." Let us notice, however, that the emotivist is not unwilling to allow the individual human being to be the ultimate judge of moral questions and issues. Ethical emotivism is therefore a type of *subjective relativism* by which we are led to believe that all moral values are the result of the psychological preferences of the individual. Hence, nothing is good or bad, right or wrong aside from my preferences and feelings, something that may remind us in some way of the speech made by Thrasymachus that we quoted in chapter 3. But as far as we can judge, the step that separates subjective relativism in ethics from what is known as *nihilism* is quite small. The nihilist, like the Marquis de Sade (1740–1814), believes that all moral values are equally good and equally bad, which in the end means that nothing is good and nothing is bad: there is a virtual absence of all morality. In our subsequent discussion of metaethics, we will return to these and similar topics.

As we have seen, in descriptive ethics we merely seek to describe values. But what about those values themselves? It is the province of *normative ethics* to announce, create, and defend moral values: normative ethics gives ethical *norms.* In general, most normative systems assume that moral values are not altogether relative to changing cultural and historical circumstances, and that there are certain universal moral claims that are applicable to most human situations. When this applicability is absolute, that is, when moral values are believed to be thoroughly independent of conditions and circumstances, then the normative ethics in question is said to be an example of *ethical absolutism*. From this point of view, it is maintained that, the varying customs and habits of human communities notwithstanding, there are universal ethical norms. In this case, the precept "Thou shalt not kill a human being" is a norm that applies to all human beings under all circumstances. The deformed child, the adulteress, the blasphemer, the criminal, the member of allegedly inferior races, and even the enemy in war—all without exception are held to possess the right to life, and the violation or abrogation of this right constitutes moral depravity. Absolute ethical norms, therefore, do not depend upon the idiosyncrasies of cultures or the dicta of moralists or legislators; they are not made by people but are found in the very nature of things.

Systems of normative ethics are often associated with religious and philosophical ideologies. Thus, the Ten Commandments and the teachings of the Gospels, as well as the canonical laws of Judaism and Christianity, are excellent examples of normative ethics. The same can be said about the ethical ideas put forward by Socrates, Plato, and Aristotle, no less than the ethical teachings of Spinoza, Kant, Hegel, Schopenhauer, and Nietzsche. The Kantian categorical imperatives, which enjoin us to act as if our actions were to become universal natural laws and to treat all human beings (including ourselves) as ends in themselves, are clearly normative in content and in intent. Nietzsche's call for the advent of the Superman, in whom the highest ethical ideals are realized, is also normative. For in all these instances, we are told that certain types of human conduct are morally better than others, and we are presented with ethical ideals towards which we are urged to strive. From this perspective, then, the great philosophers have assumed the role of moralists, and *in this respect* they have emulated the seers and holy men of religion. As moralists, they have attempted to show us the path that leads to moral excellence, even though in their carefully worked out endeavors they have exhibited the same bewildering diversity that the descriptive ethicist finds among human customs and habits.

And yet, the philosopher as a moralist differs substantially from those who expound values in the name of religion. The latter speak on behalf of a God whose will ordinary people cannot fathom, and whose holy word must be accepted without any further question. Religious ethics is therefore a matter of blind faith, something like a personal commitment one makes to accept a precept that religious traditions have sanctioned. To question the ground or basis of such precepts turns out to be a dangerous business, as it may result in excommunication and the stake in this world, and eternal damnation in the other. As some theologian observed, God "prepared Gehenna [Hell] for those who have the hardihood to inquire into such high matters," among which we may include ethical matters. But the philosopher, at least ideally speaking, remains largely unmoved by such threats. Following the example of Socrates, he reasons that if God or the gods are real, as religious people say, and if an eternal life awaits him after death, only a blessed existence can be in store for him who, while in this life, uses his mind to search into the basis and meaning of all matters, including those of ethical import. Thus, the ethical philosopher, while in the practice of advancing moral norms, does not neglect the business of adducing rational grounds for the acceptability of those norms. He replaces the blind faith of the religious man with the critical analysis of philosophical thinking and argues logically for the validity of his ethical views. He inquires candidly into the ground of moral values and is not afraid to ask why some values are more preferable than others. Consequently, every school of philosophy in which normative ethics plays a part is accompanied by a great deal of reasoning about ethics and about the meaning and import of ethical utterances, something that constitutes what today goes by the name of *metaethics*.

All this can be better understood if we linger for a moment on the structure of language in general and ethical discourse in particular. We began this chapter by introducing a distinction between *de facto* statements and *de jure* statements. The former describe matters of fact or the actual ways in which things exist, whereas the latter, let us recall, indicate how things ought to be. In the former, the ordinary syntactical structure is this: S is P, where S is the grammatical subject and P is the predicate, both being linked to each other by the verb 'to be'. In factual statements, known sometimes as "synthetic judgments," the simple analysis of the subject does not reveal anything about the predicate. In them, sense experience must provide the basis on which the linking of the subject and some particular predicate is possible. Let us take, for instance, the proposition "the sun is a yellow star." Here, "the sun" is the subject, and "a yellow star" is the predicate. The proposition itself represents the synthesis of two distinct concepts, concepts that are not necessarily or logically related, as can be seen from the fact that the sun could have been a red star or a blue star, had its cosmological origins been different. Again, we anticipate that in the future, the sun will no longer be a yellow star: it will change itself into a red mass of gas. But for the present, we are entitled to say that the sun is a yellow star, and in so saying we establish a relationship between "the sun" and "a yellow star." But on what basis are we allowed to establish such a relationship, except on the basis of empirical experience? Our eyes reveal something about the sun, and our photographic tools render the testimony of our eyes reasonably stable. Sense experience is, therefore, the ground that allows us to make *de facto* statements about the world around us. When our statements correspond to the way things are as they reveal themselves to our senses, we are entitled to assume that our statements are *true*. In any other case, our statements would be false, as when we say, in defiance of sense perception, "the sun is a blue star."

But in the instance of *de jure* statements, the situation is quite otherwise. In the first place, let us observe that in ordinary language it is possible to translate every *de jure* statement into a syntactical structure that resembles that of *de facto* language. Thus, the statement "One ought to love one's enemies" can be transformed into "Loving one's enemies is *good*" or "Loving one's enemies is *right*." In the latter statements we find, as before, the "S is P" format, and a subject (Loving one's enemies) is linked to a predicate (good or right). There is no great difficulty in understanding the meaning of the subject of this statement, as "Loving one's enemies" can be translated into a series of observable modes of behavior such as helping one's enemies in case of need, saying kind things about them, sharing one's possessions with them, and even exposing ourselves to danger on their behalf. Likewise, "hating one's enemies" can be rendered as killing them, hurting them, lying about them, maneuvering against them when their job is at stake, stealing from them, opposing their projects, injuring their families, etc. Any one of these modes of behavior is meant when we say "Hating one's enemies is evil or wrong." But in this statement, as well as in the previous, the problem centers around the meaning of ethical or moral terms such as 'good', 'bad', 'evil', 'right', 'wrong', and the like. It is the predicate of ethical utterances that presents serious difficulties, as its meaning is not quite clear. And as long as this meaning remains elusive, the basis on which we are entitled to link any subject whatsoever with a moral or ethical term cannot be fully understood. There is clearly no point in saying that the statement "Loving one's enemies is good" is better than the opposite statement, for this would clarify absolutely nothing; it would be like saying that it is good to be good and bad to be bad.

Philosophers have argued in all sorts of ways about the possible meanings of terms such as 'good', and their endeavors in this respect have given rise to systems of normative ethics and metaethical points of view that are often quite at variance with one another. On a deeper level of analysis, however, practically all their efforts converge on one single issue, and that is, on what ground or basis are we entitled to link a term such as 'good' with any particular thing or state of affairs? From the perspective offered by this question, then, the number of possible answers is truly staggering. If we say that there is in fact an objective and somehow recognizable ground or basis for making ethical statements (a ground or basis that transcends the limits of the individual who makes such statements), our ethical stance is known as *objectivism*. Ethical statements, we would claim, are objectively grounded or based on some reality that lies beyond the idiosyncratic preferences of the individual person, just as empirical statements are true or false by reference to something that is generally independent of a person's sensibility. The question in ethics is, however, what such a ground or basis is, as it is only by virtue of this that the meaning of ethical terms can be grasped.

One possible approach to the question is to say that the basis of morality is to be found in the will and revelation of God or the gods, in which case we would be justified in referring to our ethics as an example of *religious or theological ethics*. The link that connects the idea of loving our enemies with the concept of good is furnished in this instance by the alleged fact that this is what God commands. The justification of calling an adulteress 'an evil woman' rests on God's revelation as this is embodied in biblical writings. 'Good' and 'evil' are, therefore, terms that gain their meaning according to something that does not depend on any individual's preferences. When Moses ordered the killing of the Midianites' women who were not virgins, and the virtual rape of those who were (Num. 31:15–20), such an apparently dreadful injunction was perceived as a 'good' command by his people because, as they believed, Moses was acting as the mouthpiece of God. Likewise, the old Abraham had no moral scruples in preparing his own son's assassination (Gen. 22:1–11), precisely because it was God who had issued the order. It was not otherwise with the pious Euthyphro who, as Plato reports, sought to justify his indicting his own father on religious grounds:

> But I believe, Socrates, that all the gods would agree as to the propriety of punishing a murderer: there would be no difference of opinion about that.

When in his *The Morals of the Catholic Church* Saint Augustine reminds us that to be good means to pursue a life of holiness, in which the affairs of the body must be neglected, he is following, in spite of his philosophical sophistication, the same line of reasoning that once characterized Euthyphro and that is peculiar to all those whose lives are ruled by religious notions and beliefs. For the ultimate justification of the Augustinian precept is that it agrees with God's will as this is manifested either in the Scriptures or in the dictates of the Church.

And yet, even when a system of ethics based on religion is not entirely the result of blind faith or emotional commitment (in which case it would lie outside the province of philosophy), there are insurmountable difficulties that are not easy to ignore. First, what shall we say about those who, for whatever reasons, do not believe in God or gods? Shall we say that they lack thereby a basis for moral convictions, and that they are evil people? Shall we call them fools and renegades? But, obviously, this seems inappropriate: atheists are also able to develop complex systems of ethical values whose basis is removed from religious or theological considerations, and it is not difficult to find among non-believers veritable cases of human excellence that equal and on occasion even surpass the best that religion can offer. Secondly, as Socrates forcibly argued in his conversation with Euthyphro, the stories and legends about the gods are many and varied, and the sources of religious faith are often in contradiction with one another. What God or the gods have commanded human beings to do has pointed in mutually exclusive directions. Among all the religious traditions of mankind, amid the thousands of religions that have grown out of a human context, and even in one and the same religious cult, which moral norms are we to accept? The Greek gods, those Olympian examples of human worthiness, occasionally behaved in shameful ways, and their commands were not always ethical, even from their own standards. The God of the Jews, who had given Moses the universal command "Thou shalt not kill," did not hesitate to order the massacre of the Midianites' women and had Abraham attempt the murder of his son. We can well imagine that if Socrates had been in Abraham's place, he could have replied thus to the voice of his God: "Lord, I will not kill my child, not only because you once said to Moses 'Thou shalt not kill,' but also because I do not believe that a human life can be taken in order to satisfy the whim of anybody including God Himself. What you want me to do is something evil, and as such, I cannot do it, even if by my irreligious refusal I earn for myself the eternal fire of Hell."

In so speaking, Socrates would have given rise to other questions, similar to those asked by him in the *Euthyphro:* Is what the gods will *good* because they will it so, or do they will what they will because it is *good* in itself? In either case, there are serious perplexities. In the former, what is good becomes a matter of arbitrary decision on the part of God or gods, something that would be generally acceptable if God, as known by all human beings, were one and immutable, and if His commands were altogether consistent. But the facts are otherwise: human beings have known and pledged their faith to a multiplicity of whimsical gods. In the latter case, that is, if what the gods will is good because it is good in itself, we must inevitably raise a series of questions concerning what makes something good or bad *independently* of the testimony of religions. We can then say that there is something peculiar about good actions that God or the gods, being wiser than we, are easily able to recognize. But what can this *something* be? But in asking this, we are returning once more to our original question (this time leaving the divine will aside), namely, on what basis or ground we are entitled to link the predicate 'good' to any subject whatever, which is a way of posing anew the crucial ethical question concerning the meaning of the concept 'good'.

And this is what philosophers have endeavored to resolve. Those who have opted for an objectivist attitude in this regard have spoken on behalf of a variety of ethical grounds. Plato, for instance, believed that ethical values are based on a transcendent realm of reality that, as we saw in chapter 4, belongs to the Ideas or Forms. Human conduct is thereby evaluated as to whether or not it conforms with what the mind is able to know about the Ideas or Forms in the process of dialectical reasoning: The *good* man is, accordingly, he whose appetites and passions are controlled by, and in harmony with, his reason, and whose fundamental aim, while in this life, is to take care of the affairs of his soul, as we explained in the chapter on Plato. The religious overtones of this approach to ethics are undeniable, as Saint Augustine himself observed in his *The City of God,* and Plato's treatment of the concept of virtue parallels in some respects those that have emanated from religious traditions. But the strictly rationalistic elements of Plato's treatment of ethical matters do not permit us to treat him as a mere exponent of religious ethics.

In the philosophy of Aristotle, the basis of ethical statements was given one of the most interesting and clear expositions in the history of ethical thought. In his *Nicomachean Ethics,* he begins by observing that human actions can be generally divided into two classes, namely, those that are done for the sake of something else, and those that are done for their own sake. We desire some things as means for something else, and other things for themselves. For example, we choose to take a certain college course. In most cases, we do so in order to earn college credits. But why do we want to earn college credits? Simply in order to qualify for college graduation. But why do we seek a college degree? There could be many reasons for this, but one of them could well be to secure a well-paying occupation. But why do we want a well-paying occupation? Again, there could be various reasons, but often it is the desire to earn a good salary. What is the point about a good salary? Surely to secure a comfortable and pleasant life. But why do we desire a comfortable and pleasant life? The only possible answer, Aristotle would say, is that such a life would make us happy. But now it is appropriate to ask, why do we want to be happy? Under most circumstances, this question would leave us baffled: we simply want to be happy, as happiness (*eudaimonia* or well-being, as Aristotle would have said) is the *end* of all human activity; we do all sorts of things for the sake of something else, but happiness is not sought with anything else in mind but itself. Happiness, therefore, constitutes the ultimate good of human existence, and actions are judged to be good or bad inasmuch as they conduce or fail to conduce to a happy life. In the hierarchy of means and ends of human activity, happiness holds an unchallengeable position.

The problem is, however, that there have been few philosophers and few reasonable people who have disagreed with the Aristotelian view expressed in its generality. Plato's ethics also has happiness as its chief end, and the ethical systems of the Epicureans and the Stoics sought to make their adher-ents happy. The religious ethics of Saint Augustine promised nothing short of eternal happiness to those who would follow its precepts, and happiness, albeit temporal, was the main idea that set in motion the ethical and political speculations of Thomas Hobbes, David Hume, and the utilitarians like Jeremy Bentham and John Stuart Mill. Even the pessimistic ethics of Arthur Schopenhauer, in which compassion plays so important a role, had nothing but happiness in mind. Aside from philosophers, moreover, most ordinary people look upon happiness as the only real and worthy possession of a human being. Our problems begin to arise, however, as soon as we endeavor to construct a substantive definition of happiness whose applicability is not limited to an isolated person. As soon as we set out to determine what happiness is (which is, from Aristotle's point of view, equivalent to determining what the good is), significant variations emerge. These variations in their turn constitute the peculiarities that characterize objective systems of normative ethics. For Aristotle, happiness consists in a life of virtue *(arete)* in which a person seeks to attain the *golden mean* between behavioral extremes. Moderation or the pursuit of the golden mean is then for Aristotle the path that leads to happiness:

> For instance, it is possible to feel fear, confidence, desire, anger, pity, and generally be affected pleasantly and painfully, either too much or too little, in either case wrongly; but to be thus affected at the right times, and on the right occasions, and towards the right persons, and with the right object, and in the right fashion, is the mean course and the best course ... excess is wrong, and deficiency also is blamed, but the mean amount is praised and is right.

Aristotle's empirical approach did not allow him to set up an ideal of human conduct that, as in the case of Plato, would encompass all possible human situations. Instead of delineating an absolute standard of ethical excellence, as Plato did, Aristotle was satisfied with a general description of how the golden mean, as a virtuous state, can lead to the attainment of human well-being. A more complete examination of Aristotelian ethics is given in our chapter 5.

But Aristotle's concept of happiness has not been shared by other philosophers. The Epicureans identified happiness (that is, the good) with absolute peace of mind and with the absence of pain and distress. Following the teachings of Epicurus, they constructed the picture of the happy man as that of someone who knows how to enjoy mental and physical pleasures while at the same time remaining a perfect master of his desires and emotions. The Epicurean avoids becoming involved in aggravating emotional situations and minimizes the need to participate in political and social activities that lie beyond the small circle of his true friends. Thus, he creates around himself a peaceful environment where he is able to extract the best rewards that human existence can provide. Unconcerned about death and oblivious of the eternal punishments promised by religion to the irreligious, he does not fear the gods who, from his point of view, have little to do with human beings. The Roman philosopher Titus Lucretius Carus (95–52 B.C.), who inherited and assimilated the ideas of Epicurus, expressed himself in the following terms about Epicurus:

> When human life lay groveling in all men's sight, crushed to the earth under the dead weight of superstition whose grim features loured menacingly upon mortals from the four corners of the sky, a man of Greece was first to raise mortal eyes in defiance, first to stand erect and brave the challenge. Fables of the gods did not crush him, nor the lightning flash and the growling menace of the sky. Rather they quickened his manhood, so that he, first of all men, longed to smash the constraining locks of nature's doors .... Therefore superstition in its turn lies crushed beneath his feet, and we by his triumph are lifted level with the skies.

From the perspective of Epicureanism, nothing that can bring about suffering, pain, mental or physical distress can be good, and only those human activities that enhance a person's inner and outer peace can be considered to be ethically right. The very purpose of science is not really to reveal the truth about the world, so much as to relieve man's fears about the world. Nothing, absolutely nothing, is worth seeking except a lasting state of contentment and serenity, which the Epicureans called *ataraxia*.

It is a grave interpretational mistake to identify Epicureanism with simple *hedonism*, a school of normative ethics that looks upon pleasure, especially physical or sensual pleasure, as the good. This mistake reveals itself in the meaning attached to the word 'epicure' that, as the dictionary defines it, stands for "a person who is especially fond of luxury and sensuous pleasure." In this sense, it is obvious that Epicurus was not an epicure. The identification of Epicureanism with hedonism was probably the result of certain exponents of *asceticism*, who in their missionary zeal against all forms of pleasure misunderstood the teachings of Epicurus. Asceticism is a philosophical view that maintains that pleasure, in whatever form, is something morally evil and, as such, something that ought to be avoided. The ascetics, who have been often associated with certain religious tendencies, would have us believe that even the most innocent pleasures are inevitably evil. But, in reality, what could the good be for them? As Jeremy Bentham (1748–1832) observed, could the ascetics be in favor of a human life altogether *immersed* in pain? If the suffering man is a good man, could they be advocating a life of misery for everyone? But this idea seems to be truly preposterous: the ascetic, Bentham rightly noted, condemns *certain* pleasures, specifically physical pleasures, only because such pleasures may endanger our chances of ultimately enjoying the eternal pleasures of a heavenly life. Accordingly, *even* the ascetic has happiness as his ethical goal: he chooses to suffer in this life because he wants to enjoy the blessedness of an eternal existence. If, however, the reality of eternal existence is challenged or rejected, asceticism loses whatever validity it may have, as this validity is intimately tied up with a system of dualism of unmistakable religious implications.

The Epicureans would have rejected a thoroughly hedonistic philosophy, not because pleasure is evil, but simply because they knew that the indiscriminate search for pleasure often brings with it much suffering and aggravation. If the parents do not control and discipline the child's animal instinct for gaining immediate satisfaction for all his urges and desires, he will become the unhappy victim of self-destructive habits and will find himself in hosts of unpleasant situations. The child must be taught to postpone certain pleasures and avoid others so that, as a grown-up person, he may come to enjoy other more lasting and fruitful pleasures. And among all pleasures, the Epicureans asked, what could be better than a life of tranquillity and peace, in which a healthy body and a keen mind are allowed to work together in harmony? For the attainment of such a life, one must build certain useful habits that are inexorably the result of one's use of reason. What one needs, therefore, is some sort of plan or system by which one can come to be happy, and for this purpose, nothing can be more fruitful than the construction of a table of values by reference to which one may give to each pleasure its respective worth. In a word, what we need is a calculus of pleasure.

And it was precisely such a calculus that was in Bentham's mind as he set out to develop his school of *utilitarianism*. According to this view, the good must be identified with those aspects of existence that make human beings happy, not the individual and isolated human being, but the human being as he finds himself in the context of a human community. For nobody lives alone; as Plato said, human existence is by its nature a collection of inter-dependencies. Accordingly, utilitarianism does not treat ethical issues and questions as strictly personal problems, since they are always social or polit-ical. What is good for me is always a problem related to the social needs of those with whom I live. The principle of utility, as John Stuart Mill puts it,

> holds that actions are right [that is, good] in proportion as they tend to promote happiness, wrong as they tend to produce the reverse of happiness. By happiness is intended pleasure, and the absence of pain; by unhappiness, pain, and the pri-vation of pleasure.

But, let us ask, happiness for whom? For the person alone, as in the case of the 'epicure'? And happiness when? In some other life, as in the case of the religious ethicist? The happiness that the utilitarians have in mind is (1) hap-piness in *this* life, and (2) happiness for the greatest number of people.

But as the quotation from Mill's *Utilitarianism* makes abundantly clear, happiness cannot be disassociated from pleasure: to be happy is to experi-ence and enjoy pleasure, and since happiness is the declared goal of ethical life, the good must be identified with the pleasurable or pleasant, and the bad with the opposite. To say that an action is good (e.g., "loving one's neighbor is good") is tantamount to saying that it brings about more pleasure than the contrary action. Likewise, to say that something is bad or evil is tantamount to saying that it brings about more pain and suffering than its contrary. Pleasure and pain are, therefore, the ultimate court of appeal that determine the ethical value of all human activities. "Nature," wrote Ben-tham in his *Introduction to the Principles of Morals and Legislation,*

> has placed mankind under the governance of two sovereign masters, *pain* and *pleasure.* It is for them alone to point out what we ought to do, as well as to determine what we shall do. On the one hand the standard of right and wrong, on the other the chain of causes and effects, are fastened to their throne . . . . The *principle of utility* recognizes this subjection, and assumes it for the foundation of that system, the object of which is to rear the fabric of felicity by the hands of reason and law.

On this basis, Bentham proposed a pleasure calculus, that is, certain practical rules according to which reasonable people could assess the relative worthiness of specific pleasures by reference to their intensity, duration, and other characteristics. Also on that basis, John Stuart Mill proceeded to outline the details of his utilitarianism, in which the greatest happiness of the greatest number of people constitutes the ultimate ethical criterion.

Obviously, there are immense problems connected with Bentham's utilitarianism. For instance, are all pleasures equally good? Is the public good always preferable to the good of the individual? Are there no differences in the ways in which different people react to pleasures and pains? Is a happy pig better or worse (ethically) than a dissatisfied Socrates? Surely, not only Bentham and Mill, but also their followers in the twentieth century have endeavored to find adequate solutions for them, but how adequate these solutions are is itself a problem. But among the various difficulties faced by the advocates of utilitarianism, perhaps the most troublesome is related to their *identification* of what is good with what produces pleasure. It is indeed true that, as Bentham says, *nature* has placed us, along with other sentient beings, under the governance of two powerful masters, namely, pleasure and pain. By nature, we seek the former and avoid the latter, and much of what goes by the name of civilization is largely due to our ways of guiding and controlling these two inescapable human tendencies. It is therefore a perfectly valid *de facto* statement to say that human beings prefer pleasure over pain, for such is our natural constitution. And yet, one must ask, can we convert such a *de facto* statement into a *de jure* statement and say accordingly that *because* pleasure is *desired* pleasure is *desirable?* Are we justified in extracting from a natural circumstance an ethical injunction? Can the basis of morality be such an appeal to naturalism? Furthermore, there are *other natural* tendencies prevalent in the animal world in general and in human beings in particular that cannot be overlooked. For instance, we can conceivably say that it is natural for the powerful individuals of a species to dominate the weak ones, for the fittest to survive at the expense of the unfit, for the healthy to disregard the sick, and for the intelligent to take advantage of the stupid. Is this not the case among most animal species? In destroying their deformed children, then, were not the Spartans acting according to nature? The ethical philosophers who have looked upon certain evolutionary traits (e.g., the survival of the fittest) as their natural guiding light have insisted that the concept of good is independent of the pleasures of the individual and even of the happiness of the majority, and that what is good is what promotes the emergence and continuity of the strongest, both physically and mentally. When Friedrich Nietzsche attacked utilitarianism as a manifestation of "slave morality," he did so in the name of what Nietzsche deemed to be perfectly *natural*, namely, that the strong ought to dominate and take advantage of the weak. "I abhor his vulgarity," said Nietzsche in reference to John Stuart Mill, for his "vulgarity" places the happiness of the masses above that of the individual. Nietzsche's *good* man, moreover, is far removed from the hedonistic circles around which the ordinary pleasure-seeking herd-man revolves.

Which one are we then going to say is more in accordance with *nature:* on the one hand, the hedonist who instinctively and consciously searches for gratification, and the utilitarian moral agent who seeks the greatest happiness for the greatest number of people (ensuring for himself a reasonable amount of happiness), or, on the other hand, the superman who transvaluates traditional moral codes, and who, acting "beyond good and evil," declares the good to be the advantage of the stronger and superior types among mankind? Is it more *natural* to seek social reforms that bring about the welfare of the masses, work for the liberation of women and minorities, and in general alleviate the suffering of mankind at large, or to disregard the masses, subject minorities and weaklings to the domination of the strong, and create the conditions that are necessary for the advent of the Superman? In either case, it seems, it is justifiable to ask whether such types of programs are themselves *good* and ethically desirable, which demonstrates the dangers inherent in identifying the good with any set of allegedly *natural* circumstances. And, just as the utilitarians cannot claim that by saying that that which promotes the greatest happiness for the greatest number of people is good, they have established a firm ground for ethics, their philosophical adversaries cannot claim to have found a decisive answer to ethical queries. Mill himself was well aware of this. In his *Utilitarianism,* he observes that

> the only proof capable of being given that an object is visible is that people actually see it. The only proof that a sound is audible is that people hear it; and so of the other sources of our experience. In like manner, I apprehend, the sole evidence it is possible to produce that anything is desirable [that is, *good*] is that people actually desire it.

Nothing else could one say even about Aristotle's treatment of the matter. For him, as for Mill, the only "proof" that happiness is the highest good *(summum bonum)* is that ordinary people want to be happy.

But such reasonings, however, have left unmoved a number of critics of ethical naturalism. These include those philosophers who, like Immanuel Kant (1724–1804), have advanced certain *a priori* principles as the basis of morality (principles that are allegedly altogether removed from the realm of sense experience and, therefore, from pleasures, pains, and the like), and those philosophers who, like George Edward Moore (1873–1958), have insisted in the indefinability of the term 'good'. Moore begins his *Principia Ethica* by rejecting the common idea that the sole purpose of ethics is confined to the examination of how the notion of the good applies to human conduct and practice. For him, ethics is "the general enquiry into what is good" in every sense. He proceeds to argue that it is futile to define 'good' in terms of any quality whatsoever, and that *definitions* such as "the good is the pleasurable" are altogether misguided. But then, if the concept 'good' is not translatable

into other predicates, what is it that we mean when we use the word 'good'?
In the words of Moore,

> 'Good', then, if we mean by it that quality which we assert to belong to a thing,
> when we say that the thing is good, is incapable of any definition, in the most
> important sense of that word. The most important sense of 'definition' is that in
> which a definition states what are the parts which invariably compose a certain
> whole; and in this sense 'good' has no definition because it is simple and has no
> parts. It is one of those innumerable objects of thought which are themselves
> incapable of definition, because they are the ultimate terms by reference to
> which whatever *is* capable of definition must be defined . . . . There is, therefore,
> no intrinsic difficulty in the contention that 'good' denotes a simple and indefinable
> quality.

As such, then, 'good' is a quality like 'yellow' or 'soft', that is, a quality that as
an "object of thought" must be apprehended immediately by the mind, that
is, *intuited* in the process of knowledge. Hence, in this form of ethical *intuitionism*, it is argued that certain pleasures are *recognized* as being *good*, certain others as being *bad*, certain actions as being *good*, certain others as being
bad, just as we recognize the presence of yellowness in certain objects but
not in others. Intuition furnishes us, therefore, with the necessary justification to link any subject whatever with the predicate 'good'. To define 'good'
in terms of natural qualities is, according to Moore, to commit the celebrated
"naturalistic fallacy," to the exposition of which he directed some of his
efforts in the *Principia Ethica*. This fallacy entails defining 'good', which is a
simple moral quality, in terms of some sort of natural quality such as "the
pleasant," "the desirable," "that of which society approves," etc. From his
point of view, this fallacy "is to be met with in almost every book on Ethics,"
and is committed, not only by the hedonists, the utilitarians, and the ethical
evolutionists, but also by the Epicureans for whom, as we saw, the moral
good is to be found in peace of mind and absence from pain. Even those
philosophers who, like the Stoics, have identified the good with a life
devoted to reason are in some sense guilty of the naturalistic fallacy.

Stoicism, which was an offspring of the Socratic school of the Cynics, constructed the ideal of the good man in terms of a life committed to reason.
The Stoic philosopher learned to liberate himself from the pursuit of pleasure and the flight from pain that often dominate man's existence. Whether
as a humble slave (as in the case of Epictetus, 55–135 A.D.), or as a Roman
emperor (as in that of Marcus Aurelius, 121–180), he sought to remain perfectly at peace amid the allurements of pleasures and the discomforts of
pains. In a perfect mood of resignation, he accepted life as it was given to
him. Thus, Epictetus wrote,

> Ask not that events should happen as you will, but let your will be that events
> should happen as they do, and you shall have peace.

Unattached to life in general and to his particular circumstances in particular, the Stoic endeavored to reach a condition of *apathia* or feelinglessness that he identified with the highest good attainable to man. "Always observe," says Marcus Aurelius in his *Meditations,*

> how ephemeral and worthless human things are, and what was yesterday a little mucus tomorrow will be a mummy or ashes. Pass then through this little space of time comfortably to nature, and end thy journey in content, just as an olive falls off when it is ripe, blessing nature who produced it, and thanking the tree on which it grew.

But here again, we come across an effort to identify the good with a 'natural' quality, namely, a life lived "comfortably to nature," and, accordingly, we are entitled to ask the very same question we raised in the context of other ethical systems: Why is the ideal of Stoicism *good?* Why is a life of resignation and abnegation good? What is good about a life immersed in *apathia?* We may reply that such a life is good because *by definition* that is what 'good' means, something that is equivalent to saying that by a mere stipulation we have determined with finality what the good is. But this is obviously useless if we bear in mind that the hedonist, the Epicurean, the utilitarian, and the evolutionist can also do exactly the same. In the end, then, we come face-to-face with a variety of ethical goods, none of which can claim priority over the others. If we insist on supporting Moore's intuitionism, moreover, our predicament is no less severe: we must admit that different people and different cultures have had diverse intuitions concerning the meaning of the simple quality 'good'. In these circumstances, in what sense can we still support ethical absolutism? Could values be still held universally and absolutely? Does it not make more sense to lend an attentive ear to ethical relativism, and say that different moral agents and different societies have identified the good with different qualities and modes of behavior? And is this not what descriptive ethics teaches us in a convincing way?

Let us consider for one moment yet another attempt to vindicate the basis of morality as a universal and stable foundation. According to Kant, as long as we insist on linking the concept 'good' with objects of experience, little progress can be expected in ethics. The golden mean of Aristotelian philosophy, the pleasures of the hedonists, the "greatest happiness for the greatest number" of the utilitarians, the *ataraxia* of the Epicureans, the *apathia* of the Stoics, together with wealth, fame, power, friendship, and all other things that have been called 'good' by human beings are themselves *good* only sometimes and under certain circumstances. What we must find, however, is when and why they deserve to be called 'good', and on reflection we soon discover that that which renders them good is their being conjoined with something that is itself absolutely and unconditionally good. But what could this something be, the discovery of which would solve once and for

all the problems of moral philosophy? Kant's words in this respect are clear
and forceful:

> Nothing can possibly be conceived in the world, or even out of it, which can be
> called good without qualification, except a Good Will. Intelligence, wit, judg-
> ment, and the other *talents* of the mind, however they may be named, or cour-
> age, resolution, perseverance, as qualities of the temperament, are undoubtedly
> good and desirable in many respects; but these gifts of nature may also become
> extremely bad and mischievous if the will which is to make use of them, and
> which, therefore, constitutes what is called *character*, is not good. It is the same
> with the *gifts of fortune*. Power, riches, honour, even health, and the general
> well-being and contentment with one's condition which is called *happiness*,
> inspire pride and often presumption, if there is not a good will to correct the
> influence of these on the mind, and with this also to rectify the whole principle of
> acting, and adapt it to its end . . . . Thus a good will appears to constitute the
> indispensable condition even of being worthy of happiness.

If this statement from Kant's *Fundamental Principles of the Metaphysic of
Morals* is correct, then most past and present systems of normative ethics are
ultimately groundless. We cannot even speak of happiness as the basis of morality, and pleasure, a life lived according to nature, the will of God, and all
other allegedly sound ethical justifications of ethical statements become useless: pleasures could conceivably be bad, and the same can be said of the others.

But to say that only in a Good Will can we find the basis of morality is to
say little, unless the idea of a Good Will is fully elucidated, and this was precisely what Kant sought to do. Philosophers, let us remember, unlike ordinary religious moralists, do not find satisfaction in merely making moral
assertions; they do not shrink from the difficult task of adducing reasons for
them. A Good Will, Kant argues, is not good only in so far as it is able to
bring about good results, for the good consists in the intention to do good,
not in the realization of the good. The pragmatic idea that it is only in the
consequences of our actions and desires that we find moral worth was certainly far from Kant's mind. Even if a Good Will were altogether unable to
accomplish its purposes, "like a jewel, it would still shine by its own light, as
a thing which has its whole value in itself."

But still, what is it that constitutes a Good Will? That the attainment of
happiness cannot be what a Good Will wills to accomplish is clear, Kant says,
from the fact that human reason is itself a most inadequate instrument for
the attainment of happiness. Otherwise, why are most people generally
unhappy?

> Now in a being which has reason and a will, if the proper object of nature were
> its *conservation*, its *welfare*, in a word, its *happiness*, then nature would have hit
> upon a very bad arrangement in selecting the reason of the creature to carry out
> its purpose.

Indeed, it is undeniable that the more an individual or a society looks upon happiness as the ultimate goal of human existence, and the more we employ reason in the pursuit of happiness, the more misery human beings pile upon themselves: life becomes empty, and the ineludible disappointment inherent in every pleasure ultimately comes to embitter every activity. In anticipation of some of the ideas of the greatest exponent of philosophical *pessimism,* Arthur Schopenhauer, Kant concluded that the very constitution of human life did not intend to make human beings happy. This should not be construed as indicating that we ought to avoid happiness. Happiness remained for Kant a worthy goal, and there is a sense in which we are justified in saying that it is our *duty* to be happy and to make others happy. But this duty is, strictly speaking, not an absolute or moral duty, as happiness cannot be the absolute goal of morality. Happiness is rather something like an *occasionally* accompanying state of mind of moral behavior. The person of Good Will will *hopefully* be a happy person, and in the exercise of his Good Will he will *at times* experience happiness, but that which constitutes his Good Will is altogether independent of happiness as a goal and as a result of moral behavior. And if this is the case when we conceive of happiness as well-being (the Aristotelian *eudaimonia*), it is even more the case when we understand happiness in terms of pleasure.

Still, we must define a Good Will, that is, "a will which deserves to be highly esteemed for itself, and is good without a view to anything further." A Good Will, as defined by Kant, is one that acts in accordance with and for the sake of duty. Only an action done from duty can be truly said to have *moral worth:*

> An action done from duty derives its moral worth, *not from the purpose* which is to be attained by it, but from the maxim by which it is determined, and therefore does not depend on the realization of the object of the action, but merely on the *principle of volition* by which the action has taken place, without regard to any object of desire.

What is, however, moral *duty?* Duty, according to Kant, *"is the necessity of acting from respect for the law."* Yes, but what law? Divine law, as this is manifested in religious traditions? Obviously not, because in that case we would find ourselves once more in the company of Abraham as he prepared himself for the slaying of Isaac, in the company of Moses as he ordered the murder and rape of the Midianites' women, and in the company of the perplexed Euthyphro as he sought the indictment of his father. These three people were surely acting out of respect of divine law, as they understood this law to be. Then, could we be talking about "natural law"? Again no, because in that case the hedonist who searches for pleasure, the utilitarian who seeks to promote the greatest happiness for the greatest number of people, the Stoic who cherishes a life lived according to nature, and the Nietzschean advocate of the survival of the fittest—all of them would be allegedly acting in the name of the same law, which is clearly absurd. Could it then be that the law Kant has in mind refers to the moral codes of individual human cultures and societies? Surely this is impossible, since, as the ethical descriptivist convincingly shows, the moral laws by which people actually live and function are immensely varied and often in contradiction with one another. What law, then, does Kantian ethics have in mind?

In the explication of the concept of moral law, Kant developed the idea of the *categorical imperative*, on the understanding of which rests our ability to grasp the kernel of his ethical system. An *imperative* statement is one in which some sort of command is expressed: "Love thy neighbor," "Help those who suffer persecution," "Be faithful to your spouse," "Go to mass on Sundays," "Exterminate inferior people," etc. *Indicative* statements, on the other hand, are simple factual statements: "Most people are selfish," "The Christians were persecuted by the Romans," etc. The former are syntactical transformations of what we called earlier *de jure* statements, whereas the latter are *de facto* statements. There are, however, *two* kinds of imperatives, namely, those that express a hypothetical command and those whose force is absolute or categorical. *Hypothetical imperatives* take the form "If you wish X, then you must do Y"; they imply, therefore, "the practical necessity of a possible action as means to something else that is willed (or at least which one might possibly will)." Hence, the Epicurean normative statement "If you wish to have peace of mind, then you ought to avoid excessive pleasure," and the religious injunction "If you want to enjoy eternal bliss, then you ought to refrain from breaking God's laws" are typical examples of hypothetical imperatives. Conceivably, however, we can imagine someone who does not cherish the idea of peace of mind or someone who is not sufficiently interested in the prospect of eternal bliss. In those cases, then, since the antecedent condition of the hypothetical statement is denied, the hypothetical imperative has no value whatsoever. Accordingly, it is futile to look for universality and necessity in the realm of hypothetical ethical norms, since their realm of applicability is limited, and since their truth depends on the always changing circumstances of human existence. The norms prescribed by hypothetical imperative are relative to the human context from which they emerge and are contingent on conditions that are discoverable in and through sense experience. As such, then, they are all empirical statements. "Every empirical element," Kant warned,

> is not only quite incapable of being an aid to the principle of morality, but is even prejudicial to the purity of morals, for the proper and inestimable worth of an absolutely Good Will consists just in this, that the principle of action is free from all influence of contigent grounds, which experience alone can furnish. We cannot too much or too often repeat our warning against this lax and even mean habit of thought which seeks for its principle among empirical motives and laws.

And surely, from Kant's point of view, this "lax and even mean habit of thought" was at work in all those systems of normative ethics that appealed to happiness (as in Aristotle), pleasure (as in hedonism), peace of mind (as in Epicureanism), compassion (as in Schopenhauer), moral sentiments (as in Hume), or any other empirically grounded basis as a foundation of morality.

Only in *categorical imperatives* can we find the essence of morality. A categorical imperative is an ethical norm or maxim that applies universally and absolutely to every conceivable case in which a rational being (human or otherwise) is a free agent. He must be a free agent inasmuch as unless freedom is real, ethical norms have no meaning. Every moral 'ought' implies, therefore, the real possibility of acting contrary to that 'ought'. If I am not able to choose freely between two possible courses of action, I cannot be morally responsible for any of them: nobody can be blamed or praised for being a man (as opposed to being a woman), for being white (as opposed to being black), etc., because in these instances, there never was a free choice on our part. A categorical imperative, therefore, commands us to act in certain ways but recognizes the fact that ultimately it is we who must freely choose to follow or not to follow the command, and it is precisely in the act of choosing (in Kant's language, the "volitional" determination of the will) that moral worth consists.

Kant stated basically two categorical imperatives: (1) *"Act only on that maxim whereby thou canst at the same time will that it should become a universal law,"* and (2) *"So act as to treat humanity, whether in thine own person or in that of any other, in every case as an end in itself, never as a means only."* By the first, we are enjoined to act always as if our actions were to become universal norms of ethical behavior for all possible rational beings. That is, before determining the moral worth of an action I must ask: Can my action be considered a paradigm of human existence for all agents in circumstances similar to mine? Can I universalize my action? By the second, which Kant looked upon as a derivation from the first, we are commanded to treat every human being (including ourselves) as an absolute end in himself, never as a means for something else. Exploitation, abuse, cruelty, sadism, masochism, slavery, and other types of behavior in which people are converted into objects of use are hereby forbidden. Every person must strive to bring about a veritable "Kingdom of Ends" in which the dignity of all rational beings is kept intact. Should such a Kingdom of Ends transcend national boundaries, then the nations of the world would enjoy a condition of "eternal peace." The advent of this Kingdom of Ends is the ethical goal for which a rational being, in whom the will is genuinely good, ought to strive.

Ethical speculation since the time of Kant has been compelled to take into account his formidable system of values, and his influence can be detected in practically every major attempt to make sense of ethical ideas. Its architectonic structure, its claim to go beyond the realm of unreliable experience in which so many variations are possible, its insistence on the *a priori* character of true ethical precepts, and its emphasis on the necessity of universalization of moral norms—all these factors have contributed to the exalted position of Kant in the history of ethics, where he occupies a place second only to those of Plato and Aristotle. And yet, we cannot ignore the fact that many philosophers have remained unconvinced and unimpressed with the accomplishments of Kantian ethics. Georg F. Hegel (1770–1831) found it to be lacking in substance, and Schopenhauer, who in all other respects admired Kant's philosophical edifice, brushed aside the categorical imperatives as pious nonsense. John Stuart Mill expressed himself in the following terms:

> This remarkable man [Kant], whose system of thought will long remain one of the landmarks in the history of philosophical speculation, does . . . lay down a universal first principle as the origin and ground of moral obligation; it is this:— "So act, that the rule on which thou actest would admit of being adopted as a law by all rational beings." But when he begins to deduce from this precept any of the actual duties of morality, he fails, almost grotesquely, to show that there would be any contradiction, any logical (not to say physical) impossibility, in the adoption by all rational beings of the most outrageously immoral rules of conduct. All he shows is that the *consequences* of their universal adoption would be such as no one would choose to incur.

Indeed, as Mill suggests, if we disregard altogether the consequences of our behavior (as Kant insisted), what ultimate justification could there be for the categorical imperatives? And if the Good Will is good only on account of its adoption of such imperatives, in what sense can we say that such a will is truly good?

It would be unwise at this point to undertake the defense or the critical appraisal of Kant's ethics. Let it be sufficient to observe that moral perplexities have continued to plague human experience in general and philosophy in particular, in spite of the finality and sense of assurance with which Kant sought to resolve them. Certain contemporary philosophical tendencies have incorporated a number of Kantian elements into their own ways of assessing moral values, as in the case of *existentialism*, according to which, as Jean-Paul Sartre says, the realm of values is the realm of freedom in which in choosing anything whatsoever, a person must choose on behalf of everyone else: "Every person ought to say to himself: Am I someone who has the right to act in such a way that humanity itself should rule itself by my acts?" Moral behavior, therefore, must be universalizable in every respect, and this is clearly an element inherent in Kant's ethics. Furthermore, many contemporary philosophers have learned from Kant the idea that moral values are empty notions as long as they are applicable to isolated individual or even isolated communities; for moral values to gain in relevance, they must be conceived as applying to the human context in its totality. Hence, the gap that separates ethics from political philosophy is anything but real.

But, of course, such an idea can also be found in Plato, for whom, as we saw in chapter 4, the concept of justice can only be elucidated when we conceive of the person as existing in a human context that by far transcends his individuality. It is for this reason that some of the issues and questions that have been raised in this chapter will reappear, perhaps in a clearer way, in the following chapter, in which the search for values is approached from a political and social point of view.

The study of ethical issues has been characterized in the Anglo-American world, especially during the last few decades, by an emphasis on the specific problems related to ethical language. Ethical relativism has convinced some philosophers of the futility of advancing and defending impressive systems of normative ethics. This relativism, as we saw, argues that ethical values are nothing but expressions of the mores and customs by which people and social groups live. For relativism, the term 'ethics' regains once more its ancient meaning of 'habit' or 'custom'. What is good or right is, therefore, only that which is approved or commended by a social group, and this in its turn is nothing but what agrees with the positive emotions or feelings of the group. Hence, as we said earlier, it is easy to move from relativism to ethical emotivism. This view insists on translating ethical statements into psychological statements: "Loving one's neighbor is right" becomes "I (or we) find satisfaction in loving one's neighbors." Westermarck, whom we mentioned earlier, stated this view quite clearly in his *Ethical Relativity:*

> I have thus arrived at the conclusion that neither the attempts of moral philosophers or theologians to prove the objective validity of moral judgments, nor the common sense assumption to the same effect, gives us any right at all to accept such a validity as a fact . . . . In my opinion the predicates of all moral judgments, all moral concepts, are ultimately based on emotions, and, as is very commonly admitted, no objectivity can come from an emotion.

Logical positivism welcomed this attitude and made enormous efforts to show that ethical statements can be objectively neither true nor false. They cannot be verified in experience, and as all unverifiable statements, they lack meaning. Accordingly, it became a matter of embarrassment for philosophers to be in the habit of uttering *meaningless* statements such as "Loving one's neighbor is good" or "Killing innocent people is bad." Indeed, they could have abandoned altogether their interest in ethical matters, but this seemed inappropriate since the entire history of philosophy, especially after Socrates, has made ethics one of the chief concerns of philosophy. In view of this circumstance, therefore, the logical positivists and their descendants (the language philosophers) opted for an interesting and curious solution: they would no longer make ethical statements or deal in normative ethics and would avoid the role of *moralists,* a role that rightfully belongs to philosophers like Plato, Aristotle, Epicurus, Epictetus, Saint Augustine, Spinoza,

Kant, Schopenhauer, Nietzsche, and many others; instead, the new philosophers would devote their efforts to making statements about ethical statements. Remaining somehow ethically neutral, they would analyze the meaning and structure of ethical statements. It was thus that what today goes by the name of *metaethics* was formally born. The metaethicist is, therefore, someone who talks about ethical talk, and who passes judgment on moral judgments without thereby making moral judgments. How this is possible, and what benefit can come from it, are questions that the reader can ponder after having been exposed to a moderate dose of metaethical literature. It is possible, of course, that metaethics, understood in this sense, may bear wonderful fruits in the form of greater linguistic clarity and more precise philosophical discourse. But if anyone approaches these linguistic metaethicists with the aim of learning from them those solid ethical values that render human existence worth living, he will be knocking at the wrong door, and he will be as disappointed as those eager Athenian youths who anxiously flocked to the presence of the Sophists of Socrates' time. He will be told in no uncertain terms that the task of the philosopher is not to create values or defend normative systems; he will be reminded, as Moritz Schlick put it, that ethics, as a "science can do no more than *explain*" what people mean when they use moral discourse, since ethics "can never set up or establish a norm." Ethics, Schlick wrote in his *Problems of Ethics,*

> is never able to do more than to discover the rules of the judgment, to read them from the facts before it; the origin of norms always lies outside and before science and knowledge . . . . In other words: if, or in so far as, the philosopher answers the question "What is Good?" by an exhibition of norms, this means only that he tells us what "good" actually means; he can never tell us what good *must* or *should* mean.

It is not difficult to see how and why on the basis of the program proposed by the logical positivists much of contemporary ethics has become a branch of anthropology, sociology, psychology, and linguistics. Whether this is a lasting condition or merely a passing mood born out of our frustrations with old normative systems is a question that only posterity will be able to answer.

Let us now once more begin our search for values and the good life, but this time on a more comprehensive level: the political and social aspects of human life.

QUESTIONS FOR STUDY

1. Define and exemplify *de facto* and *de jure* statements. Discuss the problem faced by ethical philosophers with respect to the

relationship between the subject and the predicate of the latter statements.

2. Explain the etymological basis of the word 'ethics'. Explain in what sense the ethical relativist is closer to the original meaning of the word when he assesses moral values.

3. Define and exemplify what is meant by descriptive ethics, normative ethics, and metaethics.

4. What is meant by 'ethical emotivism'? In your view, is there any relationship between ethical emotivism and ethical relativism?

5. What are the major problems encountered in the assessment of ethical statements that are the result of a religious or theological ethical system?

6. Explain and exemplify what is meant by the terms 'hedonism' and 'asceticism'. How are Epicureanism and utilitarianism related to hedonism?

7. What did Moore mean by the naturalistic fallacy? In what sense can we say that this fallacy is found in utilitarianism?

8. What is the philosophical import of the Kantian notion of a Good Will? In your answer make specific reference to the categorical imperative.

8

Political Philosophy:
Man as a Social Being

INTRODUCTION

Political philosophy is that branch of philosophy that analyzes, explains, and evaluates social institutions in general and political institutions and practices in particular. Insofar as it is the attempt to analyze and explain, it is part of the philosophy of the social sciences. Insofar as it is the attempt to evaluate, it is similar to ethics. The exact relationship between political philosophy and ethics is something that can only be understood from within a particular theory, and it will vary from theory to theory. The further questions whether political philosophy can be distinguished from political science, whether there can be a science of politics and in what sense, and how evaluation is possible in political philosophy are all questions that make sense and can be answered only within a historical context and with reference to particular philosophies. In short, questions of methodology and evaluation are precisely why we require a philosophical treatment.

Like all branches of philosophy, political philosophy has its origins in classical Greece. Aristotle is the author of a treatise entitled *Politics,* and it was the same Aristotle who asserted that man is a political animal. What he meant by that expression is that man is a creature who reaches fulfillment in a *polis,* a Greek city-state. So, the origins of political philosophy are in the experience of the first great philosophers, the ancient Greeks, who sought to make sense of social life as it existed in the *polis.*

PLATO

Plato's political philosophy is found in three of his works: *The Republic,* the *Statesman,* and the *Laws.* There are considerable differences in these works, but it is the *Republic* that posterity has fastened upon. Given the enormous influence of that work, we shall follow the tradition of focusing upon it, but not without first warning the reader that it is not the whole of what Plato thought about politics.

Plato's analysis of social and political institutions is important for two reasons. The obvious reason is that it is a model for much later thinking upon the subject. The second reason is that it exemplifies the close connection between one's philosophy as a whole and one's views on a particular subject such as politics.

The surface details of Plato's *Republic* are clear enough. Plato begins by drawing an analogy between the individual and the community. "The State is the individual writ large." The individual human being is analyzed in terms of a personality ("soul") that has three parts: appetite, spirit, and reason. Every individual has all three parts, but in each individual one of the three parts predominates. Only that tiny minority of individuals in whom reason predominates can be harmonious or just. The analogue to society or to a just society is as follows. Every civilized society operates economically on the basis of the division of labor. Only when reason rules can there be both an efficient and a just social organization. Therefore, only when a society is ruled by philosopher-kings, those individuals in whom reason is the dominant element and who are properly trained, will there be a truly just society.

Plato advocates, it seems, rule by an elite. This elite is based upon innate natural ability, a special rigorous training, and a number of provisions such as a communal life style where rulers are not allowed to own property or to have families in the usual sense, designed to prevent corruption and the abuse of power. These qualifications are important so that the reader does not confuse Plato's elite with other elites based upon birth (aristocracy), or wealth (oligarchy), or brute power (tyranny). In all of this, and here we come to the main point, Plato presupposes that political decision making should be based upon a kind of expertise. Such expertise is possible only if there is such a thing as political knowledge and if that knowledge encompasses the relevant norms.

This is, in fact, precisely what Plato believed. As we saw in an earlier chapter, Plato believed in the possibility of objective and absolute truths, and among such truths we find knowledge of the Good ("virtue is knowledge"). Justice and virtue are objects of absolute knowledge. This kind of knowledge is not derived from experience but from acquaintance with supersensible norms. The examples of the divided line and the myth of the cave are accounts of the existence of such knowledge and its limited availability. It is no more possible for everyone to have political knowledge and insight into first principles than it is for everyone to be a creative mathematician or a nuclear physicist. No matter how well we are educated there is always the final division between those who can follow an argument and those who can formulate an argument based upon insight into the first principles.

When we take this position on the limited access to political first principles and put it together with another Platonic doctrine, Plato's conclusion becomes even stronger. That other doctrine is the Socratic maxim that "no man knowingly commits an evil act." All wrongdoing is a consequence of ignorance. Now Plato is not arguing the absurd thesis that we break the rules only because we are ignorant of the rules. That is not the kind of knowledge he has in mind. What he means is that only those individuals who see the big picture, including *why* the rules are the rules, can obey the rules. Only in those individuals in whom there is ultimate insight into the form of the Good is there a direct and unequivocal connection between knowing what is good and doing what is good. Precisely for this reason only the qualified elite should be given full power, for they are the only ones who both know the good and can do good for the rest of us. If such knowledge exists then any limit on the power of the philosopher-king and any sharing of power will inevitably lead to disaster. Any meaningful criticism of Plato's political philosophy will have to focus on whether such knowledge exists. All other criticisms are irrelevant.

A number of other points are also important. First, let us repeat that Plato believed in the existence of absolute norms of social and political organization and that these norms are objects of knowledge. Second, these norms exist outside of and independent of any actual society. Hence, we do not learn about them just by observing actual societies, past or present. Moreover, the independent existence of these norms allows them to be standards in terms of which we can judge actual societies. Actual states and political practices are good or bad depending upon whether they conform to or deviate from these absolute and independent norms. When later and modern thinkers assert that politics should be dependent upon morality, what they mean is that there are objective standards against which actual social and political practice must be measured. This view is often Platonic. On the other hand, when a thinker asserts that politics is independent of morality, what he means to deny is the existence of such external standards. Such a view is anti-Platonic.

Some critics will want to condemn Plato as being utopian, an idle visionary constructing imaginary ideal societies. They will contend either that the kind of political expertise or knowledge Plato talked about does not exist or that, if it did exist, it would be unattainable. The Platonic response to such a charge is as follows. No experiment in physical science is ever exact. There are always deviations. Usually no one takes such deviations to be an indication that there are no laws in nature. What we say is that the variables are too complex. Actual experience is an imperfect manifestation of underlying realities. Platonists would say that the same situation holds in social science. Platonic social science, like Platonic physical science, clearly recognizes the disparity between the ideal and the actual. But in both cases the claim is made that without knowledge of the ideal or a belief in such knowledge, the actual world would be unintelligible. Moreover, just as the physical scientist strives to obtain such knowledge, so does the social scientist. In addition, striving for the ideal in social science, including the objective norms, is what makes intelligent political action possible.

ARISTOTLE

Just as Plato is the source of one great tradition in philosophy, so Aristotle is the author of a second great and alternative tradition. The relationship and the differences between these two great seminal thinkers has already been discussed in the chapter on Aristotle. Much of what was said there will be relevant here. Aristotle's main work on political philosophy is the *Politics*, and although it is, as is to be expected, critical of the *Republic* of Plato, a good deal of what Aristotle says is based upon Plato's later views as expressed in the *Statesman* and the *Laws*.

One large section of the *Politics* is a critique of the ideal society found in Plato's *Republic*. Aristotle finds it to be utopian, inconsistent with human nature (as in the abolition of private property and the family), and useless as a guide to actual practice. None of this implies, however, that Aristotle rejects the notion that there are absolute and objective norms of social and political organization. Aristotle, like Plato, subscribes to the existence of such norms. Where he differs is in his conception of how we arrive at the knowledge of such norms. For Aristotle, the first principles or knowledge of the norms of social and political organization are derived from experience. Hence, a large part of the *Politics*, as well as a special project on the study of actual constitutions of the Greek city-states, involves an empirical investigation of actual social and political life in order to discover the underlying structure including the basic norms.

Aristotle's political study thus strives to be empirical and scientific as well as directed to uncovering the absolute and objective norms. How is it possible to believe that a scientific investigation can uncover fundamental values? The answer lies in Aristotle's *teleological* conception of the world.

You will recall that a teleological explanation is an explanation of a process in terms of its built-in goal or end. Aristotle interpreted everything in nature as a process with inherent goals, and these goals are empirically discoverable. The goal of an acorn is to become an oak tree, and we learn this from experience. When we apply this view to the social world we find that Aristotle believed that there were social and political structures that can only be understood in terms of processes with built-in goals.

Aristotle's analysis of social and political institutions is teleological in that he sees them as natural structures. Social institutions are not conventions but natural entities. The nature of a thing is not what it is in a primitive or early condition but what it becomes or develops into in its mature state. For example, the family may come into existence before the state does. The family is thus prior in time. But the state is needed for human beings to develop more fully in that certain human capacities can only be realized beyond the family in a larger social context. The state is thus prior by nature. Life in the state shows what human nature is intrinsically. The "natural" for Aristotle is the opposite of the "primitive" and the opposite of "instinctive." The state is the social institution in which man develops his highest powers. In this sense we can understand what Aristotle meant when he said that "man by nature is a political animal," one who develops most fully in a *polis*. To live outside the state is to be a beast or a God perhaps, but not a human being.

Aristotle viewed the social world as a set of institutions (the family, the economy, the state, etc.) wherein each institution has its own built-in end. At the same time, each institution is also a means to other institutions in the same hierarchical fashion that Aristotle attributed to the rest of the universe. The supreme institution, that institution that is the end of all of the others but is not itself a means to any other institution, is the state. The state is the top of the pyramid of social structures each dovetailing into the other. What is the ultimate end of the state? The goal of the state is to produce moral citizens who can interact with each other as both free and as equals. The goal of the state is not security, not the prevention of injustice, and not the promotion of the exchange of goods. These are the goals of lesser institutions.

Two implications of Aristotle's conception of the goal of the state are worth noting. If the state has a moral end that requires and necessitates direct participation of citizens in the life of the state, then there are strict limitations on the size of the state. Aristotle's view applies only to what has been called a face-to-face society. This accounts for his emphasis on the city-state and his ignoring of the empire, even the empire of Alexander the Great. Second, Aristotle distinguishes between natural wealth and unnatural wealth. Natural wealth is defined as what is needed for the support of life, whereas unnatural wealth is production of goods for money and gain beyond what is needed for life. Unnatural wealth is a threat to the survival of the state. Aristotle defended private property but he also advocated common use of what is produced.

Perhaps the most important element to emerge from Aristotle's conception of the social world is the complete continuity of the individual and the community. Aristotle has neither an abstract individual nor an abstract and reified community. Given his teleological view, it follows that the individual can only be fulfilled within a community, and the community exists for the fulfillment of its citizens. So, for Aristotle there is no such thing as individual rights held against or outside of society. It also follows that justice is what is created by the state, not something external to the state. Aristotle would reject the Platonic notion of external standards used to judge particular states. States can be judged, and objectively, but only by reference to their own built-in ends. These ends are discovered, not invented. Finally, Aristotle's conception of citizenship requires direct participation and excludes notions like consent and representation.

The notion that justice is created by the state raises the question of the status of law. Unlike the Plato of the *Republic*, but very much like the Plato of the *Laws*, Aristotle advocates the sovereignty of law. In his analysis of the various types of states, Aristotle offered a distinction based first upon the number of rulers, and second upon the good and bad forms of each:

	Rule by one	A few	Many
(Good)	Kingship	Aristocracy	Polity*
(Bad)	Tyranny	Oligarchy	Democracy

*(Polity is a compromise between democracy and aristocracy.)

The good forms are defined two ways. First, a form of government is good if the ruler or rulers govern for the benefit of all and not just themselves. This is what makes democracy bad, for it is mob rule. Second, governing for the benefit of all is determined by how well the laws are respected. Aristotle believed that laws embodied the collective wisdom of the past, and given his empirical-teleological view of the world, it is to be expected that the norms of past practice contain almost everything worth knowing.

MEDIEVAL POLITICAL THEORY

It is not possible in a chapter to give even a brief summary of the whole history of Western political philosophy. What is important here is to indicate how the medieval tradition continued to make use of the classical views of Plato and Aristotle. There is as well a continuity of the classical and Christian

traditions that sharply distinguishes them from modern political philosophies. A brief comment on the medieval situation will provide a needed
link and establish the contrast.

Saint Augustine (354–430 A.D.) in *The City of God* introduced the doctrine
of the "two swords." Mankind is one society but under two governments, the
sacred and the secular. Each government has its own laws. This conception
differed from previous theories because it divided men's loyalties and obedi-
ence between two ideals. The ambiguity in Augustine's position arises
because of the Platonic orientation. The city of God consists of the living pil-
grims who are predestined for salvation in the next world. The city of the
devil, which Augustine identifies with the Roman Empire, consists of the
doomed. There is no clear discussion in Augustine of precisely how the saved
are supposed to behave in actual secular states.

No such ambiguity exists in the later Aristotelian orientation of Saint
Thomas Aquinas (1225–1274). Aquinas, using Aristotle's teleological conception of the universe, sees all of nature including mankind as part of a vast
organic and hierarchical structure. Each institution has its goal and is in turn
a means to a greater good. Further, Aquinas agreed with Aristotle that the
moral purpose of government is paramount. Given that moral purpose (now
understood in Christian terms as salvation), and given the necessity of a
supreme and ruling institution within any hierarchy, it follows that the spiritual institution of the Church is superior to the secular state. On this basis the
Church has legal supervision over the secular state.

Aquinas' Aristotelian argument was useful to the Church in its conflict with
the rising national monarchies. But this same Aristotelian political philosophy was used by the Church's opponents. Marsilio of Padua (1275–1342)
argued on Aristotelian grounds that the secular state was the highest institution. His argument involved two important steps. First, Marsilio emphasized
the good of earthly life and explained it economically in terms of the division
of labor. Second, he *divorced faith from reason.* Religion's concern with salvation was relegated to the next life, and it involved as well non-rational and
supernatural considerations. This left reason to operate exclusively with
secular ends.

Despite vast differences of opinion, there is something that was universally
held by all classical and medieval political philosophies. All of them subscribed to the belief in an objective order in the world, that this order is independent of mankind in the sense that it is discovered and not invented, and
that human beings are accountable to the objective order. That objective
order exists either in Platonic forms or in the natural teleology of Aristotle or
in the divinely established order of the Bible. Justice must ultimately be compliance with that order. The classical-medieval tradition also took hier-
archies and elites seriously precisely because such elites were those who best
understood or represented the objective order. Arbitrariness on the part of the
Pope was condemned as readily as arbitrariness on the part of emperors.

MODERN POLITICAL PHILOSOPHY

If one were to hazard one broad generalization distinguishing modern political philosophy from the classical-medieval tradition, it would be to say that the moderns still believed in an objective order, but they found the objective order inside man or society and not in an external structure. The consequences are momentous. By locating the objective norms in man, we are led to believe that it is only in man's actions that those norms are achieved. Instead of conforming to an objective norm, we are taught that we must realize that norm, that is, bring it into social existence. This new conception is found in Renaissance humanism, in the rise of individualism, and in Protestantism.

When we recall that the medieval Church justified itself on Aristotelian grounds, we are not surprised to discover that the Protestant Reformation of the sixteenth century, in reacting against that tradition, went back to an earlier tradition, to Saint Augustine. But Luther and Calvin embraced determinism and predestination. That is why Luther could argue that salvation could never be obtained through good deeds and sacraments. Salvation became non-moral in the sense that it is given and not earned. What place, then, is there for ethics? Ethics can only concern this world and not the next. Insofar as we are among the elect destined for salvation, we will exemplify Christian values in our behavior, but such embodied values are not the means of salvation. In a Platonic-Augustinian sense, we manifest or reflect in this world our already achieved status in the next.

If this were the whole story, the Reformation would be as ambiguous as the *City of God* in terms of what people should do with regard to the secular state. But as a form of modernism Protestantism finds the norms in each individual who is thereby called upon to remake the world in the image of his private conscience. The literal interpretation of this position is revolutionary and anarchistic. Post-Protestant revolutionists and radicals came to interpret consent as conscious individual acceptance, whereas medieval revolutionists would have found the notion of private conscience incomprehensible.

Luther was appalled at the radical lunatic fringe generated by this view. He personally, and Lutheran churches in general, adhered to a less activist role in politics and tended to accept passively secular control of society. Calvinist churches, on the other hand, especially in Holland, Scotland, and America, finding themselves in the religious minority and in opposition to the government, ignored Calvin's own authoritarian views and emphasized the rights of revolution. Luther and Calvin both expected a greater uniformity and consensus to emerge from the appeal to individual conscience than actually did. In fact, the new locus of absolute norms in individual conscience led to the splintering of the religious community and thereby increased the power of secular rulers.

Two figures emerged as the major political theorists who grasped this new situation. Both of these men locate the absolute norms within the human world. Both rejected any external standard, including organized religion of any kind, as a check on these new norms. Both of these philosophers stressed this-worldly values. The only philosophical tradition to which they can appeal is Aristotelian, albeit in an entirely new setting. These two philosophers were Machiavelli and Hobbes.

MACHIAVELLI (1469–1527)

Machiavelli can be explained rather simply. The ultimate objective norm is the survival and expansion of the secular state, understood teleologically. All values are generated by the ultimate aim of the state. A prince is good insofar as he serves this ultimate aim. The end justifies the means, however immoral they appear to be in the light of external (and therefore irrelevant) standards. Machiavelli did not glorify violence and stealth for their own sake, rather he indicates when and where they are appropriate. He also indicates how a good prince rewards loyal citizens and encourages commerce in the service of the state. This is not a matter of cynicism, or "telling it like it is," but rather policy consistent with what Machiavelli takes to be the empirically (and historically) arrived at truth of the objective built-in end of the modern secular state.

HOBBES (1588–1679)

Thomas Hobbes does almost exactly the same thing. We say almost because Hobbes locates the objective norm of survival and expansion within each individual person instead of within the state. In this sense, Hobbes' theory is more individualistic. Despite his critique of Aristotle, and despite his pretension that he is giving a deterministic and mechanistic account of individual human psychology, Hobbes can only make sense of human nature and still discover a norm by assuming that all of the drives of each individual person form within that person a functional system whose overriding aim is the self-preservation of the system (or person). Without this teleological element, Hobbes' theory would collapse. Hobbes makes the claim that he is the first modern social scientist because he does not invoke external values, but he is not content just to describe the social world; rather he believes his theory entitles him to prescribe as well. That is because he has "discovered" a universal norm or goal in the form of individual survival.

The difference between Hobbes and Machiavelli is now worth stressing. There is a continental tradition of political philosophy that stretches from

Machiavelli to Hegel to Marx. Its philosophical origin is Aristotelian in that it finds its norm teleologically and objectively in the built-in ends of some collective whole such as the state, or the nation, or the economic class, etc. Within this particular continental European tradition, the meaning of freedom for the individual has to be fulfilling himself by playing his proper role in the collectivity. As opposed to that tradition, there is an Anglo-American tradition in English-speaking countries that owes its origin to Hobbes. In this tradition, the norm is objectively located in the built-in end of the individual. Here freedom would have to mean the absence of external constraint on the individual's pursuit of his end.

Let us return now to Hobbes. Hobbes postulates the existence of a basic human nature whose fundamental feature is self-preservation. Even the pursuit of status and wealth are subordinate to and means to personal survival. There is something fundamentally asocial about man. It is not that we shun human society but rather that we use other people as means to our ultimate ends. This is very different from Aristotle. If there were a situation in which each individual pursued his own ends in total disregard to others, it would be what Hobbes calls a *state of nature*. In the state of nature we have a perpetual war of each against all, in which life is nasty, brutish, and short. Such a state of nature is not conducive to personal survival, so reason that guides the passions, although it does not command them, suggests a more viable alternative, the formation of a community. The formation of a community or commonwealth is accomplished by means of a *social contract*. Each party to the contract agrees to surrender something, namely, their uninhibited pursuit of self-interest and the practice of seeking revenge, in return for law and order. Law and order are only possible if there is an agent who has absolute power to enforce it. That agent is the *sovereign*. The sovereign is created by the contract but is not a party to the contract. Why? If the sovereign were a party to the contract then the sovereign could, in theory, violate the contract. If the sovereign violated the contract, there would have to be an agency to which we could appeal to enforce the contract. So either we would need a super-sovereign, ad infinitum, or we would be back in the state of nature. If each individual or group reserves the right to disagree with the sovereign or to claim that he violates the contract, then we are once more back in the state of nature. For these reasons, the sovereign cannot be a party to the contract; hence he cannot violate the contract; hence he can never be unjust. What is just or unjust is what the sovereign commands.

All of this is but another way of saying that justice is integral to the system itself, and the system is defined in terms of its built-in ends. It is the classic Aristotelian response to Platonism and to religiously based theories. Hobbes continually stressed that there could be no external standard for judging the sovereign, otherwise private individuals or groups would be forever meddling with government and once more we would be thrown back into the vile state of nature.

Sovereignty for Hobbes is a formal concept and not a person. Sovereignty may reside either in one person, a small group, or a democratically elected legislative body. Hobbes preferred a monarch as sovereign, but he distinctly rejected any theory of the divine right of kings. It does not matter which person is sovereign, for sovereignty is a role. The objection to small groups and democracies is that each member of the ruling group will immediately start jockeying for power, and this will undermine law and order and lead to favoritism and corruption. If it is argued against Hobbes that monarchs can also abuse power, Hobbes replies that a true absolute monarch would have nothing to fear or to gain since he has ultimate power and status and wealth. He would be less likely to meddle precisely because he is not subject to the insecurity that breeds the abuse of power. Once you accept Hobbes' assumptions about human psychology, his conclusions follow. Finally, Hobbes notes that the only natural right you cannot surrender to the sovereign is the right of self-preservation and, again, this follows from his psychology.

A number of criticisms have been and always will be raised against Hobbes' theory or any political theory. Rather than attempt to enumerate them, let us note the types or categories into which these criticisms fall, for the same points can be made against all theories. Some critics will accept the Aristotelian-teleological starting point but then go on to disagree with the particular details. That is, they will find either different built-in ends or locate them elsewhere. Other critics will reject the Aristotelian-teleological framework and argue that values exist externally (Platonic, religious), or that values are invented not discovered, or that values do not exist in any objective sense.

JOHN LOCKE (1632–1704)

The immediate practical problem that had prompted Hobbes to write and to make revolution unjustifiable was the political instability that, he believed, had been caused by the Puritan (Cromwell) rebellion in England. The provocation for Locke's *Two Treatises of Government* (1689) was to offer a rationale for a revolution.

Locke also begins his account with a state of nature, but it is very different from that of Hobbes. Locke's is largely peaceful and marked by cooperation. It is guided by a recognition of natural law to which all men have access through reason. What does this natural law reveal? It shows us that men are God's creatures and that He has put us here to achieve certain built-in ends, that the most important of these are life (preservation of the species), liberty, and property. If it were not for a few men corrupted by an inefficient reason and environment, there would never be need for a political society. Since a few such men do exist, a social contract is necessary.

Just as the natural law of the state of nature makes social cooperation possible, so the same assumption, that there is no ultimate conflict of interest among men, is found in Locke. This assumption is built into the social contract. There are, so to speak, two contracts in Locke. The first contract, among all men, leads to the formation of a society. It creates a common social good that is sovereign. The sovereign is not an agent in Locke's theory. The second contract is a contract between two parties, society on the one hand and government on the other. The government exists legitimately only so long as it keeps its end of the bargain to serve society. When it fails, or when government violates the contract, society is justified in removing it. Hence, revolution is justified, assuming there are no peaceful ways to substitute a new government, and then only in the name of the social good.

Two things should be noted. The existence of the so-called second contract between society and the government, when terminated, does not cause us to revert to an unpleasant state of nature as in Hobbes. Rather, society remains intact. Second, the reader will recognize in Locke's theory the forerunner of the theory expressed by Jefferson in the American *Declaration of Independence.*

The remaining central issue for Locke is how and who is to determine what the social good is? Locke provides for a democratically elected legislature (property qualification) to determine the social good. Majority rule is the pattern. Why does Locke opt for majority rule? To begin with, he believes that there is an objective social good, not just individual goods, and that this social good when properly understood reveals no ultimate conflict of interest among individuals. Second, Locke is famous for an epistemological doctrine, that is, a doctrine about how men reason, and this doctrine too owes its origin to Aristotle. Locke believes that we are born with minds each of which is a *tabula rasa* (blank tablet) and that all of our beliefs are derived from experience. If men disagree (or if they misbehave in the state of nature), it is because of different experiences or inadequate knowledge. The corrective is to consult the majority and discuss the issue for the majority will more often than not be right. Since all men are fundamentally the same, it is highly unlikely that the majority would adopt a policy that would not ultimately be for the good of all.

One other doctrine in Locke's theory deserves special mention and that is his justification of private property (one of the three supreme ends). If we have survival as one of our ends, then we have the right of subsistence. In addition Locke's conception of the individual involves the curious view that we as individuals own our own minds and bodies. If we own our own bodies then we own our labor, and if we own our labor then we are entitled to the fruits of our labor, that is, the property or objects into which we have put our labor. Ownership is restricted by the fact that all men have the right to subsistence and no one is entitled to the fruits of his labor beyond what he needs to survive comfortably. So far, Locke has assumed a strictly agrarian economy in which the products of our labor are to be understood literally as perishable agriculture. This sounds almost like Aristotle. However, when the economy changed to a commercial one using money, which is not perishable, there is no limit on the amount of money that we can accumulate. In addition, Locke argues that private property increases productivity, and this serves the end of the survival of the community much better than the original communal ownership described in the Bible.

Although Locke's argument is intended to justify private property, it is easy to see what is going to happen. Later members of the Anglo-American liberal tradition will interpret the right of private property as the right to economic security. Further, following Locke's own pattern of noting historical changes in the organization of the economy, his inheritors will argue that greater government regulation and control, if not outright ownership, of property is necessitated in, let us say, an industrial or technological economy. Nor can anyone object to this arrangement, for Locke and his followers subscribe to the notion of an objective social good.

A number of paradoxes have begun to emerge in the discussion of Hobbes and Locke. Both begin with a teleological account of what is basic to man, but they disagree on what man's true end is. Hobbes says survival, whereas Locke says life, liberty, and property. As time progresses the list grows longer in the minds of some people. Since government is to provide the necessary means to the achievement of our ends, the views on the function of government changes. Hobbes anticipated that government would provide only law and order. Locke adds the protection of private property. Modern welfare-state supporters expect and demand that the government provide everything from the cradle to the grave. The entire discussion depends upon what you find to be the built-in ends of human beings. There is, unfortunately, no general agreement on this issue. Moreover, a good many social scientists believe that the issue is hopeless because they believe that the whole concept of teleology is unscientific and unempirical, that there can never be a scientific answer to what mankind needs.

The concept of freedom offers a good illustration of this paradox. To be free, for both Hobbes and Locke and all liberals, is to be unencumbered by arbitrary external constraints that prevent us from fulfilling ourselves. For the classical liberal who derives his position from Hobbes, government makes us free by providing security. For the modern liberal who derives his position from Locke, the potential list of what government must do for us is without limit. From the latter point of view, the more the government intervenes in our lives the more free we become. Modern liberals hasten to add that this interference is temporary until men are educated enough to achieve that condition Locke ascribes to a perfect state of nature wherein government will become unnecessary.

The other paradox has to do with the majority. Later thinkers like John Stuart Mill will question the validity of an assumed objective social good. If no such good exists, then majority rule can become a form of tyranny. Then there is the problem of what to do if (*a*) the majority is misinformed and (*b*) the means of communication (schools, media, etc.) are controlled by wicked men so that the majority cannot have its views properly corrected. Would this justify a revolution and a temporary dictatorship led by an elite who do know what the true objective social good is? Do they have the responsibility and the right to show us the way? Are they justified in using force to "free" us?

G. W. F. HEGEL (1770–1831)

The serious obstacle to a coherent political philosophy in the British liberal tradition that began with Hobbes and Locke was the inability to relate clearly the individual to the community. Hegel's political philosophy is, in part, an attempt to circumvent this problem by denying the abstract, rational, and calculating individualism of that tradition and its conception of individual freedom. Hegel would also argue that abstract and static individualism is part of an outmoded and static conception of political and social institutions. Hegel was among the first to take seriously the historical dimension of the social world.

In response to the foregoing, Hegel constructed a vast philosophical edifice in which ultimate reality, which he called the *Absolute,* was understood as a spiritual entity. The Absolute reveals itself in a number of ways. For our purposes we need only be concerned with how the Absolute reveals itself as objective spirit in the social world. For Hegel, the Absolute progresses teleologically. This is Aristotelianism again, but with a new twist. Aristotle had thought of the world as a cyclical one in which we constantly rediscover and reconfirm empirically the built-in end of institutions. For Hegel, teleology is historical. The whole of human history reveals a pattern that he called the dialectic. In each specifiable period there is a particular social pattern, but it must give way in the next period to a new pattern. The new pattern is not a complete novelty but retains elements of the old institutions reconstituted. The significant unit in history is the nation.

Objective spirit reveals itself in the nation in three institutions: the family, civil society, and the state. As in Aristotle, the abstract individual can only be understood in terms of his social roles and can only truly fulfill himself by participation in the larger social whole. For Hegel, the state is morally superior even to civil society. This is very different from Locke. It is only in the state that we can produce a higher level of personal self-realization and a form of society in which man gains freedom by a new synthesis of his interests as man and as citizen. Hegel opposed democracy because it encouraged consideration only of private interests. Instead he favored a corporative state, represented by various civil institutions.

KARL MARX (1818–1883)

Marx, following Hegel, rejected both the abstract individualism of the British liberal tradition and the static conception of the social world. Like Hegel, he postulated an historical teleology in which social and political institutions progress to a built-in end. But Marx also rejected some of the specific details of Hegel's view. He rejected Hegel's idealism (Absolute as spiritual), and he rejected the view that history had already achieved its final end in the nation-state. Instead, Marx argued that history had material foundations (as reflected in economic institutions) and identified the economic class as the basic historical unit. He also postulated that one more and future state of historical development was in the works.

Before continuing with our discussion of Marx, a few summary comments are in order. First, both Hegel and Marx still believe that political philosophy discovers absolute and objective norms of behavior. These norms may vary with each historical period, but within each period and in the final stage there is always an objective norm. These norms are teleological and allegedly discovered in experience (e.g., abstracted from the study of history). These norms are also internal to man via his social institutions, and in this sense both Hegel and Marx are part of the modern tradition as opposed to the classical-medieval tradition.

Second, the reader may wonder how Hegel and Marx can disagree. This question is analogous to the question of how can Hobbes and Locke disagree. Both of these questions are ways of asking how can teleologists establish that their estimation of the built-in ends is correct as opposed to what other teleologists say. The problem becomes increasingly acute when we bring in history, and most acute when we deal with the unexperienced future. Continental teleologists can no more provide a convincing answer to this problem than could British liberals. The proliferation of versions and sects of Marxism is as widespread as the proliferation of versions of modern liberalism.

Third, the teleological and hierarchical conceptions of the social world can be used to justify either an extremely conservative (Hegel) or an extremely radical (Marx) conception of policy. Within this conception of the social world, every institution has a built-in end, and each institution forms part of a larger whole in which it serves an even higher end, culminating in some one all-encompassing system. The rights of the individual are meaningless outside of the social whole, and piecemeal reform is meaningless in a world where no one social practice can be isolated from another. Either one must accept the system as a whole or restore it to its proper functioning *or* one must acquiesce in the revolution without tampering or moderating or restricting the ultimate logic of the revolution. The revolution is also built into the system.

Let us return to Marx. Briefly, the details are as follows:

Stage I (Pre-historical): There is communal ownership and an agrarian economy.

Stage II (Ancient world): Due to the division of labor, we find private property in an economy that is both agrarian and commercial. Private property encompasses not only land and objects but people (slaves) as well.

Stage III (Feudal): The economy is agrarian but ownership of the land is communal. The lord owns the land jointly with his serfs who cannot be separated from their particular plots. Serfs have rights and are in this sense not slaves.

Stage IV (Bourgeois Capitalism): The economy is now industrial and commercial, and we have private property. The capitalist owns the forces of production, but he does not own the laborers. Laborers are free to sell their labor to the highest bidder and, in this sense, are more free than serfs.

Stage V (Future): The economy will be industrial and ownership will be communal. This stage will provide the greatest freedom because we shall be working together and not engaged in destructive and wasteful competition. It will be marked by the absence of alienation (what Hobbesian man feels about the world), exploitation, and the state as the instrument of coercion and repression. In each of the above stages human relationships are the effects of economic organization, and economic organization is a reflection of a progressive unfolding of history. Shifts from one stage to the next are not deliberately planned by men but result from conflicts and contradictions within the old system in the face of a new and changing reality.

J.-J. ROUSSEAU (1712–1778)

We shall now backtrack to Jean-Jacques Rousseau and treat him as a thinker with a unique, alternative political philosophy. Like other modern political philosophers, Rousseau rejects the classical-medieval tradition of an external natural order to which we must conform and to which we have access through reason. Again, like the other moderns, he finds the norms within man. But all similarity to the other political philosophers we have discussed ends at this point. Rousseau denies the teleology of either the individual or the community. The norms are not discovered in any way, rather they are willed into existence. The norms are conventional.

The key to understanding Rousseau's political philosophy lies in his new conception of freedom, a view that greatly influenced Kant's conception of morality. For Rousseau, freedom is not the absence of external constraint (Hobbes and Locke), nor is freedom self-fulfillment within the social collectivity (Hegel and Marx). Rather, *freedom* is obeying rules that you prescribe for yourself. Since human beings have no fixed nature (no innate teleology), we are free to follow any path we will. This is not to be construed as an invitation to self-indulgence, for self-indulgence presupposes that we have needs and wants independent of our will. This is the meaning of his statement that "Man is born free . . . "

If we as individuals are free in this metaphysical sense, then how can we account for society and obligation? There is no external or internal natural order that provides for either. Rousseau's answer is to use the concept of a social contract, but it is unlike the contract in either Hobbes or Locke. Since individuals are free they can have no natural interests or rights to be protected by a contract. Here Rousseau would agree with Hegel's critique of Hobbes and Locke. The contract is not a mere matter of making and keeping an agreement. Nor is there any natural community to which we must belong. Here Rousseau would reject the views of Hegel. The social world is willed into existence and is sustained by that will. The conventional entity created by the contract is the General Will.

The *General Will* is the most controversial element in Rousseau's theory. There is little agreement among readers on what he means. But some things he says about it are clear. It is not what *I* want, nor what a *group* wants, nor what the majority wants, nor even what all of us want. All of the foregoing are transitory and unreliable. The General Will is assumed to be permanent. The General Will is also absolute and never wrong. That is, it cannot be judged by external standards (Platonic, religious, teleological, or whimsical). It is an absolute convention.

How can a convention be absolute? Conventions are absolute insofar as they are consistent with the only permanent thing we know, our freedom. So the General Will must be understood in terms of freedom. The social contract is a creation of free individuals who unanimously consent to a set of procedural rules. Having consented to the means, they must consent to the consequences or results (this is the opposite of teleology, where the end justifies the means). Since the rules are self-imposed, our freedom is intact. There are many other provisions but we note only the most important. The laws must be enforced, because if we do not make people abide by rules they have prescribed for themselves, we are not respecting their freedom. This is the meaning of "forcing people to be free."

How is the general will to be determined? Since it is a convention it cannot be discovered. Moreover, any convention or set of conventions must be continually interpreted and re-interpreted. There is never a definitive determination. There may be post-hoc modifications, that is, we can always say we were mistaken in our past determinations. That is why it is a mistake to see any totalitarian implications in this view. Nor, as Locke would have it, is the majority always right. The majority will may be but is not necessarily and always the General Will. (J. S. Mill would surely have agreed with this). Rousseau favored majority rule (if originally agreed to unanimously as a procedural rule), but he did not confuse it with the General Will. Later majorities can overturn earlier majorities. What Rousseau would have agreed with is the notion that if the majority opposes something (as opposed to favoring something), then surely at that moment what was opposed was not the General Will.

Perhaps what Rousseau meant by the General Will is best represented in the British tradition by the common law, and the reverence expressed for it by his contemporaries like Burke or his onetime friend David Hume. There is an assumed sacredness to the law and the assumption that it can evolve (not progress) and be reinterpreted, but it is nevertheless an absolute.

POLITICAL SCIENCE AND POLITICAL PHILOSOPHY

Most of the great political philosophers from Plato to Marx would have found it very odd to be told that in making recommendations and evaluations they were not being scientific. The notion of a value-free and purely descriptive political science would have seemed unintelligible to them. Where does the notion of a value-free social science come from? It is a form of empiricism (ultimately Aristotelian) in which teleology and final causes have been eliminated. It is to describe and to explain the social world without belief in the possibility of finding built-in ends. Since it is Aristotelian, it rejects out of hand any other source of value such as Platonic or religious.

Why does anyone accept the empiricist (Aristotelian) approach without believing in final causes and goals? This is a position known as *positivism*. The answer is again historical. Since the advent of modern physical science (Galileo to Newton), the belief in a deterministic and mechanical world structure instead of a teleological one has become dominant. Starting with Hobbes, this deterministic structure has been extended to man. In his political philosophy, Hobbes ignored the contradiction between his determinism and his teleology. The same can be said for Marx. If one takes the belief in determinism about man to be the literal truth, making evaluations is an incomprehensible act. One can merely note that such and such values are held. Nothing can be done about such values for they are a brute fact.

What happens when one combines a belief in determinism with a view that political thinking is to be purely descriptive and non-normative? One result is to end up seeing the social world as an unavoidable power struggle. First, it breeds cynicism and then it breeds *fascism*. As a political "philosophy" unique to the twentieth century, fascism is both an attempt to "tell it like it is" and a way of rationalizing coercion and ultimately totalitarianism. For a fascist, all political philosophy including itself is rationalization and manipulation. The only difference is that fascists do not practice self-deception. Political knowledge can only be knowledge of the manipulation of social structures.

What are the alternatives? The simple answer is to reject determinism with respect to human behavior. Beyond that one must reconsider how values are to be understood: Platonic, religious, teleological, conventionalistic, etc. Are there other possibilities?

QUESTIONS FOR STUDY

1. What did Aristotle mean when he said that "Man is by nature a political animal"?

2. "Liberalism used to mean individual liberty, but now it means state paternalism." Explain this remark.

3. Compare and contrast the doctrine of the social contract in Hobbes, Locke, and Rousseau.

4. What do Hobbes and Marx have in common? How do they differ?

5. Three different conceptions of *freedom* have emerged so far in Western political philosophy. What are they?

6. What is the major difference between classical and modern political philosophers?

9

Epistemology: The Problem of Knowledge

INTRODUCTION

Epistemology, or the theory of knowledge, is intimately related to another branch of philosophy, metaphysics. Metaphysics deals with the ultimate nature of reality. Depending upon what one believes the ultimate nature of reality and man's place within it to be, one will formulate a theory of what knowledge is. Of course, it will be asked, doesn't one already have to *know* what that ultimate reality is in order to state what knowledge is, and if so do we not then already know what it is to know? The answer is, in a qualified sense, yes. However, since different philosophers have made different claims about ultimate reality, they will invariably give different explanations of knowledge. As is to be expected, when one philosopher disagrees with another philosopher's explanation he inevitably claims that the other philosopher denies the possibility of knowledge. What he really means is that the other philosopher does not accept his preferred view of ultimate reality. Furthermore, it is not very helpful to analyze knowledge first and then use the correct analysis to find out what the world is really like. How could one know that one's analysis is correct? What language or concepts would we use for a pure epistemology? So it seems that we must presuppose a metaphysics, a view of ultimate reality, in order to engage in epistemology. Finally,

161

if we already knew completely what ultimate reality is, there wouldn't be much point to stating what knowledge is. It is because philosophers think that they know something, but not everything, that they try to formulate a theory of knowledge. The purpose seems to be to extend our knowledge, or at least articulate it clearly.

The foregoing discussion provides us with a starting point into epistemology. We shall begin with the historical claim that at different times philosophers have taken one kind of alleged knowledge and have used it as a model to see if they could extract from that model some notion of what all knowledge must be like. Since different models have been preeminent, different theories of knowledge have emerged. If this procedure on the part of philosophers seems question begging, it is good to recall what we said in the previous paragraph—namely, that no analysis of knowledge can proceed without assuming that we already have some sample or example of it. We shall find that in the history of Western philosophy, three different analyses have been given.

PLATONISM

Plato was the first to formulate the issues in epistemology. As a background to his reasons for doing so, we recall Plato's confrontation with the Sophists. Some Sophists denied the possibility of ever having objective beliefs about the world. In the moral and social realms they went so far as to advocate a kind of cultural *relativism*, the view that all norms are relative to the particular time and place in which one lives. Hence, no norms are intrinsically superior to others. Protagoras had generalized this to the thesis that "man is the measure of all things." Plato believed otherwise. He believed that there were objective and absolute grounds for preferring some norms to others. Although he believed this, the question is could he prove it? More important, did he know what a good proof was?

Plato thought he did. First, he argued that there was an ultimate reality and that it was unchanging. This is another way of saying that reality has a permanent structure. If there was to be absolute and objective knowledge, it would have to be identical to that permanent structure. Second, Plato believed that geometry was an unquestionable example of knowledge, that geometry was knowledge of the permanent underlying structure of the physical world, and that geometry gave us a clear and undisputed example of what it meant to prove something.

Geometry, then, is Plato's model of knowledge. What is geometry like as a form of knowledge? It begins with definitions of key terms like "point" and "line." What is peculiar about these definitions is that they are not empirical, nor do they define what we can imagine (picture in our mind). For example, a "point" has no dimensions. We may draw a dot on a page, like the period at the end of a sentence, and say that the dot represents the "point." But the dot is not itself a point, no matter how small we draw it. Nevertheless, we can conceive of a point (conceiving is not imagining). So knowledge begins with what is conceivable but not experienceable. Sometimes this is described as *intuition*. With these intuitions we are able to construct axioms, that is, principles that cannot be proved but are the starting points of all proofs. Given the axioms, we are able to derive (deduce, prove) theorem one. After we prove theorem one, we can prove theorem two, etc.

There are two different kinds of knowledge. There is, first, the knowledge that is proved or deduced from other knowledge. Second, there is the knowledge that is intuited, that comes to us in an act of intellectual vision, and without which there would be no proof. Inevitably, questions will be raised about this intuited kind of knowledge. Plato is adamant that it does not come from experience, that it cannot be proved (otherwise we would have an infinite regress or a vicious circle), and that there can be no definitive criterion for distinguishing correct from incorrect intuitions. Such a criterion would either have to be proved (circular argument again) or be itself intuited.

There is a kind of test that can be performed on an alleged first principle or intuited truth to determine if it qualifies. That test is to try to imagine or to conceive of the opposite of that principle. If the opposite, or contradictory, cannot be conceived or we cannot even imagine what an experience of the opposite would be, then we are secure in believing our principle to be an intuited truth. A principle that passes this test can be called *a priori* (not Plato's expression but a later technical term in philosophy). To be *a priori* means two things: non-empirical (not derived from experience), and the opposite is inconceivable. For example, the statement that a triangle has three sides is *a priori*. We cannot conceive or even imagine a two-sided or four-sided triangle. It just would not be a triangle. Nor do we learn from experience that a triangle has three sides by being shown examples. We must already know what a triangle is in order to recognize the sample.

Let us summarize the main features of Plato's theory of knowledge. First, Plato's epistemology is tied to his metaphysics. Beyond the world of our experience, there is a permanent, unchangeable, and absolute structure. To have knowledge is to grasp in some kind of intellectual vision what the structure is. Subjectively, knowledge is a kind of vision or intuition. Objectively, knowledge is access to an indubitable and unchanging structure. The object of knowledge is external to man and is there whether we realize it or not. It is because Plato thinks that there is an absolute structure that he defines knowledge in the way he does. Second, Plato does not think that we can "know" the world of our sense experience. The everyday world of our experience is unstable and changing. Since knowledge is apprehension of the unchangeable, there is no knowledge of the everyday world. Third, given what has been said so far, certain kinds of criticisms of Plato's theory turn

out to be irrelevant. All criticisms about the unreliability of everyday experience would actually reinforce the persuasiveness of Plato's theory. Moreover, arguments to the effect that the examples Plato gives from mathematics
are trivial because there is no way of showing that the ideal concepts in our
mind guarantee anything about the world of experience are also irrelevant.
Plato would not deny the *gap* between our ideal concepts and the world we
experience. Fourth, Plato's challenge to those who argue from experience is
to try and make sense of experience without using ideal concepts, that is,
concepts that go beyond our actual, if not possible, experience. Finally, we
note that Plato's conception of knowledge is not technological, that is, it is
not designed to give us control over nature. In a literal sense, we cannot control an unchangeable structure precisely because it is unchangeable. Such
knowledge as Plato allows can guide us in making the experienced world
more like the ideal.

How then would Plato respond to those Sophists who preached a kind of
relativism? To begin with, Plato would point out that there can be no disproof that an absolute structure exists. To disprove Plato we would have to
possess the kind of knowledge that Sophists say is not available. This does
not show that Plato is right, but it shows that Sophists would be making only
the modest claim that such knowledge is not presently available. To put it
bluntly, no Sophists can claim to know that we cannot know. To know that
we cannot know is to know at least one thing. Hence, the Sophist would be
contradicting himself. Almost all rebuttals of Sophists and skepticism are of
this pattern.

But there is another kind of criticism of Plato that is not so easily handled.
Suppose that instead of denying that there is knowledge, the Sophist or the
skeptic merely criticizes a particular claim to know. Suppose that I claim that
today is Friday, and suppose further that the skeptic challenges me to justify
my claim. I might try to justify my claim by showing that it is consistent with
certain generally accepted criteria for making claims. The trouble with this
is that the skeptic may challenge the criteria. Now in response to this move
by the skeptic, Plato and a good many other philosophers would point out
that the only way the skeptic can challenge one criterion is by showing that
it is in conflict with another criterion. But if the skeptic does that, he must at
least accept the other criterion. This is true. The skeptic is always committed
to some criterion or to some frame of reference, otherwise his challenge
would be meaningless. But while this is an important point, it is not to be
confused with the argument in the previous paragraph. To presume a criterion is not the same as to contradict oneself. The skeptic can easily admit
that everything he says presupposes something else, but this in no way
shows that what is presupposed is a form of knowledge. Besides, what I presuppose in one context or at one time I can challenge at another. This may
or may not be embarrassing to the skeptic, but the one thing it cannot do is
to prove that Plato is right. Here the skeptic can even turn the tables on

Plato. No skeptic can disprove Plato's position but that is because there is no such thing as proof or disproof. Proof and disproof exist only within Plato's theory. To challenge Plato's theory is to refuse to play his game. Asserting the existence of changing frames of reference is what the Sophist started out saying, and as long as the assertion refers to the frames of reference in discourse and not some ultimate reality, the skeptic is consistent. Here Plato's only reply would be to reaffirm his convictions about the absolute reality, and in so doing we shall have traveled beyond epistemology into metaphysics.

ARISTOTLE

Although Aristotle shares much in common with Plato, Aristotle's approach to knowledge is very different. Let us begin by noting the similarities and then go on to stress the differences. Aristotle accepts Plato's contention that a good explanation or argument is a deduction, that is, a proof. But Aristotle does not use geometry as his model, and he does not accept the notion of a transcendent realm of Forms. So Aristotle has to offer a different account of how we arrive at first principles. In addition, Aristotle accepts Plato's contention that the object of knowledge is external to man and, therefore, that knowledge is access to a certain permanent and unchanging structure. But that structure is embodied in the world of everyday experience. How a structure can be unchanging and still embodied in a changing succession of objects is something that we discussed in the previous chapter on Aristotle.

It is here that we can begin to understand the vast and important difference between Plato and Aristotle. Although both assert that knowledge is external to man, they nevertheless have different theories about the object of knowledge. For Plato, the object of knowledge is supersensible Forms. He frequently talks as if there is a real problem about whether there is knowledge or whether knowledge exists. What Plato is really asking is whether we can have access to supersensible Forms. Aristotle never asks whether knowledge exists or is possible. He takes it for granted that we have knowledge and concentrates on describing it, how we obtain it, and explaining its presuppositions. The object of knowledge for Aristotle is the structure of our experience. In an important sense, for Aristotle we experience our own knowledge. Right from the beginning these two theorists have conflicting theories on what knowledge is about.

Experience, then, is a kind of final arbiter for Aristotle. Our experience of the world is not to be explained in terms of something else (e.g., Platonic Forms) but is itself the explanation of everything else. Given this perspective, a number of implications follow. First, there must be some kind of *basic pure experience* unmediated by any judgment or frame of reference. This is why Aristotle gives a passive account of perception. Second, this basic pure experience is either infallible or can be overruled only by another basic experience that is infallible. Third, skeptics may be dismissed by appeal to the appropriate basic pure experience. As in Plato, Aristotle points out that the skeptic can only challenge one item of alleged pure experience by appeal to another. Any dispute can be settled by appeal to the appropriate expert or proper frame of reference. Aristotle believes that he can contain the skeptic by continually reminding us that the skeptic must himself presuppose some reference point. Fourth, once we move beyond perception to the higher and more complex forms of intellectual activity where we begin to combine concepts and to make judgments, we run the risk of error. Fifth, since the higher faculties depend upon the lower (perception) Aristotle implies that it is always possible to relate and correct errors of judgment by a return to experience (perception). Aristotle simply denies the existence of the Platonic gap between experience and our knowledge. Sixth, we should stress the role of teleology in Aristotle's epistemology, for he uses teleological biology as a model for explaining how knowledge exists and functions. There is an implicit optimistic belief that as experiences accumulate they tend to confirm the patterns in events and that in the long run the experts shall always agree. Without this teleological assumption and the functional interdependence of the perceptual apparatus and embodied forms, it is difficult to see how this theory could be taken seriously. Finally, like Plato, Aristotle does not have a technological conception of knowledge. Experience discloses a natural order external to us to which we both belong and conform, rather than one that we can manipulate.

SKEPTICISM

We have already said something about skepticism, but now we can discuss it as a movement and an epistemological tradition. Not so surprisingly, skepticism as a philosophical methodology was originally formulated within Plato's Academy in the third century B.C. The most important of the skeptics was Carneades (213–128 B.C.). These so-called *Academic skeptics* rejected Plato's own metaphysics and stressed the moral posture of Socrates' raising questions and saying that "All I know is that I know nothing." The Academics concentrated on attacking the Aristotelian position as it was then represented by the Stoics and Epicureans. Both Epicureans and Stoics had insisted upon the infallibility of sensations (even when I have a hallucination it is in some sense true that I see things like ghosts, even if only in my mind), and some Stoics believed that perceptions were infallible as signs of the true nature of reality. The Academics responded that there was no way intrinsic to experience of distinguishing between real perceptions and illusory ones.

The skeptical maneuver is as follows. Any challenge must be made from a perspective that accepts at least temporarily the truth of that perspective.

For example, I see an oar in the water and it *looks* bent. But I know that it is really not bent because when I touch it, it *feels* smooth and if I remove it from the water, it will *appear* straight. The latter two experiences are presumed reliable in order to declare the first unreliable. Although the skeptic must temporarily accept the experiences he can still remind us that they are subject to later challenge. The Aristotelian will reply that the later challenge must presuppose the reliability of still another experience. Yet here the skeptic triumphs by insisting that if the frame of reference is only assumed to be reliable, and if we keep changing our minds or can change our minds about the reliability of any frame of reference, there is no guarantee that there are permanent frames of reference. Without assuming the unproved and unprovable assumption that teleologically we shall arrive at permanent standards and frames of reference, the Aristotelian cannot reply. Perhaps this is why Platonists adhere to a belief in Forms. The skeptic cannot disprove that Forms exist; he can merely assert his disbelief. In the end we have a skeptic versus Platonic standoff. If one grants to the Aristotelian his belief in teleology as an act of faith, and not a fact, then there is a skeptic versus Aristotelian standoff as well.

A second school of skeptics, the *Pyrrhonians,* was best represented by Sextus Empiricus (200 A.D.). The Pyrrhonians attacked both dogmatists and even the Academics. Dogmatism fails to produce knowledge without a criterion, but the criterion is not itself an item of knowledge. To bring in a second criterion for the first criterion is to slip into an infinite regress. The Academics, although rejecting infallibility and certainty, apparently believed in some distinction between the probable and the improbable. Against the Academics, the Pyrrhonians argued that we can never be sure of even this distinction. For their part, some Pyrrhonians advocated trying to achieve *ataraxia,* which is the peace of mind of indifference. Other Pyrrhonians suggested a view that will become increasingly important in the later history of epistemology. They suggested that being reasonable (as opposed to certain) involved social conventions. Epistemology is concerned with norms that are conventional and have nothing to do with absolute Forms or alleged patterns in objects being duplicated in our mind or discourse. This amounts to a skeptical version of Plato's gap—it explains why our "knowledge" always exceeds the bounds of experience.

We may summarize skepticism by noting the different kinds. There is first particular skepticism, that is, skepticism about particular claims to knowledge. Here the skeptic limits his critique to some, but not all, claims to knowledge. There is second a mitigated skepticism that admits that knowledge (as certainty) is a meaningful concept but never achieveable in practice. All that is possible is limited to probability. Third, there is a form of general skepticism that denies all knowledge in an epistemological sense. This position becomes self-refuting only when it claims that we know at least that much. Fourth, there is a logical form of skepticism or metaphysical skepticism that denies that the concept of knowledge as access to an external structure is meaningful. Knowledge does exist, but it has nothing to do with grasping absolute and permanent external structures. Knowledge exists as a set of institutional and social norms or conventions that are neither absolute nor permanent. This last position shows the extent to which the theory of knowledge is tied to metaphysics.

The success of the skeptical attack on classical Platonists and Aristotelians can be gauged by the medieval response to this controversy. Saint Augustine asserted that skepticism could be overcome only by revelation. He adopted a version of Platonism in which first principles come to our soul (some of whose functions are not influenced by our body) from God. The Forms are thoughts in God's mind. Later a kind of religious Pyrrhonism flourished, as with Erasmus, wherein it was argued that we should suspend judgment and accept social or religious conventions.

MODERN EPISTEMOLOGY

Modern epistemology, like modern metaphysics, begins with Descartes. He was concerned epistemologically to defend the validity of science and to reinstate the Platonic point of view. The opportunity for doing so was presented by Galileo's introduction of the distinction between primary and secondary qualities. Galileo distinguished between those qualities or properties of objects that are mathematically measurable, and therefore both objective and real, and those qualities or properties of objects that are not measurable, and therefore subjective. Size and speed are measurable, and therefore objective. Color is not measurable and is therefore subjective. The *primary qualities* were measurable; the *secondary qualities* were not. This distinction was reinforced by studies that indicated that color varied with the condition of the nervous system and the environment. Primary qualities showed no such variation. Descartes reinforced this point by describing an experiment with a piece of wax. When viewed under one set of conditions it has one set of properties, like being solid, colored, etc. When heated, the wax changed its properties, yet we still intellectually apprehend the wax as wax.

The experiment and the distinction between primary and secondary qualities served a number of purposes for Descartes. First, it underlined the unreliability of the senses. Second, it offered a stark contrast between our experience which is subjective and the real world which is objective and not given directly to experience. Third, the real world is describable in mathematical terms. So far this state of affairs is promising to the Platonist. But the very distinction between our subjective experience and the real objective world creates a space for skepticism. How would we know for sure whether our mathematical theories describe the real world in a reliable way? Even the scientists admitted that we had no direct access to the real world.

This skeptical problem Descartes proceeded to solve. What is needed is a deductive system whose first principles can never be challenged by the skeptic. No one had ever produced such a set of indubitable and unchallengeable first principles. Descartes thought that he could do this by beating the skeptic at his own game. In his discussion of method, Descartes formulates a *methodic doubt,* an artificial device to challenge everything until he discovers what is unchallengeable. He plays the skeptical game so well that he even invents the possibility of an *archdeceiver* who sees to it that all of our beliefs are false. Just when things look like they are at their worst, Descartes hits upon something indubitable.

1. I can doubt everything except that I doubt. In order to doubt, I must doubt. Thus, the only thing that I cannot doubt is that I doubt. This is a version of the traditional response to skepticism by noting that any challenge must take something as fixed.

2. Doubt is a form of thought, so in doubting I am thinking. When I think, I perform some act. Therefore, as long as I think, at least my thought exists (even if my body does not). I think, therefore I am *("Cogito ergo sum").* At the very least, I, says Descartes, exist as a thinking (mental) being. *I exist.*

3. Among the thoughts in my mind (which are still subjective and tell me nothing yet about the objective world) there is an idea of a perfect being— namely, God. Does this idea correspond to anything in the real world? That depends upon the origin of the idea. It cannot be derived from my experience (which is unreliable anyway) because I experience nothing as perfect. I cannot have invented the idea of God as a perfect being because I myself am not perfect. *The idea of something perfect can only be caused by something that is itself perfect.* Therefore, there must be a perfect being. *God exists.*

4. Since God is perfect he would not intentionally deceive me. One of the things that God presents to us is a world that can be understood by mathematical science. Therefore, the *world exists,* and in principle science is reliable.

This argument has given rise to much controversy and has been challenged by someone or other at every point. There is one challenge that is not so controversial and that is crucial for later epistemology. The principle invoked by Descartes in the third part of the argument above is the causal principle that states that every property of the effect must be the result of an analogous property in the cause. That is what permits us to infer back from the effect to what the cause must be. That is why we cannot invent the idea of God. Earlier and elsewhere, Descartes had defended this causal principle as *a priori* and self-evident and as in the same category as the principle of contradiction. In his terms, it was a clear and distinct idea. Ironically, we of course recognize it as a principle from Aristotle's physics, originally derived from teleological biology. Despite all that Descartes does as a modern scientist to undermine Aristotle's physics, he has taken over a principle of that physics and defended it as a metaphysical truth from the Platonic point of view! There is no better example of how the history of science and philosophy are intertwined and of how what seems purely rational to one thinker can be shown to have distinct historical roots. We shall see shortly what happens when that principle is undermined.

The general response to Descartes was to strike at the perennial soft spot of Platonism, namely, the intuition of first principles. Questioning the causal principle is one example. Descartes had described the distinguishing mark of first principles as being clear and distinct ideas. Could we really know what was clear and distinct? Arguments over the content of such ideas indicated that we could not.

The specific challenge to Descartes' Platonism predictably came from those who appealed to the Aristotelian empirical tradition. But Aristotelianism also had to be refurbished in the light of modern science. In the first place, the whole of modern science seemed to be a rejection of Aristotelian physics with its teleology and its final causes. In its place, atomism was revived. Second, the distinction between primary and secondary qualities created a special problem for Aristotelians. If the ultimate constituents of reality are unperceived and perhaps unperceivable atoms, and if the immediate object of experience is so different from the ultimate object of reality, how can we appeal to experience at all? The distinction between reality and appearance becomes as acute a problem for modern Aristotelians as for classical Platonists.

There were two kinds of responses to this situation. Reversing the chronological order, we shall first discuss John Locke. First, Locke attacked the possibility of innate ideas, that is, he rejects the possibility of *a priori* knowledge. Next, he argued that the direct objects of experience, which he insisted upon calling *ideas,* are *sources of knowledge* about ultimate unperceived reality. The primary qualities really represent what the objects are like. The secondary qualities such as color do not. The secondary qualities are subjective reactions caused in us by primary qualities. For example, light waves reflected from colorless molecules strike our retina and produce images of color in the mind. We have an image of color, but the molecule is not itself colored. How does Locke or any scientist know that this is happening? The answer is an appeal to the causal principle that the properties of effects (our experience) represent properties of the causes. Not only will this principle be challenged, but some of Locke's critics like Berkeley and Hume will point out that there is no way of comparing in our experience the primary quality with the ultimate object, and, hence, there is no justification for claiming that one resembles the other.

Aristotelian-empiricist epistemology has always subscribed to the so-called *correspondence theory of truth.* According to this theory, a statement is true if it corresponds to reality and is hence checkable empirically, and a statement is false if it does not so correspond. For example, suppose I say that the cover of this book is blue. We have only to look at it in order to determine if the statement is true or false. There are two major problems that this theory has to face. First, many scientific statements are so complex and refer to unobserved, if not unobservable, entities that it would seem impractical to decide their truth or falsity in this manner. Second, if we take the theory itself and make it into a statement, there is no way of empirically checking the theory.

> S_1: "A statement is true if and only if it corresponds to reality."

Is S_1 itself true? The correspondence theory seems to make an exception of itself. In the twentieth century, logical positivists formulated a similar principle, the *verification theory of meaning*, according to which a statement is meaningful if it is either analytic (e.g., statements in mathematics; we shall discuss this term below) or empirically verifiable. But the theory itself is neither analytic nor empirically verifiable. No Platonist would be surprised by this state of affairs. Plato's gap reminds us that our knowledge and its presuppositions always exceed the bounds of our experience. This seems even truer in the light of modern science.

A more sophisticated version of empiricism is to be found in the earlier French philosophers and critics of Descartes, specifically Pierre Gassendi and Marin Mersenne. They deny that our experience is a source of knowledge about ultimate objects. Instead they argue the position that *experience is itself the object of knowledge*. Mersenne claimed that we could rely upon our experience and make predictions about future experience without having to worry about ultimate objects. Gassendi claimed that his atomic theory was a useful hypothesis for interpreting our experience. In the twentieth century this version of empiricism was defended by Moritz Schlick, who argued that scientific theories were not laws or statements about reality but rules for interpreting experience.

It is not immediately clear whether the above view is a strict form of empiricism or a sophisticated form of logical skepticism. Usually, it reverts to a form of Aristotelian empiricism because it believes that there is a strict structure to experience (a turning of experience into a peculiar kind of object) so that future developments in science and technology will allow us to describe reality behind the appearance. When the American pragmatist C. S. Peirce said that truth is what the scientists will all agree upon in the end, he was expressing the implicit teleology of this form of empiricism. The ambiguity of the relationship between reality and appearance also permits modern epistemologists to ignore the issue of how a modern conception of scientific knowledge as technology is possible in a world of permanent structures.

THE COPERNICAN REVOLUTION IN PHILOSOPHY

Hume and Kant introduced a Copernican Revolution into philosophy in the eighteenth century. Why is this revolution called Copernican? There are several reasons. In the sixteenth century, Copernicus, an astronomer not a philosopher, offered the hypothesis that the sun was the center of the universe instead of the earth. The crucial aspect of his theory for Hume and Kant was that the earth became an active participant in the solar system as it moved around the sun. Hitherto it had been thought of as a stationary object and passive spectator of the heavenly spectacle. The analogy that Hume and Kant draw is that the knower is part of the knowing process so that knowledge can no longer be explained or understood solely in terms of its object. What is revolutionary about this view is that it denies that knowledge is the attempt to grasp a structure external to man. This is not just a theory in epistemology but a metaphysical view as well. Hume and Kant are not settling for a second-best kind of knowledge and giving up on the possibility of knowing the real world. What they are saying is that the world is not composed of objects each with an essence or set of properties independent of other objects. Every object interacts with every other object. It is meaningless to talk about isolating an object and grasping its structure. In the act of knowing, we talk not about the world *per se* but about how man-knows-the-world.

In one very important sense, both Hume and Kant are rejecting the Aristotelian-empirical epistemology. The real shock produced by the Copernican hypothesis in astronomy is that there was no way of deciding by consulting experience whether Copernicus or his rival Ptolemy, and the Ptolemaic theory, was correct. We can never explain human knowledge by reference to experience alone. The Platonic gap is to be taken seriously. As we all know, the earth does not feel like it is moving, so appearances must always be interpreted. But the reason given by Hume and Kant for why our knowledge exceeds the bounds of our experience is that our knowledge consists in large part of norms that we bring to our experience. Our norms are neither derived from experience (by Aristotelian abstraction or any other way) nor are our intellectual norms justifiable by a sum of experiences in the long run (i.e., by a process of confirmation) either now or ever (no teleology). On the contrary, our experience is unintelligible in the first place unless we order it by means of our norms. Finally, the Copernican turn can make sense of technology since it is a projection of a human attitude, control of nature, not a fact about nature.

Hume's version of the Copernican revolution is often missed even by philosophers, both because he is mistakenly classified as an empiricist and because the twentieth-century logical positivists invoked him as their patron saint. Those who make this mistake about Hume inevitably find him baffling because he says things that do not fit this false mold. Often he is dismissed as a skeptic, perhaps a mitigated skeptic. But if he is a skeptic, then he is a logical skeptic who is denying a certain view about the world, not the existence of the world and knowledge understood in a Copernican sense.

Hume's epistemology is radical in several senses. First, he recognizes the extent to which alleged philosophical first principles are projections of scientific hypotheses. He points out how the traditional conception of causation used by Descartes, Locke, and just about everybody else was based upon Aristotelian physics. When Newton's physics replaced Aristotle's physics, we had to revise our concept of causation. There is now no justification for inferring that the properties of the effect are also properties of the cause. Moreover, there is no necessary connection between formal, final, and efficient causes. In fact, in Newton's physics there is nothing but efficient causation. Hume does not conclude from this that there is no external world, no mind, and no God. What he says is that those things cannot be proved using the old notion of causation. To counter Hume by saying that there is nothing sacred about Newton is, in fact, to invite Hume to make his thesis even more radical. Hume admits that there is nothing final about any set of categories we use.

Second, Hume indicates how the normative structure of reason and imagination operates. Take the belief that the future will resemble the past (this is called the principle of *induction*). How can we explain this principle? It is not *a priori* because we can imagine a disorderly and unpredictable world. Hence Platonic explanations are inadequate. It is not based upon experience, because all of our experience is of the past and the present, so we have no experience of the future. Hence Aristotelian explanations are inadequate. Belief in the principle of induction is what we bring to our experience, not what we take from it. Hume goes on to denigrate purely deductive models of explanation, regardless of the origin of first principles. Hume's model of good reasoning is the English common law, a vast array of precedents with both implicit and explicit norms. In each new situation we must decide which precedent or precedents or parts thereof most resemble the present case. This is both conservative and innovative, for every new decision itself becomes a precedent.

One of the few philosophers who appreciated Hume's new direction in epistemology was Kant, who declared that in reading Hume he was awakened from his dogmatic slumber. Kant also accepted the metaphysical implications of the Copernican revolution by realizing that we cannot understand our own knowledge unless we recognize the role of the knowing subject and the normative structure of the mind. Kant gives his own different interpretation of all this by way of some technical distinctions.

Kant begins by analyzing statements in which our knowledge is expressed. His first distinction is grammatical or logical. Statements are usually of the subject-predicate form. In some statements, the predicate adds something new to the subject. For example, if I say that "John Smith is six feet tall," the predicate is "six feet tall." This tells us something new or adds to our knowledge of the subject "John Smith," because it is not part of the meaning of the expression "John Smith" that he be six feet tall. We may recognize John Smith without ever knowing his exact height. He could be any height. These statements are called *synthetic*. In other statements the predicate does not add anything to the subject but rather spells out what is already implicit in the subject. For example, "A bachelor is an unmarried male" or "Every body occupies space." The predicate "unmarried male" really says the same thing as "bachelor." The predicate "occupies space" is part of what it means to be a body. These statements are called *analytic*.

Kant's second distinction has to do with how we relate statements to experience. Some statements are accepted as true or rejected as false because of what we find in our experience. For example, "This book is blue" is either true or false, and the truth value of the statement is determined by looking at the cover. Such statements, whose truth or falsity depends upon experience, are *a posteriori*. Other statements are in the curious position of being accepted as true regardless of our experience. Take the statement "$7+5=12$." Suppose I add 7c.c. of one liquid to 5c.c. of another, and I end up with 11c.c. of a mixture. No one would say that $7+5=11$. Rather we would say things like: the measurements were incorrect, or there was a chemical reaction in which the molecular structure of the mixture created a smaller volume (but then there is another mathematical formula that is accepted as true at another level of chemical reaction). A statement whose truth is immune to revision by our experience is *a priori*.

Kant brings together these two sets of distinctions and arrives at four possibilities.

Analytic a priori	Analytic a posteriori
1	2
Synthetic a priori	Synthetic a posteriori
3	4

It is generally agreed that Box 2 (analytic *a posteriori*) is an empty class. Analytic statements are always true, even if trivial, so experience is irrelevant. Box 1 (analytic *a priori*) is not controversial for that very reason. Analytic statements are often definitions and in this sense true even if they correspond to nothing in the world. "A unicorn has one horn" is true even if there are no unicorns. In Box 4 empirical knowledge is usually found (synthetic *a posteriori*). In a very general way, we might say that Platonists put everything in Box 1 and Aristotelians put everything in Box 4.

The controversial case is Box 3, synthetic *a priori* statements. Kant argues that there is a supremely important class of statements that tells us something new, and hence is not trivial or mere definitions, and at the same time these statements are immune to experiential revision. No amount of experience could force us to change our mind. He includes in this category all of the fundamental principles of mathematics, science, and philosophy. The reason these statements are immune is that they constitute the normative structure that we bring to experience. That is, we always interpret our experience from their point of view.

Consider the two following statements:

S_1: Every *effect* has a cause.
S_2: Every *event* has a cause.

S_1 is analytic. It is a definition that tells us something about words, namely, that where we use the term "effect," we always use the term "cause," and vice versa. But S_2 is not analytic, for it is not part of the definition of an event that it have a cause. Neither is it *a posteriori,* that is, based upon experience. For example, we do not know the cause of cancer. No one says that cancer is an uncaused tragic event. Even if we never find the cause or causes, we shall go on looking. Since Box 2 is empty, that leaves only Box 3. S_2 is a major synthetic *a priori* statement.

The reader will immediately recognize the similarity of Kant to Hume on this point. Both agree that there is something special about S_2, that it is a norm that guides our whole approach to the world and human experience. There is, however, one important difference. Kant believes that specific synthetic *a priori* statements are permanent parts of the structure of the mind, and that we can offer a definitive and final account of these norms of reasoning, and even of morality. Hume accepts the finality of our having norms but admits the possibility of our changing or revising them. In this respect Hume is more radical, and Kant, fearing the consequences of Hume's thesis, is a peculiar kind of neo-Platonist.

Hegel is the only philosopher to add a new wrinkle to this controversy. Recognizing the presence of norms, and recognizing the historical variability of norms, he argued the teleological view that there are permanent norms but we move toward them in a progressive clarification that will culminate in ultimate finality and comprehensiveness.

Post-Kantian epistemology in general has reverted to a pre-Copernican position in which reference to a knowing subject is eliminated so that we focus on methodological rules, rather than on the subject who uses the rules. The goal of much formalistic contemporary epistemology is to eliminate all consideration of the origins of rules.

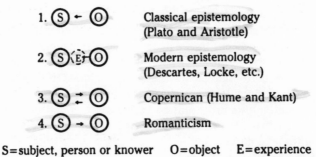

1. Ⓢ ← Ⓞ   Classical epistemology
             (Plato and Aristotle)

2. Ⓢ⟨E⟩Ⓞ   Modern epistemology
             (Descartes, Locke, etc.)

3. Ⓢ ⇄ Ⓞ   Copernican (Hume and Kant)

4. Ⓢ → Ⓞ   Romanticism

S=subject, person or knower   O=object   E=experience

In classical epistemology (1) and in much of contemporary epistemology (2), the effort is to get at the object independently of the subject. Hume and Kant agree that such a conception of knowledge is chimerical because it adheres to a false metaphysics of a world of independent objects. A thing *is* how it behaves or interacts with other objects. This, by the way, is a point that John Dewey, the American pragmatist, continually stressed in his work. Both Hume and Kant believe that there are objects in the world independent of subjects and other subjects independent of each of us, but no object has a structure or essence independent of other objects and subjects. Neither claims that the world is an illusion or a romantic invention of the subject; that would be (4).

Some of the more radical and anti-empiricist implications of the Copernican revolution have recently been stressed in the controversial work of Thomas S. Kuhn *(The Structure of Scientific Revolutions)*. If one accepts the Copernican view, then there is no totally objective (realist) explanation of science itself. By actually studying the history of science, Kuhn has punctured the teleological mythology that is usually substituted for the real history of science. Science history is usually rewritten to present a picture of unbroken progress, and the method of science is usually described as an empiricist would like to believe that it is. Kuhn has challenged empiricists to show that later theories are rationally superior, that theories can actually be tested objectively (that is, that theories fit in Box 4 above in Kant), and that self-critical standards of judgment can be presented in a non-question-begging fashion. That is, he wants to know if there is a criterion that needs no criterion. Is this a new kind of skepticism?

QUESTIONS FOR STUDY

1. Compare Descartes' methodic doubt with the Socratic method.

2. "In science and philosophy alike, an exclusive preoccupation with logical systematicity has been destructive of both historical

understanding and rational criticism" (Stephen Toulmin in *Human Understanding,* I). Comment on this statement.

3. What are *synthetic a priori* statements?

4. How would an Aristotelian respond to Platonism and Copernicanism in epistemology?

5. How would a Platonist respond to Aristotelianism and Copernicanism in epistemology?

6. How would a Copernican respond to Aristotelianism and Platonism in epistemology?

10

Metaphysics: The Nature and Structure of Reality

INTRODUCTION

Metaphysics is the fundamental philosophical task. It is basic to all other philosophical enterprises, and it is in a sense coextensive with the meaning of philosophy itself. To state one's metaphysics is to state one's philosophy as a whole. Precisely because it is so fundamental, and because there are conflicting philosophies and views about what philosophy itself is, it is difficult if not impossible to arrive at any consensus on what metaphysics is. Each different philosopher will have not only his own metaphysics, but a different view as to what metaphysics is, and this view will reflect the perspective of that philosopher. This situation is made all the more confusing when major and influential philosophers attack metaphysics itself or offer refutations of the very possibility of doing or having a metaphysics. What they are really doing is attacking the metaphysical views of other philosophers or denigrating the word "metaphysics" because the word has taken on a meaning to which they object. Therefore, it is all the more important that we avoid being misled by the use of the word. Instead, what we must do is to concentrate on *fundamental philosophical beliefs, how these beliefs relate to each other, the conception of what philosophy is, and the understanding the philosopher has of his own activity as a philosopher.*

Since we have just indicated that the word "metaphysics" is itself part of the problem and a source of confusion, it might be useful to indicate the history and development of the term itself. To begin with, none of the great classical Greek philosophers ever used the term. Neither Plato nor Aristotle employed the term "metaphysics." The term was probably introduced around 70 B.C. by Adronicus of Rhodes, a later editor and collator of Aristotle's manuscripts (see chapter on Aristotle). Andronicus used the term to refer to an untitled collection of Aristotelian writings. It means literally "after the things of nature." In the subsequent classical and medieval traditions, it was explained that the topics discussed in the *Metaphysics* were to be studied after the books on *Physics,* which deal with nature. They are to be studied afterwards because the topics deal with things further removed from the world of sense and consequently more difficult to understand. This meaning was transformed during the later Middle Ages to mean the study of things (usually theological) existing beyond nature and having a greater intrinsic reality and value. This transcendent meaning of the term metaphysics is rooted in Aristotle's discussion of the unmoved mover but is not typical of classical Greek usage. This accounts in part for the latter connotation that metaphysics deals with the spiritual or even the occult.

At the beginning of the modern period, Descartes gave to metaphysics a central role in philosophy and interpreted it to mean fundamental truths, truths basic even to the sciences that were to be deduced from metaphysical truths. In this sense a metaphysical belief is one for which we do not provide a proof or evidence but which serves as an explanation for other things. It can have this connotation even in philosophies very different from Descartes'. By the time of Hume, the word began to have the connotation of abstruse, and with Kant metaphysics came to mean speculation on questions that cannot be answered by the sciences.

Scholastic philosophers in the modern period have also distinguished several branches of metaphysics, but again usage is quite variable. Among the most prominent subdivisions are cosmology and ontology. *Cosmology* (after the Greek word *cosmos,* the conception of the *uni*verse as a single coherent whole) deals with origin and structure of the universe. Customarily, philosophers begin cosmology with the generally accepted truths of the sciences and then develop the consequences or implications. *Ontology* is the study of the most general features of reality, that is, with *being* or existence. For some philosophers, being is an independent subject matter over and above the subject matter of the special sciences. For others, ontology is the study of the basic categories or concepts for describing and explaining reality. If the distinction between cosmology and ontology seems fuzzy, it is because the distinction depends upon the specific metaphysics and cannot be explained independently.

PLATONISM

As we have seen in a previous chapter, the pre-Socratics raised most of the fundamental issues in cosmology, that is, issues about the origin and structure of the universe. Despite differences, the world of the pre-Socratics had no beginning or end in time (no creation), was finite in space, and was governed by a set of unalterable laws. Two fundamental issues raised were, first, the ultimate constituents of nature, and second, the meaning of change. One of the more popular answers to the first question was *materialism*, the view that everything is of the nature of matter; even consciousness or the activities of the mind were reducible to matter. With regard to the second issue, philosophers frequently argued that something material remained permanent during the change. What seemed a great mystery on this view was how something permanent could alter itself in the process of change. The alternatives were either to deny that change took place or to argue that some principle or law of change prevailed and that the principle was unchangeable even though everything else in the universe did change.

So far our discussion sounds like something that could have been said by scientists and not just philosophers. But it is at this point that the philosophical question arises. If there is a principle or law of change, what is its status? Is the law a thing or an object like a material object? Does the law have a supersensible or supernatural existence? Is the law merely something that exists in the minds or speech of men?

There is a long standing tradition in philosophy that says that the daily world cannot be understood on its own terms and, therefore, that however valuable science might be in telling us something about the world, science raises questions that cannot be answered by science but require philosophy, specifically metaphysics. One version of this tradition is Platonism, but it began with Plato's predecessor, Parmenides (475 B.C.). It was Parmenides who argued that ultimate reality is logical in nature, not physical. That is why reality cannot be understood through the senses. Parmenides referred to ultimate reality as *"Being,"* and the ultimate truth is that "Being is."

With Parmenides a distinction enters metaphysics, a distinction between *reality and appearance.* Reality is alleged to be unified, whereas the world of appearance, what we routinely experience, is diverse. The world of appearance cannot explain itself, but reality explains not only itself but the world of appearance. The distinction is also one of value in that reality has a greater value and comes ultimately to be identified with the divine.

Plato accepted, in part, the Parmenidean position. The physical world cannot explain itself. To explain the physical world we employ mathematical concepts like point and line, which clearly cannot be defined or explained in empirical terms. In dialogues like the *Phaedo* and *Phaedrus,* Plato specifically argued that bodies or physical objects cannot move themselves and therefore cannot move each other. There is a separate distinct entity, the soul, that can move things. We know this from the operations of our own minds. Soul is therefore the ultimate source or cause of motion, but soul (mind) is distinct from and prior to physical objects. This is perfectly consistent with Plato's theory of ideas or Forms.

Given our previous working definition of metaphysics as involving four issues, we can briefly summarize the position of *Platonic metaphysics:*

a. The fundamental reality consists of *Forms* (ideas or universals), not physical objects.

b. These Forms are related to each other in logical fashion. Platonists believe in the totality or unity of all knowledge. The highest and most pervasive trait of being (what is) is unity.

c. Philosophy is the articulation of the fundamental Forms and the deduction of the rest of what we encounter from the Forms.

d. The final objective of philosophical activity is to have as much direct contact with ultimate reality as possible—to contemplate the Forms. This can mean either an escape from the daily world, or it can mean an active attempt to make the daily world more like the ideal world.

The mysticism implicit in Platonism was openly embraced by Plotinus (204–270 A.D.). The final objective for Plotinus and the neo-Platonists is to achieve a mystical union of oneself with the One (The Form of Forms). But both Plotinus and his disciple Porphyry (232–304 A.D.) also developed some of the technical points of Platonic metaphysics. In denying that the daily world can be understood on its own terms, Platonists reject the view that properties are simply modifications of particular objects. For example, a chair is a particular object, and the blueness of a blue chair would be a property. In short, Platonists reject the view that Aristotle holds. For Platonists, properties (Ideas) are entities in their own right. Porphyry even went to the extreme of arguing that expressions that designate individuals (e.g., the word "Socrates") were predicates and hence properties.

Platonists, then, reject the distinction between a thing and its properties. This tends, of course, to put them into opposition with our familiar commonsense way of talking about the world. The technical philosophical problems raised by this approach are as follows: First, Platonists must ask if the ultimate properties can exist apart from the daily world. If so, how do they relate to the daily world? (Problem of participation). Second, Platonists must maintain that the important distinction is between the more general and the less general properties. So, in addition to having to explain how the mundane world relates to the Ideal world, the Ideal world must be explained internally in logical terms among more and less general properties. Third, Platonists must distinguish between essence and existence. *Essence* refers to what a thing is, whereas *existence* refers to whether, in fact, the thing is. This is another version of the first question, namely, whether properties can exist independently of the daily world.

ARISTOTELIANISM

The easiest way to understand Aristotelianism is negatively, as the denial of the Platonic position. Aristotle would seem to deny that there is a super-science over and above the empirical sciences, and he would deny that the first principles of the special sciences need to be deduced from this super-science. Nor is metaphysics a logically self-contained body of knowledge. Instead, for Aristotle first philosophy (his word for metaphysics) is an examination of the most comprehensive and general characteristics of existent things. It can be considered a science in its own right, but it is a special science continuous with and dependent upon the other empirical sciences.

There are two versions of Aristotelian metaphysical science. The first version is pluralistic, a critical inquiry into the individual special sciences. It tries to discuss the problems generated by the special sciences or fields of inquiry, to clarify them, and to explore the implications of their leading ideas. This sort of clarification of first principles of any particular science is to be distinguished from the application of these first principles, which is what the scientist *per se* does.

The second version of Aristotelian metaphysical science is more grandiose; it aims at nothing less than a total and unified view of the world achieved deductively. It is the attempt to interpret all of human experience, including science and man's place in the world, so as to form one systematic view of the world. This version is different from the first, for it is committed to the belief that we can generalize about reality as a whole and as a totality. The first version is not so committed. The second version also shares its claim with Platonic metaphysics, but it differs from Platonism in thinking that the basic metaphysical truths can be arrived at empirically and inductively. Aristotle himself is ambiguous about which version he favors.

Given our working definition of metaphysics, we note Aristotle's position on the four issues.

A. The fundamental realities are the commonsense things we experience in daily life. "Being" for Aristotle is neither a thing itself nor a property of any kind. "To be" (as opposed to Being) means to be a subject of thought or discourse and to have or possess properties. In a manner of speaking, to be is to be the subject of a sentence and never to be a predicate of another subject. For example, suppose this book is blue and rectangular. "Book" is a fundamental reality; "blue" and "rectangular" are properties. For Aristotle, there is no issue about the nature of existence or being. His concern is always with *what* things are, *not whether* they are. He rejected the Platonic Forms as ultimate reality. He even rejected atomism (the view that reality consists of ultimate material particles or parts). Aristotle's word for the fundamental realities is *substance.* One of the recurrent problems with substance is that it is difficult to specify what a substance is other than by enumerating its properties. That is why a logical or grammatical criterion is often used.

B. The individual objects that make up this world are related to each other in teleological fashion, that is, in terms of means and ends. These relations are discovered empirically. Man and his values are natural objects receiving the same sort of analysis. Perhaps Aristotle's specific reason for rejecting atomism is its supposition of determinism instead of teleology.

C. Insofar as the philosopher is a metaphysician, he reveals, analyzes, classifies, and clarifies problems.

D. The ultimate objective of philosophy is to explain better and more clearly that which we already know. For Aristotle, this would include our values, not just our beliefs.

MEDIEVAL METAPHYSICS

Medieval Christian cosmology differs from that of the classical Greeks because it added for our consideration such concerns as that of God's creating or annihilating the world, miracles, and the problems of freedom and evil. We must be brief and selective, so we shall focus on the so-called problem of universals, largely because it indicates how theological issues were discussed and conceived of by using classical models.

Briefly, the problem of *universals* (property, quality, relations, characteristics, etc.) is the problem of whether properties or universal terms exist apart from the individuals who possess them. This problem had a special theological dimension for the medieval Christian because concepts such as the Trinity and original sin applying to all of mankind raised questions about the status of universals. Three answers were given. Medieval *realists* such as Augustine and Anselm took the Platonic path and argued that properties (universals, attributes, etc.) have a separate existence like Forms, but in the mind of God. They used the Platonic argument that particulars could not be recognized and defined as examples of types unless we were already familiar with the type. The second answer, *conceptualism*, was derived from Aristotle. Conceptualists such as Aquinas argued that only individual things exist, and they exist apart from us, from God, and from the ideas in God's mind. Universals exist logically in our thought and speech and they exist as the structure of individual things that we can abstract.

The third answer is the most radical. It is the controversial position called *nominalism*, and it is represented in the work of William of Ockham. Nominalists agree with conceptualists, as opposed to realists, in maintaining that only individual objects exist. But nominalists disagree with conceptualists by denying that universals are abstracted from individuals. For nominalists, universals are mere words or names or human contrivances that exist only in discourse or only in the mind. Religiously, this extreme position sometimes becomes heretical. But if we refer back to one of our earlier questions we can anticipate how medieval nominalism will become important in the modern period. The earlier question concerns the status of explanations and laws in science. Do laws have a supersensible existence, are laws structures in objects that we abstract, or are laws and explanations merely human contrivances? It is now clear that the first answer is Platonic and realist; the second answer is Aristotelian and conceptualist; the third answer is nominalist.

Before moving on to the metaphysical disputes generated by modern science, let us note how problems in the philosophy of religion reflect metaphysical differences. The so-called ontological argument or proof for God's existence, an argument traditionally credited to Anselm, is based upon the Platonic realist position. All properties (attributes, etc.) are real and have an independent existence. Existence is itself a property. Therefore, existence exists. Consequently, Anselm can argue that God's essence includes existence as one of its properties, and therefore that God exists.

Aquinas attacked the ontological argument not the conclusion. Being a conceptualist (Aristotelian), Aquinas does not accept the notion that attributes or properties have an independent existence. Instead, Aquinas distinguished necessary existence from contingent existence. He then went on to use Aristotelian physics or the idea of a first cause to argue that God is necessary as first cause, hence not contingent.

METAPHYSICS IN MODERN SCIENCE

The crucial factor in post-Renaissance metaphysics is the development and preeminence of modern science. By "modern" is meant the Galilean-Newtonian view of the world: a rejection of Aristotelian physics, a reversion to atomism, determinism, and mechanism. With some qualification, we note that Descartes is a crucial figure in the development of modern metaphysics in response to the new developments in science. To understand how Descartes became the defining figure of modern metaphysics we must recount the major issues.

1. The basic question is what are the *ultimate constituents* of the world? There must be ultimate constituents, so the story goes, in order for there to be objective knowledge and values. Moreover, the ultimate constituents must be *unchangeable,* otherwise they cease to be ultimate.

2. How, then, do we account for the observation of *change?* One view is to assert that change is an illusion. The other is that change is the rearrangement of ultimate constituents. The rearrangement must be orderly, otherwise there is no objectivity.

3. The third issue is the status of the *principle of rearrangement,* the principle that change is the orderly rearrangement of ultimate constituents. There are three answers to this question:

a. The principle is not a thing but some supersensible entity. This answer makes the principle more real than the constituents. This theory can even deny that there are any ultimate constituents other than the principle itself (Platonism).

b. The principle is the abstractable structure of things (Aristotelian).

c. The principle is an invention or convention or way people have of talking about change. This position denies the external objectivity of knowledge and value (we shall call this position *Copernican.*)

Descartes restated Plato's answer and refurbished it for modern science. Physical science does not explain itself but requires metaphysical first principles. These first principles must be intuitively clear and distinct, that is, self-certifying. Moreover, physical science explains the physical world, not the mental world. Recall Plato's argument that bodies cannot move themselves. This argument plays two key roles in Descartes. First, it saves human minds from the determinism that modern science attributed to the physical world. Moreover, if the mind of man is not one of the items in the world, then it makes some sense to talk about man manipulating the world for his comfort and convenience, thereby realizing the practical advantages of modern science. It is difficult to understand this manipulation if the mind is itself one of the determined objects. Second, if physics is not self-certifying then it could presumably be reduced to mathematics, which, according to Descartes, is metaphysically self-certifying. What this means is that the principles of mathematics are the underlying principles of change. If I know the principles of mathematics I thereby automatically know the principles of the changing empirical world. For example, Descartes argued against the existence of the atom and its complementary void on the grounds that the properties of mathematics are the properties of the real world. Since mathematical space is infinitely divisible, there can be no smallest unit of matter (e.g., the atom).

Descartes' answer raised all of the special problems of modern metaphysics. First, Descartes' universe has two ultimate kinds of entities: minds (plural) and matter (singular). Through a metamorphosis of terminology, these entities were both called substances. If there are two things, then we must explain how they interact. Descartes was no more successful at doing this than Plato had been in explaining how the objects of our experience participate in the Forms. In modern discussions this became known as the *mind-body problem.*

What possible positions are there on this issue?

Descartes: two different kinds of substance (no resolution)
Spinoza: one substance with two versions (mental and physical)
Hobbes: one substance, only physical *(materialism)*
Berkeley: one substance, only immaterial *(idealism)*

Leibniz: infinite number of substances, all immaterial
Hume: no substance

The mind-body problem is not one problem but a way of focusing on a whole host of related problems. For example, those modern philosophers who tend to take the material world of modern science most seriously, Hobbes and Spinoza, invariably adopt some form of determinism. Berkeley would never have been a determinist. So the mind-body problem is connected with the problem of freedom versus determinism.

The specific position that a philosopher takes on the mind-body problem, the problem of human freedom, and the original issue of our knowledge of permanence and change vary not only with particular scientific controversies, but, as we have persistently maintained, with whether they were using the Platonic or Aristotelian framework. For example, Spinoza, using Aristotle, is committed to an identity between the order of events in the physical world and the structure of the knowing mind. Locke, who also uses Aristotle, accepts the distinction between a thing and its properties, but he admits that we have no direct knowledge of what the thing is like. Perhaps, he speculates, atomic structure will represent the thing.

Modern Aristotelians, as opposed to Aristotle himself, faced a special problem. By accepting atomism, the doctrine that the ultimate constituents of reality are not directly perceivable, they were faced with a dichotomy between what was directly perceivable and what was not perceivable. The problem is that the unperceivable items are the locus of reality. Something like the Platonic problem or distinction between reality and appearance emerges in modern Aristotelianism. What we perceive became a source of knowledge about reality rather than ultimate reality itself. Here the distinction between mind and body, where the real ultimate properties of bodies are primary, and where the derivative properties like color are secondary and "in the mind," becomes for Aristotelians a special version of the reality versus appearance problem.

Leibniz and Berkeley, using the Platonic framework, attack what they take to be a kind of complacent Aristotelianism. In the discussion of his doctrine referred to as the *identity of indiscernibles*, Leibniz argued that for two real things to be different they must be in some way distinguishable. But sometimes things differ only in their location in space and time (as two peas in a pod). But spatio-temporal relations are not themselves things but properties, and we would need to know how to identify the objects before we could identify the relationships in space and time. But as in the example of our two peas, the only way we can identify an object is through its properties. Hence, Leibniz concluded with the familiar Platonic declaration that only properties are real. Berkeley's immaterialism, one of the most misunderstood of philosophical positions, makes precisely the same point. It is not an exercise in cleverness. When Berkeley denies the existence of material substances what he is doing is denying the Aristotelian notion that there are concrete things that are the ultimate constituents of reality. Instead, Berkeley takes the Platonic view that only properties are real. Hence, the apple is not a thing with the properties of being red, juicy, and delicious, rather that collection of properties is the apple.

For Aristotelians to state simply that science discovers empirically the structure of the world is to explain nothing. Why does the world have that structure rather than another? Will it always have that structure? Remember that modern Aristotelians no longer have final causes but are stuck with determinism. In a famous controversy, Newton, speaking through Samuel Clarke, argued that the laws of nature are the laws because God wanted it that way. No further explanation is possible. Some scientists and philosophers of science now go so far as to assert that the question of why the laws are the laws cannot and should not be answered. That is, they abandon the metaphysical issue as unanswerable. Leibniz considered this an abandonment of rationality. He argued that God chose those laws (somewhat reminiscent of Plato's Demiurge) because they formed the most coherent and harmonious possibility. Both Leibniz and Berkeley distinguished between our knowledge (which is incomplete) and God's understanding, which is perfect (necessary and *a priori*).

CHALLENGES TO TRADITIONAL METAPHYSICS

Two philosophers of the eighteenth century, Hume and Kant, have challenged the traditional metaphysical enterprises. Part of their procedure is to ask the question, why do philosophers raise metaphysical issues? A large part of the answer seems to be the effort to arrive at objective knowledge and values wherein objectivity is understood as conformity to a structure external to man, the knower. For reasons discussed at length in the chapter on epistemology, both philosophers argue that there can be no such thing as that kind of certain and objective knowledge. Therefore, in an important sense, traditional metaphysics is misconceived.

Their arguments against traditional metaphysics follow a somewhat similar pattern. First, both philosophers make much of the fact that there is no consensus among philosophers on how to answer traditional questions. This is a kind of scandal. Every position is as defensible or as indefensible as every other, given the assumptions of the disputants. Second, the kind of certainty claimed by any position is always untenable. No claimant to certainty ever produces a working model, so to speak. Third, and most important, both Hume and Kant claim that knowledge is inextricably bound up with the knower and never just the object known. In short, Hume and Kant are arguing that structure is to be found in the knower or is provided by the knower and therefore is neither in a different reality beyond experience nor something built into the objects of experience.

For reasons made clear in the chapter on epistemology, this is called the *Copernican Revolution in philosophy*. Negatively, it is a rejection of both traditional Platonism and Aristotelianism. It is an alternative approach to metaphysics, not an end to metaphysics, but precisely because it rejects so much of the tradition, it is open to misunderstanding. Presently, we shall also have to distinguish between the Humean and Kantian versions. What Hume and Kant do share in common is a clear rejection of the Aristotelian notion of a world of individual objects (substances) with an inherent structure that we are capable of knowing. Hume rejects the traditional Aristotelian notion of substance altogether, whereas Kant rejects it by denying the intelligibility of the thing-in-itself. We cannot meaningfully discuss what a thing is in isolation from other things. The answer to the question what is ultimate is that nothing is ultimate. Hence, there is no discussion of how ultimate things relate.

What Hume and Kant do is to concentrate on the question about the task of philosophy. Philosophy is not a science, and science does not make sense of itself. Science, like every other pursuit, is an expression of how man relates to the world. Philosophy, and therefore metaphysics, is an attempt to answer the question of how man relates to the world. What is clear is that no science can answer that question. A scientist looks at the world or some segment of it and tries to understand and control it as an object external to the scientist. Within certain limits this may be useful, as well as dangerous. By itself, such an activity is neither intelligible nor explainable by traditional metaphysics. What can be explained, claimed Hume and Kant, is the activity of man-explaining-the-world. Neither man nor the world can be made intelligible on its own. Since neither man nor the world is an ultimate object, neither can be a strict object of scrutiny.

It is now time to distinguish between Hume and Kant. Hume was the more radical of the two, if by implication only. Hume's position with regard to the key metaphysical question is that structure exists only in the human mind (or in human discourse). He harkens back to the tradition of radical medieval nominalism. Structure is both an invention and a convention. But the mind, so to speak, cannot be the object of any scientific and empirical study. The mind is not an object. Therefore, we cannot shift all of the old questions from the external object to the internal object. The attempt to substitute psychology (as a science) will not help. That is the fallacy of *psychologism*. Neither can the answer be found in physiology. Such sciences are useful but no substitute for metaphysics. Neither can we objectify the mind as the product of culture or economics or history. That would be the fallacy of *historicism*. We may meaningfully study in what ways the mind is influenced by history, but we cannot explain the mind simply as the effect of such causes. That would once more turn the mind into an ultimate object.

Metaphysics, for Hume, is not the study of the mind of man nor the study of the world. It is the study of man-in-the-world. Mind and world are both abstractions to be explained from within the perspective of man-in-the-world. Note, the perspective is not within the mind but man-in-the-world. A great deal of what Hume says sounds like statements in psychology or history. But they are not scientific statements; rather they are metaphysical statements. These metaphysical statements (which Hume frequently refers to as common sense) involve norms. Norms are conventions but conventions modifiable with circumstances, and hence the conventions are also inventions. In a manner of speaking, the norms have no absolute status (the mind is subject to change).

We cite just a few brief examples of Hume's metaphysics. "Existence" is not a property. Instead he interprets the concept of existence as a question about whether we *believe* that something is the case. To talk about existence is to talk about how man thinks or commits himself in the world. As for "determinism," it is not a fact about the world. Necessity is a human way of construing relationships between events for human convenience.

Kant agreed with much of what Hume said, but he refused to follow Hume down the path that made our norms (both intellectual and moral) mere conventions. Kant sought a more secure and final status for our norms. Metaphysics is also for Kant the exploration and articulation of the inherent norms of all thought and action. What Kant does is to give the Copernican turn a neo-Platonic twist. He eschews the traditional Platonic quest for knowledge of absolute and unchanging supersensible reality. But he agrees that the inherent norms must be *a priori* and necessary. The mind, then, for Kant is not subject to change. There can be, for him, a final and definitive articulation of its structure, both intellectual and moral.

POST-KANTIAN METAPHYSICS

Nothing is more remarkable than the Copernican turn in metaphysics. Nothing, that is, except what followed it. If it is possible to take Hume's radical position and Platonize it, then is it possible to Aristotelianize it? The answer is yes, and the man who did it was Hegel.

G. W. F. Hegel (1770–1831) begins with a critique of Kant. On Kantian terms and in full agreement with the rejection of traditional metaphysics, Hegel does to Kant what an Aristotelian can be expected to do to a Platonist. First, he attacks the radical separation of the forms of thought from the objects of our experience. The forms are only revealed within experience. Unlike traditional Aristotelians, Hegel did not believe in a world of a plurality of separate, particular objects. For Hegel, there is only one all-encompassing substance (a kind of mind-world unity), the *Absolute.* Not only is there one ultimate object but the plurality of individual minds is merely part of the Absolute mind. Like Spinoza, Hegel argues that there is an identity between connections in thought and the structure of things. Each is an aspect of the Absolute. Logic and metaphysics coincide. There is only one technical problem raised here. If mind-world is a unity, why is there no immediate and total self-consciousness of it or of itself? That is, why do we not have immediate and full comprehension? To answer this question (which in a way is why there have been so many different philosophies), Hegel employs a second Aristotelian notion, namely, teleology. The Absolute unfolds itself gradually and progressively toward its ultimate aim of absolute self-consciousness. Metaphysics is the autobiography of the mind in its itinerary from naive self-consciousness to absolute knowledge. Hegel called this itinerary *phenomenology,* and he considered himself the last and final spokesman.

One other noteworthy post-Kantian development in metaphysics has been an astonishing rejection of the Copernican turn by some philosophers. These philosophers, very broadly referred to as *analytic philosophers,* have either steadfastly retained the Aristotelian position or have reverted to it. Beginning with the notion that truths about the world are discovered by the sciences, they go on to argue that metaphysics is an inductive and empirical science of its own that examines problems left over by the special sciences. Analytic philosophers can be divided into two camps. Those following the lead of Bertrand Russell examine and analyze the language of the sciences. This analysis is designed to reveal the elements that any formally correct assertion must have. It is assumed that corresponding to these elements there will be necessary structural elements in the objective world. What is sought are the ultimate objective categories of reality.

This first camp tends to be scientistic in aiming at one coherent and systematic view of the world and man, and in believing that the details are discovered by the special sciences from physics to psychology. It assumes that all of the major issues are settled and concentrates on the language. It tends to emphasize formal linguistic structures as in modern logic. *Formalists* avoid issues about the relation of mind to body or the problem of human freedom, etc., by declaring these to be issues to be decided by the future developments in the sciences, such as psychology. The implicit teleology is the assumption that there is real progress in science and that science will answer any meaningful question. At the same time, formalists avoid saying anything about philosophy itself except that it is formal analysis. The reason they avoid making such statements is that a detailed description of philosophical activity will have to be the subject matter of the science of psychology. But we note that, as a science, psychology will use a language whose formal structure can be analyzed by the philosopher, so this is not to be confused with psychologism. It is difficult to imagine how this web of assumptions can be sustained without subscribing to an implicit determinism in which all human activity, including philosophy, is subject to scientific explanation of a rigid sort.

A second camp of analytic philosophy originating with Ludwig Wittgenstein does not aim at one coherent and systematic view of the world, nor does it believe that the whole of human experience is captured by science. Instead this form of philosophy analyzes the statements of *ordinary language* (which covers all subjects). But this analysis does not reveal the necessary structural elements in the objective world. Rather it reveals or aims to reveal the structure of our talk or thought about the world. What this form of analysis does is to make an object of our talk or thought about the world and then analyzes it as in any empirical science. In treating talk or mind as an object, this movement ignores the Copernican turn. When it analyzes language, it is referred to as the philosophy of language. When it analyzes our mental activity, it is called philosophy of mind. There is no clear separation.

Copernicans would argue that ordinary language analysis, insofar as it aims to give an accurate and definitive rendering of the structure of language or mental activity, is a form of the fallacies of psychologism and historicism. It fallaciously attempts to treat something that is not an object (namely, human thought) as if it were an object. Since ordinary language philosophers don't believe that structures are *a priori* but empirical, they cannot believe that structures are impervious to change. They must deal with how language changes. This they do not, and some would suspect cannot do, without invoking an inner teleology to language and thought. When ordinary language philosophers go outside their analysis to discuss how and why the object of their analysis changes, they are doing non-philosophical work. Formalists criticize ordinary language philosophers precisely on this point. There is nothing, by the way, that prevents ordinary language philosophers from becoming radical Copernicans by taking the turn and realizing that there can be no definitive analysis, hence no science of mental activity and language.

In opposition to the scientism of formal analysis and in opposition to the narrow internalism of ordinary language analysis, there is another large and amorphous movement very broadly referred to as *phenomenology and existentialism*. The term "phenomenology" is borrowed from Hegel, but under the leadership of Husserl and Heidegger, the term has taken on new meanings. Phenomenologists accept the Copernican turn and focus their study on man-in-the-world. One thing that phenomenology is definitely not is Platonic, for no phenomenologist believes in an *a priori* structure outside of man-in-the-world. Beyond this point there are great differences. Husserl, for example, changed his position several times, but at one time he seemed to understand phenomenological analysis as a kind of Aristotelian analysis of the implicit structure of man-in-the-world. His later writings indicate a more radical understanding of phenomenological analysis. Husserl came at last to stress what he called the *"Lebenswelt,"* which is the analogue to common sense in Hume and, as in Hume, prior to science itself.

Heidegger has always taken a more radical path in stressing the normative and emotional elements of man-in-the-world, emphasizing such things as our concern about death. He has also gone to great pains to show that something like the history of thought, now called the "history of Being" is the history of our understanding of being. This is not historicist anymore than it is psychologistic. It is a position about how the history of man-in-the-world is integral to man-in-the-world, the way that a person's conception of who he is becomes an important element in who he is.

There is something that can be called rigorous phenomenological analysis, but, of course, it varies with the particular philosopher. Since phenomenologists do not subscribe to scientism, analysis is not given a mathematical or quasi-mathematical format. More often than not it uses striking literary devices. This has led formalists to deride phenomenologists as poets rather than philosophers. The charges and countercharges are not descriptive and not very informative. Rather they are symptomatic of different philosophical commitments.

QUESTIONS FOR STUDY

1. What is metaphysics?

2. Why is the problem of change so crucial for metaphysics?

3. Compare and contrast Platonic and Aristotelian metaphysics.

4. What is the difference between medieval realism, conceptualism, and nominalism?

5. Why do Platonists tend to defend human freedom?

6. In what way do Hume and Kant challenge traditional metaphysics?

11

Philosophy of Religion:
Reason and Faith

1. THE DEFINITION OF "GOD"

At the beginning of his *Faith and Reason,* the contemporary philosopher John Hick attempts to define the concept of God. He writes that "God . . . is (1) the unique, infinite, personal Spirit, (2) 'holy, righteous, wise, and loving,' (3) who has created the existing universe, and (4) who is preparing souls for eternal fellowship with Himself, through their own free responses to the environmental challenges and opportunities which He appoints." A long definition! Do you think that most people who believe in God (or, for that matter, who deny that God exists) would recognize in this definition the being that they pray to? Hick believes that this is what Christians mean when they speak of God; we might go further and suggest that this fine definition captures what members of the two other great Western religions, Judaism and Islam, mean by God. However, this God is unknown to the adherents of the Eastern traditions, which we shall explore in chapter 12.

Let us begin with an examination of Hick's definition.

The first part appears to define God's *essential nature: God is unique,* or as the Moslem says in his prayer, "There is no God but God." The Western religious tradition since the time of the Hebrew prophets has been staunchly *monotheistic* and has not only refused to acknowledge the gods of other peoples, but has denied that they exist. This has usually led to an insistence on the *universality* of religion; the God of Abraham, Isaac, and Jacob is God to *all* peoples. *God is infinite,* not quantitatively infinite like the number system, but qualitatively infinite: God is without limits to his existence—perfect, all-encompassing, omnipresent, omnipotent. This has led some thinkers to deny a distinction between God and the world. That theory is called *pantheism,* and it has usually been condemned by the mainstream of Jewish, Christian, and Moslem believers. It remains an important logical difficulty in the Western tradition, however, that God is conceived as being infinite, and yet as *not* being the world.

God is personal: God may be infinite, and hence not just another entity among the entities that make up the world, but He is nonetheless conceived as a personal deity. This means that God is not simply a supernatural cosmic force, an unmoved mover, or pure act, as natural theologians, in their efforts to understand God's nature, have asserted. Rather, God is analogous in *some* respects to the human being: man is created in God's image; God feels emotions and hears our prayers; He rewards and punishes according to our just deserts. It is significant that the seventeenth-century Dutch philosopher Spinoza was turned away from the Jewish community of which he was a member because, among other heresies, he *denied* that God was conscious of the world and concerned about mankind. *God is spiritual:* Jews, Christians, and Moslems identify God's essential nature with the highest and most noble part of mankind, our spirit. Men may possess animal natures and an intelligence that serves that nature, but we also possess an element of spirit, which emerges in our pursuit of the higher values—beauty, truth, and goodness—for their own sakes. The believer identifies the substance that underlies these spiritual pursuits with the very essence of God.

The *second* group of categories defines God's *moral* nature. He is *holy:* a value term that can be understood only by contemplating the kinds of things we call holy—a holy book, a relic, a saint, a holy place. God is *righteous:* He is perfectly just, and the religious believer trembles before His righteousness. He is *wise:* this is the most difficult moral value of all to define, but it signifies that God is farseeing, and His providence is unerring. And He is loving: this is a central category of Christianity, in which it is believed that the world is a product of, and is kept in existence by, the divine love that was made manifest in the self-sacrifice of Christ.

The third part of Hick's definition describes God's *activity:* He has created the world. And the long, concluding passage describes God's *purposes:* each of us is placed upon the earth not by chance, but because God is inviting us to risk our lives in an enterprise whose goal is in the next world. Life is an opportunity to go upon a pilgrimage—we are asked to create from the unique human material we were born with, and from the gifts or handicaps of the environment into which we were born, a personality that is not merely a "sometime thing," like an inanimate object or a mere animal, but one that is *worthy* of eternal life: we are called upon to "live as though we were already immortal."

2. THE STUDY OF RELIGION

What kinds of questions do philosophers ask about God? And where do we look for answers to these questions? We can identify *three* central issues and three "routes to knowledge of God," which we will consider in the light of Hick's definition.

A. *Is this definition correct?* That is, does it in fact describe what Jews, Christians, and Moslems mean by God? Is that understanding of God properly based in *Scripture* (the Old Testament, the New Testament, and the Koran), and in *reason?* This we may call the question of *revealed theology;* scriptural revelation is said to be the *first* route to God.

B. *Does the being so defined exist?* The philosopher will develop, analyze, and criticize *arguments* purporting to prove the existence of God, or at least to show that belief in God's existence is in conformity with standards of rational belief, and that faith, therefore, is not blind or irrational. This we may call the question of *natural theology;* reason, thus, is the *second* route to God.

C. *If God does exist, what significance does that fact have for the conduct of life?* It is possible that God may exist, and yet take no interest in the affairs of mankind. Or it may be that God has created individuals for a purpose, which is dimly revealed in the scriptural texts, and we are called upon to realize that purpose. We may call this the question of *religious faith.* Religious experience is the *third* route to God.

In the eighteenth century, when people began to interest themselves in the study of religion as a historical phenomenon, a distinction was made that will make the meaning of the questions of *natural theology* and *religious faith* clearer to us. That distinction was between *positive* or *objective* religion and *subjective* religion. The term "positive religion" refers to all aspects of religion that have to do with an established community of believers: the existence of *churches,* an *ecclesiastical hierarchy* of priests, rabbis, or mullahs who possess spiritual authority and sometimes social and political influence, a set of prescribed *prayers, festivals, rites* and *rituals,* and a *theology* that consists *at least* of a set of holy books and their interpretation. Of course, each of these elements may be more or less developed in different religions. Judaism has very little in the way of a complex ecclesiastical hierarchy like that of Roman Catholicism, but the number of holy books of the Law in its possession far exceeds that, say, of modern Protestantism.

All of these "objective" books, buildings, prayers, and priests would be empty, however, without *subjective* religion. Subjective religion refers to the piety of the individual believer. Here we encounter the act of faith of the believer, his personal prayers and petitions to God, and his special relationship to God, which may appear in such emotional states as the "experience of being saved," or its opposite, despair over his sinful state (the "dark night of the soul"); the feeling of the presence of God in the world; the sense of the mystical; religious ecstasy; and the serenity of soul that is said to come with faith. Such matters are not simply of interest to the psychologist. They are presented to us by believers as living options by means of which each individual can seek and experience his own salvation. As such, they are of *philosophical* interest, for they constitute one possible route on the way to the Good Life, the perennial target of philosophical searching. And we will consider the reflections that philosophers have made about subjective religion when we consider the question of religious faith.

Positive religion, however, has usually been the first aspect of religion that has attracted the attention of philosophers. For religion is a social institution, and as such has often had to defend itself against attack by diverse dissenters. It usually justifies itself by claiming to represent a traditional set of beliefs that are not only personally satisfying to believers, but are literally *true*. And it is this *claim to truth* that has summoned up a host of critical thinkers committed to defend or to demolish the basis of that claim. The starting point of these philosophical struggles that make up natural theology are the *proofs of the existence* of God, some of which we must now consider.

3. PROOFS OF THE EXISTENCE OF GOD

The traditional proofs of the existence of God are generally classified as *cosmological, ontological,* and *teleological.* All three conclude, of course, with the statement, "therefore God exists." All of them involve an appeal to some *synthetic a priori principle,* that is, a principle that is known to be true by the mind alone, but that is *not* a tautology or a definition (chapter 6). And all three have a long history extending, in the case of the cosmological argument, to antiquity, and in the case of the ontological and teleological arguments, to the Middle Ages. Consequently, the number of formulations each has received and the number of significant objections and counterarguments to them is enormous. We will state each proof in what we take to be its simplest, if not most rigorous, form and then discuss two key objections that have been raised against it. Our ending with objections should not leave the student with the impression that each of these arguments contains a fatal flaw, for with some of these objections, at least, a powerful case can be made for the view that the supposed objection is not genuinely compelling. Such controversy is the stuff of philosophy. You should, in any case, supplement your study of the arguments as stated here by examining their formulations by Artistotle, Saint Anselm, Saint Thomas Aquinas, Descartes, Spinoza, and

Leibniz, to name some of those thinkers who have based, at least in part, their religious beliefs upon rational argument.

A. The *cosmological* argument:

1. There is change in the universe (observable fact).
2. All change can be brought about only by an antecedent agent, to which it can be traced as an effect to its cause. (Principle of causality: every event has a cause different from itself; thus, things cannot produce themselves.)
3. But if any given change must be traced to an antecedent causal agent, then that causal agent must also be traced to an antecedent agent that caused it, and so on ad infinitum (follows from 2).
4. A causal series must have a starting point, that is, there must be a *first* cause, an agent that effects change without itself being the effect of a cause (synthetic *a priori* principle: a chain of causes cannot reach back indefinitely, or more simply, the world *cannot* have existed from all eternity).
5. Thus a cause of change that is itself unchanged or uncaused must have originated the change in the universe (follows from 1–4).
6. But an unchanged changer (unmoved mover, first cause) is what is meant by God.
7. Therefore, God exists.

Statement 4 has, of course, caused most difficulties for both believers and skeptics. First, it is not clear why the world *could not* have existed for ever. Saint Thomas Aquinas claims that the *impossibility of an infinite regress* is evident to reason alone, even if divine revelation did not assure us of the creation of the world by God, and it is this impossibility that is the basis of the conclusion that God exists. But many traditions have affirmed the eternity of the world. For the Greeks of Homer's time, the cosmos has always existed; similarly, the Chinese appear to have believed that Heaven and the world are eternal. A modern cosmologist may speak of the origin of the universe in a cataclysmic explosion or "big bang" some fifteen billion years ago, but that event, according to the cosmologist, might have been preceded by events that reach back into the indefinite or limitless past. So point four does not seem to be evident to the reason of all men in all traditions.

Furthermore, it seems *arbitrary* to end the causal series with some uncaused being whom we then identify with God. For one thing, the argument appeals to the principle that every event has a cause. It then reaches the conclusion that one thing at least does not, namely, God. This seems *paradoxical,* also, and makes us wonder whether the concept of an unmoved mover makes any sense at all. Spinoza spoke of God as *causa sui,* or cause of itself, but the mind boggles at such a thought; we wonder if it does not make more sense to assume that the universe is eternal.

Of course, to the person who says, "God must exist. Otherwise, who created the world?" such objections may seem uncompelling. For many of us have a root intuition that this world cannot account for its own existence; that it is, in fact, dependent for its existence upon some higher realm. Nevertheless, we cannot say that the cosmological argument has *explained* the existence of the world or given us a "deeper understanding" of the world by its reference to God as first cause, until we can account for God's creative activity itself. For only then will we have an explanation in the sense in which that concept was explicated in chapter 6: a deduction of the existence of the world from the laws governing the will and the activity of God. And it must be realized that the connection between the unmoved mover and the God revealed in scripture (premise six) is tenuous at best.

B. The *ontological* argument.

1. God is conceived by everybody as a being greater than which nothing can be conceived.
2. Such a being must possess all possible positive attributes to an infinite degree (God must be infinitely good, infinitely loving, infinitely wise, etc.); otherwise, he would not be the being greater than which nothing can be conceived.
3. But it is clearly greater to exist than not to exist.
4. To deny existence to God would thus involve a contradiction: that is, it would imply that the being greater than which nothing can be conceived is *not* the being greater than which nothing can be conceived, for an existing being greater than which nothing can be conceived would be greater.
5. But a contradiction cannot be asserted.
6. Therefore, God's non-existence is unthinkable; God exists necessarily.

Although its conclusion is *not* a tautology, the argument is entirely *a priori;* its premises are either about definitions or logical rules, and yet the conclusion asserts a purported fact about the world! It is, in some respect, similar to a proof in geometry. Imagine that you were to ask a child about the geometric figure we call an isosceles triangle. You would tell him that the term refers to a three-sided plane figure with two equal sides (definition). But if you then asked him what *new* facts he could tell you about such triangles, he probably could not give a reply. But with a little application of Euclidean axioms and some rigorous thinking, you could show him that the above definition implies that all such figures have equal base angles. In general, concepts may have implications of which we are unaware, even if we use the concepts every day. Similarly, Saint Anselm tells the biblical "fool who says in his heart that there is no God" that his own concept of God implies His existence! God's perfection (and even the atheist conceives of God as a perfect being) implies that He exists, for existence is a perfection: it is better to exist than not to exist (again, even the atheist would agree to that!).

It is difficult to locate and identify what is wrong with this argument. Perhaps it is this very difficulty that has kept alive the debate about its merits, despite the fact that very few people—except, perhaps, those who are already convinced that pure thinking alone will give us knowledge of existence—have ever confessed to having been brought to a belief in God, or even to having had their religious belief reinforced by this argument. And yet, even in very recent years, some of the most subtle minds in philosophy have tested themselves upon the logic of this argument. Again, let us confine ourselves to *two* observations about this delightful puzzle.

Although both the believer and the atheist agree that the term "God" properly refers to a "being greater than which nothing can be conceived," or to a "being possessing all possible positive attributes to an infinite degree," it is *not* clear that the term thus defined is *understood* by them. What, after all, do we mean by the term "infinite being" or "perfect being"? Since the very definition states that God is greater than all other conceivable beings, can we be sure that we know what we are talking about when we speak of Him? And if we are uncertain as to what the concept *means*, how can we be certain as to what it *implies?* How do we know that an "infinite being" is a *possible* being? This difficulty of insuring that our efforts to speak of God are *meaningful* efforts will be discussed in a later section of this chapter. But surely I cannot be as clear about the meaning and implications of the term "God" as I can be about the term "isosceles triangle."

But there is another difficulty with reference to our comparison of the ontological argument to an argument in geometry. Euclid's axioms and definitions are *rules* (which he claimed to be self-evident) for using the concepts of plane geometry, and for drawing out consequences (theorems) from them. They are all *a priori* in the sense of requiring no experience for their confirmation. They are either stipulated definitions (a triangle has three sides) or tautologies. Geometry thus weaves out the fabric of ideas implied in its axioms and definitions; its theorems are all about the imaginary objects we call triangles, squares, and the like. There is nowhere a claim made that any of the objects spoken of by the geometer *exist*. But the ontological argument does attempt to go from *concepts* to *existence,* and there is something strange at best, and at worst unclear, about such a move. Saint Anselm would of course deny our first objection, and claim that not only is the concept of God comprehensible, it is also self-evident, like a Euclidean definition. The fact that existence is posited in the conclusion may be strange, but it is due to the uniqueness of the concept of God: God is the *only* entity whose existence can be proven in this fashion.

Nevertheless, the ontological argument has forced philosophers to *rethink the concept of existence.* Saint Thomas Aquinas, who denies the soundness of the ontological argument, believed that existence is discoverable only by beginning with the *a posteriori* encounter with the world. And Kant, whose rejection of the ontological argument is perhaps most famous, suggested that *existence is not a predicate at all,* and hence that you cannot derive it from the other predicates of an object. He asked us to compare ten dollars in our pocket with ten imaginary dollars. Both have the same predicates—they are both described in precisely the same fashion—but one does not exist! Kant's point is that when we say that something exists, we do not thereby contribute to the *description* of the thing; the two are different *kinds* of claims: and hence we cannot conclude that God exists from a description of Him. We might also note that Saint Anselm's argument implies that existence comes in degrees and kinds (point 2: God must possess all possible positive attributes to an infinite degree, and that therefore God must possess the attribute of existence to an infinite degree. And in another formulation of his argument, Saint Anselm says that it is better to exist *in two ways* rather than in just one, viz., in reality and in the understanding). But are there degrees of reality, such that some things are more real than others, as some things are bigger, or some acts are more just than others? Some philosophers have argued this point along with Saint Anselm; Plato is a case in point. However, philosophers today tend to believe, along with Saint Thomas Aquinas and Kant, that a claim to existence is an either/or affair made on the basis of a physical encounter with the thing said to exist or its manifestations, and that existence does not admit of degrees. Yet it is perhaps this lingering uncertainty about the meaning of "existence" that continues to bring serious thinkers back to the ontological argument.

    C. The *teleological* argument

      1. The world contains ordered, harmonious structures (observable fact).

      2. But order and harmony are always the products of intelligent design (synthetic *a priori* principle).

      3. Therefore, the world is a product of intelligent design.

      4. But an inteligent designer great enough to have designed and created the world is what we mean by God.

      5. Therefore, God exists.

This argument has probably brought more skeptics to God than any of the others; even David Hume, its most severe critic, admitted that it has a "tough inner core" and allowed one of the more sympathetic characters in the *Dialogues on Natural Religion* to confess that the argument shows that the world was possibly due to a designer who "bears a remote analogy to human intelligence." Some examples, indeed, of the "order" and "harmony" of the world spoken of in premise one may be borrowed from Hume:

> Look round the world: contemplate the whole and every part of it: you will find it to be nothing but one great machine, subdivided into an infinite number of lesser machines, which again admit of subdivisions, to a degree beyond what human senses and faculties can trace and explain. All these various machines, and even their most minute parts, are adjusted to each other with an accuracy, which ravishes into admiration all men, who have ever contemplated them. The curious adapting of means to ends, throughout all nature, resembles exactly, though it much exceeds, the productions of human contrivance; of human design, thought, wisdom and intelligence . . .

Premise two was supported in a famous argument by William Paley (1743–1805), who compared the world to a watch. Imagine that you were walking on the surface of an alien and apparently uninhabited planet when, among rocks, debris, plants, and the remains of animals, you should come upon a watch lying on the ground. You would surely assume immediately that the watch had been made by some intelligent being who either inhabited this planet or was a visitor to it. You would never conclude that the watch had been created by mere accidents of wind and weather acting upon bits of metal and stone. Analogously, think of the examples of order and harmony to be found in the world. Must we not also assume that these, too, are products of an intelligent, ordering being? The present writer recalls one of his teachers at the high school he attended once saying with great emotion, "I do not know how anyone could deny the existence of God who had seen the human arm dissected, with its fantastic array of muscles, veins, sinews and nerves, all needed to make possible even the simple act of turning on a light switch."

Again, we will confine ourselves to describing two fundamental objections to this argument. They are taken from David Hume, who is considered to have demolished this argument despite his own worried concessions to it. First and most damaging is the lack of analogy between a world and a machine, which becomes evident when we look a bit closer at the first premise. For although all of us may easily observe, say, a watch in the making in the watchmaker's shop, none of us has ever seen a world in the making. How can we tell, then, whether intelligence is required to make a world? As we learn more about the world, we are better able to understand the forces that produced the seemingly machinelike structures mentioned above. In fact, few scientific explanations rely upon the assumption of a goal-directed intelligence underlying the world. Darwin, as is well known, is generally considered to have succeeded in his efforts to explain the familiar phenomenon of adaptation, the fact that a creature seems to have been created with biological structures that are needed to survive in the environmental niche that it inhabits, *without* reference to a creative God. Again, a watch is not like the human arm in that, although both fulfill a certain human purpose, we know only the purposes of the watchmaker, not those of God. Am I fulfilling God's purposes when I use my arm? Of course, the answer is "yes," if you accept the biblical account of God's purposes, but the arguments for the existence of God are intended to succeed without presupposing the truth of revelation. And the teleological argument is not able to show that any of the orderly and harmonious structures that it argues from are in fulfillment of the divine plan. Another way of expressing this objection is to note that premise one may be criticized for not supplying an objective criterion for identifying something as a harmonious design. How are we to tell whether any given object is "orderly" except insofar as its structure serves some human purpose? Viewed from a different standpoint than the human, the world might appear to be totally chaotic.

The second target of Hume's objections concerns the identification of God with the intelligent designer. And some of these objections could be made to apply as well to Saint Thomas Aquinas' identification of God with the unmoved mover or first cause. The teleological argument supplies no basis for asserting the *omnipotence, continued existence,* or *benevolence* of God. Not for the omnipotence of God, for God need be only powerful enough to have created the world: we need not assume that world creation requires infinite power, for we do not know that the world is an infinitely great place! The designer-God asserted by the argument, Hume notes, might have been a beginner who gave up on the world when it was half-completed. It supplies no basis for asserting the continued existence of God, for the watchmaker may die or move to another profession after the watch is made and sold! And it supplies no basis for asserting the benevolence of God, for, considering that earthquakes, cancer, and famine are part of the orderly structures of the world, we might conclude that the orderly designer created this world to realize his malevolent purposes, and whatever good we find here is the result of sheer chance!

D. *Other Arguments for God's Existence.* Of course, philosophers and natural theologians have reached beyond such formal proofs as these three in their efforts to render the belief in God plausible. There is, for example, the *argument from universal consent:* the very fact that all known peoples since the earliest beginnings of mankind have practiced some form of religion is itself a kind of evidence, it is said. For although some religions are more primitive than others, and although many great religious traditions do not acknowledge a God in the sense defined at the outset of this chapter, nevertheless all mankind has sought a world beyond, even if they have placed the locus of their religious concerns in a "spirit world" like the primitives, a transcendental principle, like the Hindu *Upanishads,* or in the Judeo-Christian-Islamic God. Such universality argues in favor of the reality of its object.

Now the logic of this argument appears to be weak; it assumes that belief is a criterion of truth. Today the skeptic might refer to the psychological theories of Sigmund Freud in response to this argument. Freud believed that religious faith could be shown to be a kind of *neurosis,* in which the son's conflict over his infantile rejection of his father is resolved by the worship of an all-powerful deity, whose aspects of frightful power and all-forgiving love are similar to the child's ideal image of his father. Of course, Freud's theory cannot account for religions that worship no gods or even for the religious devotion of women, it appears. But its threat to the argument from universal consent is clear: if we can show that human beings are motivated to seek God by a psychological need whose origins are transparent to modern science, then the plausibility of the contention that religious belief reveals transcendental truth diminishes.

Another argument bases itself upon the testimony of prophets, apostles, persons who have seen miracles performed or who have seen or spoken with

God or His angels. This is the argument from *religious experience:* men have spoken with God, hence God exists. Alas, the persuasiveness of such evidence seems always to be restricted to those who have had such experiences. To them, the existence of God is not a matter of faith but of fact. But the rest of us must base our belief upon our willingness to accept the testimony of the favored ones. In his famous refutation of the argument that biblical or contemporary miracles are an adequate basis for religious faith, David Hume noted that when I receive a report of such a miracle (as, say, the raising of Lazarus from the dead by Christ, or the appearance of the Virgin Mary to the children at Fatima), I must ask myself whether it would be more miraculous for the person giving me the report to be insane, confused, or plotting my deception than for the event to have occurred. Since I have had no experience of men being raised from the dead or of miraculous apparitions, but much experience of persons who are mad, deceived, or themselves deceivers, reason will always be opposed to the miracle, for reason always chooses the side with the preponderance of evidence.

An argument in favor of positive religion, if not of subjective religion, is that from the *salutary influence of religion.* "Religious faith may not be necessary for educated and strong-minded people," it is argued, "but the masses of mankind *need* religion: it not only supplies them with a reason for living, however chimerical, but it gives them a *powerful motive for moral behavior* in the promise of Paradise and the threat of hellfire. Without it, the masses, who do not possess the resources of fortitude and self-discipline needed to restrain the chaos of their passions and the selfish desire for personal gain, will turn to indolence and crime. Therefore, although there may be no God, we always do well to support religion." A frequent response to this argument points out the *pernicious* consequences of religious belief: its support of dogma and its impeding of scientific progress; its frequent furnishing of motives for conflicts between nations; and, more profoundly, its substitution of the authority of the revealed will of God for moral insight in matters of behavior—fear of hell is a poor reason for doing what is right! But the question of the positive and negative contributions of religion to civilization is always hotly debated by religious believers and skeptics. Two powerful arguments have been developed *against* positive religion; let us quickly sketch them.

Ludwig Feuerbach (1804–72) observed that my belief in God makes it impossible, or at least dangerous, to be the friend of a person who does not share my religious outlook. For, from my point of view, all persons who do not worship God as I do are among the outcast and the damned; indeed, I would have to fear that God will cast me out if I were to love His enemies. Of course, persons who worship other gods are inclined to view me in the same fashion! And thus, argues Feuerbach, we have the origin of seething animosities towards other peoples, even a powerful motive to go to war with them. Karl Marx (1818–83), a younger contemporary of Feuerbach who claimed to have learned a great deal from the older man, developed the view of religion that has shaped the thinking of the communist nations today: religion is an *instrument of domination* of the lower classes by the upper or ruling classes; it stands upon an eternal and unchanging authority—its "holy scriptures"— and thereby resists change; it is the "opium of the people," lulling them to sleep while the upper classes pick their pockets, making the misery of their lives more palatable by promising them "pie in the sky when they die." Religion is conceived not as having grown out of the longing of the soul for transcendence, but rather as an expression of an underlying and intractable discontent with the world as it is—a discontent that is purged in the act of worship. The liberation of mankind from the class society will lead to the rapid disappearance of the institutions of religion—and where it does not, as in most of the communist world, one can always simply close the churches.

The final argument in support of positive religion that we will consider is called *Pascal's Wager*. Blaise Pascal (1623–1662), a French mathematician and philosopher, made an extraordinary personal search for the meaning of life, which he describes in a notebook, published after his death, called simply *Thoughts*. Troubled by a lack of certainty in religious matters, he conceived of the problem of whether to believe in God as follows: Either I believe in God, or I do not. If I do, I will live a religious life and take care lest my soul be corrupted. If I do not, I will attempt simply to enjoy life. But either God exists, or He does not. The possibilities are as follows:

	God exists	God does not exist
I believe in God and live a religious life	I am rewarded with eternal bliss	I have wasted my life on religion
I do not believe in God and simply enjoy myself	I suffer the pain of eternal damnation	I have enjoyed myself in life

The payoff, if I believe in God and am right, is *infinitely* greater than the loss I incur if I do not believe in God and am wrong. With such odds in favor of the religious life, it would be sheer madness to bet that God does not exist. Of course, we cannot post any odds on whether God exists, but they surely cannot be as great as the qualitative distance between heaven and hell—who would trade eternal bliss for a few years of raising hell here on earth?

Were the possibility of believing in God real and living for a person, this argument might be compelling. But if the conviction that there is no God sits very deeply in your mind and soul, you will probably shrug your shoulders at Pascal's Wager. An interesting feature of this argument is that Pascal seems to assume that the Good Life in the City of Man is different from, incompatible with, and inferior to the Good Life in the City of God. Is this so?

Would the happiest human life be odious to God, and must a life pleasing to God be one that no human being would want? The Western tradition in religion does not speak with one voice on this issue, but in general Christianity seems to share Pascal's supposition: at bottom, we really don't want to be pious or even moral. Many contemporary Christians, however, deny that God saves only those who deny the passions of the flesh, or sacrifice themselves for the sake of others. Perhaps the highest human life is the one spent rejoicing in life! It is unclear, therefore, how much I am giving up of what I really want for the sake of my one winning chance to get into heaven.

On the other hand, Pascal's Wager seems not to speak at all of the act of *faith* that seems to be a part of all true religious living. I may believe *that* God exists without necessarily believing *in* God. For religion does not seem to be simply a theoretical alternative to agnosticism or to a naturalistic metaphysics. One does not believe in God the way one believes in, say, the theory of relativity. Religion has always demanded of the believer a subjective *commitment* to God, an attitude of *trust* that God will not fail him, a humble attempt to speak to God in *prayer,* and the *living experience* of His presence: all these things that are a part of faith. Pascal's Wager seems to imply that one can win the heaven-lottery just by buying a ticket and showing up at church at regular intervals! But now that we have introduced the student to some of the issues concerning positive religion and have outlined the most significant arguments that impel men either to faith or to skepticism, we will examine the concept of faith itself. And in this way we will explore the possible *significance* of God's existence for the life of the believer.

4. FAITH

We noted earlier that a personal God might exist, and yet take no interest in the affairs of men. However, the Western religious tradition has insisted upon the role of God in the individual human being's life and in human history. God is said to have chosen the Jewish people to form a special covenant with Him, Christ is said to have come to save all mankind from sin, and Mohammed received the Glorious Koran from God as a message to all mankind. And, of course, each individual person is called upon to "work out his salvation with diligence," for the life we live on earth has eternal significance. Eternal significance! That is the key to faith. In an often-quoted phrase, the contemporary theologian Paul Tillich spoke of religion as the area of our "ultimate concern"—*ultimate,* because we encounter here the eternal and the absolute dimension of life before which all else pales in significance; and *concern,* because we deal here not with abstract and theoretical questions, but with those of choosing our commitments, our hopes, our direction in life. But where do we encounter this eternal and absolute dimension? Let us first consider the case of Spinoza.

A. *Spinoza.* Spinoza's religiousness was not typical of the Western religious tradition, as we noted earlier. He denies the personhood of God, a passage in his *Ethics* implies his rejection of the divinity of Christ, and he denies the holy books of Judaism to be the word of God. Yet his life work, the *Ethics Demonstrated in Geometrical Order,* reveals a profound religiousness; indeed a later thinker, the German Romantic poet Novalis, was led to describe Spinoza as a "God intoxicated man." The source of this intoxication was "Nature, or God," which Spinoza discloses as an all-encompassing, unified, logical system, in which every event bears upon every other. "God" is not identified with each individual thing or event, but is conceived of as the *laws* according to which all things come to pass, and the *power* by which all things exist and act. Thus for Spinoza, "all things express, in a certain and determinate manner, the eternal and infinite essence of God." This is a classical statement of *pantheism,* the doctrine that God and the world are in some sense identical. Pantheism is more frequently encountered in Oriental religions than in the West, but in all cases it is accompanied by a heightened sense of the holy. For Spinoza, that sense of the holy impelled him to search for rational understanding of the laws of nature, for they constitute the *element of the eternal* in all things. Since reason teaches us that each event is a necessary consequence of immutable laws, we may come to contemplate each event, no matter how personally distressing it may be for us as individuals, under the aspect of eternity. This contemplation will inspire us to experience the most profound joy, which Spinoza identifies as the *intellectual love of God.* My own earthly existence, too, has an eternal aspect, insofar as it is a necessary expression of the infinite essence of God; I am part of the eternal scheme of things, and what I do while I am alive will influence, in some small manner, the totality of what is to come. Moreover, although God is not personal, in my love of Nature, Nature comes to love itself, for I, too, am a part of Nature. This concept of faith is *not* based upon a personal encounter with God (for God is not considered to be a person), nor is it a hope in God's providence (for everything is as it must be). It does not involve prayer, but reason; and yet it is a loving encounter with the whole of Reality, and we may call it *faith,* and not just rational science. A religiousness like this is surely not intended for Saturday or Sunday services but is a total attitude toward existence that one carries within one throughout the week, and that fills us with stoical courage, as well as with joy in life.

B. *Schleiermacher.* Spinoza was a *rationalist,* and it is not surprising that his mode of encountering God was through the faculty of reason. In the Romantic era, more emotional and subjective approaches to God were sought. And one of the most profound doctrines, as well as the most influential within Protestant Christianity, was that developed by the German pastor and theologian Friedrich Schleiermacher (1768–1834). Schleiermacher's view of religious experience was similar to that of Kant, who spoke of the "feeling of the noumenal" when we contemplate the starry skies or the vast reaches of nature; such feelings intimate a world beyond whose presence we sense but cannot grasp. Kant believed, however, that religion is built upon our moral life alone, and that to have faith is to view the moral law as commanded by God. Schleiermacher insisted that the experience of the "noumenal," the "encompassing," the "transcendent" be brought to the forefront of religious experience instead of morals. Religion, he says, is a *kind of feeling*, the feeling of dependence upon God. Indeed, not only do I feel the dependence of the *world* upon God, but my personal existence is felt to be dependent upon God, not merely in the sense that I am a creature of God, but that I could not possess a sense of self-identity unless I stood in some sort of God-relation, the highest of which is faith. In the Christian religion, Schleiermacher believed, I comprehend my own inner existence, my own "ego" with its personal history, in terms of my relationship of dependency to Jesus Christ. In his philosophy, therefore, faith becomes a personal engagement of myself with God. Faith, however, is erected upon a basis of feeling and not of reason, but Schleiermacher does not describe in great detail the *kind* of feeling that the feeling of the God-relation is. Such work was left to men like Rudolf Otto (1869–1937) in the twentieth century, who attempted to describe kinds of religious feelings—especially those of religious *awe* and religious *fascination*, by which our soul, if not our reason, comes to know God. Here the important contribution to religion is precisely the subjective component of religious awareness: a feeling, an uncanny and inexpressible sensation that the world is not exhausted by the realm of natural occurrences, but that we stand in the presence of God. And, realizing this, our view of the world and of ourselves is profoundly altered.

C. *Kierkegaard.* The Danish philosopher and theologian Søren Kierkegaard's (1813–1855) essential life-problem was: How do I become a Christian? And, as such, we might be led to believe that his work is of interest only to Christians. But what makes Kierkegaard of universal importance is that he considered the problem of faith from the outside, as it were, asking how an individual might attain to religious faith, and whether faith constitutes the *highest* kind of life attainable for a human being. This concern with the human being engaged in a personal struggle for faith, or for some kind of personal meaning in life, has given Kierkegaard his position as one of the founding fathers of the contemporary philosophy known as existentialism; and we will consider Kierkegaard as an existentialist in a later chapter. Kierkegaard's thought is difficult, and he often writes not in his own name, but in the names of various invented characters who represent different points of view in the struggle for understanding. Consequently, his work is more a series of question marks in terms of which each reader can pose the question of the meaning of his or her own life, rather than a set of doctrines or philosophical theories. Indeed, Kierkegaard called himself the "Socrates of Christianity," meaning that he tries to help others discover religious faith within themselves while he is yet unable to give final form to his own answers to life's questions.

Although, then, Kierkegaard sees himself as moving towards Christianity, he grants that the arguments for God's existence are inconclusive. Moreover, he recognizes the inherent difficulty of basing one's aspirations to eternal life upon a historical claim—the life and mission of Christ—whose historicity can be questioned. Even more, from the point of view of this side of faith, many of the traditional doctrines of Christianity appear to be impossible, even incomprehensible and absurd: that God became man in the person of Christ, that God is "eternal," that God may interfere in the natural order by performing miracles, that even evil men can be saved—who could believe such things but a fool or a desperate man? But the point is that we *are* desperate, according to Kierkegaard, although we may conceal this fact from ourselves: we are born into this everyday world, but with something very un-everyday within us, namely, an eternal element that longs for the absolute, the beyond, the perfect. And so we feel ourselves impelled toward God, toward something that we cannot understand, but that we can relate ourselves to in a subjective act of appropriation: we take a *leap of faith,* we project ourselves toward what our mere intellects cannot understand, we begin to live as though we were eternal, as though we stood before the eyes of God. We believe *although* it is absurd; the religious message then becomes true *for me* and not simply true as some indifferent fact about the world is true: I make the religious message *my own.* How we are able to do all of this is, in part, a mystery, although we can describe what the religious man, the Knight of Faith, is like: we have Kierkegaard's famous description of Abraham who was able to make ready to sacrifice his own son on the command of God—an act that, from a merely human point of view, appears as the monstrous act of an evil or insane man. Venerable father Abraham! says Kierkegaard. Who can understand you? Yet faith makes all things possible, it saves us when we are lost, swimming over fifty fathoms of water; it makes us whole, we who are a confused amalgam of the finite and the eternal. Without this leap, Kierkegaard believes, the human spirit is doomed to be divided within itself.

5. FAITH UNDER ATTACK

About a century ago, the German philosopher Friedrich Nietzsche (1844–1900) proclaimed the death of God: the Western religious tradition, he said, was no longer providing its civilization with the underpinnings of its existence. Clearly, our lives are no longer God-centered, and our *best knowledge—* science—makes little or no reference to God. And, indeed, the typical American community today seems to be centered more about its school and its shopping center than about its church. Nietzsche not only documents the death of God among us, he helps to bring about His demise. Let us consider first his attack and then the attack of contemporary philosophy upon what we have been calling subjective religion.

Nietzsche's argument represents a form of *humanism* that we will later encounter in the existentialist Jean-Paul Sartre. The death of God is welcomed by Nietzsche, although with a certain dread that mankind might sink into nihilism without some thought of a God beyond the horizon of our world. But up to now, religion has served the weak-minded masses as a *kind of crutch* supporting wasted lives, as a *consolation* for being lost, confused, and exploited (indeed, Nietzsche believes that Christianity has even *encouraged* weakness, foolishness, and poverty). Moreover, religion has tempted men to reject those values appropriate to this life in favor of those of the next—has made men, in effect, *long for death*. It has robbed men of their courage and has taught them to despise this world. Thus, instead of being a challenge to the most profound yearnings of the human spirit, as in Kierkegaard, religion reveals itself in Nietzsche as a *denial* of the best part of us, as a *threat* to life, and to joy, and to the life-serving spirit. O my brothers, Nietzsche says, do not indulge yourselves in other-worldly hopes! *Remain true to the earth!* And Nietzsche draws up in great detail his bill of accusations against religious faith. He opposes to religion a humanistic vision of a race of supermen who, by remaining true to the earth, perfect the resources of spirit that ages of evolutionary development have stored up in mankind. In each of us, says Nietzsche, is a god waiting to be born: something new, unique, and creative can be brought forth from us—if only we risk everything during the brief moment we are on earth, if only we have the courage to say that not God's purposes, but my own joy, however brief, justifies existence itself.

In the Anglo-Saxon world, the attack upon religious faith often takes the form of a claim that religious faith is *empty*, in that the believer himself *does not know what it is he believes in.* This was the import of our first objection to the ontological argument. The God defined at the outset of this chapter is attacked *not* as not existing, but rather as a *meaningless* concept. And this powerful reproach to religion was expressed in terms of a parable told by a contemporary philosopher with the appropriate name of John Wisdom. The story goes something like this. Imagine, says Wisdom, two gardeners, Don and John, who return to their garden after a long vacation. "The flowers are still growing," says Don. "Some gardener must have kept up our garden in our absence." "That is a possible hypothesis," says John, "let's put it to the test by asking the neighbors if they have seen anyone in our garden." They ask, and the test is negative: no one has seen a mysterious gardener. Instead of dropping the hypothesis as disconfirmed, however, Don *qualifies* it in various ways: "Perhaps the gardener came by night," or "perhaps the gardener is invisible." Of course each new qualification suggests a new test: we can test for the presence of invisible gardeners by using electronic sensors, for example. But finally Don runs out of qualifications. Still, he says, "I shall continue to believe in a mysterious gardener who has helped us out in the past, and who is, perhaps, helping us right now. Even though we cannot see him, hear him, or feel him, even though we *cannot test for his presence in any way*, I believe in his existence." At that point, John might simply chalk up this attitude of Don's to an act of faith on his part, a faith that he does not share, but that he cannot disprove. But instead John asks Don a question that changes the direction of their argument. "What is the difference," he asks, "between a gardener whose existence cannot be tested for—and *no* gardener at all? Indeed, *what difference does it make* if your mysterious gardener exists? You have qualified him out of existence: all we can say about him is that he is unlike any gardener we've ever encountered. He has no body, uses no tools, is seen by no one, acts without being physically present, and the like. In fact, we don't know what he's like; and you don't even have the right, without *some* sort of test, to claim that he is a gardener or has any specific qualities at all. Therefore, you cannot use your belief in this gardener to *explain* anything that goes on in the garden. So why not *forget about him?*"

The objection to religious faith contained in this story is a powerful one. Unless we know what we mean by a concept contained in a claim, we cannot find our whether the claim is true, any more than I could go searching for glumpfs, unless I knew what they looked like or what properties they were supposed to have. And if I *cannot* describe the properties of glumpfs, then I not only could never find one (even if one was in this room right now, I couldn't recognize it as a glumpf), but I would not know what it is that I was looking for. And we do *not* know what we mean by God: think for a moment about what it means to be "infinite" and "eternal." Do you know what it would be like to encounter such a being? Kierkegaard speaks of a "leap of faith" in which we embrace a being that is infinite and eternal. But if we don't know what these terms mean, then our leap is truly a leap in the dark. Moreover, if there are no possible tests for God's existence, then how does believing in God differ from believing that there is an invisible monkey on my back just now? One might argue that belief in God does at least make a difference in the life of the person who believes in Him (as Kierkegaard believed), and that this change justifies faith; but if there is no check on the truth of the claim, doesn't that argument give me the right to believe in *anything* I wish to believe? And should we not have the *courage* to reject any belief that is blind, that is based only in my will to believe?

Let us close at this point. Indeed, the debate about God could go on, even though this final argument seems to show that the debate is *futile:* what is the point in trying to make sense about something that by definition is beyond sense? But we do not seem to be able to dispense with God, to dispose of Him as a useless concept, like that of entelechy in biology, or the ether in physics. During the past several centuries there has been a tendency to move God from his position at the center of Western society to a place on the periphery of our consciousness. We spend six days a week thinking in worldly and rational concepts, and only one hour a week thinking about what transcends reason and the world. The effects of this slow contraction of the religious dimension of life will be one of the subjects of our study of the philosophy of man in our final chapter.

QUESTIONS FOR STUDY

1. Restate the arguments for the existence of God in as strong a fashion as you can. Then discuss at least one of the objections to each argument that was raised in this chapter, and attempt to show that it does not effectively weaken the argument.

2. Jean-Paul Sartre attacks subjective religion from the standpoint of atheistic humanism in his play *The Flies*. Read this play and attempt to state in the form of an argument Sartre's charges against religious faith.

3. Develop a Marxist critique of positive religion by arguing that religion, both historically and essentially, resists change and thus is supportive of the social and political *status quo;* and that it supports the interest of the upper rather than the lower classes.

4. Contrast *insight,* which is often claimed to be a route to religious experience, with what philosophers call *reason.* To what extent does insight depend upon emotion? Is insight more likely to be perverted by "wishful thinking" than reason? To what extent, do you believe, is it possible to "know" the truth of a proposition apart from reason and experience?

5. Discuss Pascal's Wager. Would such a proof be convincing to a person who had *no other reason* to believe in God?

6. Nietzsche appears to look upon religious faith as a crutch for the weak-minded, whereas Kierkegaard considers the leap of faith to be one of the most difficult feats to which a person can aspire. Develop the reasons in support of both points of view.

12

The Legacy of the Orient

1. WEST AND EAST

It may occur to you to ask why all the philosophers we have discussed up to now have been Europeans. Is this because the authors are especially narrow-minded, and interested only in their own traditions? Or is philosophy itself something that is found only in the Western world? But surely there were philosophers and philosophy in ancient China or India! These are fair questions and reasonable expectations, but the answers to them are not easy to discover. The philosophical tradition we have been discussing here does not have roots in the ancient history of other great civilizations. This is due, to a great extent, to geographical factors, for Eastern and Western cultures were effectively sealed off from each other until quite recently. The caravans that made their way across Africa, the merchants of silk that slowly transported their goods from China to Europe by way of Samarkand, even the armies of Alexander the Great that conquered India all failed to transmit philosophical insights from one people to another in any but the most superficial fashion. Europe's intellectual culture has influenced the peoples of Asia and Africa only during the past two hundred years, the age of colonial domination. And Asia and Africa have made their spiritual traditions felt in Europe and America for even a shorter period of time. Perhaps we today are still seeking a basis for a world philosophical outlook that would draw upon the spiritual, cultural, and intellectual heritage of all mankind. But Western philosophy, as described in this book, is the unique tradition of thought that originated among the ancient Greeks and developed in relative isolation among the Jews, Christians, and Moslems of Europe, North Africa, and the Near East.

But aren't the traditions of China and India, for example, "philosophical"? Or are they what we call "religious" traditions? Now this is a semantical issue— that is, it concerns the meanings of a term, namely, "philosophy" and what it properly designates—but it is an important issue. Remember that what we have called "philosophy" is a variety of *doctrines, activities* and *attitudes* all concerned with a subject matter that is itself difficult to define. (Ask yourself what philosophy is "about"!) If one means by "philosophy" a set of *doctrines* and *beliefs* concerning the nature of the world, man's role in the world, and mankind's hopes for a future life, then surely all civilizations have philosophical traditions. However, if by "philosophy" one means the uninhibited exploration of the cosmos by reason unencumbered by tradition or dogma, as we find in Thales, or the unrestricted criticism and self-criticism of unexamined beliefs, as we find in Plato's dialogues, or the Aristotelian confidence in the life of rational activity as the Good Life, then the question of whether other civilizations "do philosophy" becomes doubtful. Doubtful but not entirely implausible, however, for there are elements of all three of these dimensions of Western philosophy in the thought of other civilizations, although they may not be as firmly rooted there.

But just as we would not call Western thought "Buddhist," although there are elements of Buddhist thought found in it, so perhaps it would be better to use the term "philosophy" to designate only the Western tradition that begins with the Greeks, and use those terms that Eastern thinkers themselves devised to describe the traditions from within which they speak: "Hinduism," "Confucianism," and "Buddhism." Such terms do more than designate an individual philosophy or system of religion; they refer to the thought, religion, and especially in the case of the first two, even the social system of entire peoples and regions of the world. These are traditions that have developed, like philosophy, over the course of more than two thousand five hundred years, and, like philosophy, contain different and often contradictory visions of the world.

When one begins the study of a tradition vastly different from one's own, one normally starts by comparing the foreign tradition with the familiar one. The reasons for this are twofold. First, there is the difference in language. If one knows Sanskrit or Chinese or Pali or Japanese, it is possible to plunge into the scriptures of Hinduism or Buddhism or Confucianism directly; one learns unfamiliar usages of terms from the context in which they appear. If one does not know these languages, one is forced to search for equivalences in one's own language, and that is often quite difficult. English lacks exact equivalences for such terms as Brahman or Tao or Satori, which we will discuss later in this chapter. Of course, you may not know Greek either, and yet we plunged without further ado into Plato and Aristotle. But we must not forget that the English language, like other European tongues, has been profoundly influenced by Greek; its very structures and its vocabulary bear the imprint of the philosophical vision of the Greeks. We see the world, so to speak, in categories similar to theirs. Not so with Eastern thought; there we need to provide ourselves with new spectacles, beginning by altering the only ones we have. Indeed, any Westerner who seriously considers the attempt to share one of the religious and philosophical visions of the East, or even to become a convert to Buddhism or Hinduism, ought to begin by learning one of the languages through which those traditions give themselves expression.

Second, we can find *some* authentic and significant traces of Eastern cultures, beliefs, and concerns in our own traditions. After all, despite profound differences of language and outlook, we all share a common humanity and are able to recognize ourselves in other peoples, no matter how strange they may initially seem. Understanding the Oriental legacy is not unlike making friends with a person from an Asian country. After awhile, we come to recognize shared concerns and common beliefs; we begin to see that the presuppositions of our own lives and our actions are similar to those of our new friend, although they seem to operate within a different context and receive different expression from him. For example, we are both capable of being insulted, but our Oriental friend may understand the insult as unanswerable in the social context in which it was given and respond to it by smiling—until the appropriate day of reckoning arrives! This kind of thing is, of course, part of our social behavior, and not the expression of a religious or philosophical belief, but the idea of getting to know foreign thought the way we come to understand the way of life of foreign peoples is not farfetched. Both involve starting from our own standpoint and sympathetically reaching out toward a common standpoint, a point at which our human natures touch, and then moving from that common ground to a detailed understanding of the world our neighbors inhabit. The attempt is a great adventure, and one that is sure to deepen our own vision and to expand our own world.

2. HISTORICAL SURVEY

That much said, let us begin by sketching the historical origins and development of the three major Oriental traditions we will study in this chapter: Hinduism, Confucianism, and Buddhism. We will then point out a few parallels between Eastern and Western thought and show how the two differ even at points of intersection. And finally, we will offer a description of several of the most important *religious concepts* of Eastern thinkers, especially those that are foreign to the West.

Just as it is fair to say that the Western religious tradition was born in the area around today's Israel and spread as Judaism, Christianity, and Islam throughout the world from the Himalayas through northern Africa, Europe, and the New World, so we may say that the Oriental traditions were born in northern India, and eventually spread as Hinduism and Buddhism to China, Southeast Asia, and Japan, meeting with and influencing the native Shinto cult in Japan, and the Confucian and Taoist traditions in China. Let us arbitrarily take 1500 B.C. as the date of the earliest beginnings of civilization in both China and India and begin with the native tradition of China. In China at that time (more exact dates will be found in the table on page 216), the earliest historical dynasty, the Shang, was established. In the thousand years that followed, classical Chinese civilization developed, Confucius lived, and the so-called Six Schools sprang up to debate the ideas of Confucius. Two philosophical concepts that had evolved in the centuries before Confucius, and that appear to have been assumed by him, include the notion of *Tao*, or the Way of Heaven, which manifests itself in the way of things on earth; and the *yin-yang*, which designates the forces underlying all change in nature. These terms will be described in our final section.

By the time of the first three centuries after Christ, the period of the later Han dynasty, the fundamental character of Chinese civilization was fixed—except for the more mystical and otherworldly element of Buddhism, which, in the eyes of some Chinese, was invited from abroad, and in the eyes of others, had invaded the seemingly self-sufficient Chinese people after 400 A.D. The early civilization of China tended to be this-worldly and humanistic. Except for the relics of animism and ancestor worship and the more mystical philosophy of the semi-mythical Lao tzu, the father of Taoism, the thrust of Chinese thought was toward the problems encountered in this world. It concerned itself with the problem of how to live well despite frequent social disruptions, and of establishing the proper relationship of the individual to his society and the individual to the other persons around him: to the king, the father, the spouse, the brother, and to the child. For that reason, it has often been asked whether the thoughts of Confucius, whose subtle, conservative mind gave answers to these and similar questions—answers that have remained vital and alive in the minds of the Chinese for two thousand five hundred years—ought to be called a religion, an ethical philosophy, or simply a set of wise maxims for ordering our earthly affairs. The question is again a semantical one, of course, but it is an important and enlightening fact that when such other-worldly and mystical religions such as Taoism and Buddhism were developed in China, they did not supplant Confucianism but coexisted with it on a different plane, so to speak. However, Confucius was awarded a more and more godlike place in the popular Chinese mind as the centuries passed, and his yearly festival was the occasion of great celebrations throughout China until 1949.

In the centuries following 1500 B.C., India was subject to repeated waves of invasion by a people we call the Aryans—a term meaning simply "lord" or

CHRONOLOGY

CHINA	INDIA	JAPAN
B.C. 1500 Shang Dynasty, c. 1800–1120	Invasion of Arya; destruction of Indus valley civilization. Rig-Veda complete by 1000; oral tradition	
Chou dynasty, 1000 1120–221 Development of the classical texts of Chinese civilization	Vedas complete by 800 Upanishads after 800	
	Jains: Mahavira, died c. 526 Buddha, c. 563–483	
Lao tzu?		
500 Confucius, c. 551–479	Epics: Ramayana after 400 Mahabarata	
"Six Schools"	Ashoka, Buddhist emperor of India, c. 274–237	
Ch'in dynasty, 221–207: Great Wall Early Han dynasty, 206–A.D. 9		
0 Later Han dynasty, 23–220 Confucian cannon fixed Buddhism penetrates China after 100	Bhagavad-Gita, c. 1st century A.D. Gupta age, c. 300–540 Buddhism expelled from India after c. 400	Earliest beginnings of Japanese civilization
A.D. 500 T'ang dynasty, 618–906		Yamato: first known emperor
Sung dynasty, 960–1279	Vedanta: Shankara, philosopher, c. 788–820	Buddhism penetrates Japan after 552
1000	First Islamic invasions after 900	
Confucian revival 1260: conquest of China by Moghuls	Ramunuja, philosopher, 1175–1256 Madhva, philosopher, 13th century	Development of Zen Buddhism: Eisai, 1141–1215 Nichiren, 1222–1282
Ming dynasty, 1368–1644		
1500	Akbar, greatest Moghul emperor, 1542–1605	Rise of Tokugawa shogunate after 1600
Ching dynasty, 1644–1912	Sikhs: Nanak, 1469–1538	

"noble." They were related to the Greeks, and we get the name of Iran from them. These people spoke a language that is related to our own, for both English and their language (a later dialect of which is called Sanskrit) are members of the Indo-European language group and are distinct from the Oriental, African, Amerindian, and Semitic tongues. The Aryans brought with them a bardic tradition of hymns, tales, and magical formulas that, in interaction with the literate civilization of the Indus river valley that they apparently destroyed, and with the native Dravidian religions of central and southern India, was to form the basis of the religious tradition of India for over three thousand years. This oral tradition was eventually put into writing and constituted the earliest Hindu scriptures. These are called the *Vedas*, of which the most famous, the *Rig-Veda*, was completed in about 800 B.C., approximately the time that the Homeric epics in Greece were given the form by which we know them today. Indeed, they contain as their chief characters gods and goddesses who are unmistakably related to those of ancient Greece. The three major gods of the earliest Vedas are Indra, a warrior-god; Varuna, god of order and morality; and Agni, the god of fire. The general character of the Vedas reflects the spirit of fighting, carousing, self-assured warrior kings, and they contain no marked tendencies toward asceticism or mysticism. However, the Vedas assert the priority of a priestly class, the Brahmins, over the warrior caste, or nobility (kshatriya); the beginnings of *caste* as a fundamental Hindu social structure has its roots in these very ancient Indian traditions. The proliferation of castes, the definition of the obligations and rights attached to each caste and the general rigidity of caste (one was fixed in the caste to which one was born for life; working your way up the social ladder to a higher caste would be impossible and even immoral) came only much later. The Vedas were later supplemented by appendices, called *Upanishads*, some of which were written before and some after the two great heresies of *Jainism* and *Buddhism*.

Jainism was founded in the sixth century B.C. by Mahavira, who is said by his followers to be the last of a succession of Enlightened Ones who point the way of salvation to mankind. Its most remarkable characteristic (perhaps especially from a Western point of view) is its extreme *asceticism* (at one time it was considered meritorious by Jains to fast to the death), which, in the case of the so-called "sky-clad" Jains, included even the renunciation of the wearing of clothing, and its extreme reverence for life. Indeed, Jains are known to sweep the streets with a small broom as they walk along, to insure that they will not tread upon insects that might happen to be in their way. The Jains claim two million members in India today.

Buddhism's early history is among the most colorful and striking of the great world religions. The tale of Gautama Siddhartha, a prince of northern India who left his father's palace to seek salvation, should be part of every person's heritage. The religion Gautama ultimately found is a rejection of both the social and religious structures of Vedic religion. The importance of caste is denied, and the extremes of Jainist and Brahmin asceticism were abandoned by Him. The gods, although apparently admitted to exist, were given little status by Gautama. But it was through his doctrine of the no-self that His influence has been felt through the ages. For Gautama denied the existence of a soul-substance that constitutes my personal identity, and that is subject to successive reincarnations. "I" *do not exist:* because I continue to imagine myself as an entity inhabiting a world distinct from myself that desires to possess, exploit, and enjoy, I become *bound to* the world. But this world of everyday perception, which our own cravings create, is, Gautama taught, *dukkha:* pain and suffering. And thus the main thrust of Buddhism is toward *liberation* from this everyday world. This avenue consists in the renunciation of desire and in reestablishing the fundamental *unity* of all things. We must learn to experience the world without reference to a self that is the subject of that experience. The religious consequences of this remarkable doctrine will be explored in the final section.

Eventually, Buddhism was to divide itself into two fundamental sects, each of which fostered numerous schools. Historically the most important of the sects is the one called *Mahayana,* or Greater Vehicle Buddhism. This sect developed a complex scholarly tradition that emphasized devotion to the celestial Buddhas and the Buddhas-to-be who figure in an elaborate mythology and, in some schools, reintroduced the doctrine of reincarnation or, as in Pure Land Buddhism in China, the immortality of the soul. The other sect of Buddhism is called *Theravada,* or the Ways of the Elders. It seems to be closer to primitive Buddhism than Mahayana. It preaches the renunciation of, and eventual withdrawal from, the world and emphasizes meditation rather than worship of Buddha-figures; it is inward-looking and unworldly. Perhaps for that very rason, Theravada never appealed to the broad masses of the peoples of Asia, who, like the masses of people everywhere, prefer to seek their salvation in more tangible things—in myths, rites, and images. Nevertheless, by about 700 A.D. Buddhism had left India entirely, forced out by the growing strength of the Brahmins, who reasserted the Vedic traditions in the new and more profound way that was to become Hinduism.

Before it left, however, Buddhism occupied central stage in India for a few centuries, thanks to the work of one of the most remarkable men in the history of the world—the emperor Ashoka. This great conqueror almost succeeded in a feat that has eluded the peoples of India during all of its history: the unification of the subcontinent under a single native leader. Nevertheless, when still a young man, Ashoka renounced all warfare and violence, became a convert to Buddhism, and proceeded to spread Buddhist doctrines and the arts of peace throughout his realm. His great capital at Pataliputra, which was supposedly modeled after the Persian capital Persepolis, has entirely vanished today. All that remains are the testimony of foreign visitors (for the Indians wrote little about their own history), some beautifully polished marble statues, and Ashoka's famous iron pillars upon which Buddhist precepts were carefully engraved.

Some of the greatest works of the Hindu tradition were written in the centuries following the rise of Buddhism and Jainism. Among these are the *Upanishads.* Some of the Upanishads are metaphysical works in that they are concerned with the ultimately real constituents of the universe. Then there are the *epics,* which contain the tales of the gods, their humanlike incarnations, and their struggles with each other and in the affairs of men. These epics have provided the basis of popular religion to Hindus up to the present day, much as the biblical stories and the lives of the saints, with their wondrous events and symbolic representations of the Divine Will, provide spiritual nourishment to both sophisticated and simple Christians. The first of the Hindu epics is called the *Mahabharata;* it is the longest poem in the world. Like the *Iliad,* it tells the story of a battle that is supposed to have taken place before recorded time. The famous *Bhagavad-Gita,* or *The Celestial Song,* is considered to be part of this epic; in its magnificent poetry, it expresses a simple ethics of renunciation and devotion to the will of some one god (bhakti). The second epic is the *Ramayana,* in which the trials and misadventures of a princely couple is recounted. Hindus look upon Prince Rama and his spouse Sita as models of the highest virtue (dharma) because of their fidelity, piety, and thankless devotion to justice during their struggle with the demon chieftain of Ceylon, Ravana.

The first centuries after Christ were a time of the highest flowering of Buddhist and Hindu culture in India. It is called the age of the Gupta Kings. During this time, Buddhism established its canon of sacred writings, created the magnificently decorated caves at Ajanta and Ellora, and developed its typical architectural form—the stupa—which was later to influence the building of monuments in China and Southeast Asia. But Hinduism was to be the victor in the bloodless struggle with Buddhism, and the later Gupta period and the Middle Ages were to see a renaissance of speculation and sacred writing in a Hindu key. The *Vedanta* or "end of the Vedas," a set of philosophical commentaries upon the Vedas and the Upanishads, and their philosophical articulation by various learned Brahmins became a part of the Hindu tradition after about 500 A.D. Included here would be the great speculative systems of Shankara and Ramanuja. This great outpouring of culture and thought occurred despite frequent invasions of the subcontinent by various peoples; indeed, with the exception of the high points of the Gupta period, there was no central rule in India from Ashoka until the Moghul emperors in the sixteenth century A.D. India was composed of petty kingdoms of native nobles and of the descendents of foreign invaders, such as the great Kushan king Kanishka I, who ruled northern India during the first century A.D. Eventually, however, the Brahmins, who had been so successful in absorbing foreign invaders into the Hindu religious and social systems, were forced to confront an unassimilable foe: these were the Moslem invaders from Persia, who began expeditions of plunder into the subcontinent as early as the tenth century and then stayed on to establish sultanates in Delhi. These sultans were eventually superseded by a Moslem empire of Turks and Mongols, the Moghuls, whose greatest emperor, Akbar, sought to replace Hinduism with a hybrid religion of his own.

The reason why the Moslems could not be assimilated as had been the earlier invaders of India is an interesting one. The Hindus had developed on the basis of the Vedic traditions a religion whose fundamental percepts were flexible. They seem to recognize the frailty of the human intellect and the great distance between man as he is and man in his enlightened state; and they acknowledged the great differences between individuals in temperament, inclinations, and ability. Thus, they held, we ought not to expect that there is one single true road to the divine. Moreover, no one metaphysical system was considered by Hindus to possess absolute truth, any more than any one of India's numberless gods are said to be ultimate. Rather, philosophical viewpoints are just that—viewpoints, or *darshana,* from one of which you or I may get a clearer view of what lies beyond all words, all philosophy, all cognition.

The Moslems, on the other hand (like the Christians whom the Hindus were later to encounter in the form of the British imperialists), believed in a single, ultimate truth, one that brooked no disagreement; they believed in the virtue of having faith in a single, universal God, and, at times, even in forcing others to share that faith. Disagreements among men as to the true philosophy, they seem to believe, are not due to any inherent human frailty, but to a self-inflicted, pernicious blindness on the part of unbelievers. But the Moslems were not enormously successful in suppressing Hinduism, although they won many converts and mingled with the population. One of the religious results of the Moslem invasions was the establishment, after years of bloody struggle, of a Moslem-Hindu religion, that of the *Sikhs,* whose membership today is centered in the Punjab, the northwest border region between Pakistan and India.

It is impossible in a short chapter to recount the vicissitudes experienced by Buddhism when it established itself outside of India. By the fifth century A.D. it was well represented in China, as we have seen, where it contributed elements of popular ritual that were to appeal to the lower classes, and a powerful scholarly and speculative tradition that found favor among Chinese intellectuals who were weary of a Taoism that had begun to compromise with popular superstition and a Confucianism that had grown rigid. When the Japanese began to borrow extensively from the Chinese in the development of their own unique culture, Buddhist monks and Buddhist writings were invited to Japan, along with the secularly cultivated mandarins. Japan had, of course, an indigenous religion, called *Shinto,* which is characterized by the worship of ancestors and of a native Japanese pantheon of *kami,* or things divine—including, as you may know, the beautiful mountain called

Fuji, which has become the symbol of all Japan. But the greatest of the *kami* was the goddess of the sun, Amaterasu, who is said to have chosen the Land of the Rising Sun as her residence, where she gave birth to Jummu, the mythical first emperor of Japan. The first historical emperor, a member of the family of the Yamato, was believed to have been Jummu's descendent, and it is a fact that the current emperor, Hirohito (as he is called in the West), is the descendent of the Yamatos in an unbroken line—by far the oldest known family in the world. For this reason, before the Second World War, the sophisticated Japanese presented to the world the strange and seemingly archaic practice of worshipping their emperor as a deity.

Buddhism, on the other hand, became the transcendental religion of the Japanese and took on many forms, most of which have an esoteric (secret) and exoteric (popular) form. The most famous of the esoteric religions— esoteric because it requires, initially at least, that studies be conducted as a monk in a monastery—is that of Zen Buddhism, which had its earliest origins in China. Zen, like all of Buddhism, is a doctrine of liberation from the everyday world and from the self, whose cravings and whose habits of thought cause our bondage. In Zen, we learn to experience reality in a new way, and this requires a discipline of the body as well as a discipline of the mind. We will describe a typical practice of Zen training in the section following this one.

3. CONCEPTUAL CONTRASTS

History alone gives us no direct insight into the inwardness of the religions whose history we study. For that, we must attempt to understand the categories in terms of which the realm of the divine is thought, and we must study the actual practices of the religious believers whose religious experience we seek to understand. But what are the fundamental conceptualizations that underlie Western thought? We are generalizing in a very broad way, of course, but we might venture the suggestion that the concepts of *substance*, of *God*, of *idea*, and of *history* are fundamental to Western thought. Just because they are so basic to Western thinking and because they are *not* as fundamental in the East, the contrasts they suggest are interesting and revealing.

A. Substance.

The concept of substance was first analyzed by Aristotle. It is discussed in our chapter on Aristotelianism, and it figures in our chapters on logic and metaphysics. Substances, for Aristotle, as for most subsequent Western thinkers, are the individual physical objects that make up the world, and which we cognize in terms of the concepts of our language. "Socrates" is a substance, as is the paper I am writing upon, and as is the dog sitting at my feet. The logical difficulties that have been discovered clinging to the concept of substance, as well as the various qualifications of the term, make up the greater part of the Western debate about the nature of Ultimate Reality. But the mainstream of Western thought has tended to follow Aristotle in attributing *primary,* and, as the case of materialism, *ultimate* reality to the world of our everyday experience. In fact, if a metaphysical or epistemological theory had the unreality of the physical world as a consequence, this was often held to be a *prima facie* reason for rejecting that theory. Bishop Berkeley, for example, was believed to have denied the reality of the physical world, and his opponent in philosophy, Dr. Johnson, is reported to have claimed to have refuted Berkeley by kicking a stone. This story illustrates the strong conviction of the Western thinker in beginning the search for reality with what is often called the "world of common sense."

The East, however, has tended to welcome doctrines that preach the illusory or derivative nature of the physical world. This assertion must be approached with caution, however. There is an element of materialism in both Indian and Chinese thought. And many Western thinkers (recall Nietzsche) have criticized Christianity for its element of other-worldliness, and its suggestion that events in this world are of little significance in comparison with what awaits us in the next. Thus the contrast we are asserting is one of emphasis rather than of principle. Nevertheless, in much of Eastern thought it is precisely this everyday phenomenal world that the Eastern thinker wishes to penetrate, overcome, and go beyond. We have already encountered the Buddhist doctrine of the no-self, which teaches that an illusory dualism of self-world is responsible for mankind's bondage. In the system of Vedanta Hinduism developed by Shankara, the phenomenal world—including the gods and men—is *Maya* or illusion. The everyday world is a mere magic show conjured up by selfish craving! Like Zen, the goal of Hindu religious practices—including yoga and meditation—is to penetrate the veil of Maya, and enter into a direct relationship with the ultimate reality, called the Brahman, that lies within all things. To succeed, one must achieve enlightenment about, and release from (moksha) the everyday world. This liberation is akin to what we in the West call salvation, although here there is no reference to a personal God.

In more popular forms of Hinduism, devotees of the Great God Shiva imagined this deity as dreaming the dream of everyday reality; each of us, in this view, exists only insofar as we appear in Shiva's dream. His awakening means the destruction of the physical universe and the beginning of a new cycle of rebirth and recreation. Thus Shiva is known as both the creator and the destroyer, and is often pictured as a four-armed man, whose graceful dance sets in motion the cyclical wheel of the universe. In Him is reality (but again perhaps not the highest reality, which honor is reserved, in some Hindu philosophies, to the impersonal cosmic force called Brahman). The world is not his creation as the painting is the creation of the artist; that is the image of creation familiar in the West, where God's creation is not a part of the divine nature, any more than the painting is part of the artist. Rather, the phenomenal world is Shiva's creation, as the dream is the creation of the dreamer, and has no existence outside of the dreamer's mind.

In the earliest Buddhist scriptures, we find a rejection of everyday styles of life in the name of a higher spirituality. The Buddha teaches that this world is the realm of pain; *life is essentially suffering.* And yet there is an *escape* from suffering; this involves adopting a new and totally different approach to life called the "Noble Eightfold Path." The exact interpretation of the eight steps along this path has varied through history and is subject to different and widely varying translations into English. It is fair to say, however, that Buddha taught a kind of ascetic withdrawal from the things of this world as uninteresting, as unworthy of man, and as snares that bind us more securely to the diseases of life, rather than help us to find release from them. The everyday world, which the Western thinker thought to conquer and bend to his will, is a place from which the Buddhist seeks release, or *nirvana.* This desire for release refers also to release from bondage to ourselves: individual personality, indeed all sharp distinctions between "this" and "that," between "mine" and "yours" need to be repressed and escaped from; what is desirable is selflessness, for this is the way of release from all worldly attachments.

Heinrich Zimmer, a leading Western student of Indian philosophy retells the following traditional Hindu tale: A young prince had a *guru,* or teacher, who visited him regularly at the palace to give him instructions in philosophy and in the true wisdom. Part of the guru's wisdom, which he sought to impart to the prince, was just this sense of the illusory quality of the world and of the self. But the prince, like most young men, did not wish to learn that the things of the world, which gave him such pleasure, and which he was fortunate to be able to enjoy in such abundance, were mere chimeras. So one day he decided to teach a lesson to his guru: he had his men allow a furious bull elephant to roam about the grounds of the palace just as the guru was expected to arrive. When the guru encountered the elephant, he was at first petrified with fear but then managed, just in time, to escape the animal's tusks by climbing a tree. The prince and his men arrived on the scene, all roaring with laughter. "Why did you turn pale and run away, O teacher, if the elephant, like all else in this shadowy and dismal world, is merely an illusion?" said the prince to the guru, after ordering his men to drive off the elephant. "Because, my prince," said the guru, "there was on the surface of my soul a desire not to have the illusion of being trampled to death by an elephant."

Thus it would seem that for the mainstream of Western philosophy, the substances we physically encounter are considered the primary reality, whereas in the East, what is revealed in special meditative states or through philosophical speculation is considered primary, and the everyday world is considered to be a shadow—sometimes a very undesirable shadow—of the world we glimpse within. However, semantical differences like this one may color not only the perception of the world by a people but also make a tangible difference in the directions and goals of their activities. The way the concept of individual substance, and its correlative concept of *causal relations* between substances were developed in the Western world have surely helped to establish the typical forms of *scientific analysis* in the West—the controlled experiment, the description of substances in quantitative rather than qualitative terms, and the exploitation of theories for the satisfaction of practical needs. Westerners have been attracted to the uses of knowledge in obtaining control over the physical environment, rather than in the quest for liberation or salvation. In general, modern philosophy has been profoundly influenced by the development of science; indeed, Professor Zimmer believes that the single chief difference in outlook of the East and the West can be traced to the West's concern with science and technology. Natural Science has provided a model of true knowledge to Western philosophers (recall the case of Kant); it has posed many of the questions that philosophers try to answer; its standards of clarity and logical rigor and its ability to limit its own inquisitiveness have persuaded many philosophers to abandon the perennial philosophical search for ultimate reality. The East, which has lacked this powerful input from the physical sciences, has evolved different standards and different techniques of analysis.

B. God.

In the West, "religion" is a very general term. It refers to (1) a set of beliefs regarding the ultimate nature of reality, the origin and purpose of the world, and the proper course for man. These beliefs are not considered to be mere theories but are given as articles of faith in which the individual is expected to believe; and to (2) a prescribed method of communal worship, based on tradition and on the revealed word of God, which is organized and presided over by specified individuals. Now it is striking that the Sanskrit language, in which the holy books of Hinduism were written, contains no term equivalent to the English "religion." For the Hindu, it seems, the differences between the various "religions" of the world are not significant; in all of what we call the religions of the world, there is a reaching out to what is sacred. Moreover, the practice of religion is not to be distinguished from the practice of philosophical inquiry, or the participation in society. All such practices have something sacred about them. But if all significant activity is sacred, then why does one need a term "religion" to distinguish the practice of religion from other phases of one's life? Are not all things holy?

This attitude towards what we call "religion" in the West is reflected in the

Hindu (and, in some measure, the Buddhist) concept of God. The concept of God that is assumed by Jews, Christians, and Moslems was defined in chapter 11. The Hindu and the Buddhist would not recognize this definition as describing the focus of their worship. The contrast is striking. The Eastern thinker would agree that God or the gods were spiritual and holy, but he would surely reject the *uniqueness, personality,* and *infinity* of God. God is not unique, for there are many gods, and although some of them are more powerful than others, they are usually conceived of as each other's peers—as, for example, in Greek and Roman religion. The gods are hence not infinite, for each limits the other's activities—although, in the act of worship, the devotee of any one god may speak of that god as the only god!

Now although the gods are depicted in the sacred writings as having superhuman personal form, Hinduism and Buddhism quite often suggest that there is a reality greater even than the gods, which is called the Brahman or the Absolute, and that the gods or the Buddhas-to-be (Bodhisattvas) are incarnations of, or manifestations of, the supreme reality. If the gods are only manifestations of an even higher, impersonal reality, how are those who desire to approach this reality to begin their quest? For this supreme or ultimate reality, again unlike Western conceptions, does not appear to be a substance at all! The way of approaching the realm of the ultimate and most sacred, therefore, must be negative: the religious novice is taught by his guru that God is "not this" or "not that," not any one thing, but in all things—until the novice is capable of a direct, intuitive, and wordless awareness of the divine.

Another approach to the Absolute, well known in the West because of its logically absurd character, are the koans of Japanese Zen Buddhism. These are questions directed by the guru at his students that are intended to boggle the imagination and thus cut a path for the mind to travel toward what is most mind-boggling of all—mind-boggling only because we are accustomed to confront the world in terms of the neat categories of everyday experience, and the Absolute is always not this—not that—not *any one* thing. Koans are thus questions like "What is the sound of one hand clapping?" or "Where does your lap go when you stand up?" (not an authentic example!) If you were to reply to the latter question by saying "The term 'lap' designates a configuration of bodily parts, and has no reference to a substantially existing thing; hence the predicate 'goes' does not apply to it," your guru might bow politely and give you a whack with a stick he carries for such purposes—although your philosophy professor in America would most likely be very pleased with your answer!

The ultimate form taken by such a negative thrust toward the Absolute is a sudden return to Earth; as the Hindu philosopher Shankara said, "Only the one who has abandoned the notion that he has realized Brahman is a knower of the Self, and no one else"—for the state of bondage to the illusion of the world is itself illusory! And the Zen masters often note that upon achieving enlightenment (satori), the things of this world become once again the prosaic, individual substances we originally apprehend them as being. As in the New Testament, we become once again like children—we are *reborn*, but after having passed through the fire of new understanding. So radical is the rejection by some European adepts of Hinduism or Buddhism of the transcendental and the Absolute as a substantial, independent entity, however, that it often appears that they have rejected the concept of the Divine or the supernatural altogether and possess a belief in a kind of materialism that is different from atheism only in its perception of the world within us and, indeed, the world as a whole as sacred. Again, everything is holy, and no specific focus of holiness or divinity is needed, such as a God or gods or even an impersonal cosmic force such as Brahman. This is the path that each of us must tread, say many representatives of Eastern religion: from mere worship of deities to the struggle for a higher perspective—and then back to the everyday world, now transformed, mystical, beautiful.

C. Idea.

The Eastern thinkers do not manifest the same tendency to understand the world in terms of discrete entities called *ideas* as we do in the West. The concept of "idea" was introduced into Western philosophy by Plato, although we observed in chapter 2 that the pre-Socratic philosophers believed that the world was comprehensible by means of the disciplined conceptual analysis that we call *reasoning*. Plato, on the other hand, made ideas prior to physical reality and posited a realm in which are found substantial entities called Forms, or *Idea*. These forms are available to the human mind through intuition and by means of the dialectic and serve as the patterns or models that physical reality imitates. There is an eternal form of everything for which we have a name, and hence the world as we perceive it fits entirely into these patterns, except insofar as it possesses an irrational or merely finite element. Each man, for example, is modeled after the form of manhood, and differs from the pattern only insofar as he is finite, temporal, and physical.

Now this way of perceiving reality is foreign to the East. In the West, it created the tendency to see all things categorically, that is, as members of a class of things; differences between individuals were conceived of as insignificant; the object of rational discourse was the universal, the lawful, the underlying structure, the idea of things. It is this tendency against which the mystical spirit, both East and West but so markedly in the East, revolts. What is significant, says the mystic, is the individual rather than the universal, the emotional, rather than the rational, the wordless awareness, rather than the chatty dissection of entities in terms of universal ideas. Of course, the difference is again one of emphasis and is not absolute. Nor is it a useless conflict, for the tension between the mystical and the rational impulses has caused a great deal of creative ferment in both the Eastern and the Western traditions.

D. History.

Another striking absence from the center stage of intellectual concern in the East, one that is the product of a very special kind of rational dissection in the West, is the idea of history. In chapter 6, we noted that the writing of critical and interpretive history was first attempted by the Greeks. History represents a special form of self-consciousness in that it places one's own time and place in a broader context and thus enables individuals to see themselves as part of the total history of mankind, and as having a determinate place in that history. But Western historians did not rest content with interpreting the past; they wished also to establish a *pattern* of some kind, so that a picture of the sense and significance and direction of all history might emerge. A story that has fixed itself in the Western imagination is that of the Roman general Scipio, who wept when he threw salt upon the ruins of conquered Carthage as the symbol of its complete destruction. He wept, he said, at the thought that one day his beloved Rome would suffer the same fate. And, of course, he was right. But why would he expect that Rome, too, was doomed? Because to the Romans the sense and significance of history was to travel eternally about in a circle: civilizations are born, evolve up to a point, and then begin their inexorable decline. Each event draws significance from the role it plays in the completion of the circle. Historians can try to "make sense" of history by discerning this pattern and fitting their data into it. Other patterns of history have, of course, exerted an influence upon the writing of history in the West. One might cite the belief of Christians that all of history is the tale of God's providence, in which man was created, fell, was redeemed by Christ, and now is moving through the successive empires mentioned in the Bible towards Armageddon and the Second Coming. And the modern theory of Karl Marx proposes that history is the successive unfolding of class societies and will be terminated when the final class struggle results in the establishment of a classless society.

Eastern thought generally refuses to tie together all of history into such neat little patterns whose seeming inevitability has done so much to influence political attitudes in the West. Indeed, Eastern peoples tend to think of the world as endless, although perhaps subject to cyclical phases of creation and destruction. Jainism speaks of history as having seen the birth of a succession of twenty-four tirthankaras, or "ford-makers" of which the last was Mahavira; but no absolute terminal point is asserted: the world possesses a moral order but it does not progress, and it does not exist for the sake of an eventual redemption. Moreover, the Eastern imagination speaks in terms of temporal dimensions that would have staggered the Western imagination before modern cosmology began to fix the age of the universe as somewhere between ten and twenty billion years. For example, the age of Brahma—the deity considered by ancient Vedic religion to be one of the greatest of the gods, whose births and rebirths fix the universal cycle of events—was said to be equivalent to the amount of time it would take for a bird who flew over the Himalaya mountains once every thousand years with a silken cloth in its beak to wear the mountains down to sea level. (Do *you* have a better way to imagine twenty billion years?)

This lack of a concern with history as evolution, as change *in some direction* and *for some reason,* denied to the Eastern world an important mode of *becoming an object to itself.* But the picture of the physical world and the human scene as always existing and as fundamentally static is a source of strength, too. It sanctifies tradition and enables the old wise man to say: Thus has it ever been. It is in this way a source of the social cohesiveness that has long characterized India, China, and Japan. It enhances the moral status of the individual, who is not conceived of as an agent of historical forces (Adam *had to fall* if there was to be Christ)—but as the unique manifestation of an eternally repeating, non-sequential cosmic force, who, in the typical scenarios of life—maintaining a family, working as a peasant or a monarch, seeking liberation—shows his mettle or his lack of it. Each person has a place in such a culture, and at each place is repeated what was done in ages gone by. If the level of virtue has declined since the times of our ancestors, as Confucius moaned, that is not because of ineluctable historical forces, but because of the moral failure of individuals: thus the high value placed upon learned teachers of virtue in Eastern cultures.

4. CONCEPTUAL STRUCTURES AND MODES OF WORSHIP PECULIAR TO THE ORIENT

Up to this point we have been discussing philosophical contrasts between East and West. Here a dialogue between the two cultures is easy and unforced, because traces of Western ideas were always to be found in the Orient, and traces of Eastern ideas were to be found in the West. When one comes to the specific forms of worship practiced in the East, however, contrasts become too distant to be effective, and we must instead try to penetrate the underlying conceptualizations and their language, as foreign to the Western ear as they may be. Again, of course, we will have to generalize very broadly and to leap over the barriers established by time between the various Oriental cultures and schools, if we are to convey the flavor of Eastern religion and the nature of the opening toward the divine that it seeks to establish. We will do this by studying two groups of concepts: Those concerning the religious life: *bhakti, zen, tao;* and those concerning the ultimate ends of man: *moksha, nirvana, satori.*

A. The Religious Life.

The proper relationship between man and God, between the finite and the infinite, the transitory and the eternal has occupied mankind throughout history. Persons perceive themselves as standing within a mysterious and encompassing realm to which they desire to respond in some way, whether to placate the gods, or in order to understand their role in the ultimate scheme of things, or to realize in their actions the dimension of eternity that they feel within their own souls or in the familiar objects around them. The familiar English term that we use to describe one form of that response is worship. We have seen that for the Indian tradition, the locus of the sacred is not, as in the West, a unique infinite personal being whom we call God, but rather a transcendent reality called Brahman. Brahman is not personal, so there is no question, say, of communicating with Brahman in the act of prayer or holy celebration. However, there is in the Hindu tradition a distant but significant and beautiful relative of our concept of worship; it is called *bhakti.* Let us begin our brief investigation of the Eastern religious life by examining this concept.

We have seen that during the course of the evolution of Hinduism, various philosophical interpretations of the world were developed. These philosophies, we noted, were not intended to represent any final truth, but rather were points of view, *darshanas,* which the individual is invited to share as a point of departure for his personal struggle for *moksha,* that is, enlightenment and release. Indeed, the Hindu tradition recognizes that just as there are natural divisions among men, such that each person inhabits a distinct caste as a reward or punishment for the good or evil he has done in a previous lifetime, so too are some methods of seeking release more appropriate to some persons than to others. The way most appropriate for a given individual will depend upon the state of his soul. Some persons are more equipped for the physical life and take to rigorous discipline of the body; they seek salvation through the practice of yoga, which, by perfecting the mind's control of the body, releases the mind and enables it to give birth to pure thoughts. For others, who possess great gifts of mind, the way of philosophical knowledge (jnana) may be appropriate; here we seek to incorporate within ourselves the thoughts of things, to live the life of the mind, to accept conflict and contradiction, to stand at no one final point, but to reflect the changing appearances of all things as idea. Still others in whom the spirit is strong may seek release through the practice of meditation. The key philosophical concept here is that of the identity of the Brahman with the principle of *Atman,* or world-soul, which was so beautifully developed in the Upanishads. In the famous *Chandogya Upanishad,* the young man Svetaketu is taught by his father that all things—the wind whistling through the trees, the frog in its pond, your own most profound self—*tat tvam asi,* that thou art. The soul that animates all things, the soul within each one of us is one, is *Atman,* and the Atman and the Brahman are one and the same. The function of meditation, then, is to cut through the mere appearances of things, especially through the merely phenomenal parts of ourselves (what we in the West call the empirical ego, or the "personality") to the underlying principle of Self, which is not mine, not yours, but is all things. This road is the highest of all to tread and is reserved only to a few persons who have the moral and spiritual fiber to accept the renunciation of all the particular things of the world that it implies for the sake of *moksha.*

The great masses of men, however, possessing no great resources of body, mind, or spirit, are not forgotten by Hinduism. Just as salvation in Christianity is not reserved for great saints or heroes of the spirit but is open to those whose faith is simple but real, so too in Hinduism is release—if not in this life, then at least in a future life—from the wheel of *samsara,* the cycle of birth and death and rebirth, promised to those who practice *bhakti* in accordance with *Dharma.* Bhakti is the worship of some God or gods as the incarnation of Brahman. It manifests itself in India in the form of the innumerable temples of worship dedicated to some divinity or other, in the rites and rituals performed at various times, in the reciting of the songs and hymns of the Vedas, and in the meditation upon the great works of the gods that are told about in the epics. What to the haughty conquerors of India, the Moslems and the Christians, appeared to be the superstitious worship of "bloomin' idols made o'mud," to use the words of one of Kipling's characters, is the worship of manifestations of the divine that, as the believer himself recognizes, is the first and simplest way a mere mortal can approach the Mystery. All things may, under certain circumstances, be looked upon as bearing the divine in themselves; thus, we have the very ancient practice, so strange to Westerners, of cow worship, whose origins in India are obscure. Indeed there is in the holy city of Benares a temple, sometimes frequented by Gandhi, whose god is a huge map of India. This India-temple as it is called is not a monument to nationalism, but a way of recognizing what so many peoples feel but rarely give religious expression to, namely, that the very soil is holy upon which their daily work of survival is consummated.

Dharma is dimly translated into English as virtue, although it has many other meanings. Worship is not enough; the individual must also practice good works. These good works usually require no special moral excellence; a person must simply abide by the rules for marriage, worship, and work set down for the caste into which he was born, and for which the good or bad works (which are called karma insofar as they affect the soul of an individual) he performed in a previous life have determined him. Hindus recognize also some typical "stages on life's way" and the type of virtues appropriate to each. These stages or *ashramas* are universal and cut through caste differences, although the specific demands made upon persons in each of the first three stages may vary with one's caste. They are (1) that of the young student during his initiation into the religious life; (2) that of the householder, citizen, and family man, who practices virtue while immersed in the affairs of life; (3) that of the wandering ascetic, who has renounced his affairs upon the completion of his duties to his family and his fellow men and has gone to seek salvation; (4) that of the *sannyasin,* who has achieved *moksha;* he is the equivalent of our wise man or saint. Again we see that in India the lines between the purely secular and sacred are indistinctly drawn. Everything in life may have religious significance: meditation and philosophy, worship and the carrying out of the obligations imposed by one's station, marriage and family, and even the soil upon which one labors.

The forms of worship and the holy life in China and Japan are more difficult to sketch; their traditions are not as highly unified, and they do not penetrate what we call the secular sphere as profoundly. We have seen that in China a form of Mahayana Buddhism, one with a mystical and salvationist tradition, and that also provided the masses with simple forms of worship, was at first grafted onto and ultimately transformed the more literate, secular, and humanistic world view that we call Confucianism. But although Confucianism ultimately took on the trappings of a somewhat transcendental and ceremonial religion, even in its original form it represents a kind of reverential approach to life that can be called religious. Confucius himself did not care to speculate about worlds beyond, claiming that he had enough difficulty making sense out of how we ought to live in this world. But he accepted without question a realm of the sacred that the Chinese call heaven, and he believed in the manifestation of that realm that was called *Tao,* or the Way. *Tao* is a philosophical principle and might be compared, however distantly, with the Greek concept of the *logos:* the word or reason or principle that makes all things to be the way they are. For example, it was said of an imperial butcher in China that he never had to sharpen his cleaver; for he knew so well the *tao* of animals that his blade was able to separate the limbs at the joint with a single stroke. The forces of nature, which operate according to the *tao* of each thing, are the *yin* and *yang: yin,* the light and feminine principle, *yang,* the heavy and masculine principle. If we think of these categories in terms of our Western vocabulary (which, of course, we must do at first), we may compare the *yin-yang* principles to some of the dynamical conceptions of nature developed here: the damp and the dry of the pre-Socratic philosopher Anaximander, the principles of Good and Evil of the Zoroastrians and the Manicheans, and even (to take a great leap) to the id and superego of Freudian personality theory—principles complementary to each other that, by their very differences, produce instability, change, and diversity according to fixed patterns or *tao.*

There is in such philosophical schemata profound and nourishing material for the religious imagination; they heighten our sense of wonder, of mystery, of a realm behind things if not beyond them. Confucius was a genius who used the philosophical givens of his time to mold the elements of a reverential and serious, if not transcendental, world view, one that stresses good works over worship, justice and a concern for duty over meditation and withdrawal from the world, and a sort of sad, uncertain love for his fellows over devotion to a God. Many persons in the West do not consider Confucianism in its original form to be a religion because of the apparent lack of the sacred, the transcendental. Here semantical questions become unenlightening; let us simply say that Confucianism represents a religious concern for living rightly and in accordance with what its founder perceived to be the *tao* of all things.

B. The Ends of Life.

From what has been said in the preceding pages, a broad and general vision of what is Highest and Best for human beings can be discerned. Most forms of Eastern thought and religion begin with a dissatisfaction with life as it is ordinarily lived—we recall Gautama's claim that all is *dukkha,* pain and suffering, and the Upanishadic belief that we are not what we think we are—and seek, therefore, a *release* from this self-created illusion we call life. This release may consist simply in overcoming our usual passionate or habitual desire for the things of this world—that is, by learning renunciation and living according to the Noble Eightfold Path—or it may involve a complete restructuring of our ordinary modes of thought and perception, as in the case of meditation, yoga, or the practice of Zen. The release that follows from this restructuring is called satori in Japanese, nirvana in Buddhism, and moksha in Hinduism. The roads to this end vary, and the interpretations of the nature of the final release vary as well. Let us begin with Japan, and confine ourselves to one form of Japanese religion, that of Zen Buddhism and its concept of *satori.* Satori is the enlightenment that *constitutes* release—release from the constraints placed upon us not simply by the pressures of life, or by the fact we have a fleshy body, but from the constraints placed upon us by words—words that lead us to make distinctions, posit substantial existing things, chop up experience into discrete parts, and prevent us, therefore, from encountering existence directly. We noted earlier that Zen employs peculiar techniques to drag the mind of the student away from the habits of discursive reason—the koans posed by the guru. If successful, the student is brought into a closer, more profound and authentic relationship with the world. The breach between what is myself and what is not myself, the breach between thing and thing, created by the analytical mind, is bridged in this wordless encounter, I become all things, and all things become me. The very mystical oneness of things is achieved, which alienated Westerners have sought in art, in drugs, in sexual love, in a return to their own unconscious. The path of Zen is arduous, however, and many who have attempted to follow it—Japanese and foreigners alike—have failed, for the habits of thought it attempts to overcome are deeply ingrained; indeed it might be said that they are the habits of thought typical of Western philosophy and science. The goal of this overcoming, satori, is of course indescribable—how absurd to attempt to describe an experience that, by its very nature, involves the overcoming of all words! Zen, like many byways of Eastern thought, is a gateway with an invitation to enter inscribed above it and is not a doctrine that can be learned, but a way of life that must be appropriated by the individual.

Nirvana seems especially paradoxical to the Western religious imagination. Nirvana is described by Buddhism as a "going out of the flame," the becoming nothing. For Buddha denied the reality of the self, or ego, and hence the doctrine of reincarnation. Therefore it would appear that the desire for nirvana is nothing more than the desire for death. But if life is pain, the incredulous utilitarian outsider might ask, then why not just kill oneself? We must remember, however, that when the Buddhist speaks of "nothing," he points not to the lack of existence, or to the absence of a thing, but to what is no-thing. This world, in our everyday view of it, is made up of things. But when we seek the world beyond, we must take the "negative" path spoken of earlier: "It is not this, not that, not some other thing." To become no-thing, therefore, is not simply not to exist, but to be beyond the pale of beings, to approach Being itself. The nature of this state is not described by the Buddha himself in the sayings attributed to him, but it is not the perdurance of my personhood or ego after death. Again, however, to describe nirvana in words, to speak of it as "bliss," for example, is both senseless and useless, for, again, it is no-thing, and things alone can be described by words.

Like nirvana, the Hindu concept of moksha refers to the going-out of the flame, the annihilation of Self, and the emancipation of the individual from all finite limitations of existence. And like nirvana, it is attainable in this life only through the practice of Dharma and the discipline of mind and body. The path has been blazed by Ford-Makers and Enlightened Ones of the past; it requires only the courage to renounce desire and the craving for gain. When it is achieved, the terrible cycle of birth and rebirth, which is produced by good and bad actions (karma) clinging to our soul at death, will be ended, and all suffering will cease. In this world a road lies open to us: we can escape from the daily demands of life, and the quiet life of wandering, fasting, meditation, and prayer will beckon to us. Our soul grows, the view of the Beyond becomes clearer; we enter the ferryboat, as the Buddhists teach, and begin our journey to the Farther Shore.

QUESTIONS FOR STUDY

1. Assess the degree of contrast between Eastern and Western thought. What differences between the two are most significant,

in your view? Which least significant? Where might a person who was trying to bring the two traditions together begin to search for the closest point of contact?

2. Write an essay on the concept of the monotheistic God found in the West and its apparent absence from the Eastern traditions. How is the Western concept an expression of Western philosophy? How has it in turn affected that tradition? How has the absence of that concept in the East influenced the outlook of Eastern peoples?

3. Read through at random some of the sacred literature of Hinduism or Buddhism. Find a text that has significance to you. Write an essay on that text in which you seek to express its religious dimension, its philosophical outlook, and its relevance to your experience of the world.

4. Some Eastern religions tend to view all things as both holy or sacred, and at the same time as not ultimately real. Explain this apparent paradox. In the West, the view that all things are divine is called pantheism. Study this concept and contrast it with similar beliefs in Eastern thought.

5. In recent years, many Westerners have been attracted to Eastern religions. Some have donned the robes of Hindu ascetics (Hare Krishna); some have submitted themselves to Zen Buddhist or Yogic disciplines; some have traveled across Asia to join a Buddhist monastery in Nepal or to sit at the feet of a Himalayan guru (the Beatles). Write an essay discussing the sources of this phenomenon, and attempt to isolate those elements of Eastern thought that Westerners tend to find most attractive.

13

The Philosophy of Man: Existentialism

There is an old story that tells of seven blind men who approached an elephant. One of them touched the tail of the elephant and remarked, "This beast is very much like a rope!" Another felt the leg of the elephant and exclaimed "It is clear, the elephant is quite like a tree!" And on they went, each understanding the whole of the animal to be like the part that had touched him. And since they were blind not only to the elephant, but to the limited validity of each other's perceptions, they could not form a single picture of the whole.

Now we have arrived at the final chapter of our letter of invitation to philosophy. We are still attempting to generalize about the big beast, philosophy, which seems to elude all attempts to pin it down, and to sum up its nature or the nature of its many parts. No simple formulas seem to be adequate. And nowhere is this inability to grasp what philosophy is all about more apparent than in the case of contemporary philosophy. There have been an abundance of philosophical schools in this century; and yet these schools not only contradict each other, but have members whose work contradicts the work of other members. There has been a proliferation of jargon and an emphasis upon technical virtuosity that has made it difficult for professional philosophers to keep up with the work being done in different branches of their discipline. Thus the understanding one has of the nature and the aims of philosophy today will depend to a great extent upon the door by which a student enters the field; and, like the blind men in the tale, he may easily confuse the whole of the elephant with the part of the beast that touched him first. The only cure for the resulting narrowness of vision is to read widely and to read well.

In the twentieth century, four very general tendencies of philosophy may be distinguished. Three of these have figured in other chapters, and one will be the subject of our attention here. All are concerned, of course, with the perennial questions of philosophy: questions of the nature and limits of knowledge, the structure of the world, the contents of the Good Life, and our hopes for a future life. What distinguishes these tendencies lies in their commitments to, or their reaction against, older philosophical traditions and techniques of analysis—especially *empiricism* or *rationalism*—and their concern with some specific area of experience, often to the neglect of other areas. Their mutual lack of sympathy and understanding, indeed their blindness to each other's concerns, may be attributed to the social and political chaos of our age, or to the gradual breakdown of the Western philosophical tradition, which Nietzsche and others prophesied. These tendencies may be sketched as follows.

LINGUISTIC ANALYSIS

It is fair to say, we think, that this is the direction of thought that is dominant in the English-speaking countries today. And it is fair to say that the theory of linguistic analysis developed out of a reflection upon the later work of Ludwig Wittgenstein (1889–1951). Wittgenstein's *Philosophical Investigations* insist upon the fundamental importance of a study of language, especially the ordinary language of everyday discourse, for the elucidation of traditional philosophical questions. For example, we have encountered the problem of the nature and limits of *knowledge* at various points in this book; these are the concerns of the philosophical discipline called epistemology. A linguistic analyst might suggest that we begin an inquiry into the nature of knowledge with an example of the way speakers of English normally use the term "knowledge" in some everyday situation, and then consider what the user of the term is attempting to communicate to others thereby. Quite often (but not inevitably), the linguistic analyst will then identify the meaning or meanings of the term with the range of its proper uses (this is called the *usage theory of meaning*, and the analyst speaks of the range of its proper uses as the "logic" of the term). In the case of one typical usage of the term "knowledge," the linguistic analyst may ask what *kind of information* is communicated by the use of the term. If I say, "I know who shot Lincoln; it was John Wilkes Booth," I am communicating the claims (1) that "John Wilkes Booth shot Lincoln" is *true* (otherwise I wouldn't say that I knew it, but rather "I thought so," or "it might be so," etc.); (2) that I *believe* the statement is true (Do not confuse this claim with the first! I may claim that something is true without believing it myself; a typical case of this is what we call "lying."); (3) and that I have reason to believe (have evidence!) that the statement is true (otherwise I could not claim that I knew it to be so, but only that I believe, or hope, or "have heard" that it is true). By considering other usages of "knowledge" and comparing their similarities and differences, we may explore further dimensions of the term.

Linguistic analysts, in general, agree upon two epistemological principles that underlie and underwrite their method of philosophy. The first is that language, to use Wittgenstein's expression, is a kind of "game," in which persons abide by a complex set of rules (such as those governing the term "knowledge") in order to communicate with one another in endlessly diverse ways. The rules of language are conventions, but they are not arbitrary, in the sense that the rules of baseball are arbitrary. A given language may be relative to a cultural group, and the use of language may be a human invention, but its rules develop in the process of that cultural group's interaction with the "world" his language designates and with other persons. Indeed, language is mankind's window onto the world. All our claims to knowledge are couched in a language; this language conditions our perceptions and, ultimately, our understanding of the world. To explore the usages of terms, therefore, is to clarify our perceptions of the world.

The second principle is that it is futile to peer beyond the usages of terms in order to discover a supposed "ultimate" and mysterious Platonic meaning behind them. Wittgenstein argued that it was an error of Plato to assume that each term *must* have a single meaning (that there must be a single ideal language game!), which we can approach by dialectics and finally apprehend in intellectual vision. "Justice" does not function in any single way in the English language (or for that matter, in Greek); what we mean by a "just" law is surely not the same as we mean by a "just" man: the logic of "justice" is different in each case. Indeed, justice *as such* does not exist; it was in vain that philosophers throughout the Western tradition searched for such a thing. Thus we must expect as the reward of philosophy no ultimate knowledge of the meaning of things but rather greater clarity about the legitimate and the questionable uses of terms, and learn to trace philosophical perplexities to misuses of language, rather than to an inherently mysterious quality of things.

LOGICAL ANALYSIS

This second direction of contemporary philosophy can trace a part of its heritage to the early twentieth-century school known as *logical positivism.*

The logical positivists were greatly impressed by the success of science in uncovering new knowledge. Indeed, empirical science was slowly absorbing domains that had traditionally been a part of philosophy and establishing them as independent sciences—such as those nineteenth-century inventions, psychology and sociology. If science continued to progress, it was asked, what tasks would ultimately be the inheritance of philosophy? If the only legitimate questions were those that could be investigated scientifically, wouldn't philosophy be forced to break camp and to vanish into the desert? Logical positivists were confident that at least one set of questions that were of a genuinely philosophical sort would survive the growth of science: those are the questions that concern the *criteria of scientific reasoning itself.* After all, it was argued, it is not the function of the physicist to discuss the nature of physics itself, or to disclose and analyze the logical relationships between physical theories and the data that are intended to support them. These are *logical* questions, not scientific ones.

Now it so happens that in the second half of the nineteenth century, logic, which had to a great extent lain dormant since the end of the Middle Ages, began to be developed in new ways. In the work of G. Frege (1848–1925) and Bertrand Russell (1872–1970), symbolic logic became a powerful tool in the philosophical analysis of the conceptual problems raised by the new sciences. Most notable were the efforts of Russell and Alfred North Whitehead (1861–1947) to develop a logical language that would enable mathematicians to express, in the terms of that language, the fundamental relationships that occur in arithmetic. Today, logical languages are being developed that make it possible to chart the logical relationships occurring in theories in any of the sciences. In common with linguistic analysis, its efforts in constructing these new and flexible tools are intended to make clear the logical relationships between conceptual structures—although it is more concerned with those that occur in the specialized sciences than those in everyday discourse. And, in common with all forms of empiricism, it tends to be skeptical of the efforts of philosophers to establish metaphysical systems, to obtain insight into supernatural realms, or to attain absolute knowledge in matters of morals and right conduct.

MARXISM

The state of contemporary Marxism reflects the enormous political divisions in the contemporary world. The metaphysical and historical theories developed in the nineteenth century by Karl Marx and his associate Friedrich Engels eventually became the state philosophy of the Soviet Union, and were used to justify its political and economic policies. A bridge between Marx's philosophical theories and political action was constructed by V. I. Lenin for his historical context, that of the revolutionary struggle within Russia. However, Marx's moral condemnation of the repression of the great masses of mankind under the economic system prevalent in his day, and his peculiar approach to the analysis of institutions have not lost their appeal. The changing historical scene has failed to obscure the revolutionary message of Marx and Engels; their ideas are reworked and accommodated to historical and political events wherever persons have become conscious of their enslavement to ruling cliques. Additions to, or "revisions" of, Marxist philosophy with reference to different historical contexts were made by Mao Tse-Tung in China, Ho Chi Minh in Vietnam, and Fidel Castro and Che Guevara in Latin America—to mention just three examples.

In the modern industrial nations of Europe and America, the mainstream of Marxist thought has come to be known as *"critical theory."* Its adherents seek to uncover the techniques of political repression hidden within the social and cultural institutions and philosophical beliefs of a society and *open them to criticism.* Logical analysis is criticized for uncritically assuming the essential correctness of one mode of communication among men: that of scientific discourse; and one proper method for solving practical problems: that of rational technology. All other approaches to problems are deemed irrational. These glib assumptions encourage repression within modern industrial society as they lead us to a neglect of the human dimension of the sciences and leave us with the impression that all rational activity is scientific activity. Moreover, the belief of empiricists that matters of morals are not capable of being investigated scientifically takes the question of social justice out of the arena of rational discourse and gives it over to the politicians and media experts and their economic masters. Linguistic analysis is criticized for beginning and usually ending with an analysis of "ordinary" language games, forgetting the social and political concerns that shape the usages of words. In fact, linguistic analysts have tended to restrict themselves to a study of the "language games" played by Cambridge professors! And existentialism, the fourth direction of modern thought we will discuss here, is condemned by most Marxists as a decadent philosophy for socially disaffected middle-class individualists whose obscurantist metaphysical theories tend, in the end, to sanctify rather than to undermine the *status quo* and whose nihilistic hedonism encourages a neglect of the plight of the working class.

EXISTENTIALISM

Nevertheless, our book will conclude with a consideration of existentialism, despite its admitted limitations as a world view, for its concerns, more than those of the other three, seem to reach out beyond academic philosophy to the streets and alleys where men and women live out their lives. It seeks to bring into focus the speaker of language, the creator of science, the social being who stands in need of liberation—namely, man himself, man the individual, who, in this century at least, has tended to see himself not primarily as a rational or a social animal, but as an undefined being standing at the abyss, with warfare, concentration camps, and dead idols behind him, and the threat of atomic destruction and no guarantee of personal immortality before him. Existentialism seeks to *describe* the nature of the human situation and to explore possible *responses* to that situation with the hope of attaining insight into the age-old question with which Socrates began philosophy: How should I live?

Let us begin a discussion of existentialism with two observations. First, it appears that existentialists are concerned not primarily with the abstract analysis of concepts but with human existence in its concreteness, that is, with the ways in which human beings live out their lives. For that reason, most existentialists have at one time or another given *literary* expression to their ideas. In poems, novels, plays, or short stories, we are shown persons going about the business of living, making choices, and choosing their responses to the unique situations in which they find themselves. Those who, like Camus or Simone de Beauvoir or Dostoyevsky, are primarily novelists, also write essays, diaries, or letters that explore the philosophical horizons of the persons and situations they depict in literature. And some of those who are primarily philosophers, Kierkegaard, Nietzsche, Sartre, and Marcel wrote literary works of one kind or another; you will find some examples of them listed in our bibliography.

Second, the lives of the existentialists themselves are examples of the spiritual crises that existentialists endeavor to interpret and deal with. In most existentialist writings there is the sense of tension, uncertainty, anguish, and of intensely lived experience that is seeking to give itself expression. Few of the existentialists were university professors; Martin Heidegger is a notable exception to this rule. Most supported themselves on the income from their writings. All of this is unusual for, since the eighteenth century, philosophy has become an academic enterprise, in which most philosophers enjoy security and bourgeois respectability as teachers. This seems to be true even for the Western Marxist philosophers, with the exception of Karl Marx himself. It is perhaps for this reason that existentialism has had such a wide appeal among those intellectuals who imagine themselves to be living on the fringes of society, struggling to find a meaning to life that would be, as Kierkegaard put it, "true for *me*," rather than simply accepting prefabricated ways of life and living what passes for a meaningful existence among everyday people.

THEMES IN NINETEENTH-CENTURY EXISTENTIALISM

The term "existentialism" came into use only in the twentieth century, and there is little agreement about how the term ought to be defined. In fact, only one major philosopher, Jean-Paul Sartre (1905–1980), has used the term to refer to himself, although many thinkers could be identified as having done philosophy in an existentialist key, so to speak. That "key" is a set of themes, attitudes, and concerns that began to appear in philosophical writings as early as the middle of the last century. By the second quarter of this century, some philosophers became aware of these key elements as comprising a unique approach to philosophy and began to appropriate the special techniques of a philosophical methodology known as *phenomenology* to study the problems they discovered in the writings of these earlier authors. Of these nineteenth-century "existentialists," we will mention three: the Dane Søren Kierkegaard (1813–1855), the Russian Feodor Dostoevsky (1821–1881), and the German Friedrich Nietzsche (1844–1900), and we will abstract from the enormous corpus of their work one or two themes that they developed and passed on to our own age. In the next section we will look at the origins of modern existentialism and then conclude with a study of the work of Jean-Paul Sartre.

A. Kierkegaard: The Demand for Subjectivity.

Philosophy in the West has generally been thought of as an adventure of the mind. It investigates critically the uncertain areas of experience, and, much like science, the other great adventure of the mind, it attempts to give us knowledge, or at least some insight into the limitations of knowledge. It has always been distinguished from *faith*, that is, from belief unwarranted by sound evidence, and from *art*, which is the adventure of the imagination. Philosophy and science have pretended to give us objective knowledge—that is, claims to truth based upon evidence that anyone would accept.

However, can man live by objective knowledge alone? I am born, thrown into this world to live, and will someday die. Objective knowledge may be available about the nature of my physical environment, about physiological and psychological laws that apply to my body and my mind as well as to everyone else's, and perhaps even about the nature of right and wrong. And religion may offer me a faith in the ultimate goodness of all things, and some arguments in favor of the reasonableness of its beliefs. Thus armed with philosophy, science, and religion, it would seem that I had all the guidebooks and maps I needed to chart my course in life. However, a nagging doubt about the adequacy of objective knowledge and institutional religion for the pursuit of the good life came to the surface in the thought of Kierkegaard.

What is lacking in our science, philosophy, and "positive" religion, says Kierkegaard, is a sense of the individual who must *appropriate* all this "knowledge" and make it *work for him*. If it is to be more than a pleasant adventure of the mind, it must enable me to *live ethically*, and, ultimately, to realize within myself the element of the eternal possessed by every human being. Now if you have been reading thoughtfully, you will recognize this theme of the *relationship of knowledge to living well* as similar to that which we encountered in our study of Socrates in the second chapter. Socrates, like most Greeks, never could have imagined a kind of knowledge that had no applications to human life, but unlike most Greeks, he sought knowledge that was not merely useful in the practical affairs of life, but that helped us care for our most precious possession: our own soul. Kierkegaard recognizes this connection with Socrates. Like Socrates, he gently chides us for losing our soul to material possessions and to objective knowledge. And like Socrates, Kierkegaard wishes to lead us to an adventure in subjectivity, to a quest for selfhood. But unlike Socrates, he does not point out to us our own *ignorance* but rather demonstrates to us the nakedness and emptiness of our inward selves. Kierkegaard in effect exhibits to us the simple truth of the scriptural admonitions:

> Thou sayest, I am rich, and increased with wealth, and have need of nothing, and knowest not that thou art wretched, and miserable, and poor, and blind, and naked (Rev. 4:17–18).

We are poor in spirit, believes Kierkegaard, for we have neglected our own existence while constructing the marvelous edifice of science—which, in the end, cannot tell me who I am, or what I ought to be about, or what it means to die. We have "built an enormous palace, which we admire from afar, while we choose to live in a little hut alongside of it." But of course! Only I, not science and philosophy, can tell me who I am, and what I am to believe in! But *do I know who I am?* And thus Kierkegaard begins his search for something to believe in, something that will be true for him, something that he will *make* his truth by the inward force of his own passion for self-knowledge. He conducts his search under many disguises: he writes books under assumed names, engages in dialogues with his readers and with imaginary characters, writes a voluminous journal in which he records his changing moods and states of soul, tries out, imaginatively, various styles of life— that of the young pleasure-seeker, the tormented lover, the earnest judge, the old priest—he looks at life from various standpoints and sums up the personal truth contained in each, notes their limitations, and marches ahead. We recall from chapter 11 that the eventual outcome of Kierkegaard's search is a "leap of faith" in which he attempts to enter, as a finite self, into a relationship with an infinite being, a leap that seemed always objectively questionable to him (after all, he says the "objective" arguments we discussed in chapter 11 are inconclusive) but for which his passion for himself in his eternal truth furnished the final impulse.

The lesson of Kierkegaard seems to be that objective thought may help make sense out of the world, but it cannot assist me in making sense out of my life. Modern philosophy thus receives an *expansion* in Kierkegaard: it becomes again, as in Socrates, a way of life, an expression of the yearning for enlightenment about the state of our soul, our subjective self: philosophy again turns inward to see what has been stored up inside of our selves, and finds *nothing there*—except a possibility and autonomy, a freedom to seek and create the person I will become.

B. Dostoyevsky: The Constriction of Freedom.

The characters of Dostoyevsky's fiction seem to suffer from an excess of self rather than a lack of self. They are intensely self-aware and vulnerable people, who seek in excess, even in crime, to announce their presence to the world; yet beneath their frantic self-seeking activity, one senses an emptiness, a hollowness, that has haunted modern man. Like Kierkegaard, Dostoyevsky sees the strong individualism of his characters as threatened. And like Kierkegaard, the Russian writer looks to Christian faith as the only hope for salvation in a world that is "drenched with tears from its crust to its center." Again, Christian faith is not primarily a matter of belief in Christian dogmas, but rather the *subjective appropriation* of Christ's message, and the practice of the active love of one's neighbor. But the threat to selfhood includes in Dostoyevsky not only the new objective science of "those damned Germans," who threaten to make mankind itself into another object of its inquiry, but the entire modern world, which, with its factory system, its industrial cities, and its state bureaucracies, threatens to reduce the individual to nothing more than a cipher, an "organ stop" that responds to pushing and pulling in a preprogrammed way. In his *Notes from the Underground,* Dostoyevsky invents a strange character in whom adolescent petulance and venomous rejection of other persons become his only defense against a world that seeks to mold him according to its needs. He refuses to behave the way others expect him to behave—he refuses to do a "good day's work," to be a "decent fellow," an "enjoyable chap to be with"—because he fears becoming what others want him to be—and hence losing his own self.

How much greater, then, thought Dostoyevsky, is the threat to selfhood posed by the modern state—which, for better or worse, Dostoyevsky identified with technology and socialism. Here Dostoyevsky has sounded a theme that has echoed through the vast impersonal factories and the dreary, uniform Levittowns where we of the twentieth century live. What will happen to the individual if men, like spare parts, are interchangeable with one another? What will become of the "care of the soul" that Socrates spoke of if modern science convinces us that we are no more than "respondent organisms"? What will become of courage and fortitude and striving for excellence if we are all to be treated equally and cared for from the cradle to the grave? And finally, what will become of freedom if, in the name of "universal humanism" or the "love of the fatherland" or merely in the name of the efficiency of production and distribution, men are organized in mass societies under the leadership of a few—hopefully benevolent—despots?

Although Dostoyevsky is remembered for the intensity of his characters—we think of their unique personalities and the intense passion with which they seek their own salvation or experience damnation even in this world—it is easy to recognize this theme of the loss of the self to modern technology as the one that has inspired much of modern literature. You may be familiar with some of these works. The fantastic, machinelike world of Franz Kafka, in which individuals are subject to unfeeling bureaucracies; the fearsome, closed, mechanical world of the future depicted in Huxley's *Brave New World*, where individuals are factory-produced to meet the needs of their society; even the supposedly benevolent communal system constructed by behavioral technologists, which is proposed by B. F. Skinner in *Walden II* as a desirable antidote to the chaotic world in which we live—all of these books have in common a concern for, or a rejection of, the individual person in his privacy and autonomy. Have we, indeed, lost something very precious as we entered the industrial and technological world?

C. Nietzsche: The Death of God.

In fact, all of the existentialists in this century and in the nineteenth speak of some sort of *loss* by mankind that, in their view, is as significant and as far-reaching as man's supposed loss of innocence when Adam and Eve ate the apple in paradise. Friedrich Nietzsche speaks of our loss of religious faith, of which, he says, we are not as yet entirely aware. In a characteristic passage in *The Joyful Wisdom,* he tells a parable about a madman who entered the marketplace crying "I seek God! I seek God!" When the people laughed at him and said they did not know where to look for God, he shouted:

> "Where is God? . . . I will tell you! *We have murdered Him*—you and I. We are all His murderers! But how have we done this? How were we able to drink up the sea? Who gave us the sponge to wipe away the horizon? What did we do when we unchained the earth from its sun? Whither is it moving? Whither are we moving? Away from all suns? Are we rather not continually falling? Falling backwards, sideways, forwards, in all directions? Is there still an above and below? Are we not lost wanderers in an infinite nothingness? . . . God is dead! God remains dead! And we have killed him! Where shall we find someone to comfort us, we murderers of all murderers? The holiest and most powerful thing that the world has possessed until now has bled to death under our knives—who shall wipe the blood from our hands?" . . . At last [the madman] threw his lantern upon the ground, so that it broke in pieces and went out. "I come too soon," he said then, "the time has not yet come. This terrible event is still in the making, and wanders about—the ears of man have not yet heard it. . . . This act is even farther still from man than the farthest star—and yet *man has done it himself!*"

We noted in chapter 11 that Nietzsche in fact welcomed the death of God and used this historical observation to launch an attack upon religion as a threat to the life-instincts, even as an enemy to all that is excellent in man. This attack was continued in the twentieth century by some of the existentialists, who spoke out in the name of humanism against a religious belief that tended to make man the mere plaything of God. It is to be noted in the above passage, however, that the madman does not perceive the Death of God as a liberation; on the contrary, it is apparently God's absence that has cost him his sanity. For if it is true that we have lost our faith in God, if we no longer believe that the world and our existence is a part of the Divine Plan— then *what is the ultimate meaning of life?* The question hits us with a terrible shock. We recall that in an earlier chapter we spoke of the doctrines of materialism and naturalism, which, like existentialism, deny the existence of God and of an immortal soul and thereby force us to accept our future non-being. Adherents of the first two doctrines have normally encouraged us to rejoice in our day's labors and to look to the future with merely finite hopes—hopes for a better world but not for a future life. The nineteenth-century existentialists, however, believed that the situation is not so simple, for man by nature aspires to the infinite. We must give birth to new gods—or go mad. And yet, they noted, nihilism, the belief that nothing in life is of meaning or value, is conquering our culture and slowly penetrating the mind of each of us. It is felt by the madman in his parable as the cold wind of Nothingness, meaninglessness, absurdity that chills our souls when we peer into the darkness of infinite and empty space. We no longer sense that our lives are encircled by a horizon that beckons to us, that conceals the answer to all questions, that will someday reveal to us the meaning of each moment in each human lifetime.

Despite this insistence that the world and human existence is meaningless and without ground because it is not the fulfillment of the Will of God, most modern existentialists affirm the value of life. If they did not, they would hardly bother to write books about the human situation. If they were honest they would commit suicide, and if they were less so, they would adopt a philosophy of hedonism and seek to enjoy life as much as possible before death rings down the curtain upon this senseless existence. As we recall, the Marxists criticize the existentialists for furnishing a rationale for dropping out of the struggle for a better world. But it is at least debatable whether the phenomena of piggish materialism, alcoholism, drug addiction, and either despairing indifference to life, or the frantic search for religious salvation, all of which seem to characterize life in industrial societies today, is inspired by the nihilistic message of existentialism or is rather a response to the underlying human situation diagnosed by the existentialists. In any case, most of the philosophers, playwrights, and novelists who write in an existentialist key seek to *escape* from nihilism. They append to their diagnosis of the human situation a *doctrine of salvation* of some kind and point to ways in which individuals may construct their own values and thereby give meaning to their lives. Come, let us create ourselves anew! they seem to say. Kierkegaard spoke of the leap of faith, Dostoyevsky taught the practice of authentic Christian love, and Nietzsche developed his famous doctrine of the Superman. Autonomy, freedom, the loss of God, the infinite within us, all beckon to us to become gods ourselves, to create a meaning of life worthy of us since life in itself is without meaning or purpose. Even Albert Camus, who once asserted that the only real question for him was "why not commit suicide"—even he, despite moments of the darkest despair, in which life itself seemed stale, flat, and unprofitable—was able to find reason to go on living. But before we can explore further the diseases of life and their proposed cures, we must examine one peculiar component of twentieth-century existentialism.

PHENOMENOLOGY

Phenomenology was established as a school in Germany at the beginning of this century. Its leading exponent was Edmund Husserl (1859–1938), who assembled about himself a number of graduate students and young teachers, much as Socrates once attracted young men like Plato to a new way of doing philosophy. The way of phenomenology involves a rejection of metaphysical and epistemological speculation such as had been the practice among the followers of Hegel and Kant during the nineteenth century. Instead, it calls upon us to return to the immediate facts of our everyday world, but from a new perspective—from that of what Husserl called the transcendental ego. Very roughly, Husserl invites us to reflect upon the *subjective* component of all knowledge, that is, upon the *way* we experience reality. Since the mind is active in processing data given to it through the senses, an investigation of the ways in which this processing takes place will enable us to clarify the essential content of the givens of experience. Husserl thus undertakes an analysis of the various modes and structure of the transcendental ego as the psychic center through which all experience takes place. In the sphere of ethics, for example, phenomenology tends to *describe* the values we encounter in the world and the *way* we apprehend these values, rather than attempting to establish what is preeminently valuable or what the ultimate nature of values are.

The link with the themes we have discussed in the previous paragraphs was provided by Husserl's younger colleague, Martin Heidegger (1889–1976). Heidegger conceived of phenomenology not simply as an investigation into the way humans experience the world, but as the way we *exist* in the world. Heidegger's most notable contribution, in his first major work, *Being and Time* (1927), was an analysis of the peculiar way in which the human experience of time gives structure to our mode of existence—*our* mode, that is, insofar as human existence differs from that of an insect or an inert object. Humans are, of course, both conscious of a world and *self-conscious*: that is, I am conscious of the world *as* the object of my consciousness; I can always relate what I experience back to the *subject* of that experience, namely, to myself. This self always and essentially experiences itself as "strung out," so to speak, in time. I am never "located" at a particular instant; I am always moving towards a future from out of the past. Indeed, if I were not always conscious of future and past, I could not be self-conscious at all. My present activity of writing, for example, is both conscious activity (I am aware of what I do) and self-conscious activity (I am aware that I am doing it). But it is clear that I could not understand what I am doing at this moment unless I was somehow aware of myself moving towards a future in which this present project of writing will make sense (I am aware of a time when I will stop writing for the day, eventually complete this book, use it in the classroom, and so forth), and out of a past that the present either completes or rejects or interprets anew. (In this case my awareness of the past includes my having begun the work on this chapter, the reasons why I am writing it, and the original learning of the materials and ideas I give expression to here.) Phenomenological reflection enables us to penetrate these temporal structures and other peculiarly human ways of existing in the world. Temporality, indeed, opens us to *possibility*—for possibility is, after all, my apprehension of a future state in which something *can be* that *is not now.*

In the end, the total picture of the human situation revealed by Heidegger's reflection upon how man exists is a somber and perplexing one. Man's ultimate possibility, he says, is death—that is, I am aware of a future possibility in which all other possibilities cease, and I am aware of this as *my* possibility. Moreover, human existence is revealed to involve a kind of *lack* that is part of man's essential nature. Since the future is the "place" in which my present activity will be completed—indeed, the future is the *meaning* of the present— my present activity has an *emptiness* about it: something is aimed at in what I do now, but it is not present to me yet. Thus my activity is not complete in itself; it points beyond itself: man is forever ahead of himself and is never entirely in the present. This eternal lack of completeness, this sense of "I am not . . . " is experienced by us as anxiety, guilt, and dread.

Much of modern culture—especially its art, its frenetic pace, the eternal desire for change, the fact that its popular culture never allows us to stop and think, to collect ourselves—can be interpreted in terms of the abstract categories of Heidegger's phenomenology; indeed, it stands as the most complete and insightful diagnosis of the cultural illnesses of our age. And although Heidegger was to reject the designation of "existentialist" for his thought, he provided for that school the most complete analysis of the human situation as it was first revealed by the nineteenth-century existentialists. Like them, Heidegger stresses subjectivity, warns against the loss of the self in the complex technological and bureaucratic systems of modern society, and thinks through the consequences of the collapse of absolutistic philosophical and theological systems that formerly gave people a sense of meaning, order, and direction.

Attending Heidegger's lectures in Germany during the early thirties was the Frenchman Jean-Paul Sartre. Heidegger's concept of man as fundamentally conditioned by his futurity and thus as possibility has an upbeat flavor, however securely it may be fastened to man's sense of lack and its consequent anguish. But it seems also to underwrite a belief in human *freedom* and to invite individuals to re-create themselves, according to the message of Kierkegaard and Nietzsche. It is this aspect of Heidegger's thought that Sartre was to pursue, along with his own efforts at a phenomenological examination of the human situation or the "human way of existing."

THE EXISTENTIALISM OF JEAN-PAUL SARTRE

When Sartre returned to France after his two-year sojourn in Germany, he began to produce an amazing variety of works that have made him the leading French man of letters in the twentieth century. He wrote novels, such as *Nausea,* which are standard fare in literature courses; plays, such as *The Flies* and *The Devil and the Good Lord,* which are performed by repertory companies throughout the world; he contributed to the theory of socialism in articles and in a major work, the *Critique of Dialectical Reason;* he was founder and editor of one of France's leading journals; he fought against the Nazis and was a loud and persuasive voice for socialism in France; and, finally, he was a philosopher, whose *Being and Nothingness* is one of the major philosophical works written during this century.

Although he was widely influential, like most men who have philosophical ideas of great significance and who attempt to make them known to a broad public, he was nevertheless often attacked and roundly disliked for his radical stances. His novels were attacked for their depiction of the raw and seamy side of life. His concern with such categories as anguish, death, and the absurdity of life was called defeatist and pessimistic by those of his readers who neglected the humanistic aspects of his philosophy. He added to his unpopularity by helping to organize an "international war crimes tribunal" that conducted a mock trial of the United States for its alleged crimes in Vietnam, and by refusing the Nobel Prize in literature as a meaningless token of the bourgeois culture he despised. Finally he was rejected even by the communists, with whom he had hoped to make common cause, and he withdrew from the Communist Party of France after the Soviet invasion of Hungary in 1954. Sartre died in 1980 at age 74.

A. The World.

The key to Sartre's world view is its subjectivity, which he inherited, in a certain sense, from that most French of philosophers, René Descartes. But Descartes' lonely ego, who thinks and who is present to a world outside himself, is radically transformed by Sartre in the light of Kierkegaard's and Heidegger's philosophy. For Sartre, the greatest adventure is the adventure of subjectivity, the adventure of discovery of the Self. Selfhood is, for Sartre, based upon *consciousness;* and it is consciousness that distinguishes the being of man from the being of all other things and creatures. Man is called by Sartre the *being-for-itself,* for only man can be an object to himself: only man is aware of his own existence. All other things belong to the realm of *being-in-itself;* they possess no capacity for reflection upon their own existence or upon the world they inhabit. This much seems obvious. But the consequences drawn by Sartre from this doctrine of a cleavage between the for-itself and the in-itself are surprising and profound. Let us begin with his analysis of the *in-itself.*

The realm of the in-itself, which is roughly equivalent to the collection of material or physical objects that we call "the world," is characterized by Sartre as *undifferentiated,* as *non-temporal,* and as *meaningless.* Now the question of what the world is like apart from our human perception of it has always perplexed Western philosophers, beginning with those who, like Locke, attempted to draw out some of the consequences of Descartes' subjectivism. Colors and sounds, and the shapes I perceive by means of them seem to be the result of mental processing of raw data—data that consist not of colors and shapes themselves, but of light and sound waves that, in themselves, are not colored or audible. Physical events exist in themselves, but it is only through the activity of consciousness that something called a "world" emerges from the raw data of perception. People perceive "trees" and "dogs," that is, they see them as those things, they give *names* to them, *distinguish* them from other things, and *evaluate* them in the light of their own needs and desires. Try to think of a "tree" apart from the typically human way of apprehending trees as objects of consciousness! The tree, simply as existing in itself, cannot be described; indeed the very attempt to grasp the pure givenness of objects causes a feeling of nausea in us, Sartre believes: the tree is there, and I am present to it; it is *not*-me, and yet it has no meaning or value beyond what I choose to give it. Its existence is *de trop,* gratuitous, formless, without value in itself.

The world is meaningless apart from the meaning we give to it! But don't *we* have to conform to the "world"? Every child is taught that we must "play the rules of the game" or the world will destroy us; that the world doesn't care what *we* think of *it.* This is true, says Sartre, only insofar as we let ourselves be dictated to by the world; quite possibly, we secretly wish to be told by the world what it is we must do and who we are. But always it is we, in fact, that bring meanings into the world, and we do this in various ways. Consider two examples, the first of which is a variation of one of Sartre's own. A poor man is standing on the beach in New York, thinking about members of his parents' family who live in Europe whom he has never seen. He longs to visit them one day, but he can't afford it. To him, the Atlantic Ocean is an unsurmountable barrier; the empty space above the ocean has a reality for him that seems to mock his own longing. The rich man, on the other hand, who could easily purchase his own airplane and travel to Europe, may have the objects of all his desires contained in one small part of New York; to him the Atlantic is not only not a barrier, it exists only as a meaningless space at the periphery of his awareness.

And what were the heavens above to men in ancient times? A region of things divine, incomprehensible, for the most part, to them; a place where things follow rules quite different from those they were accustomed to on Earth. The heavens were not part of their world, however much their imagination may have populated them with mysterious beings strangely like themselves. To modern man, however, the heavens are an extension of our own world; we think we understand the physical structure of the galaxies. We see the planets and stars beckoning to us, inviting us to know them better. We think we can travel to the farthest stars ourselves, and therefore their immense distances from us become a barrier to our curiosity, an obstacle to be overcome.

It is we, then, who create the world we inhabit, our consciousness gives meanings to things, and even values are created by human subjectivity; man alone is conscious of his existence, and man alone pronounces things either meaningful or meaningless. This does not mean, of course, that we can accomplish whatever we please; the world has a certain "facticity" that can't be overcome by a mere wish. I can't jump out the window and fly to Seattle, but I can decide to entertain such a wish, and only then does the project of "doing the impossible" become significant. At bottom, then, the world in itself is without significance, or, as Sartre and other modern writers have asserted, the world in itself is *absurd.* This term has a deeper sense, however, and to penetrate that sense we must examine the human being as he exists within this sphere of the in-itself.

B. Man.

But what then is man, the for-itself whose consciousness gives meaning to things? Where does man's significance come from? And here, says Sartre, we hit upon the deepest paradox. Think about the pen I am using to write these words. It has a clear meaning—for me. It has been constructed at a factory according to a design created by some engineer. It has been shaped to fit my hand, to permit ink to flow onto paper, in order to be sold to people who will use it to write, as I am now doing. Its meaning is thus circumscribed within narrow limits: it is there for—some particular purpose. But now think about the person who is using the pen, namely, myself. Heidegger, as you recall, notes that I am conscious of myself at a moment in time as working towards the completion of some end, namely, the completion of this book, and as having come out of a past in which this project of writing took shape for me. But how is it that I have this project and am fulfilling this function, that of writing this book? You will say that I decided to do it, took advantage of an opportunity, wish to be the person who writes these words, desire to make this communication to other persons, and the like. But the pen was determined by some one else to fill its particular role; who determined me to fill mine? Alas, at this point, all recourse to further "reasons" stops: only I myself determined myself to do these things. But who am I, apart from these choices and decisions, and apart from the role I choose to fill? I feel the ground slipping out from under my feet!

In the case of man, says Sartre, *existence precedes essence.* In the case of the pen, its essence is determined by the engineer or the designer and by the needs to which they respond. The pen *is,* but only insofar as that design, and that need, are previously given. But first I exist, and only then do I set out to create an essence, a personality, a reason for being. I chose to be a writer, but the pen did not choose to be a pen. I could choose—well, I could choose to do anything, whether I succeed in doing it or not; I could even choose to destroy myself, but the pen cannot choose to be destroyed. But then, again, what is this existence that I call mine and about which I can make these choices? My existence is a consciousness, says Sartre; I am conscious of myself in a world. And what is the essence of this consciousness? Its essence is a nothingness, a null point, a *lack:* it is simply the point from which a ray of awareness goes out towards the undifferentiated and meaningless in-itself and comes back towards itself as the empty possibility of being. We can say no more about consciousness than such vague and general descriptions as that it is an X through which possibility enters the world; it is the locus of a going-beyond and a coming back, the point at which a physical organism is first able to have a world as its possibility, and to be forever beyond itself. For the fact I am conscious makes it impossible for me to be fixed at a point in space or time; I am always going beyond myself towards the possibility of being what I am not now.

In this way, the for-itself constantly *transcends* itself. For example, I look back upon the past that I was as upon what has now become for me a possibility, for I *can* reinterpret my own past as I choose. And I look towards a future that I am not yet, and I make choices concerning it that are determined by no one—except myself. I go *beyond* myself to what I no longer am, or am not yet, and I give meaning to my existence. *In itself,* my "life" has no meaning whatever, no more than the objects outside of myself. Rather, the meaning of my life will be determined by my choice of courses of action. Man is thus lost and alone, amidst things that are meaningless in themselves, and surrounded by a sea of possibilities of being among which I must choose, and, in so doing, choose myself. I am not what I am, says Sartre: I am a host of possibilities, none of which is completely realized; and I am what I am not: I am no longer the past that I was, and am not yet the future that I will be. Completeness is always beyond my grasp. Again, this pen is simply what it is: one of a universal type whose existence is determined by man. But a man is not one of a universal type, for he is "spaced out" in time and in possibility; he can't be all he could be at once.

For Sartre, the fact that the meaning of my life is without external and universal foundation is a source of anguish. And this anguish is not occasioned by some specific fear—not, for example, by the thought that I ought to be about something else than the writing of this book, or even by the thought that I ought to be a farmer, or active in workers' or consumers' or ecological movements, rather than a bourgeois professor. Rather it is occasioned by the thought that I ought not to be anything particular at all—that what I am doing with my life is not what I must or ought to do with it, but simply that there is no ultimate reason why I do one thing rather than another, except for the fact that I have chosen to do it. This is the sense in which Sartre says I come in anguish to realize that my life is without external foundation, that it is in fact ultimately meaningless or absurd. I am a being without foundations, and yet I must create my own foundations, and no one or nothing can dictate to me what I ought to be about. I *cannot* be like this pen—unless I choose to kill myself and become a mere corpse; but even that act I will have chosen, and, in so doing, will have chosen to make that act the meaning of my life.

Nevertheless, in that anguish over my foundationless existence, I discover my *freedom:* I can strive to become . . . anything, for nothing is dictated to me. And in this glimpse of freedom is the core of man's salvation, Sartre believes. But first let us consider the peculiar nature of that freedom. Sartre's literary works show a constant concern for those special situations—such as Sartre's own, in which he chose to risk his life in the resistance against the German occupation of France—in which human freedom asserts itself. We are never more free, says Sartre, than when we are placed in a situation in which the necessity of a life-or-death choice brings us face-to-face with the ultimate groundlessness of our existence. But why should this be so? Because normally our anguish impels us to *flee* our freedom, to imagine that we cannot but do what we now are doing—such as when we have the sensation of being merely an instrument in a design that has been imposed upon us by fate, or by God, or by other persons. It is easier to be an object for others, like this pen, than to be forced to the realization that I have chosen to do what I am doing and, hence, am entirely responsible for my actions. But when I am forced to choose between my life and that of my friend, between torture and the freedom of France, between fighting in a war and the conquest of my country, then I see in all clarity that I alone can and must choose, and nothing is forcing me to make the decision one way or the other. You say fear of pain made you choose to run away? But who is responsible for making the fear or the pain unbearable, if not you yourself? You say you ran away because you are a coward? But "cowardice" is not a universal essence that inhabits our consciousness and makes us do things; *you chose* to be a coward, that is, to think of yourself as belonging to a universal type. And yet who would, in the end, choose to be an inert object like the pen or like the corpse? Don't we flee from objectivity too? Yes, we do, says Sartre, and this flight places us in the most paradoxical position of all: we choose both to be entirely free, to be our own possibilities, and at the same time we choose to escape those possibilities and to exist without possibilities, like an object. We all aspire to be a for-itself and an in-itself at the same time. The absurdity of human existence consists in this discrepancy between our aspirations and our possibilities. In effect, we wish to be God, says Sartre, in a telling passage in *Being and Nothingness:* a being that *is* all of its possibilities. But this is impossible; we cannot rid ourselves of the worm of nothingness, of unrealized possibility at the core of our being: *man is a useless passion.*

This innate longing for ultimate completeness, which all of us experience at times, became especially painful to twentieth-century intellectuals such as Sartre, when Nietzsche revealed that God, who was once the object of such longings for the infinite, was dead. With the death of God, all certainty has vanished, and the myth of a perfection in which man could share has been stripped away. Now mankind stands alone and naked in a world he is free to make, but his freedom is limitless and agonizing, for all reasons for being lie only within each of us. If this is truly the human situation, how are we to respond to it? And respond we must, for we cannot not act; even trying to forget about the necessity of choosing our course in life is a choice we freely make. As we noted earlier, all of the existentialists believed that there is hope for mankind, each of them developed a doctrine of "salvation," which is usually called the "authentic" way of life. Sartre's doctrine is only one among many, for others have felt the urgency of the problem that he has articulated so masterfully. We will sketch briefly some of these ways of authenticity. But for more complete answers you must turn to the individual existentialists themselves, for the answer, by its very nature, can only be a personal one, and you should hear them spoken in their author's own voices.

C. Authenticity.

Very generally, the authentic life is one lived in the light of the human situation as sketched above. Sartre calls upon each person to live his life in full realization of its groundlessness and its absurdity, rather than attempting to conceal our transcendence and our boundless possibilities from ourselves. But does the distinction between authentic and inauthentic existence have ethical implications? One would expect that existentialists would claim that the authentic life is *morally better* than the inauthentic life, and not simply better for such practical reasons as that it is happier, or more intense. However, with the possible exception of Sartre, none of the existentialists has attempted to work out an ethical system. The reasons for this lack seem clear: the existentialists believe in the complete moral autonomy of individuals. I am free to create the values by which I shall live. Moreover, to imagine that I must obey a moral law that hangs over me, as it were, like Kant's categorical imperative, would invite me to justify my actions by reference to that law, whereas Sartre, as we have seen, believes that all of my actions are without external foundation. To imagine otherwise is precisely a case of inauthenticity. For these reasons, the existentialists appear not to be concerned with questions of right and wrong, or of duty, right, and obligation, but choose instead to leave such matters to the individual. Rather, they attempt to make a case for a particular way of life or attitude of mind as being *higher* or *more worthy* of human dignity and human freedom, and this they call the authentic life.

The inauthentic man, we have seen, tries to avoid the problem of existence, tries to flee from it, by denying either that he is an autonomous agent, responsible for his own life, or by imagining that his true self is not the one that acts, and this act of bad faith costs him his dignity. Consider the arguments of Kierkegaard. He lived within a community that was nominally Christian. Everyone went to Church on Sunday, and heard sermons about the glory of God. But such sermons, Kierkegaard seems to believe, produce only inauthentic Christians: people for whom Christianity is both a comfortable and a comforting way of life: it reassures them that their lives are worth living, that their mediocre existences are beloved of God, that the world is as it ought to be. Kierkegaard's "leap of faith" is his response to the human situation: it is the attempt, born of despair and anguish over one's freedom, to construct a truly Christian life upon no guarantees other than the little light of infinity that seems to glow within our souls—that light which, in Sartre is our absurd aspiration for completeness. Sartre declares that such completeness is impossible; Kierkegaard confesses that he does not know how it is possible to relate oneself to infinite being, but he will try.

Many existentialists have been more passionately affected by one of the features of the human situation than the others. In the Christian existentialist Kierkegaard, that feature was the longing for the infinite. In the case of the Jewish thinker Martin Buber (1878–1965), the theme of cosmic loneliness predominates. We have lost ourselves among things, suggests Buber in his early work *I and Thou*: not that we have turned ourselves into objects, but we treat things, and even the other people we encounter in the world along with ourselves, as mere utensils to be used to obtain some gratification for ourselves. But we can approach objects and persons as beings to be *addressed*, to be *spoken to*. Not only must we treat other persons as ends, never as means, as Kant wrote, we must also attempt to open up a dialogue with other persons and even with other things, such that this communication may fill the vacuum of loneliness created by the modern world, where autonomy and subjectivity are stressed at the cost of community and spiritual presence in the world. Sartre, of course, denies that the subjectivity of the lonely consciousness can ever be bridged; each of us looks upon the other person as a threat or as a refuge from ourselves, a place where we can escape from our freedom. But Buber believes that true subjectivity does not imply the lonely Cartesian ego who peers at the physical world from the outside, as it were, and lays plans to subdue Nature to his will. It is possible to make my personality, my soul, my spirit present in the world, and to appropriate the spirits of other persons and other things to myself. Ultimately, Buber believes, it is possible to apprehend the spirit of God in the universe and to respond to it, like Adam, with the prayerful words, "Here I am."

Martin Heidegger's work, at least during his earlier years, concerned the phenomenological analysis of how human beings exist. In his later years, however, he moved closer to an underlying theme that had troubled him throughout his life. That theme was the question of Being itself, which, in the Western world, we first encounter among the Greeks. When we speak of Being itself, we are not referring to the individual things that make up the world. You recall that for Sartre and, again, for Buber, things are the individual objects that we use (or which at times seem to use us), and which we choose to interpret and evaluate in various ways. To Sartre, the realm of the in-itself as such is mere undifferentiated and massive givenness, which stands opposed to the for-itself and to its projects. But to Heidegger, Being is what encompasses both the for-itself and the in-itself. For Heidegger, "Being" is not the word for a mystery that laughs at our efforts to grasp it, or for an all-powerful God who transcends our understanding. Being does not lie in a world beyond: it is close to us; it can be forgotten, but it is not incomprehensible. And it is our fate, he believes, to have forgotten the mere being of things—forgotten not things themselves, but the unobjectifiable, inexpressible realm out of which things appear to us and human projects take shape. Being is not another thing among things, but rather what gives all things the ability to be. It is a non-thing; it is that horizon upon which things appear and our attempts to understand them begin. Authenticity is a kind of attunement to Being itself, and a rejection of that frenzied desire to conquer nature, which, since the time of Plato, and especially since the time of the scientific revolution, has characterized Western civilization. The authentic man tries to stand simply in the light of Being itself, and, like a man who attempts to look at the light itself rather than at what it illuminates, to let Being be. Eastern thought, in its search for Brahman and associated conceptualizations, furnishes a clear parallel with Heidegger's search for Being, and Heidegger himself has noted that the state of satori sought by Zen Buddhists approaches what he means by authenticity.

Sartre's philosophy contains warnings against the excessive pursuit of technique and the exploitation of Nature similar to those we find in Buber and Heidegger, and he calls us to return to an existence more reflective and spiritual than that prevalent in the West. But his concept of authenticity also stresses our intense participation in life as an adventure, rather than encouraging the spiritual contemplation of the world or of God or of Being itself. I do not just stand in the light of Being or the Presence of God; I must learn to cast my own light. But what am I to do with my life? Only I can determine that. And the authentic person chooses his actions in the full realization of the limitlessness of his freedom. But Sartre appears to believe that just because I am so free, I am responsible to others for my actions. This responsibility does not mean that I have an obligation to make use of my freedom, for Sartre denies that my freedom is limited by any moral obligation. But it is true that my actions influence the actions of others, and that by making or failing to make use of my freedom I establish precedents for others. Sartre freely accepts an obligation to other persons to live well, and to work for the extension of both political rights and the sense of existential freedom to all mankind. In a famous passage in *Existentialism is a Humanism,* he writes:

> I cannot be sure that (my activity as a socialist) will necessarily lead to the triumph of the proletariat . . . nor can I be sure that comrades-in-arms will take up my work after I am gone and carry it to the maximum perfection, seeing that those men are free agents and will freely decide tomorrow, what man is then to be . . . If I ask myself, "Will the social ideal as such, ever become a reality?" I cannot tell, I only know that whatever may be in my power to make it so, I shall do; beyond that, I can count upon nothing.

Will all persons show such commitments in the light of the unlimited freedom granted to us by Sartre? Or will mankind return to God, or to blind commitments to their nations, or to their people, or to some powerful leader in an attempt to get rid of their freedom, to offer it up on the altar of an all-consuming belief? Or, perhaps even worse, will people see in this foundationless existence proclaimed by Sartre the license to abandon discipline and to selfishly pursue pleasure, as the Marxists say is the last heritage of existentialism? Sartre himself would merely note: These questions are as yet undecided; the future of man has yet to be made.

QUESTIONS FOR STUDY

1. Develop a concept of authenticity, and contrast your concept with that of Jean-Paul Sartre. Show how your concept is related

to what you consider to be the fundamental features of the human situation.

2. Some existentialists are of the "religious" variety (Buber, Kierkegaard), whereas others are of the "atheistic" type. Speculate on the reasons for this controversy among existentialists, and upon how it is related to the fundamental questions raised by the existentialist writers.

3. Marxists criticize existentialists as furthering selfishness, subjectivism, and hedonism. Suggest avenues by which an existentialist might reply to this charge.

4. Write an essay on Sartre's famous statement, "Man is a useless passion." Re-state in your own words his reasons for this claim as stated in our text, and then formulate and attempt to justify an opinion on whether it is a correct and fair description.

5. The first two schools described at the beginning of this chapter, logical analysis and linguistic analysis, have tended to be hostile towards existentialism. Their criticism seem to be of two kinds: 1) that existentialism is a *confused* doctrine, for its language is unclear; and 2) existentialism is *incorrect* in its depiction of mankind as prey to anguished freedom, absurdity, and meaninglessness. Make a case for both criticisms.

Postscript

Before we leave you, we would like you to reflect with us again upon the nature of philosophy. The question is an important one, for philosophy appears to be unlike any of the other courses you are likely to take at college. Why should this be so? And why is it so difficult to define philosophy?

Most of the sciences refer in their very names to the subject matter they study. Many have the suffix '-logy,' from the Greek *logos*, which originally meant 'reason,' and later 'word,' but has come to mean 'study of.' Thus anthropology is the logos of anthropos, the word about man, and this science attempts to give an account of the behavior and culture of primitive man. In contrast, in the first chapter we noted that the word "philosophy," from *philosophos*, means the love of wisdom.

Now, a certain kind of love of wisdom animates all of the sciences. Without a love of what it studies, science would become merely mechanical, technical, or utilitarian. But what kind of love is the philosophical love? And what is wisdom? Doesn't the term "love" imply that philosophy is *not* just one study among others, but that it is an attitude, a state of feeling, a yearning for something? Yet if philosophy is not just a study, but also a kind of love, then how can it be taught? For example, you can't be taught to love another person, you have to fall in love with him or her. So, too, with philosophy, it appears: you have to *need* philosophy, to *desire* enlightenment, to have a loving *concern* for life that only a deeper understanding of it can satisfy. One

258

can learn, say, about Descartes' philosophy of mind, but one can't learn love of wisdom and, in that sense, *be* a philosopher.

Still, the love of wisdom must have *some* direction. What is the philosopher trying to understand? And how does he go about his undertaking? Here the puzzle becomes even sharper. You see, the question of what philosophy's proper method and proper content may be is itself a philosophical question. Philosophers may speculate upon the nature and limitations of other disciplines; they may ask, for example, "What is science? What are its proper methods? What kind of knowledge is scientific knowledge?" Such questions make up the philosophy of science. Notice that the scientist himself rarely asks such questions; he is concerned primarily with the extension of knowledge in his own area. But the philosopher has no one to ask what it is that he is to do—except other philosophers.

What do philosophers have to say about the nature of philosophy? Have they arrived at any consensus as to its nature? Can we find an underlying unity in the separate subjects we have studied in the course of this book? We will venture the opinion that philosophy is essentially *four* interrelated activities. And we will suggest that this analysis helps to clarify the strange paradox we have just encountered: that philosophy is a love that can't be taught, and yet we try to teach it, and that philosophy is a need for something that seems to have no special content.

1. PHILOSOPHY IS THE ANALYSIS OF CONCEPTS

Some philosophers have claimed that of all of mankind's characteristics that distinguish us from the animals—our upright posture, our opposable thumb, our large brain—it is language that is most significant: it is speech that makes us man. But language is something of a blunt instrument. It often lacks precision and universality (words may have different meanings even in the same language), and there are so many languages! That is why logicians, linguists, and mathematicians have tried to develop precise symbolic languages that have simple grammatical rules and terms with precise meanings. But our everyday language has grown up with us, the people who speak it. It is used to make endless kinds of communications and is sometimes as vague and confused as life itself can be.

Still, we see the world through the medium of language, and, many people believe, philosophy should begin with an exploration of how we use language. If we are sometimes confused, perhaps the fault lies not within ourselves or in the world, but rather in the language we use to express our thoughts. G. E. Moore once said that it is not the world that he found interesting, but rather the curious things that people *say* about the world. A case in point: imagine some people arguing about whether it is wrong for one of them to break a promise to another party even when, by breaking the promise, he could cause a great deal of good to be done in his community. One person might say that whether the act is wrong depends on how much good is done to the community, and how much harm to the person to whom the promise has been made. Another person might suggest that the important thing is how "serious" the promise is. A third might argue that the matter is simple: it is always wrong to break promises. But after struggling in this way awhile, someone is sure to ask the simple question of language: "What does 'wrong' mean, anyway?" This question, you will recall from the chapter on ethics, is a central question of metaethics. It calls upon us to become clear on what ethical terms mean before we start using them to describe things. And so philosophers ask: Is "wrong" a descriptive term? Is wrongness a characteristic of things? What kinds of things? Or is "wrong" simply an evaluative term? If so, what are the typical contexts in which it is used? What is communicated by its use?

Such questions are typical of philosophical activity. Here we have a process in which persons polish the instruments of their thought, and in this way avoid falling into the errors and confusions that result from misusing language. The key terms that have been the object of distinctively philosophical analysis are 'truth', 'knowledge', 'mind', 'justice', 'causality', 'space and time', and 'existence', and many others that became the subject of our reflections throughout this book. Plato, of course, describes this philosophical war with words in the form of imaginary dialogues between two or more people. In the *Laches,* for example, a general and Socrates struggle to come up with a coherent definition of 'courage'. Both know how to use the term, both can easily point out examples of courage, and both of them are courageous persons. But neither succeeds in bringing to word a definition of the term that is satisfying to both of them. But their wrangling is not merely "about words," and hence trivial. For words designate objects, and actions, and events, and we perceive those things in the light of the supposed meanings of words. If we let words trick us, if we don't learn how slippery they can often be, if we imagine that we are speaking sense when we are in fact confused, then, in one sense, we are truly prisoners in Plato's cave. In a very real way, you *are* the language you speak; and philosophy helps us to take care of our language and, hence, of ourselves.

2. PHILOSOPHY IS A WRITTEN TRADITION

Many students have told us that they enjoy the activity of philosophical analysis. They like to take apart concepts, and then try to be clear about what the words they use mean. And most see the importance of applying these analyses to the clarification of the broad and general problems that philosophers like to discuss. "But why do we have to learn what Spinoza's concept of substance was, or that it was Anselm who developed the first ontological argument? Why do we have to read their original texts? Why not just discuss ideas? After all, most of Descartes' theories are no longer accepted by anyone!" This is a difficult question to answer *before* a student has had a chance to read the great philosophers. Fortunately, the experience of reading them is frequently so exhilarating and so rewarding, and provides such excellent exercise to the mind that the question tends to be forgotten before the semester is over!

But the question is a serious one. The fact is that philosophers continue to read and reflect upon books that are, in some cases, two thousand five hundred years old, much as religious men read and reflect upon scriptures that are often even older. Karl Jaspers once wrote:

> Wherever men engage in philosophical thinking, an acceptance of the great philosophers and their works—similar to the canon of Holy Scriptures—takes shape . . . . It is in their company . . . that we can attain to what we ourselves are capable of being.

Nevertheless, philosophers today do not treat the works of their predecessors as scripture in one important respect. They are not treated as a special revelation from a higher realm. Philosophers consider themselves free to disagree, to criticize, and even to try to demolish and consign to oblivion the ideas of some of the earlier thinkers. But it is impossible to reject them all. The road to understanding must begin somewhere, and in philosophy each new generation begins with a reappraisal of what went before, as a first step in defining what we are today, how far we have come, and what is still to be done. Everyone taking professional training in philosophy is therefore expected to have mastered the works of the past and to be able to criticize them intelligently. A thinker who did not learn past traditions would be at point zero, so to speak; he would have to learn only from his own mistakes, and he would never know how much he owed to the past. And he would owe something to the past, in any case, although he might not be aware of it. For philosophical ideas fill the atmosphere we breathe in as children; they have structured our language and made the world we inhabit in the West somewhat different from the world that philosophy has helped to create in the East, as we saw in chapter 12. There is no escaping history. Far better that we learn that history than to imagine that we can do without it.

3. PHILOSOPHY IS A VIEW OF THE WORLD

The writings of the great philosophers, past and present, are not merely clever works of the imagination that reflect an individual's subjective views on God, the structure of the world, or how society ought to be organized. Each represents an effort to say something about the world that is *true*. They appeal to the reason of all persons and are intended to have universal validity. If none of them has won acceptance among all persons, that is perhaps not a sign of their failure, but rather an indication that the world is so complex that no human mind can encompass all things. Life is, after all, confusing; should philosophy be any less so, when it attempts the bold task of trying to understand life?

Philosophy is not like the individual sciences, although like them, it is animated by a love of understanding. For it does not confine itself to any given region of experience—the nature of primitive man, human behavior, or matter in motion—anthropology, psychology, or physics. It borrows from the knowledge obtained in these sciences and tries to give a synoptic picture, a picture of the whole of reality. Its typical questions, to quote the philosopher Kant, are such as "What can we know?" (not just "What have we learned?"), "What ought we to do?" (not just "How do we behave?"), "What may we hope for?" (not just "What do we want?"). And thus, in answer to these questions, were developed the great world views we have glimpsed at in this book: Platonism, Aristotelianism, Hinduism, Rationalism, Existentialism. These represent very broad options that the mind can adopt in its search for understanding; they *are* ways of understanding the world that offer themselves to us, not dogmatically, but persuasively. They are founded upon evidence that each individual can examine and accept or reject and attempt to correct, improve, and perhaps even replace with a *new* view of things that, similarly, will address itself to all mankind.

4. PHILOSOPHY IS THE SEARCH FOR THE GOOD LIFE

The logical analysis of concepts is a skill that can be acquired, although, unlike the skill involved in playing a piano, it is not one that can be easily measured, or one that has a clear criterion of success and failure. And the ideas of the great philosophers can be taught, and learned, and mastered, although, unlike knowledge of physics or of medicine, it is not clear just what use we are to make of such knowledge. But philosophy, we have seen, is not just a skill, or a certain kind of knowledge, it is also a love—a love of understanding, of wisdom, for their own sakes. Plato believed that the philosophical love was a love not of any one thing, but of all being and essence. It is a desire to take in and to understand truly all of reality, not just a few things that happen to please us at the moment. To be as fully conscious of life as possible—that is the philosopher's quest.

And in this way, philosophy becomes a certain kind of life—a life that Plato personified in the character of Socrates, and which other persons have led both then and now. The life of the philosopher, like the life of the artist or the writer or the man of God, is a life of the spirit. All of us possess spirit, that is, all of us are capable not just of knowing facts or doing useful work, but of understanding. However, in each of us the spirit takes a slightly different form. What any of you who have mastered the skills of philosophical analysis and have learned about the philosophical tradition will do with what you have acquired is your own affair. For no one can teach you how to live, or what to love, or what are the fundamental truths about life. You must decide that for yourself. That is the secret of your life, and mankind's most prized possession—our freedom, our autonomy, our ability to search by ourselves for those things that we perceive to be the best, the highest, the most true. All that teachers can do—even Socrates, the greatest of them—is wish you well, and send you on your way.

Glossary

Glossaries are always either complete or satisfying, but not both. This is an attempt to be satisfying.

Absurdity. According to existentialism, a fundamental characteristic of human existence. There is no reason why I exist, and the choices I make of a course in life are undetermined by any factors external to those choices. Hence I create the meaning of my life; my life as such is without meaning, hence, absurd.

Aesthetics. Branch of philosophy whose major concern is the study and clarification of the meaning, principles, and criteria of art.

Agnosticism. Philosophical view that denies the possibility of absolute knowledge, especially about matters related to God, the ultimate nature of reality, the soul, and the universe at large. The agnostic's denial of knowledge is often based on his assertion that the limitations of the human mind forbid us to make absolute assertions.

Analytic/Synthetic. A distinction between kinds of statements. *Analytic* statements are true or false either by definition (All parents have children) or by virtue of their logical form (A square is a square). A *synthetic* statement is true if it correctly describes some state of affairs (Newton was born in 1642), and false if it does not (Poland is south of Czechoslovakia). The distinction between analytic and synthetic statements, and the concept of truth upon which it depends, has been subject to intense debate among contemporary philosophers. See also *a priori/a posteriori.*

Ancient Philosophy. Traditionally, ancient philosophy is said to be the period of Western philosophy encompassed between the years 600 B.C. and A.D. 450: as such then, ancient philosophical developments of the Greco-Roman times of antiquity.

Anthropomorphism. From the Greek words *anthropos* and *morphe* ('man' and 'form' respectively), anthropomorphism is the tendency to invest non-human beings and objects with human characteristics. Exemplified in the child's behavior towards his teddy bear who becomes for the child another child, anthropomorphism can be widely found in religions and cults in which God and the gods assume human characteristics.

Apathia. Greek term used in the context of the philosophy of the Stoics. *Apathia* literally means 'no feeling'. According to the Stoics, the ideal ethical life is one in which the person learns to subdue his feelings and emotions under the rule of strictly rational principles.

A posteriori. Latin term used to designate those modes of knowledge for which sense perception is the basis. Our knowledge of the physical world, inasmuch as this knowledge is the direct or indirect result of sense perception, is said to be empirical or *a posteriori*. Like *a priori, a posteriori* is an epistemologically relevant concept.

A priori. Latin term used to designate those modes of knowledge in which sense perception plays either no role at all or a secondary role. It has often been argued that mathematical knowledge is *a priori*. Innate ideas and knowledge based on recollections (when these recollections are of things experienced in some previous non-physical life) are also said to be *a priori*.

Arché. Greek word that meant 'beginning', 'basis', or 'principle'. In Aristotle's language, *arché* was used to designate the primordial substance or element of which the Milesian philosophers spoke. Thus, water was for Thales the *arché* of the universe, *number* for Pythagoras, etc.

Argument. In logic, a set of statements about which it is claimed that one of the statements is true because the others are true.

Aristotelian. Any philosophy with the following characteristics: (1) all knowledge and value ultimately are discoverable within experience; (2) the belief that processes in nature or in man (acquiring knowledge, apprehending values, social organization, history, etc.) function teleologically.

Asceticism. Ethical point of view that considers pleasures, especially physical pleasures, to be undesirable. The ascetic looks upon pleasures as fundamentally detrimental experiences. Asceticism has been advocated by certain Christian and Jewish groups, as well as by a number of philosophical schools, some of which trace their ancestry to Plato.

Ashramas. In Hinduism, the four stages of life ideally appropriate to man: specifically, those of student, father of family, anchorite, and holy man or sannyasin.

Ataraxia. Philosophical concept associated with the ethics of Epicureanism. *Ataraxia*, a Greek term, designated the ethical ideal of Epicurus, an ideal that included complete serenity and tranquillity, the absence of physical and mental pain, and a lasting peace of mind.

Atheism. Philosophical view that denies the existence of God or gods. The atheist often adduces arguments to support his position. Among these arguments, for instance, the argument from evil is quite important. It is said that the mere existence of evil in the world precludes the existence of an omnipotent and benevolent God.

Atman. In the *Upanishads*, the impersonal eternal element in man; the cosmic Self to which the individual may attain through meditation. In the philosophy of Shankara, the atman is identified with Brahman.

Atoma. In the philosophy of Leucippus and Democritus, the *atoma* (literally the indivisible or unbreakable) are exceedingly small bits of matter that by a process of aggregation constitute physical things. The *atoma* or atoms are invisible, indivisible, eternal, homogeneous in content, and heterogeneous in form. They float in empty space.

Authenticity. In existentialism, man's distinctive possibility, characterized by the free commitment of the individual to self-chosen goals and opposed to the escape from freedom in bad faith.

Bad Faith. In Sartre's philosophy, a kind of self-deception practiced by an individual without his being fully aware of the deception. Bad faith may take two central forms: a person may attempt to escape from his freedom by imagining that he is, like an inert object, entirely determined by factors beyond his control; or he may imagine that he is entirely without any foundations in the world about him, denying, for example, that his own past bears any relation to his existence in the present. See also *absurdity, facticity.*

Being. Whatever exists. In Platonism, being is ultimate reality.

Bhakti. In Hinduism, the devotion to, and worship of, one god or goddess as a way of salvation. The *Bhagavad Gita* contains one of the earliest examples of Bhakti in Arjuna's devotion to Krishna. Mahayana Buddhism stresses bhakti in the form of the worship of the Lord Buddha.

Brahman. In Hinduism, Absolute Reality. The concept is developed philosophically in the *Upanishads.* Brahman cannot be described, for it lies "beyond" all possible descriptive terms, but it can be approached by various paths, such as those of religious devotion, meditation, philosophical speculation, and the practice of yoga.

Categorical Imperative. In the ethics of Immanuel Kant, the categorical imperative is an absolute norm or precept of ethical behavior that depends on no condition or circumstance of a hypothetical nature. It constitutes the verbalization of the moral law that in its turn defines the Good Will. The categorical imperative is this: "Act in such a way that your action may become a universal law of nature." A second precept is derived from this: "Treat humanity, in your person and in others, always as an end in itself, never as a means towards an end."

Categorical Statement. A statement whose subject and predicate denote classes of objects, as in "All swans are white birds." Categorical statements can be either affirmative or negative, either universal or particular.

Category. In Aristotle, one of ten possible classes of predicates: (1) substance; (2) quantity; (3) quality; (4) relation; (5) place; (6) time; (7) position; (8) state; (9) activity; (10) passivity. In Kant, one of the twelve transcendental structures by which the mind interprets incoming data and forms a judgment. In general, any phenomenon that is a central concern to a given philosopher, as Sartre is concerned with the categories of freedom, anxiety, and absurdity.

Cause. In Aristotle, to give the cause is to give an explanation. He distinguishes four kinds of causes. The material cause is the matter that undergoes change; the formal cause is the principle in terms of which the change occurs; the efficient cause is that which initiates the change; the final cause is the goal. In nature, the formal, final, and efficient causes are identical. In classical and modern philosophy up to Hume, the *principle of causality* states that whatever property we find in the effect must also be present in the cause. In modern Newtonian science, only efficient causes are accepted. The question of the nature and the justification of such judgments has been a philosophical problem since the time of Hume.

Conceptualism. In Medieval philosophy, the position that universals can not exist apart from particular objects, but such universals can be abstracted by the mind.

Confirmation. The justification of a statement by appeal to experience (observation or experiment).

Consciousness. A primary phenomenon of human existence that is difficult to define without circularity, for our understanding of related terms (awareness, perception, thinking) seems to depend upon our understanding of consciousness. Phenomenologists note that consciousness is always consciousness of something or other, but is there an ego which is the source of this consciousness? Or does the self arise out of consciousness? Such questions are central to epistemology, and to the existentialist analysis of the human situation. Some animals merely respond to external stimuli. But some animals monitor their behavior. People, alone, can monitor their monitorings (be aware of being aware) and are thus conscious. To be conscious is to be capable of commenting on our actions. This permits both self-deception and self-correction.

Contemporary Philosophy. Generally, the philosophical developments of the twentieth century.

Contradiction. In logic, the affirmation and denial of a single statement. "All swans are white, and some swans are not white" is a contradiction.

Copernican. Having to do with the Copernican revolution as understood by Hume and Kant. Any philosophy with the following characteristic: All knowledge and value consist of structures which, in part or in whole, are provided by man and not wholly by external realities.

Correspondence Theory of Truth. A statement is true if it relates to experience. This is sometimes contrasted with the coherence theory of truth in which a statement is true if it is consistent with an acceptable system of statements (e.g., a theorem in mathematics).

Cosmology. Traditionally, the branch of philosophy and science that studies the general structure and the development of the universe at large. Obviously, it is related to astronomy and physics (from which it derives its data and descriptive content), but its emphasis is philosophical as it seeks to give a rational account of the totality of physical reality.

Cosmos. Greek word whose original meaning was order and beauty. By the time of Plato, its meaning had been extended to embrace the concept of Univers, a concept that for the Greeks never lost the ancient meaning of order and beauty. The Latins coined the word *universum* in order to find an adequate translation for *cosmos*.

Cynicism. Socratic school of philosophy that supported a number of ideas such as (1) the reality of natural law; (2) the equality of all human beings; (3) the groundlessness of most human conventionalities; and (4) the identification of virtue with a simple and rational life. Originally, the word 'cynic' meant 'doglike,' as the cynics were often compared to dogs by the opponents of this philosophical school.

Darshana. Literally, "point of view"—a philosophical interpretation of the world, such as the systems of the Vedanta, thought to aid the mind in the search for enlightenment, but without laying claim to absolute truth or to adequacy as a theory of the ultimate nature of reality.

Deduction. An inference from at least two premises to a conclusion that is claimed to necessitate its conclusion by virtue of its logical structure.

De Facto Statements. *De facto* statements, otherwise known as informative or indicative statements, are those linguistic structures by means of which we seek to convey information about matters of fact or states of affairs. "The sky is blue," "The sun is a yellow star," and "Deformed children were killed in ancient Rome" are examples of *de facto* statements.

De Jure Statements. As used in ethical discourse, *de jure* statements are those utterances that express ideas concerning how things ought to be, how people ought to behave, etc. A system of normative ethics is made up of *de jure* statements. The statement "The ancient Romans should not have killed deformed children" is a *de jure* statement, whereas the statement "The ancient Romans killed deformed children" is a *de facto* statement.

Descriptive Ethics. Aspect of ethical inquiry in which the emphasis lies on the description, classification, and anthropological and sociological explication of norms or ethical values. The descriptive ethicist does not generally delve into the question of philosophical justifiability of ethics, nor does he assume a given ethical view *vis-à-vis* the values he describes.

Determinism. The view that every event, including human action, is totally dependent upon, caused by, and predictable from prior events.

Dharma. A Sanskrit term with a wide variety of meanings in Asian religious traditions. It may refer to a true teaching, such as that of the Buddha; to the moral virtues of justice or adherence to duty; or to the cosmic order itself conceived as a moral order.

Dialectic. In Greek, debate by use of question and answer, as in a dialogue. In Hegel and Marx, a theory that the process of social change operates through opposing forces whose clash leads to self-transformation.

Dialectics. As relevant to Socratic philosophy, dialectics designates Socrates' method of inquiry, a method that consisted in subjecting a person to a series of logically arranged questions. Socrates' dialectics is clearly exemplified in Plato's *Euthyphro.*

Dualism. Philosophical view according to which reality is fundamentally made up of two realms or dimensions of being. In Plato's philosophy, dualism appears in his belief in the existence of two worlds, namely, the true world of the Forms or Ideas, and the world of change and imperfection that Plato identified with the physical world. Both in Plato and in Descartes, the belief that man is made up of a soul and a body is a manifestation of dualism.

Dukkha. Pain or suffering; in Buddhism, the fundamental character of human existence.

Emotivism. A theory about the nature of ethical judgments. It holds that ethical judgments, such as "American society is fundamentally just," are intended to express the feelings of the speaker and to influence the attitudes of others, and hence are not objectively true or false.

Empiricism. A philosophical school first developed in the eighteenth century that opposed itself to rationalism, and whose general principles still dominate Western thought today. Very roughly, empiricism holds that all knowledge depends upon, and cannot transcend in any significant way, the data given in experience to the mind through the senses. Thus it denies that metaphysical knowledge (that is, knowledge of the ultimate nature of experience itself) is possible. A central idea of empiricism is that *a priori* knowledge of the truth or falsity of synthetic statements is impossible.

Epicureanism. A philosophical school formed by the Greek philosopher Epicurus (fourth century B.C.) whose major tenet was the identification of the good with the attainment of *ataraxia* (peace of mind). The Epicureans believed that the highest ideal for a human being was the liberation of the mind from all those thoughts that create fear, insecurity, unhappiness. The classical Epicureans did not advocate a life of pleasure but a life of peace and tranquillity.

Episteme. Greek word whose ordinary denotation was 'knowledge.' In this sense, *episteme* stood in contrast with *sophia* (wisdom) and *doxa* (opinion). The typical scientific knowledge of an astronomer of Alexandria was, for instance, referred to as *episteme.*

Epistemology. From the Greek word *episteme,* epistemology is the branch of philosophy that studies the problem of knowledge. This problem embraces issues such as (1) the nature of knowledge, (2) the kinds of knowledge, (3) the sources of knowledge, (4) the limits of knowledge, and others.

Essence. In Medieval philosophy, the nature of a thing considered independently of its existence. In Greek, 'ousia' means both essence and substance. In Latin, it is the idea or principle of a thing.

Ethical Absolutism. An ethical view that maintains that certain ethical values are absolute and immutable regardless of the changing conditions of human existence. These values are regarded as being, therefore, independent of human needs, desires, laws, etc.

Ethical Relativism. An ethical view that maintains that ethical values are relative to either the individual or the social group. What is right or wrong, good or bad, depends entirely on the human context in which ethical judgments are made. There are no universal norms or precepts in ethics; like fashions and customs, ethical values are simply the peculiarities of diverse social and cultural groups.

Ethics. From the Greek word *ethos* (custom), ethics is the branch of philosophy whose main concern is the problem of human values. It studies the meaning and use of concepts like 'good', 'right', 'evil', etc. See "descriptive ethics," "normative ethics," and "metaethics."

Ethos. Greek word whose original meaning was 'custom' or 'habit.'

Eudaimonia. Greek term that can be best translated as 'well-being.' It is also often translated as 'happiness,' and this translation is adequate, provided that by 'happiness' we do not mean those transitory states of physical or mental excitement brought about by pleasure.

Evolution. Change through time without any implication that later is better or more progressive. Mechanistic evolution is opposed to teleology.

Ex Nihilo. Latin phrase that means 'out of nothing'. In the cosmology of Saint Thomas Aquinas, we are told that God created the Universe *ex nihilo,* that is, out of nothing. Likewise, the contemporary advocates of the steady-state theory in cosmology also speak of the universe coming into being constantly *ex nihilo.*

Facticity. In Sartre's philosophy, the singular facts and features of the world, which, in themselves, are merely contingent, but which provoke some response on the part of the individual. I did not cause World War II, nor is World War II a necessary feature of existence, but the event has determined to some extent the course of the history of the postwar world into which I was "thrown." Facticity limits my freedom (I have to make choices in and about a situation I did not create), but my freedom is still my own (I involve myself in the world as I see fit).

Freedom. When applied to human decisions, the theory that such decisions are not completely determined or caused by prior events but could have been otherwise. In ethics, the view that people are responsible for their decisions. In political philosophy it has been interpreted at least three ways: as absence of external constraint (Hobbes, Locke); as fulfillment within one's proper social role (Hegel, Marx); as living according to rules that one prescribes to oneself (Kant, Rousseau).

General Will. In Rousseau, the collective absolute end of a community and the ultimate source of sovereignty. Not always identical with the will of the majority.

Golden Mean. In Aristotelian ethics, the golden mean is the middle point between the states of excess and deficiency in human behavior. Virtue consists in attaining the golden mean in our activities. For instance, to be virtuously courageous entails the avoidance of rashness and the deficiency of timidity, etc.

Guru. A holy man functioning as a spiritual teacher or guide. The term originated within the Hindu tradition but is widely used in Asian religions.

Hedonism. An ethical view or attitude that identifies the good with pleasure. Something is therefore good if and only if it brings pleasure.

Hypothesis. A guess, made on the basis of a preliminary investigation of a phenomenon, about the causes of the phenomenon, or about the yet unsuspected relationship of the phenomenon to other phenomena. An acceptable hypothesis must be observationally testable, at least in principle, to be considered "scientific."

Idealism. A fundamental principle of certain metaphysical theories, all of which assert the priority of ideas over material things. *Subjective idealism*

(Berkeley) holds that reality can be reduced to the collection of ideas in the minds of individuals and of God; it denies that ideas refer to or are caused by independently existing material things. *Objective idealism* (Hegel, et al.) holds that reality is essentially idea and is grasped with more or less adequacy by individuals during the historical development of mankind.

Immediate Implication. An inference made on the basis of an examination of one and only one statement that another statement is either true or false. If "All men are mortal" is true, one can immediately infer that "Some men are not mortal" is false.

Immortality. When this concept is applied to the soul, one of two views is entertained: either (1) that the soul is an entity that entirely transcends all temporality and is, therefore, eternal, or (2) that the soul, as God's special creation, has a beginning in time but can never be destroyed. The former view is associated with Plato, whereas the latter constitutes an idea of Christian philosophy as this is conceived by Saint Augustine.

Induction. A kind of reasoning that yields only probable knowledge on the basis of the evidence given. A typical example is the inductive generalization, which goes from a set of statements about individual members of a class to a claim about unexamined members of that class.

Intuition. Knowledge that is obtained without prior reasoning or without need of further justification.

Intuitionism. An ethical view according to which 'good' is a quality that cannot be defined in terms of any other quality. As such then, 'good' is indefinable. The quality 'good' can only be recognized by means of a direct intuition. The English philosopher George Edward Moore gave a comprehensive exposition and a cohesive defense of intuitionism in his *Principia Ethica*.

Kami. In Japanese Shinto tradition, a collective term referring to the things that are sacred and to the power that animates them. Gods are Kami, but then too the thunder is Kami, as is also an awesome mountain, such as Fuji.

Karma. In Buddhism and Hinduism, the metaphysical principle that all actions have inevitable consequences, and that hence the actions of an individual determine that individual or other individuals in a future life. According to Hinduism, it is karma that dooms a person to continue to be in bondage to illusion in a next life.

Koan. In Zen Buddhism, an impossible or paradoxical question posed by a guru to his students. By meditating upon the koan, the student comes to realize the limitations of reason and of intellectual doctrines of all kinds in the search for true enlightenment, or satori.

Leap of Faith. In the philosophy of Kierkegaard, the term refers to the necessity of subjectively engaging oneself in a relationship with God by an act of faith, in the absence of objective proofs of God's existence.

Logic. From the Greek word *logos* (reason or word), logic is primarily concerned with the process of reasoning and the laws of inference.

Logical Positivism. Philosophical school of the first half of the twentieth century that insisted, among other ideas, on applying a strict criterion of verifiability to all non-analytical or factual propositions. According to the logical positivists, meaningfulness entails verifiability, so that only those factual propositions that are verifiable in sense perception are said to have meaning. Thus, metaphysical, theological, and ethical propositions became meaningless.

Logos. Originally 'word' or 'reason' in Greek; in early Christian speculative theology, the Divine Reason according to which the world was created by God, and which became incarnate in the person of Jesus Christ.

Mahayana. The "Great Vehicle" of Buddhism; the form that Buddhism takes in most Buddhist countries today. It stresses personal devotion to the Lord Buddha and His successive reincarnations and has evolved an elaborate tradition of myths, rituals, and speculative doctrines.

Materialism. Philosophical view that maintains that existence can only be predicated of physical or material objects. The materialist therefore denies the existence, as well as the possibility, of nonphysical entities. The philosophies of Democritus and Karl Marx are examples of materialism.

Maya. Literally, 'illusion' in the sense of an illusion in magic. Typically, in Hinduism, the world as it appears to common sense or to normal waking states, as opposed to ultimate reality.

Medieval Philosophy. Philosophical developments of the Middle Ages are said to be 'Medieval.' Medieval philosophy accordingly embraces the philosophers of Western Europe who lived between the fall of the Roman Empire (about A.D. 450) and the emergence of the Renaissance (around the sixteenth century).

Metaethics. Aspect of ethical inquiry in which the emphasis lies on the analysis of ethical language. In metaethics, we do not seek to advance, defend, or attack ethical values; we seek only to clarify the meaning of ethical terms and propositions.

Meta Ta Physica. Greek phrase which means 'after the physics'. This phrase was used by the Alexandrian scholar Andronicus of Rhodes in order to identify an untitled work of Aristotle that became then known as the 'meta ta physica' or simply the 'metaphysics', as it was written or catalogued after Aristotle's famous *Physics.*

Metaphysics. From the Greek phrase *meta ta physica*, metaphysics has come to mean the general branch of philosophy that deals with the meaning and significance of reality at large. In Aristotle it had a meaning wide enough to make it identifiable with philosophy. According to Kant, metaphysics is the philosophical endeavor to deal with these questions: (1) Does God exist? (2) Is the human soul immortal? (3) Is there a free will in man?

Methodic Doubt. In the philosophy of René Descartes, the methodic or systematic doubt is a methodological device by which he subjects all his ideas and beliefs to a careful scrutiny in order to determine which ones possess the attributes of absolute clarity and certainty. Through the methodic doubt, Descartes arrived at the initial conclusion that the only clear and certain idea was the awareness of his existence as a thinking being: "I think therefore I am."

Modern Philosophy. This designation generally applies to the philosophical developments of the centuries between the Renaissance and our own time.

Modus Ponens/Modus Tollens. In truth-functional logic, two examples of valid deductive structures. They are forms of valid hypothetical syllogisms. Both arguments have a hypothetical statement "If p, then q" as their first premise. If the antecedent p is asserted, then the truth of q can be concluded; this is Modus Ponens. If the consequent q is denied, then the falsity of p can be concluded; this is Modus Tollens.

Monism. A view that maintains that all things are the manifestations of one universal substance or element. In the case of Thales, we encounter a clear example of monism, insofar as according to him, all things are viewed as transformations or modifications of water.

Mos. Latin word that serves as a translation for the Greek *ethos*. Its meaning as 'habit' or 'custom' remained unchanged until Cicero coined the derivative *moralis* that can best be translated as 'moral' or 'ethical'.

Naturalistic Fallacy. As defined by G. E. Moore, the naturalistic fallacy consists in defining the ethical concept 'good' in terms of a 'natural' quality such as 'pleasurable', 'expedient', 'useful', etc. According to Moore, this fallacy was committed by those utilitarians who, like J. S. Mill, insisted on defining 'good' in terms of the principle of utility.

Nihilism. From the Latin word *nihil* that means 'nothing'. Nihilism can have two related meanings: (1) the view that existence in general and human life in particular are meaningless or pointless, and (2) the view that ethical values are altogether groundless.

Nirvana. In Buddhism the "blowing out" of the flame of life; that is, the ending of a person's bondage to the conditions of this world, including bondage to an illusory self; the cessation of all desire.

Nominalism. In Medieval philosophy, the position that universals are mere words or names and represent nothing real.

Normative Ethics. Aspect of the ethical inquiry in which the emphasis lies on the actual enunciation of ethical norms or precepts. In general, the ethical systems of the major philosophers of the past contain clearly normative components inasmuch as they were often interested in advancing and advocating specific moral points of view.

Objectivism (1). As employed in the context of chapters 2, 3, and 4, this term designates the tendency of early Greek philosophy to devote itself mostly to the study and investigation of the objective world of physical reality. *Objectivism* should be contrasted with *subjectivism*.

Objectivism (2). As employed in the context of chapter 7, this term designates the view that ethical norms are based on certain objective or factual conditions that are not dependent on the subjective circumstances of the moral agent.

Ontology. The study of being. Traditionally, it was the study of the nature of substance. In contemporary discussions, it is the study of the ultimate concepts in terms of which we understand being.

Pali Canon. The scriptural tradition of Buddhism, first put into writing at the fourth great council of Buddhist monks held in Ceylon in 25 B.C.

Pantheism. The belief that God and the world are in some sense identical. The intended sense could be either that the individual phenomena are themselves God, or God dwells within objects; or that the world manifests a holy but impersonal Power or Reason.

Philosophia. Greek word probably coined by Pythagoras. Originally its meaning was the desire or love for wisdom, as its etymological roots were *philos* (desire or yearning) and *sophia* (wisdom).

Philosophein. Greek verb widely used by Greek philosophers (especially Aristotle), whose meaning was 'to search for wisdom'. According to Aristotle, this search for wisdom is the outcome of the sense of wonder experienced by people as they confront the mysteries of the universe.

Physis. This ancient Greek term originally stood for the regular and cyclical processes of nature which can be observed in phenomena like the seasons, the tides, and others. The Romans translated physis by means of the word *natura* which in turn gave rise to the English 'nature.'

Platonism. Any philosophy with the following general characteristics: (1) knowledge is *a priori;* (2) absolute values exist externally to man and to social institutions and are also *a priori.*

Plato's Gap. Our knowledge or concepts of knowledge always exceed our actual and possible experience. Our knowledge can never be totally explained by reference to experience alone.

Pluralism. As employed in chapter 2, this term designates those systems of cosmology that, as those of Empedocles and Anaxagoras, postulate a variety or plurality of primordial substances as the underlying elements of nature. It should be contrasted with *monism.*

Polis. Greek word that meant 'city'. The concept of *polis* is essential for an understanding of ancient Greek history and political philosophy. The *polis* was the political and social unit of Greek life, and it was to the *polis* that a Greek citizen owed his primary allegiance. The enormous importance of the *polis* as a source of ethical values can be seen in the latter parts of Plato's *Crito.*

Political Philosophy. The branch of philosophy whose concern is the study of values as these apply to the political and social context.

Positive Religion. The dimension of religious practice that is given institutional form within a community. Such elements of religion as the Church, its hierarchy and organization, formal prayers, rituals, holy books, and an established orthodoxy are elements of positive religion.

Predication. In Aristotelian logic, the attribution of some characteristic to a subject. "Socrates is bald" predicates baldness of Socrates. Aristotle claimed that predicates can be classified under ten and only ten rubrics, which he called 'categories'.

Primary Qualities. Those qualities that are objective, i.e., in the object independently of their being perceived. They are usually measurable qualities.

Proof. An explanation or argument that is deductive and alleged to be both valid and sound.

Rationalism. A philosophical outlook developed in the seventeenth century. Its leading exponents were Descartes, Spinoza, and Leibniz. Rationalists believed that the mind alone, even apart from observation and experimentation, is capable of true, absolute, objective knowledge of the nature and the structures of reality and the Good Life for man.

Realism. In Medieval philosophy, the position that universals can exist apart from actual exemplification in the objects of our experience or even our knowledge. In epistemology, the view that we can, through experience, have direct knowledge of the real world.

Reason. A term descriptive of certain functions of human thought, which, although the term has played a central role in Western thought, are difficult to identify. Generally, human reason has been conceived of as the instrument whereby the human mind passes beyond the simple givens of everyday experience to the discovery of the arché, or the principles underlying experience.

Samadhi. In Hinduism, a mystic or hypnotic state in which final enlightenment and release from samsara-karma is achieved.

Samsara. In Hinduism, a fundamental concept descriptive of the human situation. Man is trapped in the wheel of birth, decay, death, and rebirth by the effects of karma. Liberation consists in the experience of samadhi, or enlightenment.

Sannyasin. In Hinduism, the fourth stage of life in which one experiences final enlightenment and release from the wheel of birth and death.

Satori. In the Zen Buddhist tradition, the experience of enlightenment.

Scientism. The theory or belief that science can ultimately explain everything and anything without remainder.

Secondary Qualities. Those qualities that are not in the object but are caused in our minds by the object, e.g., color.

Skepticism. Any philosophical position, in general, that denies the possibility of a specific kind of knowledge. The denial may be about the possibility of obtaining reliable knowledge (epistemological) or about the existence of the alleged realities (ontological).

Social Contract. A theory that explains the origin and legitimacy of a society or government by reference to an agreement, implicit or explicit, of all of its members. Important differences are to be found in the respective versions of Hobbes, Locke, and Rousseau.

Solipsism. A type of subjective idealism. It holds that one can be justified in attributing reality only to the ideas entertained in the mind of that person at any given moment. The world, in effect, is my own idea.

Sophia. Originally, this Greek word meant skill or practical knowledge. By the time of Pythagoras, its meaning had sufficiently changed; it was used to signify wisdom or understanding as opposed to mere information or knowledge.

Sophism. A philosophical movement that developed during Socrates' time. Its adherents, the Sophists, were itinerant teachers of philosophy, rhetoric, and politics, whose preoccupations included the training of the youth in the art of social and political success. Sophism is characterized by an emphasis on the subjective and strictly human aspects of the philosophical enterprise. Often they advocated metaphysical skepticism and ethical relativism.

Sophist. Originally it meant a person of remarkable skills and experience. Its meaning changed, and it was used to designate particularly 'wise' persons. The "Seven Wise Men of Antiquity" (among whom Thales was often included) exemplifies this usage. During Socrates' time, however, 'Sophist' had a different meaning. This latter meaning we indicate by writing 'Sophist' with a capital 'S'.

Soundness. Characteristic of a valid deductive argument in which the premises are in fact true. By extension to informal logic, the term may refer to an argument that is convincing by virtue of the completeness of its premises and their relevance to the conclusion.

Sovereign. The ultimate and independent source of political authority.

State of Nature. Either the way men lived prior to forming social groups or the way they would live without a common authority.

Stoicism. School of philosophy that developed out of the school of the Cynics. Its name is derived from the Greek word for 'porch' (stoa) since its original adherents were in the habit of meeting under one of the Athenian porches. The Stoics advocated, among other ideas, a life lived according to nature. They saw themselves as integral parts of a universe thoroughly governed by Reason (*logos*). In ethics, they insisted on equating virtue with a life ruled by rational principles.

Subjective Religion. The dimension of religion in which the individual is engaged in a personal relation to God. Such phenomena as personal prayer, meditation upon Scripture, mystical states, and the feeling of God's presence in the world are examples of subjective religious states and practices.

Subjectivism. As used in the context of chapters 2 and 3, this term designates the tendency of Sophism and Socratic philosophy to shift the interest of philosophy *away* from the objective world *towards* the human world where values and specifically human issues occupy the foreground.

Substance. A word coined by Marcus T. Cicero in order to translate into Latin the Greek word *ousia*. *Ousia* meant simply 'what is', 'something which exists', or 'something which remains in spite of change'. In Cicero, however, *substantia* (substance) is also used to translate the Aristotelian *arché*, the underlying thing that remains permanent in the process of change.

Summum Bonum. Latin expression that means 'the highest good'. In ethics it has designated the highest human ideal or that which ought to be sought for its own sake. In Aristotle's ethics, for instance, the *summum bonum* is happiness or well-being (*eudaimonia*). In Medieval writings, God was often spoken of as the *summum bonum*.

Syllogism. A deductive argument having two and only two premises. In a *categorical* syllogism, the premises and conclusion are categorical statements; in a *hypothetical* syllogism, at least one of the premises is a hypothetical statement.

Tao. In Chinese tradition, the Way of Heaven. The Tao came to be identified with the lawful structure of the universe itself, and with the right or proper rules of the conduct of human life. A good life, for the Taoist, is one lived in accordance with the cosmic order.

Tautology. A statement that is necessarily true by virtue of its logical structure, especially if the subject and the predicate of the statement are identical ("All bachelors are unmarried males"), or if the statement is an instance of some logical rule ("Today is Tuesday or today is not Tuesday").

Teleology. The study of the ends or purposes of things. Aristotle introduced the idea of a final cause of events, e.g., that the changes undergone by an acorn as it develops are due to the end toward which it is moving, viz., the state of being an oak tree. All present events, according to Aristotle, are thus determined by some future state. This concept has played a central role in the development of Western thought, though it tends to be ignored by modern science.

Theological Ethics. The view that maintains that the basis of moral judgments is the will of God or gods, the precepts contained in sacred scriptures like the Bible, or the canon laws of religious institutions.

Theravada. Literally, "the way of the elders," referred to as the "lesser vehicle": An orthodox sect of Buddhism that attempts to adhere to the Buddha's original teachings, as revealed in the Pali Canon. Its adherents stress meditation more than bhakti, and the monastic life plays a central role in its practices.

Tirthankaras. Literally, a finder of fords, or places where a crossing to the Farther Shore may be made. In Jainism, the twenty-four enlightened ones, the last of whom was Mahavira, the founder of Jainism.

Transcendence. In the philosophy of religion, the existence of God beyond the world as its creator. Opposed to *Immanence,* the existence of God within the world as its sustainer. Most theologies attempt to develop a theory of the Divine Nature such that God may be correctly and coherently described as both transcendent and immanent. In existentialism, the doctrine that the world intended by consciousness is essentially beyond consciousness; man hence experiences his situation as a lack, or a negation; consciousness is not self-sufficient.

Universal. In Medieval philosophy, a property or quality that can be attributed or predicated of many individual things, e.g., "man" is a universal term that applies to Tom, Dick, Harry, etc.

Upanishads. Philosophical writings produced in the two or three centuries after the completion of the *Vedas.* The *Upanishads* attempt to make clear the vision of the world believed to be implicit in the earlier sacred writings.

Utilitarianism. School of ethical philosophy according to which the good can best be defined in terms of the principle of utility. This principle states that something is good if it promotes the greatest happiness for the greatest number of people. Utilitarianism is associated with the writings of the English philosophers Jeremy Bentham and John Stuart Mill.

Utopia. Greek word that literally means 'no place'. This term is often used to describe ideal constructions of man and the social state, which, on account of their perfection, are not expected to belong to the actual world. They serve, however, as ideals towards which, as in Plato's *Republic,* we are urged to strive.

Validity. Characteristic of deductive arguments. An argument is valid if and only if, by virtue of the argument's structure, it is not possible for the premises to be true and the conclusion false. "All men are mortal and Socrates is a man; therefore Socrates is mortal" is a valid deductive syllogism.

Vedanta. Literally, "the end of the Veda"; specifically, the philosophical darshanas written about the Vedic writings, especially the Upanishads, that constitute the core of modern Hindu thought.

Vedas. The Holy Books of Hinduism, based on an oral tradition completed in about 800 B.C. The four Vedas are the Rig-Veda, Yajur-Veda, Sama-Veda, and Athara-Veda.

Yin-Yang. In Chinese tradition, the two forms of cosmic energy that animate all things. The yin is the passive, feminine, wet principle, and the yang is the active, masculine, dry principle.

Bibliography

If your instructor asks you to write a term paper on philosophy, or to research any of the discussion questions we have placed at the end of each chapter, you would do best to begin work at the card catalogue of your library. If your topic is very general, you can look under the subject heading "Philosophy" itself. You will find that heading to be subdivided under such headings as "Philosophy—Greek," or "Philosophy—Modern." In addition, a library will normally have separate headings for many of the areas to which each of the chapters of this book have been dedicated, for example, "Epistemology" and "Existentialism." Finally, you will find the names of individual philosophers listed as both authors of their own works and as subjects of books.

To research a topic such as "Plato's Concept of God," you might first locate a general book on Plato and check in the index for a listing of "God" or "Gods"; you might find a large, collected edition of Plato's works and see whether it has an index, and whether there is a listing under "God"; and you might look for listings under such diverse subject headings as "Religions—Greek," "Plato and Platonism," or "God."

In general, books on philosophy are of five types. There are *anthologies,* which contain a collection of articles or excerpts on philosophy in general, on one area of philosophy, on one problem of philosophy, or even on one philosopher. Second, there are *textbooks* on philosophy, such as the book you have been reading, that attempt to give people an overview of the entire field of philosophy, its problems, and its leading exponents. Third, there are books that reflect upon the *nature* of philosophy and try to tell us what philosophy is and what its uses and limitations are. Such books therefore assume a prior familiarity with the problems of philosophy and the ideas of the great philosophers. Fourth are *histories* of philosophy. These are books that tell the story of the lives and ideas of the great philosophers, the times in which they lived, and what they accepted and rejected in the works of their predecessors. And fifth are the original contributions to philosophy themselves, that is, the books that make up the philosophical tradition.

The books listed here fit into all five of these categories. They cover most of the topics discussed in this book. The list is short, but we have chosen for it those books that our students have enjoyed, and which we found useful when we started out on the philosophical quest. Your college library will own most of them, and the starred books are easily available in paperback.

I. REFERENCE BOOKS, GENERAL HISTORIES OF PHILOSOPHY, AND BOOKS ON THE NATURE OF PHILOSOPHY

* Bontempo, Charles J., and S. Jack Odell, eds. *The Owl of Minerva: Philosophers on Philosophy.* New York: McGraw-Hill Paperbacks, 1975.

 Bullock, Allan, and Oliver Stallybrass. *The Harper Dictionary of Modern Thought.* New York: Harper & Row, 1977.

* Capaldi, Nicholas, and Navia, Luis E., eds. *Journeys Through Philosophy: A Classical Introduction.* Buffalo, N.Y.: Prometheus Books, 1977.

* Copleston, Frederick, S. J. *A History of Philosophy.* 8 vols. Westminster, Md.: The Newman Press, 1946–80.

* Danto, Arthur C. *What Philosophy Is: A Guide to the Elements.* New York: Harper & Row, 1968.

 DeGeorge, Richard T. *A Guide to Philosophical Bibliography and Research.* New York: Meridith, 1971.

 Edwards, Paul, ed. *The Encyclopedia of Philosophy.* 8 vols. New York: Macmillan, 1967.

* Frost, S. E., Jr. *Basic Teachings of the Great Philosophers.* rev. ed. Garden City, N.Y.: Doubleday & Co., 1962.

 Hospers, John. *An Introduction to Philosophical Analysis.* 2nd ed. Englewood Cliffs, N.J.: Prentice-Hall, 1967.

 Kolenda, Konstantin. *Philosophy's Journey: A Historical Introduction.* Reading, Me.: Addison-Wesley, 1974.

 Lamprecht, Sterling P. *Our Philosophical Traditions: A Brief History of*

Philosophy in Western Civilization. New York: Appleton-Century-Crofts, Inc., 1955.

Magill, Frank N. and Staff. *Masterpieces of World Philosophy in Summary Form.* New York: Harper & Row, 1961.

Randall, John H. *The Career of Philosophy.* 2 vols. New York: Columbia University Press, 1962–65.

* Russell, Bertrand. *The Problems of Philosophy.* New York: Oxford University Press, 1959.

Stumpf, Samuel Enoch. *Socrates to Sartre: A History of Philosophy.* 2nd ed. New York: McGraw-Hill, 1975.

Titus, Harold C., and Smith, Marilyn. *Living Issues in Philosophy.* New York: American Book Co., 1974.

* Toulmin, Stephen. *Knowing and Acting: An Invitation to Philosophy.* New York: Macmillan, 1976.

Urmson, J. O. *Philosophical Analysis.* Oxford: Clarendon Press, 1956.

* Woodhouse, Mark B. *A Preface to Philosophy.* Belmont, Calif.: Wadsworth, 1980.

II. CLASSIC WORKS MENTIONED IN THE TEXT: INDIVIDUAL WORKS AND COLLECTIONS

* Aiken, Henry D., and Barrett, William C., eds. *Philosophy in the Twentieth Century.* New York: Random House, 1962. Anthology.

Aristotle: McKeon, R., ed. *The Basic Works of Aristotle.* New York: Random House, 1941.

Beardsley, Monroe C., ed. *The European Philosophers from Descartes to Nietzsche.* New York: Modern Library, 1960.

* Buber, Martin. *I and Thou.* 2nd ed. New York: Charles Scribner's Sons, 1958.

* *The Empiricists* (Locke, Berkeley, Hume). Garden City, N.Y.: Doubleday, n.d.

* Feuer, Lewis, ed. *Basic Writings on Politics and Philosophy: Friederich Engels and Karl Marx.* Garden City, N.Y.: Doubleday Anchor Books, 1959.

* Freud, Sigmund. *The Future of an Illusion.* New York: Random House, 1960.

————. *Totem and Taboo.* New York: Norton, 1976.

* Heidegger, Martin. *Basic Writings.* Edited by David Krell. New York: Harper & Row, 1977.

* Kant, Immanuel. *Critique of Pure Reason.* Translated by Kemp Smith. New York: St. Martin's Press, 1965.

* Kaufmann, Walter, ed. *Existentialism from Dostoyevsky to Sartre.* New York: Meridian Books, 1956.

Kierkegaard, Søren. *A Kierkegaard Anthology.* New York: Modern Library, 1959.

* ———. *Either/Or.* Translated by W. Lowrie. 2 vols. Princeton, N.J.: Princeton University Press, 1944 and 1959.

Montesquieu, Charles Louis de Secondat. *The Spirit of Laws.* Berkeley: University of California Press, 1977.

* Navia, Luis E., and Kelly, Eugene, eds. *Ethics and the Search for Values.* Buffalo: Prometheus Books, 1980.

* Nietzsche, Friedrich. *The Portable Nietzsche.* Edited by W. Kaufmann. New York: Viking, 1959.

Oates, Whitney J., ed. *The Stoic and Epicurean Philosophers.* New York: Modern Library, 1940.

Otto, Rudolf. *The Idea of the Holy.* Translated by John W. Harvey. 2d. ed. New York: Oxford University Press, 1958.

Plato. *The Collected Dialogues of Plato.* Edited by E. Hamilton and H. Cairns. Bollingen Series: vol. 71. Princeton, N.J.: Princeton University Press, 1961.

* ———. *The Last Days of Socrates.* Translated by Hugh Tredennick. London: Penguin, 1954. Includes *Euthyphro, Apology, Crito,* and *Phaedo.*

Rousseau, Jean-Jacques. *The Social Contract and Discourse.* New York: Dutton, 1973.

* Saint Anselm. *Proslogium.* Edited by S. Deane. LaSalle, Ill.: Open Court, 1974.

Saint Thomas Aquinas. *Basic Writings.* Edited by A. Pegis. New York: Random House, 1945.

Sartre, Jean-Paul. *Being and Nothingness.* Translated by Hazel E. Barnes. New York: Philosophical Library, 1956.

Schleiermacher, Freidrich Ernst David. *On Religion, Speeches to Its Cultured Despisers.* New York: Harper & Row, 1958.

III. SPECIAL TOPICS

A. Greek Philosophy

* Burnet, John. *Early Greek Philosophy.* London: Black, 1958.

———. *Greek Philosophy from Thales to Plato.* New York: Macmillan, 1960.

Bambrough, R., ed. *The Philosophy of Aristotle.* New York: New American Library, 1965.

Friedländer, Paul, ed. *Plato: An Introduction.* Translated by H. Meyerhoff. New York: Pantheon, 1958.

* Guthrie, W. K. C. *The Greek Philosophers: From Thales to Aristotle.* New York: Harper Torchbook, 1960.
* Randall, John H. *Aristotle.* New York: Columbia University Press, 1963.
————. *Plato: Dramatist of the Life of Reason.* New York: Columbia University Press, 1970.
Robinson, John Mansley. *An Introduction to Early Greek Philosophy.* Boston: Houghton Mifflin Co., 1968.
* Ross, W. D. *Aristotle.* New York: Meridian Books, 1959.
* Taylor, A. E. *Socrates.* New York: Doubleday, 1952.
————. *Plato: The Man and His Work.* Ann Arbor: University of Michigan Press, 1964.
————. *Aristotle.* New York: Dover, 1955.

B. Epistemology and Metaphysics

* Ayer, A. J. *Language, Truth and Logic.* New York: Dover, 1946.
* ————. *The Problem of Knowledge.* New York: St. Martin's, 1956.
* Bergson, Henri. *An Introduction to Metaphysics.* New York: Bobbs-Merrill, 1949.
Capaldi, Nicholas. *David Hume.* Boston: Twayne, 1975.
Dray, William. *Laws and Explanation in History.* New York: Oxford University Press, 1957.
* Hook, Sidney. *From Hegel to Marx.* Ann Arbor: University of Michigan Press, 1962.
* Lovejoy, Arthur O. *The Great Chain of Being: A Study of the History of an Idea.* Cambridge, Ma.: Harvard University Press, 1936.
Maritain, Jacques. *A Preface to Metaphysics: Seven Lectures on Being.* London: Sheed, 1948.
Pears, D. F., ed. *The Nature of Metaphysics.* London: Macmillan, 1957.
Popkin, Richard H. *The History of Scepticism from Erasmus to Spinoza.* Berkeley: University of California Press, 1979.
* Schaffer, Jerome A. *The Philosophy of Mind.* Foundations of Philosophy. Englewood Cliffs, N.J.: Prentice-Hall, 1968.
Sprague, Elmer. *Metaphysical Thinking.* New York: Oxford University Press, 1978.
* Taylor, Richard. *Metaphysics.* Englewood Cliffs, N.J.: Prentice-Hall, 1963.
* Wilshire, Bruce. *Metaphysics: An Introduction to Philosophy.* Indianapolis, Ind.: Bobbs-Merrill, 1969.
Yolton, John W. *John Locke and the Way of Ideas.* New York: Oxford University Press, 1968.

C. Logic and Philosophy of Science

Copi, Irving M. *Introduction to Logic.* New York: Macmillan, 1972. Various editions.

Harré, R. H. *The Philosophies of Science.* New York: Oxford University Press, 1974.

* Hempel, Carl. *The Philosophy of Natural Science.* Englewood Cliffs, N.J.: Prentice-Hall, 1966.

Kaminsky, Jack, and Kaminsky, A. R. *Logic: A Philosophical Introduction.* Reading, Ma.: Addison-Wesley, 1974.

* Nagel, Ernest. *The Structure of Science.* New York: Harcourt Brace, 1961.

D. Social Philosophy and Ethics

Barnes, Hazel. *An Existential Ethics.* Chicago: University of Chicago Press, 1978.

* Frankena, William. *Ethics.* Englewood Cliffs, N.J.: Prentice-Hall, 1959.

Garner, Richard, and Rosen, B. *Moral Philosophy.* New York: Macmillan, 1967.

* Hare, R. M. *The Language of Morals.* New York: Oxford University Press, 1950.

MacIntyre, Alasdair. *A Short History of Ethics.* New York: Macmillan, 1966.

* Strauss, Leo. *Political Philosophy.* Edited by Hilail Gildin. Indianapolis, Ind.: Bobbs-Merrill, 1975.

Warnock, Mary. *Ethics Since 1900.* London: Oxford University Press, 1958.

———. *Existentialist Ethics.* New York: St. Martin's, 1967.

E. Philosophy of Religion and Eastern Philosophy

* Capitan, William H. *Philosophy of Religion.* Indianapolis, Ind.: Bobbs-Merrill, 1972.

Conze, Edward, ed. *Buddhist Scriptures.* Harmondsworth: Penguin, 1959.

Collins, James. *God in Modern Philosophy.* Chicago: Regnery, 1967.

* Gard, Richard A., ed. *Buddhism.* New York: Braziller, 1961.

Hick, John. *Faith and Knowledge.* 2d. ed. Ithaca, N.Y.: Cornell University Press, 1966.

* ———. *The Philosophy of Religion.* Englewood Cliffs, N.J.: Prentice-Hall, 1963.

Holmes, Arthur F. *Faith Seeks Understanding.* Grand Rapids, Mich.: Eerdmans, 1971.

Hutchinson, John A. *Paths of Faith.* 2d. ed. New York: McGraw-Hill, 1978.

Matson, Wallace I. *The Existence of God.* Ithaca, N.Y.: Cornell University Press, 1965.

Puligandla, Rama. *Fundamentals of Indian Philosophy.* Nashville, Tenn.: Abingdon Press, 1975.

* Renou, L., ed. *Hinduism.* Great Religions of Modern Man. New York: Braziller, 1961.

Smart, Ninian. *The Religious Experience of Mankind.* New York: Scribner's, 1969.

* Smith, Huston. *The Religions of Man.* New York: Mentor Books, 1958.

* Watts, Alan W. *The Way of Zen.* Harmondsworth: Penguin, 1957.

* Zimmer, Heinrich. *The Philosophies of India.* Princeton, N.J.: Princeton University Press, 1951.

* Zaehner, Robert C. *Hinduism.* London: Oxford University Press, 1966.

Zaehner, Robert C., ed. *Hindu Scriptures.* New York: Dutton, 1976.

F. Contemporary Philosophy

* Barrett, William C. *Irrational Man.* New York: Doubleday, 1958.

Blackham, H. J. *Six Existentialist Thinkers.* London: Routledge, 1952.

Collins, J. *The Mind of Kierkegaard.* Chicago: Regnery, 1953.

Grene, Marjorie. *Introduction to Existentialism.* Chicago: University of Chicago Press, 1970.

Hartnack, Justus. *Wittgenstein and Modern Philosophy.* New York: Doubleday, 1965.

* Lauer, Quentin. *Phenomenology: Its Genesis and Prospect.* New York: Harper & Row Torchbook, 1965.

* Marcuse, Herbert. *Reason and Revolution: Hegel and the Rise of Social Theory.* 2d. ed. New York: Humanities Press, 1968.

* Olsen, Robert G. *An Introduction to Existentialism.* New York: Dover, 1962.

Passmore, J. *A Hundred Years of Philosophy.* London: Penguin, 1957.

Schmitt, Richard. *Martin Heidegger on Being Human: An Introduction to Sein und Zeit.* New York: Random House, 1969.

Spiegelberg, Herbert. *The Phenomenological Movement: An Historical Introduction.* 2 vols. 2d. ed. New York: Humanities Press, 1969.

* Stevenson, Leslie. *Seven Theories of Human Nature.* New York: Oxford University Press, 1979.

Waismann, F. *The Principles of Linguistic Philosophy.* Edited by R. Harré. New York: St. Martin's, 1965.

* Zaner, Richard M. *The Way of Phenomenology: Criticism as a Philosophical Discipline.* Indianapolis, Ind.: Bobbs-Merrill, 1970.

Index of Names

This index is intended to include the names of major philosophers and philosophically relevant persons mentioned in the chapters of the book.

Index of Subjects

293